The Crime of Aggression and Russia's Invasion of Ukraine

Jennifer Trahan

The Crime of Aggression and Russia's Invasion of Ukraine

ASSER PRESS

Springer

Jennifer Trahan
Center for Global Affairs
NYU
New York, NY, USA

ISBN 978-94-6265-762-5 ISBN 978-94-6265-763-2 (eBook)
https://doi.org/10.1007/978-94-6265-763-2

Published by T.M.C. ASSER PRESS, The Hague, The Netherlands www.asserpress.nl
Produced and distributed for T.M.C. ASSER PRESS by Springer-Verlag Berlin Heidelberg

This T.M.C. ASSER PRESS imprint is published by the registered company Springer-Verlag GmbH, DE, part of Springer Nature.
The registered company address is: Heidelberger Platz 3, 14197 Berlin, Germany

Foreword

This book tells a narrative, perhaps a dispiriting one, about a vision to create an international criminal tribunal to prosecute the crime of aggression committed against Ukraine. It is a dispiriting tale because the vision that states and individuals had for a tribunal established through the United Nations, which would have created the strongest precedent against high-level leaders who invade another state, was not to be. Other powerful states did not wish to set a strong precedent for prosecuting the crime of aggression or for prosecuting a head of state for the crime of aggression and would only agree to a much weaker tribunal.

At the same time, the invasion has proven a tragedy for the people and country of Ukraine, and the victims deserve justice. The tribunal agreed on, formalized by agreement between Ukraine and the Council of Europe, is not what it should be. Yet it would be far worse for there to be no tribunal, given the existence of a widely accepted definition of the crime of aggression that builds on the legacy of the International Military Tribunal at Nuremberg. As of this writing, it is critically important that states join in endorsing the tribunal—a Special Tribunal for the Crime of Aggression in the Situation of Ukraine—and provide it with sufficient funding and support. We can only hope that the tribunal will provide at least some measure of justice and accountability. The tribunal's existence would simultaneously make the statement that it is profoundly wrong to invade a neighboring state or commit other acts of aggression, in this case, resulting in the death and injury of over 1 million people.

The book also poses the question of when states will be willing to make a broader commitment to the rule of law and prosecuting the crime of aggression, wherever and by whomever committed. This commitment is sorely needed to enforce the provisions against the aggressive use of force contained in the UN Charter, as the crime of aggression does. In a world where states are facing multiple threats and incursions against their territorial integrity, this commitment must be made, so that others do not needlessly suffer the same fate as the people of Ukraine.

Johannesburg, South Africa
October 2025

Richard J. Goldstone

Acknowledgements

I would like to thank all the many individuals who contributed to the book and/or supported me in the process.

First, I would never have written on the topic had I not been inspired by former Nuremberg Prosecutor Benjamin B. Ferencz, who toiled for years proclaiming to anyone who would listen the horrors of war and the need for the crime of aggression to be meaningfully prosecuted. Ben, who was a prolific scholar, knew what war meant firsthand, having traveled with the US military in 1945 and helped to liberate concentration camps. It was his dedication to the topic, his son Don Ferencz's passing the baton to me to serve as Convenor of the Global Institute for the Prevention of Aggression, as well as my own belief in the critical importance of the topic, that inspired my focus on the crime of aggression.

Over the years, I have been privileged to work with a group of hugely talented individuals and scholars, from Ambassador Christian Wenaweser, who, among other positions, led the negotiations of the Special Working Group on the Crime of Aggression, to the handful of academics and others who have been committed to seeing the crime defined and a workable solution as to jurisdiction achieved, including: Astrid Reisinger Coracini, Claus Kreß, Sina Alavi, Jutta Bertram-Nothnagel, Enid Adler, Carrie McDougall, Roger Clark, Noah Weisbord, David Donat Cattin, Marion Crepet, Stefan Barriga, Jörn Eiermann, and Leena Grover.

Numerous friends and colleagues contributed ideas and proofreading assistance. They include: Mark Shulman, Gleb Bogush, Belinda Cooper, Astrid Reisinger Coracini, Roger Clark, Rebecca Shoot, Annegret Hartig, Patrycja Grzebyk, Amber Lewis, David Donat Cattin, Iva Vukusic, Enid Adler, Carrie McDougall, Ari Brose, Andrea Olejar, Tristam Yale, and Andreas Schüller. I am also indebted to the legal advisers to UN Member States who permitted me to interview them.

A profound debt of gratitude also goes to Erin Lovall for formatting and editorial assistance, and to my NYU student assistants Muna Abdelwahab and Anakaren Iniestra. It has also been a pleasure working with Kiki van Gurp, Frank Bakker and Inge Klompmakers at T.M.C. Asser Press. My work was financially supported by a Dean's Research Grant from NYU SPS.

Thank you to all those who have supported me in this process, including my beloved children, Teddy and Nicole Rashkover.

I dedicate the book to the people of Ukraine: may you see justice done.

Contents

About the Author

Jennifer Trahan is a scholar and expert in the areas of international justice, international criminal law, and public international law, with a particular focus on the crime of aggression. She is a Clinical Professor at NYU's Center for Global Affairs, where she directs the Concentration in International Law & Human Rights. She is also Convenor of the Global Institute for the Prevention of Aggression. Starting shortly after Russia's invasion of Ukraine, she commenced serving as a special advisor to states and others on the establishment of a special tribunal for the crime of aggression against Ukraine.

Professor Trahan's prior book, "Existing Legal Limits to the Veto Power in the Face of Atrocity Crimes" (CUP 2020), won the Book of the Year Award from the American Branch of the International Law Association. She is featured in the documentary film "The Veto", produced by Tim Slade. The film and her writings have been part of an effort to seek an Advisory Opinion from the International Court of Justice recognizing existing limits to the veto power of the permanent members of the UN Security Council created by other obligations of international law.

She has also authored digests on the case law of the International Criminal Tribunal for the former Yugoslavia and the International Criminal Tribunal for Rwanda, published by Human Rights Watch, where she served as Counsel to the International Justice Program earlier in her career.

Chapter 1
Background on the Crime of Aggression and Structure of the Book

Contents

Abstract Russia's invasion of Ukraine has reignited focus on the crime of aggression. This book raises the question: if the international community fails to ensure that the crime is prosecuted when there has been such a clear violation of the UN Charter, then what is the utility of this crime? After exploring the historical foundations that led states to adopt an updated definition of the crime, the book provides an overview of the tragic consequences of the 2022 full-scale invasion of Ukraine. The book then describes how the elements of the crime could be proven in the situation. Yet, a gap exists in the international legal architecture—namely, the International Criminal Court ("ICC") cannot exercise jurisdiction over the crime in the situation of Ukraine. Given this impediment, the book turns to the more difficult conundrum of examining where the crime could be prosecuted. It primarily examines the negotiations to establish a special tribunal on the crime of aggression for the situation of Ukraine—tracing them from the proposal for an ad hoc international criminal tribunal for the situation to be established through the United Nations, to the agreement reached on a tribunal to be established through the Council of Europe. The book also makes the case for addressing the issue more systematically by amending the ICC's Rome Statute so that the ICC would possess more comprehensive jurisdiction over the crime. The book explores the efforts of states and others in pursuing these two tracks, and how well (or not) they have tackled these challenges. This introductory chapter provides an overview of these topics, sets forth the aim, structure, and approach of the book, and defines key terms.

J. Trahan, *The Crime of Aggression and Russia's Invasion of Ukraine*,
https://doi.org/10.1007/978-94-6265-763-2_1

Keywords Crime of aggression · International justice · State responsibility · Individual criminal responsibility · Invasion of Ukraine · Rome Statute · International Criminal Court

1.1 Introduction and Relevance of the Topic

In addition to causing untold suffering and threatening the global order, Russia's 2022 full-scale invasion of Ukraine and illegal annexation of Crimea in 2014 highlighted a significant gap in international law. Precedent exists for prosecuting the crime of aggression, as the Allies did before the International Military Tribunal at Nuremberg (the "Nuremberg Tribunal") and the International Military Tribunal for the Far East (the "Tokyo Tribunal").[1] Moreover, the crime has an updated definition contained in the Rome Statute of the International Criminal Court ("ICC").[2] And yet, the ICC is unable to prosecute the crime in the situation of Ukraine.

This book begins by explaining the history of the crime of aggression, the development of the current definition of the crime, and how this gap in the ICC's ability to exercise its jurisdiction over the crime came to exist. It then provides an overview of the facts concerning Russia's invasion of Ukraine (as well as its earlier illegal annexation of Crimea), and discusses the harms inflicted and crimes committed during and as a result of the invasion. Based on this factual background, the book both details the elements of the crime of aggression and analyzes how these elements could be proven against Russian or other political and military leaders.

The book then transitions to examining where the crime of aggression in the situation of Ukraine could be prosecuted. It commences by looking at efforts pursued since early 2022 to create a special tribunal on the crime of aggression for the situation of Ukraine. The book delves into the legal issues involved (for example, the issue of immunities), as well as the political dynamics of the negotiations. Specifically, it considers the two initial positions taken by states.

The first approach was to press for the strongest precedent: the establishment of an international tribunal created through the United Nations—an approach Ukraine strongly favored. The second approach advocated for a much weaker precedent of utilizing a hybridized Ukrainian chamber. This option was initially put forward by Germany, the United Kingdom, and the United States, and later supported by the full "G7" group of states.[3] The book explores the potential motivations of some of these states in taking such negotiating positions.

---

[1] See Charter of the International Military Tribunal (1945) 85 UNTS 251 ("London Charter 1945"); International Military Tribunal for the Far East, 19 January 1946, Special Proclamation by the Supreme Commander to the Allied Powers at Tokyo, amended 26 April 1946 ("Tokyo Charter 1946").

[2] Rome Statute of the International Criminal Court (1998) 2187 UNTS 90 (as amended) ("Rome Statute (1998) (as amended)"), Article 8*bis*.

[3] The Group of Seven (G7) consists of Canada, France, Germany, Italy, Japan, the United Kingdom, and the United States.

The book next turns to the compromise result that has emerged (a third approach), and which is the solution that has been agreed on. It is a Council of Europe-led tribunal that potentially allows for states from other regions to join in supporting the tribunal's establishment. While not the ideal solution—an international tribunal would have set the strongest precedent—this approach still shows significant promise. Most essentially, *not* to prosecute the crime through a credible tribunal in the current situation would carry considerable downsides.

In parallel with these efforts, states and civil society organizations additionally have begun a process to amend the ICC's Rome Statute to harmonize the ICC's jurisdiction over the crime of aggression with its jurisdiction over its other three core crimes (genocide, crimes against humanity, and war crimes).[4] If successful, there would be less need for such ad hoc solutions in the future, as the ICC would have considerably more jurisdiction over the crime of aggression than at present. The book argues that it is important for the ICC's Assembly of States Parties ("ASP") to successfully conclude such negotiations and amend the Kampala crime of aggression amendments to strengthen the ICC's ability to prosecute the crime. Unfortunately, in July 2025, powerful states blocked this amendment process, effectively delaying negotiations until 2029.[5]

The author served as a special advisor regarding the efforts to establish a special tribunal through the United Nations and has been involved in the efforts to amend the Rome Statute. In writing this book, she draws on concrete tribunal proposals. She also includes the views of states, gleaned from interviews with representatives who attended meetings of a "Core Group of States".[6] This group met from January 2023 through spring 2025 in order to reach consensus as to how to establish an aggression tribunal for the situation of Ukraine. The group reached agreement on the form of the tribunal in spring 2025, with the agreement signed between the Council of Europe and Ukraine.[7] However, as Chap. 7 details, before the tribunal can be set up and commence operations, sufficient funding and endorsements by additional states must be obtained. These remain outstanding as of late 2025.

Aggression prosecutions are only one aspect of a broader effort required to ensure justice for the victims. Prosecutions will need to operate in tandem with a separate reparations process (a Register of Damages and Claims Commission)[8] to assist with the rebuilding of Ukraine. Aggression prosecutions also will need to operate in conjunction with prosecutions by the ICC and other authorities, including domestic

---

[4] Rome Statute (1998) (as amended), note 2, Articles 6, 7, 8.

[5] See Chap. 8.

[6] The full name of the Core Group is "the Core Group on the Establishment of a Special Tribunal for the Crime of Aggression against Ukraine".

[7] Agreement between the Council of Europe and the Government of Ukraine on the Establishment of the Special Tribunal for the Crime of Aggression against Ukraine (2025) https://rm.coe.int/agreement-and-statut-english/1680b66127. Accessed 28 September 2025.

[8] For the Register of Damages, see Committee of Ministers, Council of Europe 2023. "The Claims Commission will serve as the second integral element of Ukraine's international compensation mechanism, alongside the Register of Damage for Ukraine, established by the Council of Europe". Didkovska 2025 (emphasis omitted).

authorities in Ukraine and elsewhere, who are pursuing war crimes and crimes against humanity cases.[9]

A question often raised in discussions about the creation of a special tribunal for the crime of aggression for Ukraine is why such a tribunal should be established if it is unlikely that the President of the Russian Federation, Vladimir Putin, or other high-level leaders, would end up in its dock.[10] The answer is three-fold. First, never say never. During the early years of the work of the International Criminal Tribunal for the former Yugoslavia ("ICTY") and the Special Court for Sierra Leone, it appeared extremely unlikely that former Serbian President Slobodan Milošević would be tried before the ICTY[11] or that former Liberian President Charles Taylor would be tried before the Special Court[12]—and yet they were. More recently, the former President of the Philippines, Rodrigo Duterte, was transferred to the ICC to stand trial for crimes against humanity.[13] These cases illustrate that what appears inconceivable can become possible as political situations and alliances transform over time. However, as will be explained in Chap. 7, in negotiating the tribunal's statute, certain states made it *more difficult* for President Putin and other top-level leaders (referred to as the "troika") to be tried.[14]

Second, despite this setback, it is also clear that President Putin is not the only individual who potentially bears responsibility for the invasion of Ukraine—which

---

[9] Justice is being initiated at three levels—before the ICC, in third countries, and within Ukraine. See International Criminal Court nd (list of ICC suspects); Bardelle and Mora 2025 (at least 14 EU Member States and several non-EU members have launched extraterritorial criminal investigation into core international crimes committed in Ukraine in the context of the invasion); Reuters 2024 (quoting Ukrainian Prosecutor General Andriy Kostin on probing over 122,000 suspected war crimes for domestic prosecution). For discussion of some indications of genocidal intent, see Chap. 4, note 176.

[10] For President Putin's role in planning the invasion, see Chap. 4, Sect. 4.2.

[11] The case was terminated midway through trial upon the death of Milošević. See International Criminal Tribunal for the former Yugoslavia nd (proceedings terminated on 14 March 2006 after his death on 11 March 2006).

[12] Special Court for Sierra Leone (2012) *Prosecutor v. Charles Ghankay Taylor*, Trial Chamber Judgment, SCSL-03-1-T. https://www.rscsl.org/Documents/Decisions/Taylor/1283/SCSL-03-01-T-1283.pdf. Accessed 4 May 2025; Special Court for Sierra Leone (2014) *Prosecutor v. Charles Ghankay Taylor,* Appeals Chamber Judgment, SCSL-03-01-A, Special Court for Sierra Leone. https://www.rscsl.org/Documents/Decisions/Taylor/Appeal/1389/SCSL-03-01-A-1389.pdf. Accessed 4 May 2025.

[13] Deutsch and van den Berg 2025.

[14] Under the agreement reached on a Special Tribunal on the Crime of Aggression against Ukraine ("Special Tribunal") President Putin, as well as other members of the so-called "troika" (i.e., the Head of State, Head of Government, and Minister of Foreign Affairs), will have proceedings against them suspended while in office. Charges could be issued, but not confirmed. See Chap. 7, Sect. 7.4.2.2. This unfortunate outcome could have been avoided had the tribunal been structured as an international one formed through the United Nations. See Chap. 5 (advocacy for such a tribunal). It also potentially could have been avoided through a Council of Europe-led tribunal if sufficiently internationalized and if the Tribunal's statute had remained silent on the issue. See Chap. 7, Sect. 7.4.2.2.

arguably commenced with Russia's attempted illegal annexation of Crimea in 2014.[15] The crime's current definition in the Rome Statute covers leaders "in a position to effectively exercise control over or to direct the political or military action of a State".[16] A number of individuals within the Russian Federation would fall within that category,[17] as would some in Belarus (or, possibly, the Democratic People's Republic of Korea).[18] While both the Presidents of Russia and Belarus (and other members of the troika) remain in power, it is individuals lower in the chain of command who would likely initially end up in the dock or be tried *in absentia*[19] (if a tribunal is established).

Third, a strong argument can be made that justice should be pursued regardless of the feasibility of effectuating arrests. After all, the ICC has not shied away from issuing an arrest warrant against President Putin for the "unlawful deportation and transfer of Ukrainian children from occupied areas of Ukraine to the Russian Federation",[20] despite the difficult odds of seeing him transferred to The Hague for trial before the ICC. Even the issuance by a tribunal of an indictment—something the Council of Europe-led Special Tribunal would be able to do even against the highest-level leaders (the troika)[21]—can prove a powerful statement.[22]

---

[15] On the illegal annexation of Crimea, see Chap. 4, Sect. 4.2.1.

[16] Rome Statute (1998) (as amended), note 2, Article 8*bis*. This requirement is also in the Special Tribunal Statute. See Chap. 7.

[17] See Open Society Justice Initiative 2022 (model indictment against Vladimir Putin, Nikolai Patrushev, Sergei Shoigu, Sergei Naryshkin, Valentina Matviyenko, Sergei Beseda, Sergei Lavrov, and Valery Gerasimov).The "leadership clause" would likely cover additional individuals. Tom Dannenbaum writes:

> It is difficult to know at this stage how many individuals might satisfy the leadership element as it pertains to the invasion of Ukraine. However, the broadcast of Russia's Security Council meeting in advance of the war revealed a range of senior officials participating in what could be characterized as part of the planning or preparation for aggressive war.

Dannenbaum 2022.

[18] As will be discussed, in placing Belarus' territory at the disposal of Russia for the launch of part of the invasion, Belarus' political and military leaders potentially have criminal exposure. See Chap. 4, Sect. 4.2.3 (role of Belarus); Chap. 4, Sect. 4.4 (analysis of responsibility). For the involvement of North Korean forces, see Chap. 4, Sect. 4.2.4; Chap. 4, Sect. 4.4 (analysis of responsibility).

[19] As will be detailed, the agreed on Council of Europe-led Special Tribunal would permit trials to be held *in absentia*. See Chap. 7, Sect. 7.4.2.4.

[20] Statement by Prosecutor Karim A. A. Khan KC on the Issuance of Arrest Warrants Against President Vladimir Putin and Ms Maria Lvova-Belova (2023). https://www.icc-cpi.int/news/statement-prosecutor-karim-khan-kc-issuance-arrest-warrants-against-president-vladimir-putin. Accessed 4 May 2025.

[21] As will be detailed, it is "confirmation" of charges that would not be permitted under the Special Tribunal's statute or the issuance of arrest warrants. See Chap. 7, Sect. 7.4.2.2.

[22] As Ukrainian President Zelenskyy movingly conveyed:

> the very fact of preparing indictments and issuing arrest warrants for those who planned and ordered the beginning of this aggression will be the most powerful signal to all other potential aggressors in the world that war is inevitably punished, and the guilty are held accountable; that the law is always valid and the law always prevails ….

Another question frequently posed regards the necessity of pursuing *crime of aggression* charges, given that the ICC already has issued arrest warrants for war crimes and crimes against humanity in Ukraine, and the Ukrainian authorities and third states are pursuing similar charges as well.[23] The unfortunate answer is that no matter how many cases are brought, justice inevitably will be incomplete. Prosecutions likely will cover only a fraction of the total number of crimes committed. Moreover, war crimes and crimes against humanity charges will not encompass the crime of the invasion itself.[24] All of the harm Ukraine has suffered is due to the "original sin" or the "supreme crime", as the crime was termed in the Nuremberg Tribunal's Judgment.[25] Russia's invasion was at one level an act by a state against a state, but a state is only an abstract entity that acts through individuals[26]—hence, the need to additionally pursue individual criminal responsibility.

Furthermore, it is the people of Ukraine who have borne the brunt of the harm, and they deserve to see the crime prosecuted. The victims also include soldiers—whether Ukrainian, Russian, or other nationals[27]—none of whom should have had to fight or die in an illegal war.[28] The victims additionally include all the civilians who have perished, including those whose deaths are categorized by the euphemism "collateral damage".[29] Those fatalities could not be prosecuted as war crimes.

Zelenskyy 2022. But see note 21.

[23] See note 9 (three levels of justice).

[24] Ukraine also is pursuing aggression cases (potentially in the absence of the accused). See Leshkovych and Labuda 2024 ("According to the [Office of the Prosecutor General], at the time of writing, there are 99 criminal cases registered pertaining to Russian aggression against Ukraine. These cases include 689 suspects".). Yet, Ukrainian cases (particularly for higher-level accused) would lack the authoritative weight and appearance of impartiality that could be achieved through more international proceedings. The troika could not be tried in Ukrainian courts due to the application of personal immunities.

[25] International Military Tribunal (1946) Judgment of 1 October 1946, in The Trial of German Major War Criminals. Proceedings of the International Military Tribunal Sitting at Nuremberg, Germany, Part 22 (22 August 1946 to 1 October 1946), p. 421.

[26] The Nuremberg Judgment famously stated: "Crimes against international law are committed by men, not by abstract entities, and only by punishing individuals who commit such crimes can the provisions of international law be enforced". Ibid., p. 55.

[27] For the involvement of North Korean troops and Russian recruitment efforts in Nepal, see Chap. 4, Sect. 4.2.4.

[28] In this way, the crime of aggression has a broader victim base than war crimes. International Humanitarian Law ("IHL") permits the targeting of combatants during international armed conflict (i.e., it is not a war crime to do so), but they too are victims of the crime of aggression. For background on the victims of the crime of aggression, see Pobjie 2017.

[29] IHL permits a certain amount of killing of civilians and destruction of civilian objects around a permissible military target. See Protocol Additional to the Geneva Conventions of 12 August 1949, and Relating to the Protection of Victims of International Armed Conflicts, Article 51(5)(b) (1977) ("Protocol I"). Yet, such civilians are victims of the crime of aggression and the civilian objects are part of the damages inflicted, even if their targeting does not amount to IHL violations or war crimes.

Pursuing justice for the crime of aggression also enforces the rule of law—in this case, consequences in the form of individual criminal responsibility for a seemingly blatant violation of the UN Charter's prohibition against the aggressive use of force.[30] Upholding the rule of law can serve many purposes. One is to express the wrongfulness or condemnation of the conduct. Arguably, this is especially needed where the alleged[31] aggressor state is a permanent member of the United Nations Security Council. Because a permanent member holds veto power over the issuance of substantive Security Council resolutions,[32] the United Nations essentially is paralyzed from taking any kind of binding enforcement measures in such instances.[33] Thus, consequences are limited at the level of state responsibility, at least through the United Nations. Pursuing the rule of law in the form of individual criminal responsibility in the current instance would deliver a powerful statement that even a permanent member of the Security Council may not blatantly invade a neighboring state without its leaders incurring responsibility. Conversely, the borders of all states are less secure when what appears to be a clear violation of the UN Charter goes unchecked at both levels.[34]

Accountability for the crime of aggression additionally conveys that it is profoundly wrong (as well as illegal and criminal) to start an aggressive war—where over one million individuals have been killed or wounded.[35] It is hoped that acting on this messaging also will serve as a deterrent[36]—potentially discouraging

[30] Article 2(4) of the UN Charter states: "All Members shall refrain in their international relations from the threat or use of force against the territorial integrity or political independence of any State, or in any other manner inconsistent with the Purposes of the United Nations". See Charter of the United Nations (1945) 33 UNTS 933 ("UN Charter (1945)"), Article 2(4). It is read in conjunction with the Security Council's ability to authorize forceful measures under Chapter VII, and the permissibility of states to utilize individual or collective self-defense in response to an armed attack. See ibid., Chapter VII, Article 51.

[31] If prosecutions are pursued against Russian (or other nationals, such as those of Belarus), for the crime of aggression, the act of aggression by the state would need to be proven. At this point, there is only "alleged aggression". Internationally accepted due process standards mandate the presumption of innocence of the accused, and that the burden of proof remains on the prosecution.

[32] Ibid., Article 27(3) (providing for the veto, i.e., a negative vote by a permanent member). For questions about the legality of a permanent member using its veto to shield its own aggression, see Trahan 2023 (arguing the veto can be *ultra vires*, as contrary to the obligation not to aid, assist, or maintain a serious breach of a peremptory norm of international law, and contrary to the UN Charter's Purposes and Principles).

[33] For an analysis of the response by the UN General Assembly and lack of response by the UN Security Council, see Trahan 2024. The UN General Assembly, except in extremely limited situations, may only issue recommendations. See UN Charter (1945), note 30, Articles 10–14 (General Assembly powers). Thus, the General Assembly is no substitute for a functioning Security Council. On the need to make more use of obligatory abstention when the Council is voting on a resolution under Chapter VI of the UN Charter, see Trahan 2024.

[34] On why the UN Charter violation appears to be a manifest one, see Chap. 4, Sect. 4.4.3.

[35] Pancevski 2024.

[36] For whether deterrence is effective at the international level, see, e.g., McAllister 2020; Miller 2023.

future would-be aggressors. It could reinvigorate the precedent (admittedly somewhat dormant since the Nuremberg and Tokyo Tribunal prosecutions),[37] that a clear violation of the UN Charter will not be countenanced and that individual criminal responsibility can follow. Conversely, the lack of accountability in this instance would risk conveying the opposite and dangerous message that a leader of a permanent member of the UN Security Council may cause the invasion of a neighboring country with impunity.[38]

Given that the invasion of Ukraine is hardly the only aggression committed since the prosecutions at Nuremberg and Tokyo, the question additionally arises why *this aggression* should be prosecuted when aggression in other situations has not been. For example, the lack of prosecution related to the US-led war in Iraq commencing in 2003 often is raised.[39] While the United States did have a legal theory purportedly justifying the war—that it was implicitly authorized by certain older, open-ended Security Council resolutions related to Iraq's earlier invasion of Kuwait[40]—the argument was not entirely convincing.[41] It also is worth noting that in 2003, states had not yet reached agreement on the current definition of the crime of aggression, with the negotiations then ongoing.[42] The ICC's ASP also had not yet adopted the definition,[43]

[37] Many international and hybrid tribunals have been established subsequent to the prosecutions at Nuremberg and Tokyo. See Sect. 1.3.2. Yet, those tribunals, with the exception of the ICC, were established to prosecute crimes internal to their situations (genocide, crimes against humanity, and/or war crimes), not aggression—which was largely not implicated in those contexts.

[38] The UN General Assembly has condemned the invasion, but its resolutions are essentially recommendations. See Chap. 4, Sect. 4.4.2 (General Assembly resolutions condemning the invasion). The United States and European Union have also implemented economic sanctions and various countries have been providing military assistance to Ukraine; obviously, neither measure constitutes accountability. See Chap. 4, Sect. 4.3.1 (on assistance provided to Ukraine).

[39] Similar legality questions exist, for example, about the June 2025 Israeli and US military strikes against Iranian nuclear installations. See Rosen et al. 2025.

[40] On the "revival argument", see Dunoff et al. 2020, p. 682. US military strikes against Venezuelan boats are raising similar concerns. See, e.g., Nevitt 2025.

[41] The legal justification for going to war in Iraq was largely rejected in the UK's Chilcot Inquiry report. See Maxwell 2016. The Bush administration's argument of the need to enlarge the doctrine of self-defense to include "pre-emptive" self-defense (a concept broader than anticipatory self-defense) has found little support in international law. See, e.g., Rabinovitch 2021 ("[James] Crawford notes that state practice since 1945 has generally opposed pre-emptive self-defence. This divergence in *opinio juris* and lack of state practice indicate that the right of pre-emptive self-defence is not established as [customary international law]".), citing Crawford 2019, p. 724; Clapham and Gaeta 2014, p. 561.

[42] Negotiations on the definition of the crime and conditions for the ICC's exercise of jurisdiction over it occurred in 2003–2009 before the Special Working Group on the Crime of Aggression ("SWGCA"). The definition of the crime used at Nuremberg was not utilized as it is quite minimal and circular. See London Charter 1945, note 1, Article 6(a).

[43] The definition of the crime was adopted by consensus of all Rome Statute States Parties in 2010 in Kampala, Uganda, at the ICC Review Conference. See International Criminal Court, Assembly of States Parties 2010.

and the ICC's jurisdiction over the crime had not yet activated.[44] Furthermore, international criminal law may not be applied retroactively,[45] even if Iraq or the United States had been States Parties to the Rome Statute. They were and still are not, nor have they ratified the Kampala crime of aggression amendments.[46]

To those unconvinced by this admittedly somewhat technical answer, I would argue that if the international community is ever to achieve a more peaceful world, where serious consequences flow from a leader causing his or her state to manifestly violate the UN Charter's prohibition against the use of force, the crime of aggression needs to be prosecuted at the international level. Repercussions cannot occur only where the political cards align such that the UN Security Council can act. Of course, the crime cannot only be prosecuted when Russian nationals are in the dock. It must be enforced apolitically, across the board, difficult as that may be to accomplish. This is why amending the Kampala crime of aggression amendments to create jurisdiction over the crime more broadly is also imperative.[47]

The globe is awash in war and has for time immemorial.[48] The UN was founded "to save succeeding generations from the scourge of war. . .".[49] While a third world war has to date been averted, the death tolls in the wars since World War II are staggering.[50] If the international community is ever to reach this lofty goal articulated in the UN Charter—indeed, as *one of the founding purposes* of the United Nations[51]—prosecuting the crime of aggression is one of the tools at the disposal of the international community, waiting to be utilized.

---

44 Activation of the ICC's jurisdiction over the crime occurred at the 2017 meeting of the ICC's ASP, effective 17 July 2018. See International Criminal Court, Assembly of States Parties 2017.

45 See, e.g., Rome Statute (1998) (as amended), note 2, Article 24 (non-retroactivity).

46 Under one reading of the ASP's 2017 Activating Resolution, in order for the ICC to be able to exercise jurisdiction over the crime: (a) both the aggressor state and the victim state would need to be States Parties to the Rome Statute; (b) both would need to have ratified the Kampala crime of aggression amendments; and (c) the aggressor State Party also would need to have not opted out of the ICC's crime of aggression jurisdiction. See International Criminal Court, Assembly of States Parties 2017; Chap. 3, Sect. 3.2.4 ("narrow interpretation"). Even under the "broad interpretation" of the resolution, either the aggressor *or* victim state would need to be a State Party that has ratified the Kampala crime of aggression amendments and the aggressor state would need to have not opted out of jurisdiction. Chap. 3, Sect. 3.2.4.

47 See Chap. 8.

48 For example, "[s]ince 1800, more than 37 million people worldwide have died while actively fighting in wars". Herre et al. nd. "The number would be much higher still if it also considered the civilians who died due to the fighting, the increased number of deaths from hunger and disease resulting from these conflicts, and the deaths in smaller conflicts that are not considered wars". Ibid.

49 UN Charter (1945), note 30, preamble.

50 See Herre et al. nd (chart showing that several million people have died in conflicts in the years following World War II).

51 UN Charter (1945), note 30, Article 1.1 ("The Purposes of the United Nations are:. . . [t]o maintain international peace and security, and to that end: to take effective collective measures for the prevention and removal of threats to the peace, and for the suppression of acts of aggression or other breaches of the peace. . .".).

1.2 Aim, Structure, and Approach of This Book

The aim of this book is to explain the history and significance of the crime of aggression. While populations in any region of the globe are at risk of becoming victims of the crime, the book primarily focuses on Russia's invasion of Ukraine. By examining the harms inflicted in Ukraine, the book illustrates the severity of the consequences that can flow from the commission of the crime—potentially all stemming from the decision of one individual to go to war. In delving into the issue of immunities that can attach in prosecutions before national courts, the book explains why the crime is one that particularly needs to be prosecuted at the international level.[52] In detailing the efforts to establish a special tribunal on the crime of aggression for the situation of Ukraine, the book examines which states played roles in blocking the strongest form of accountability and which strove to ensure it. The book secondarily makes the case that the Rome Statute's jurisdiction over the crime of aggression must be amended (i.e., harmonized with that of the ICC's other three core crimes), so the crime may be prosecuted more broadly before the ICC in the future.

1.3 Terminology

The most central term in the book is the crime of aggression, the prosecution of which is part and parcel of the system of international justice. Aggression is simultaneously something that states commit and a crime in which individual political and military leaders may be implicated. Thus, both state responsibility and individual criminal responsibility exist in parallel. Potentially, the crime could be prosecuted before the ICC (if the ICC were to have sufficient ability to exercise jurisdiction), or there could be an ad hoc solution, such as creation of a freestanding tribunal for the situation of Ukraine—although that leaves aggression in other situations unaddressed. While there is some potential for the crime to be prosecuted at the domestic level, that is not the focus of this book due to the inherent limitations of such proceedings.[53]

---

52 As will be detailed, the issue of immunity for top leaders was not, in this author's view, addressed well during the negotiations to establish a Special Tribunal. See Chap. 7, Sect. 7.4.2.2 (suspending proceedings against the troika while in office). That outcome could have been avoided had there been the political will to do so. See also note 53.

53 The highest level leaders are likely to have immunity from prosecution at the domestic level, making the crime ill-suited to domestic prosecution, at least vis-à-vis such leaders. On immunities, see Chap. 5, Sect. 5.3.4.3.

1.3.1 Crime of Aggression

The crime of aggression was prosecuted before both the Nuremberg and Tokyo Tribunals, although it was then known as "crimes against peace".[54] Various states thereafter included the crime in their domestic criminal codes,[55] the UN General Assembly affirmed the principles of the Nuremberg Charter (including recognition of crimes against peace), and the International Law Commission ("ILC") included the crime in its Draft Code of Crimes against the Peace and Security of Mankind.[56] By 1974, the General Assembly had also adopted a definition of aggression for purposes of evaluating state conduct.[57] In 1998, the crime of aggression was included in the Rome Statute of the ICC as one of the four core crimes over which the court would have jurisdiction.[58] However, agreement on the definition of the crime and the conditions for the ICC's exercise of jurisdiction over it was delayed until later negotiations.[59] These were agreed on and adopted by consensus at the 2010 Review Conference on the Rome Statute held in Kampala, Uganda.[60] The decision to activate the ICC's jurisdiction over the crime occurred at an ASP meeting in 2017, with activation becoming effective on 17 July 2018.[61] Yet, the ICC's quite limited jurisdiction does not, as will be described in the book, encompass the situation of Ukraine (or many other situations).[62] The content of the definition of the crime is detailed in Chaps. 3–4.[63]

1.3.2 International Justice

The field of international justice describes the international and hybrid criminal tribunals established to prosecute crimes such as genocide, crimes against humanity, and war crimes, as well as (somewhat inconsistently) the crime of aggression. Some also might include prosecutions of these crimes before domestic courts, conducted

---

54 London Charter (1945), note 1, Article 6(a); Tokyo Charter (1946), note 1, Article 5(a).

55 For legislation, see Reisinger Coracini 2017, pp. 1038–78. Years later, after the crime was included in the ICC's Rome Statute, additional states incorporated it into domestic law on the basis of the Rome Statute's definition of the crime. For domestic legislation following the 2010 Review Conference, see Hartig 2023, Chap. 6.

56 UN General Assembly Resolution 95(I) (1946); International Law Commission 1954, Articles 2.1, 2.2.

57 United Nations General Assembly Resolution 3314 (XXIX) 1974.

58 Rome Statute (1998) (as amended), note 2, Article 5(1).

59 See ibid., Article 5(2) (since agreed to be deleted).

60 International Criminal Court, Assembly of States Parties 2010.

61 International Criminal Court, Assembly of States Parties 2017.

62 See Chap. 3, Sects. 3.2.3–3.2.5 for details on crime of aggression jurisdiction before the ICC.

63 See Chap. 3, Sect. 3.2.2 (the definition of the crime); Chap. 4, Sect. 4.4 (applying the elements of the crime to the situation in Ukraine).

on the basis of universal jurisdiction or other jurisdictional theories.[64] In addition to the ICC, the following international and hybrid criminal tribunals have been established: the Nuremberg Tribunal; the Tokyo Tribunal; the ICTY; the International Criminal Tribunal for Rwanda; the State Court in Bosnia-Herzegovina; the Special Panels for Serious Crimes (in Timor-Leste); the Extraordinary Chambers in the Courts of Cambodia; the Special Court for Sierra Leone; the Special Tribunal for Lebanon;[65] the Extraordinary African Chambers within the Courts of Senegal (prosecuting crimes committed in Chad); the Special Criminal Court in the Central African Republic; and the Kosovo Specialist Chambers and Specialist Prosecutor's Office (and prior to that, Regulation 64 Panels within Kosovo's court system). With the exception of the ICC, the establishment of each of these tribunals was ad hoc—that is, they were intended to have jurisdiction over crimes only in a particular situation—while the ICC is a permanent standing institution. Of the tribunals, only the Nuremberg and Tokyo Tribunals and the ICC have had or have jurisdiction over crimes against peace/the crime of aggression,[66] as the other tribunals were established to prosecute crimes internal to their respective situations.[67]

1.3.3 State Responsibility versus Individual Criminal Responsibility

There are acts for which states may be held responsible and for which individuals can also incur criminal responsibility, with these types of responsibility operating in tandem. For example, a state can be responsible for the commission of torture, with obligations set forth for states parties in the Convention Against Torture and Other Cruel, Inhuman or Degrading Treatment or Punishment.[68] Torture is also a violation of a peremptory norm of international law (*jus cogens*),[69] with the International Law Commission having detailed the responsibility states hold vis-à-vis such norms in its

---

[64] See, e.g., Trial International nd.

[65] The Special Tribunal for Lebanon is an outlier, as it prosecuted the crime of terrorism. See Statute of the Special Tribunal for Lebanon (2007) attached to United Nations Security Council Resolution 1757 (2007), Article 2(a).

[66] London Charter (1945), note 1, Article 6(a); Tokyo Charter (1946), note 1, Article 5(a); Rome Statute (1998) (as amended), note 2, Article 8*bis*.

[67] The tribunals listed were established to prosecute crimes in the former Yugoslavia, Rwanda, Bosnia, Timor-Leste, Cambodia, Sierra Leone, Lebanon, Chad, the Central African Republic, and Kosovo, respectively. The Extraordinary African Chambers in the Courts of Senegal had jurisdiction over crimes committed in Chad. See Statute of the Extraordinary African Chambers within the Courts of Senegal Created to Prosecute International Crimes Committed in Chad between 7 June 1982 and 1 December 1990, Article 1 ("Statute of the Extraordinary African Chambers 2011").

[68] Convention Against Torture and Other Cruel, Inhuman, or Degrading Treatment or Punishment (1984) 1465 UNTS 85 ("Convention Against Torture 1984").

[69] See, e.g., International Law Commission 2019, Conclusion 23 and Annex (providing a non-exhaustive list of peremptory norms).

Articles on the Responsibility of States for Internationally Wrongful Acts.[70] Where jurisdiction exists, states may bring disputes alleging violations of state responsibility to the International Court of Justice ("ICJ") in The Hague.[71] Torture is simultaneously a crime for which individual criminal responsibility attaches and can constitute (if the appropriate contextual elements are satisfied) part of the crime of genocide,[72] a crime against humanity,[73] and/or a war crime.[74] These latter three core crimes could be prosecuted before most of the tribunals listed above,[75] or, where the appropriate legislation exists and jurisdictional conditions are satisfied, before a state's domestic courts.[76] However, certain immunities can apply in prosecutions at the domestic level that can be avoided when prosecutions are conducted before an international tribunal.[77]

1.3.4 The International Criminal Court

The ICC was established by states through a multilateral treaty, known as the Rome Statute because the final treaty negotiations, conducted in June and July 1998, occurred in Rome, Italy.[78] The court sits in The Hague, The Netherlands. As of late

---

[70] International Law Commission 2001, Articles 16, 41.

[71] Convention against Torture 1984, note 68, Article 30(1) (disputes about interpretation or application of the convention referable to the ICJ). An example is the case of Canada and The Netherlands against Syria brought in 2023 before the ICJ. See International Court of Justice (nd) *Application of the Convention Against Torture and Other Cruel, Inhuman or Degrading Treatment or Punishment (Canada and the Netherlands v. Syrian Arab Republic)* ("International Court of Justice nd").

[72] See, e.g., Rome Statute (1998) (as amended), note 2, Article 6(b) (genocide encompasses "serious bodily or mental harm"). To date, there is no case where a court has found torture *alone* to constitute genocide. Given the high threshold necessary for satisfying the special intent requirement of genocide (*dolus specialis*), torture is more likely to constitute one aspect of a genocide case.

[73] See, e.g., ibid., Article 7(f) (torture as a crime against humanity).

[74] See, e.g., ibid., Article 8 (2)(a)(ii) (torture as a war crime in international armed conflict); ibid., Article 8 (2)(c)(i) (torture as a war crime in non-international armed conflict).

[75] The Special Court for Sierra Leone and Kosovo Specialist Chambers did not have jurisdiction to prosecute the crime of genocide. See Statute of the Special Court for Sierra Leone (2002). https://www.refworld.org/legal/constinstr/unsc/2002/en/43606. Accessed 20 March 2025, Articles 2–5 (jurisdiction over war crimes, crimes against humanity, and crimes under domestic law); Republic of Kosovo 2015, Articles 13–15 (similar). The Extraordinary African Chambers within the Courts of Senegal, along with having jurisdiction over genocide, crimes against humanity, and war crimes, additionally had jurisdiction over torture. See Statute of the Extraordinary Africa Chambers 2011, note 67, Article 4. As previously mentioned, the Special Tribunal for Lebanon prosecuted the crime of terrorism.

[76] For a listing of states that have implemented Rome Statute crimes into their national legislation, see The Clooney Foundation for Justice and Justice beyond Borders 2025. For states that have implemented the crime of torture into their national legislation, see OPCAT Database nd.

[77] On immunities, see Chap. 5, Sect. 5.3.4.3; Chap. 7, Sects. 7.3.2, 7.4.2.2.

[78] Rome Statute (1998) (as amended), note 2.

2025, it has 125 States Parties.[79] The court has jurisdiction to prosecute genocide, crimes against humanity, war crimes, and the crime of aggression.[80] Investigations and prosecutions may be initiated by UN Security Council referral, referral by one or more States Parties, or the Prosecutor acting on his or her own (*proprio motu*).[81]

As to genocide, war crimes, and crimes against humanity, jurisdiction exists: (a) over crimes committed in the territory of a State Party; (b) over crimes committed by a national of a State Party; (c) where the Security Council has made a referral;[82] or (d) where a state has accepted jurisdiction on an ad hoc basis.[83] As detailed in Chap. 3, a more limited jurisdictional regime exists regarding the crime of aggression.[84] Specifically, as a result of negotiations conducted at the 2010 Review Conference on the Rome Statute, crimes committed by the nationals of non-States Parties and those committed on the territories of non-States Parties were excluded from the ICC's jurisdiction over the crime.[85] At the Review Conference negotiations, states also agreed on the possibility for States Parties to "opt out" of jurisdiction.[86] Furthermore, a restrictive reading of jurisdiction that was incorporated into the 2017 ASP resolution that activated the ICC's jurisdiction over the crime of aggression[87] truncated, or arguably truncated, jurisdiction even further.[88] A group of states led by Germany in spring 2025 proposed an amendment to the Rome Statute to harmonize the ICC's jurisdiction over the crime of aggression with the ICC's jurisdiction over its other three core crimes, which would create considerably more jurisdiction before the ICC over the crime.[89] As of this writing, States Parties have not adopted the amendment.

---

[79] See UN Treaty Collection nd. Hungary has filed for withdrawal from the Rome Statute, which, once effective one year after filing its instrument of withdrawal), would reduce the number to 124. See Human Rights Watch 2025. In September 2025, Niger, Mali, and Burkina Faso also announced an intent to withdraw. Reuters 2025.

[80] Rome Statute (1998) (as amended), note 2, Article 5.1.

[81] Ibid., Article 13(b) (referral by the UN Security Council); Article 14 (referral by a State Party); Article 15 (the Prosecutor initiating an investigation *proprio motu*). Where the Prosecutor acts *proprio motu*, as to the crimes of genocide, crimes against humanity, and war crimes, approval of an ICC Pre-Trial Chamber is additionally required to commence an investigation. See ibid., Article 15.3–4.

[82] Ibid., Articles 12(2), 13(b). As to the territory of a State Party, if the crime was committed on board a vessel or aircraft, the State of registration of the vessel or aircraft would need to be a State Party. Ibid., Article 12(2)(a).

[83] Ibid., Articles 12(3).

[84] For details, see Chap. 3, Sects. 3.2.3–3.2.5.

[85] Rome Statute (1998) (as amended), note 2, Article 15*bis*(5).

[86] Ibid., Article 15*bis*(4).

[87] International Criminal Court, Assembly of States Parties 2017.

[88] Ibid. *compare* Trahan 2018 (arguing that the attempted modification of jurisdiction was invalid); McDougall 2024, p. 552 (same); McDougall 2021 (setting forth the argument in detail).

[89] See Chap. 8.

1.4 Overview of the Chapters

After this introductory chapter, the book is structured as follows.

Chapter 2 discusses the development of the crime of aggression from the 1800s to the 1998 Rome Conference, where states agreed to the Rome Statute that established the ICC. The chapter commences by tracing the crime's early roots in *jus ad bellum* theory and the peace movement of the 1800s, as well as historic developments related to limitations on the conduct of war (*jus in bello*). The chapter then examines two different methods by which states have attempted to rein in aggressive war—at the level of state responsibility and the level of individual criminal responsibility. The chapter traces the first approach from the aspirations behind the founding of the League of Nations, as well as the 1928 Kellogg-Briand Pact in which states reached the historic agreement to prohibit aggressive war. After the horrors of World War II, states additionally pursued the second approach, prosecuting individuals for crimes against peace before the Nuremberg and Tokyo Tribunals. Prohibiting aggressive war was also the central animating purpose behind the founding of the United Nations in 1945, with the UN Charter's prohibition of the use of force constituting one of its core provisions. The chapter concludes by tracing legal developments during the Cold War and leading up to the 1998 negotiations, where the crime was poised to be included as one of the four core crimes under the Rome Statute.

Chapter 3 continues to discuss the development of the crime of aggression, covering the years 1998 through the present. The chapter starts by focusing on the decision by states—following the precedent of the Nuremberg and Tokyo Tribunals and development of the field of international justice more generally—to include the crime of aggression as one of the four core crimes within the ICC's Rome Statute. Yet, as will be explained, the definition of the crime, as well as conditions for the ICC's exercise of jurisdiction over it, needed to be agreed upon through later negotiations. The chapter traces these developments, and examines both the content of the definition of the crime contained in the Rome Statute and the ICC's jurisdictional regime over the crime. As to the latter, the chapter examines the agreements reached by States Parties to the Rome Statute at the 2010 Kampala Review Conference and the 2017 meeting of the ICC's ASP at which states activated the ICC's jurisdiction over the crime, subsequently becoming effective on 17 July 2018. With this background, the chapter turns back to the situation of Ukraine and explains why the ICC cannot exercise jurisdiction over the crime of aggression in the situation, despite the fact that Ukraine had earlier accepted the ICC's jurisdiction, and, on 1 January 2025, became a State Party to the Rome Statute. The chapter concludes by exhorting states to create additional jurisdiction over the crime of aggression, both by establishing a special tribunal on the crime of aggression for the situation of Ukraine and by amending the Rome Statute to cover future similar situations.

Chapter 4 chronologically traces the events leading up to and including the Russian Federation's 2022 invasion of Ukraine. It addresses key actors, the composition of forces, command structures, and the number of civilians and military personnel killed. While focusing on the 2022 invasion, the chapter acknowledges Russia's 2014 illegal annexation of Crimea as the start of the aggression. The chapter also discusses Belarus' actions in placing its territory at Russia's disposal for launching the invasion, the role of North Korean forces, and the role that cyber-attacks have played as an additional modality by which Russia's invasion has been perpetrated. The chapter also surveys the war crimes and crimes against humanity allegedly committed since the invasion, as well as other harms suffered, none of which would have occurred without the original crime, the crime of aggression. The chapter culminates in a preliminary analysis of how the invasion, as well as the earlier illegal annexation of Crimea, fall within the definition of act of aggression contained in the Rome Statute, and suggests some of the Russian and other political and military leaders who might potentially be implicated in the crime of aggression.

Chapter 5 next turns to efforts to establish a special tribunal on the crime of aggression for the situation of Ukraine. Shortly after Russia's full-scale invasion, calls began to mount for accountability for the invasion. Because the UN Security Council was essentially paralyzed from acting due to Russia's veto power, it became clear that the Security Council would neither be able to refer the situation to the ICC for prosecution of the crime of aggression nor be able to utilize any other of its typical enforcement measures under the UN Charter. Scholars, states' representatives, and non-governmental organizations began to call for the establishment of an aggression-specific tribunal for the situation and suggested various possible forms the tribunal might take. By June 2022, a group of scholars at the Yale Club in New York City put a concrete proposal on the table. The proposal was for a fully international tribunal to be created by agreement between the United Nations and Ukraine, upon the recommendation of the UN General Assembly. For many reasons, including the powerful precedent it could set, and particularly due to the ability of an international tribunal to avoid the application of personal immunity that otherwise could prevent the prosecution of top Russian leaders, this was seen as by far the strongest method by which to create the tribunal. A tribunal established through the UN also would carry the greatest legitimacy and appropriately convey that aggression is a global threat—an offence against the international order. Yet, the proposal was not supported by the G7 group of states, and, absent such support, the concern later arose that the tribunal would not garner a sufficiently persuasive number of votes within the UN General Assembly. Another reason for concern about the vote was that states from other regions had begun questioning (to some extent rightly) why so much focus was being put on creating a tribunal to address Russian aggression but not aggression in other regions.

Chapter 6 explores the competing proposal tabled by Germany, the United Kingdom, and the United States, which they described as a "hybrid tribunal", but which was basically a plan to use a Ukrainian chamber with international features or support. For many reasons, this proposal appeared to be far weaker than the proposal for an international tribunal established through the United Nations. It faced potential constitutional impediments within the Ukrainian system and would result in personal immunity for top Russian leaders. Nor was it seen to carry nearly the same precedential weight as an international tribunal, because having Ukrainian judges adjudicating cases of Russian aggression—potentially *in absentia* as is permitted under Ukrainian law—would lack the appearance of impartiality, even if actual impartiality could be achieved. The G7 states came to endorse this Ukrainian hybrid model; meanwhile Ukraine opposed it. Thereafter, months of negotiations ensued within a Core Group of States working to establish consensus on how to move forward with a crime of aggression tribunal for the situation. Yet, during the first year of negotiations within the Core Group, deadlock resulted between those states that supported the establishment of an international tribunal and those that supported utilizing a domestic Ukrainian one. Clearly, a third way would need to be found in order for a crime of aggression tribunal to be established in the situation of Ukraine.

Chapter 7 discusses the proposal that eventually emerged and was accepted by both groups of states in the Core Group. They agreed that the Special Tribunal on the Crime of Aggression against Ukraine would be formed by agreement between Ukraine and the Council of Europe, with states from other regions able to join in endorsing the Tribunal. Such broader backing could increase the Tribunal's base of support beyond being solely a regionally backed tribunal, making it more international. As of late 2025, hurdles remain. Specifically, states in the Council of Europe (and beyond) must decide whether to become parties to a certain Enlarged Partial Agreement[90] and/or enter into cooperation agreements with the Tribunal. They must also ensure that the Tribunal has sufficient funding to operate. Key issues as to the Tribunal's operations have been resolved. These include the question of immunities, the issue of trials *in absentia*, and whether there will be a fully independent prosecutor or cases will be referred from Ukraine. The Tribunal will utilize a definition of the crime that is similar, but not identical, to the internationally accepted definition of the crime of aggression found in Article 8*bis* of the Rome Statute. The compromises reached on some of the issues—particularly recognizing personal immunity for top Russian (and other) leaders—present the question of when too many compromises suggest that one should decline to pursue the establishment of a tribunal. The author does not suggest that point was reached, since failing to pursue accountability for the crime of aggression in the situation would prove to be a profound mistake. Yet, the chapter details how powerful states lobbied to weaken the Special Tribunal's statute (particularly on the issue of immunities), making it a less powerful one than it could have been. The chapter closes by addressing some of the challenges ahead if or when the Tribunal becomes operational. Above all, the Tribunal, if established, must prove itself to be a fair and credible one in its operations so that the potential to ensure at least some measure of justice and deterrence is not squandered.

The final chapter acknowledges that creating a tribunal to adjudicate the crime of aggression in the situation of Ukraine would not resolve the gap in ICC jurisdiction that exists vis-à-vis the crime. This must be resolved if the crime is to be meaningfully prosecuted and state actors are to be deterred (to the extent deterrence is possible) from committing the crime in the future. The chapter considers why States Parties to the Rome Statute should amend the Statute (specifically, the Kampala crime of

---

[90] Council of Europe (2025) Draft Resolution Establishing the Enlarged Partial Agreement on the Management Committee of the Special Tribunal for the Crime of Aggression against Ukraine. https://www.riigiteataja.ee/aktilisa/2170/2202/6002/760XV_Ukraina_ingl_k_L1.pdf.

aggression amendments)[91] to harmonize the ICC's jurisdiction over all four of its core crimes. Such an amendment would create considerably more jurisdiction before the ICC over the crime of aggression than presently exists. The chapter makes the case that there is no coherent reason for the ICC to have only the sliver of jurisdiction that it possesses over the crime, a situation that only entrenches double standards, exceptionalism, and impunity. Harmonizing the ICC's jurisdiction also would provide a broader answer to states that question the focus on the crime of aggression only in the situation of Ukraine. It would make it clear that this is not a crime that should be enforced only in one situation, but prosecuted more systematically in order to try to make a meaningful contribution to global stability and world peace. Unfortunately, in a Special Session of the ICC's ASP held in July 2025, a limited group of influential states was able to block the negotiations that could have resulted in the ICC having more jurisdiction over the crime, deferring the topic to future negotiations to be held in 2029.

In conclusion, the book asks whether, when it comes to the crime of aggression, states are really ready to go beyond the one-sided approach to justice, "victors' justice", that was imposed before the Nuremberg and Tokyo Tribunals. In weakening the Special Tribunal's statute (particularly, suspending proceedings against the troika while in office), powerful states appear to be acting not out of a desire to "protect" President Putin from prosecution, but out of a concern about setting a precedent for trying high-level leaders that could come back to haunt them. Unfortunately, the same dynamic arose in the context of the July 2025 negotiations to amend the Rome Statute to harmonize the ICC's jurisdiction over all Rome Statute crimes, where G7 states (except Germany, which led the amendment process), blocked progress. This behavior begs the question why powerful states appear to want the leeway for their leaders to be able to *manifestly* violate the UN Charter without ramifications in terms of individual criminal responsibility, since, as will be detailed, the crime of aggression only applies where there has been such a manifest violation of the Charter. These states should be embarrassed into explaining why they cannot stand behind the UN Charter's use of force provisions, where manifestly violated.

References

Bardelle A, Mora A (2025) "No Safe Haven" Is Not Enough—Universal Jurisdiction and Russia's War of Aggression. EJIL:*Talk!* https://www.ejiltalk.org/no-safe-haven-is-not-enough-universal-jurisdiction-and-russias-war-of-aggression/. Accessed 5 May 2025

Clapham A, Gaeta P (2014) The Oxford Handbook of International Law in Armed Conflict. Oxford University Press, Oxford

Committee of Ministers, Council of Europe (2023) Resolution CM/Res (2023) Establishing the Enlarged Partial Agreement on the Register of Damage Caused by the Aggression of

[91] International Criminal Court, Assembly of States Parties 2010.

the Russian Federation against Ukraine. https://rd4u.coe.int/documents/358068/372244/CM_Res%282023%293+-+Statute.pdf/2cebbb65-c86d-61c6-06c2-dca378ecd900?t=1708702115594. Accessed 8 August 2025

Crawford J (2019) Brownlie's Principles of Public International Law, 9th edn. Oxford University Press, Oxford

Dannenbaum T (2022) Mechanisms for Criminal Prosecution of Russia's Aggression Against Ukraine. Just Security. https://www.justsecurity.org/80626/mechanisms-for-criminal-prosecution-of-russias-aggression-against-ukraine/. Accessed 4 May 2025

Deutsch A, van den Berg S (2025) ICC Takes Philippines' Duterte Into Custody to Face Murder Charges for Drug War Killings. Reuters. https://www.reuters.com/world/asia-pacific/plane-carrying-philippine-ex-president-duterte-icc-delayed-flight-tracker-shows-2025-03-12/. Accessed 4 May 2025

Didkovska M (2025) Kyiv Initiates Talks on Claims Commission Treaty for Ukraine. The Gaze. https://thegaze.media/news/kyiv-initiates-talks-on-claims-commission-treaty-for-ukraine. Accessed 12 August 2025

Dunoff J, Hakimi M, Ratner S, Wippman D (2020) International Law Norms, Actors, Process: A Problem Oriented Approach, 5th edn. Wolters Kluwer, New York

Hartig A (2023) Making Aggression a Crime Under Domestic Law. T.C.M. Asser Press, The Hague

Herre B, Rodés-Guirao L, Roser M, Hasell J, Macdonald B (nd) War and Peace. https://ourworldindata.org/war-and-peace. Accessed 4 May 2025

Human Rights Watch (2025) Hungary: Orbán Government Withdraws from ICC. https://www.hrw.org/news/2025/06/16/hungary-orban-government-withdraws-from-icc. Accessed 15 June 2025

International Criminal Court (nd) Situation in Ukraine. https://www.icc-cpi.int/situations/ukraine. Accessed 4 May 2025

International Criminal Court, Assembly of States Parties (2010) Review Conference, The Crime of Aggression, ICC Doc. RC/Res.6

International Criminal Court, Assembly of States Parties (2017) Activation of the Jurisdiction of the Court Over the Crime of Aggression, Res. ICC-ASP/16/Res. 5

International Criminal Tribunal for the former Yugoslavia (nd) Case Information Sheet, Slobodan Milošević, "Kosovo, Croatia & Bosnia" (IT-02-54). https://www.icty.org/x/cases/slobodan_milosevic/cis/en/cis_milosevic_slobodan_en.pdf. Accessed 4 May 2025

International Law Commission (1954) Draft Code of Offences against the Peace and Security of Mankind

International Law Commission (2001) Draft Articles on the Responsibility of States for Internationally Wrongful Acts, with Commentaries (adopted), UN Doc. A/56/10

International Law Commission (2019) Report on the Work of the Seventy-First Session, UN Doc. A/74/10

Leshkovych T, Labuda P (2024) Prosecuting the Crime of Aggression in Ukraine and Beyond: Seizing Opportunities, Confronting Challenges and Avoiding False Dilemmas. Just Security. https://www.justsecurity.org/94104/prosecuting-aggression-ukraine-and-beyond/. Accessed 4 May 2025

Maxwell D (2016) Iraq: A Basis in Law? Law Society of Scotland. https://www.lawscot.org.uk/members/journal/issues/vol-61-issue-08/iraq-a-basis-in-law/. Accessed 4 May 2025

McAllister J (2020) Deterring Wartime Atrocities: Hard Lessons from the Yugoslav Tribunal. International Security 44: 84–128

McDougall C (2021) The Crime of Aggression Under the Rome Statute of the International Criminal Court, 2nd edn. Cambridge University Press, Cambridge

McDougall C (2024) Expanding the ICC's Jurisdiction over the Crime of Aggression. Journal of International Criminal Justice 1: 543–64

Miller A (2023) Without an Army: How ICC Indictments Reduce Atrocities. Journal of Peace Research 60: 573–87

Nevitt M (2025) Using Labels, Not Law to Justify Lethal Force: Inside the Venezuelan Boat Strike. Just Security. https://www.justsecurity.org/119985/labels-ustify-lethal-force-venezuelan-boat-strike/. Accessed 21 November 2025
OPCAT Database (nd) Association for the Prevention of Torture. https://www.apt.ch/knowledge-hub/opcat. Accessed 21 March 2025
Open Society Justice Initiative (2022) Model Indictment for the Crime of Aggression Committed Against Ukraine. https://www.justiceinitiative.org/publications/model-indictment-for-the-crime-of-aggression-committed-against-ukraine. Accessed 4 May 2025
Pancevski B (2024) One Million Are Now Dead or Injured in the Russia-Ukraine War. Wall St. Journal. https://www.wsj.com/world/one-million-are-now-dead-or-injured-in-the-russia-ukraine-war-b09d04e5?msockid=0671e85760f5627530dce108617263c3. Accessed 4 May 2025
Pobjie E (2017) Victims of the Crime of Aggression. In: Kreβ C, Barriga S (eds) The Crime of Aggression: A Commentary. Cambridge University Press, Cambridge
Rabinovitch B (2021) The Crime of Aggression and Pre-emptory Self-Defense. Global Justice Journal Queen's Law. https://globaljustice.queenslaw.ca/news/the-crime-of-aggression-and-pre-emptory-self-defence. Accessed 4 May 2025
Reisinger Coracini A (2017) (Extended) Synopsis: The Crime of Aggression under Domestic Criminal Law. In: Kreβ C, Barriga S (eds) The Crime of Aggression: A Commentary. Cambridge University Press, Cambridge
Reuters (2024) Ukraine Probing Over 122,000 Suspected War Crimes, Says Prosecutor. https://www.reuters.com/world/europe/ukraine-probing-over-122000-suspected-war-crimes-says-prosecutor-2024-02-23/. Accessed 4 May 2025
Reuters (2025) Mali, Burkina Faso and Niger Announce Exit from International Criminal Court. https://www.reuters.com/world/africa/mali-burkina-faso-niger-announce-exit-international-criminal-court-2025-09-23/. Accessed 3 October 2025
Rosen B, Bridgeman T, Gerami N (2025) The Day After US Strikes on Iran's Nuclear Program: Law & Policy. Just Security. https://www.justsecurity.org/115234/policy-legal-iran-nuclear-strikes/. Accessed 4 May 2025
The Clooney Foundation for Justice, Justice beyond Borders (2025) Justice Beyond Borders Data Set. Airtable. https://airtable.com/appceDWWzmrL1awQi/shrNhgLXq2g3Z3nSy/tblNt3dQ9b6F32QTU. Accessed 20 March 2025
Trahan J (2018) From Kampala to New York—The Final Negotiations to Activate the Jurisdiction of the International Criminal Court Over the Crime of Aggression. International Criminal Law Review 18: 197–243
Trahan J (2023) Legal Issues Surrounding Veto Use and Aggression. Case Western Reserve Journal of International Law 55: 93–146
Trahan J (2024) The Role of the UN Security Council and General Assembly In Responding to the Invasion of Ukraine. Polish Review of International and European Law 12: 23–64
Trial International (nd) Universal Jurisdiction Review. https://trialinternational.org/wp-content/uploads/2023/11/UJAR-2023_13112023_updated.pdf. Accessed 4 May 2025
Zelenskyy V (2022) We Must Create a Special Tribunal on the Crime of Aggression Against Ukraine—Address by President Volodymyr Zelenskyy to the Participants of the Public Debate "War and Law" in Paris. https://www.president.gov.ua/en/news/mayemo-stvoriti-specialnij-tribunal-shodo-zlochinu-agresiyi-78285. Accessed 5 May 2025

Other Documents

Agreement between the Council of Europe and the Government of Ukraine on the Establishment of the Special Tribunal for the Crime of Aggression against Ukraine (2025) https://rm.coe.int/agreement-and-statut-english/1680b66127. Accessed 28 September 2025
Charter of the International Military Tribunal (1945) 85 UNTS 251

Charter of the United Nations (1945) 33 UNTS 933

Convention Against Torture and Other Cruel, Inhuman, or Degrading Treatment or Punishment (1984) 1465 UNTS 85

Council of Europe (2025) Draft Resolution Establishing the Enlarged Partial Agreement on the Management Committee of the Special Tribunal for the Crime of Aggression against Ukraine. https://www.riigiteataja.ee/aktilisa/2170/2202/6002/760XV_Ukraina_ingl_k_L1.pdf

International Court of Justice (nd) *Application of the Convention Against Torture and Other Cruel, Inhuman or Degrading Treatment or Punishment (Canada and the Netherlands v. Syrian Arab Republic)*

International Military Tribunal (1946) Judgment of 1 October 1946, in The Trial of German Major War Criminals. Proceedings of the International Military Tribunal Sitting at Nuremberg, Germany, Part 22 (22 August 1946 to 1 October 1946)

International Military Tribunal for the Far East, 19 January 1946, Special Proclamation by the Supreme Commander to the Allied Powers at Tokyo, amended 26 April 1946

Protocol Additional to the Geneva Conventions of 12 August 1949, and Relating to the Protection of Victims of International Armed Conflicts (1977)

Republic of Kosovo (2015) Law No.05/L-053 on Specialist Chambers and Specialist Prosecutor's Office

Rome Statute of the International Criminal Court (1998) 2187 UNTS 90 (as amended)

Special Court for Sierra Leone (2012) *Prosecutor v. Charles Ghankay Taylor*, Trial Chamber Judgment, SCSL-03-1-T. https://www.rscsl.org/Documents/Decisions/Taylor/1283/SCSL-03-01-T-1283.pdf. Accessed 4 May 2025

Special Court for Sierra Leone (2014) *Prosecutor v. Charles Ghankay Taylor,* Appeals Chamber Judgment, SCSL-03-01-A, Special Court for Sierra Leone. https://www.rscsl.org/Documents/Decisions/Taylor/Appeal/1389/SCSL-03-01-A-1389.pdf. Accessed 4 May 2025

Statement by Prosecutor Karim A. A. Khan KC on the Issuance of Arrest Warrants Against President Vladimir Putin and Ms Maria Lvova-Belova (2023). https://www.icc-cpi.int/news/statement-prosecutor-karim-khan-kc-issuance-arrest-warrants-against-president-vladimir-putin. Accessed 4 May 2025

Statute of the Extraordinary African Chambers within the Courts of Senegal Created to Prosecute International Crimes Committed in Chad between 7 June 1982 and 1 December 1990 (2011) African Yearbook of International Law Online/Annuaire Africain de Droit International Online 19: 443–58. https://doi.org/10.1163/22116176-01900021. Accessed 4 May 2025

Statute of the Special Court for Sierra Leone (2002). https://www.refworld.org/legal/constinstr/unsc/2002/en/43606. Accessed 20 March 2025

Statute of the Special Tribunal for Lebanon (2007) attached to United Nations Security Council Resolution 1757 (2007)

United Nations General Assembly Resolution 95(I) 1946

United Nations General Assembly Resolution 3314 (XXIX) 1974

United Nations Treaty Collection (nd) Status, Rome Statute of the International Criminal Court. https://treaties.un.org/Pages/ViewDetails.aspx?src=TREATY&mtdsg_no=XVIII-10&chapter=18&clang=_en. Accessed 4 May 2025

Chapter 2
The Development of the Crime of Aggression: Historical Background to the 1998 Rome Conference

Contents

Abstract By the time states, in 1998, included the crime of aggression in the Rome Statute of the International Criminal Court, they were building on the foundations of centuries-old attempts to limit aggressive war-making through the rule of law. These efforts trace back from early *jus ad bellum* theory and the work of peace activists in the 1800s, to the 1920 founding of the League of Nations, the 1928 conclusion of the Kellogg-Briand Pact, and the 1945 founding of the United Nations. The years 1945–1946 also saw the Allied prosecutions before the International Military Tribunal at Nuremberg and, in 1946–1948, those before the International Military Tribunal for the Far East (Tokyo). These developments—attempting to rein in aggressive war either through the framework of state responsibility or individual criminal responsibility—provide the foundations for the inclusion of the crime of aggression in the Rome Statute and the overall rationale for prosecuting the crime.

Keywords Crime of aggression · Nuremberg Tribunal · *Jus ad bellum* · Just war theory · *Jus in bello* · Peace movement · Peace Palace · UN Charter · Prohibition on the use of force · League of Nations · Kellogg-Briand Pact · International Court of Justice · UN Security Council · Permanent members · Veto power · Rome Statute

J. Trahan, *The Crime of Aggression and Russia's Invasion of Ukraine*,
https://doi.org/10.1007/978-94-6265-763-2_2

2.1 Introduction

This chapter discusses the development of the crime of aggression from the 1800s to the 1998 Rome Conference, where states agreed to the Rome Statute that established the International Criminal Court ("ICC").[1] The chapter commences by tracing the crime's early roots in *jus ad bellum* theory and the peace movement of the 1800s, as well as historic developments related to limitations on the conduct of war (*jus in bello*). The chapter then examines two different methods by which states have attempted to rein in aggressive war—at the level of state responsibility and the level of individual criminal responsibility. The chapter traces the first approach from the aspirations behind the founding of the League of Nations, as well as the 1928 Kellogg-Briand Pact in which states reached the historic agreement to prohibit aggressive war. After the horrors of World War II, states additionally pursued the second approach, prosecuting individuals for crimes against peace before the International Military Tribunal at Nuremberg (the "Nuremberg Tribunal") and, later, the International Military Tribunal for the Far East (the "Tokyo Tribunal"). Prohibiting aggressive war was also the central animating purpose behind the founding of the United Nations in 1945, with the UN Charter's prohibition of the use of force constituting one of its core provisions. The chapter concludes by tracing legal developments during the Cold War and leading into the 1998 negotiations where the crime was poised to be included as one of the four core crimes under the Rome Statute.

2.2 *Jus ad Bellum, Jus in Bello,* and the Early Peace Movement

2.2.1 Early Jus ad (contra) Bellum *Theory*

The law against aggressive war-making by states is part of a field of international law referred to as *jus ad bellum*. This translates as the laws (or justness) of going to war—although it could also be thought of as *jus contra bellum* (the laws against going to war).[2] Just war theory has ancient roots, starting with ancient Egyptian,[3] as well

[1] Rome Statute of the International Criminal Court (1998) 2187 UNTS 90 (as amended) ("Rome Statute (1998) (as amended)").

[2] As Salmon O. Levinson wrote in 1917: "We should have, not as now, laws *of* war, but laws *against* war; just as there are not laws *of* murder or *of* poisoning, but laws against them". Salmon O. Levinson to Jacob Schiff, 25 August 1917, quoted in Hathaway and Shapiro 2017, p. 108.

[3] Cox 2017. The Indian Hindu epic, *The Mahabharata* (roughly 400 CE), discusses "righteous war". Robinson 2017. For Chinese theory on war, see Kwon 2023. Aristotle (384–322 BCE) wrote on the topic in 350 BCE in *Politics, Book 1.* Ancient Roman writers included Cicero (106–43 BCE) and Livy (59 BCE–17 CE) writing on "just cause" for war. See Atkins 2023, pp. 170–204.

as theological, ones. The latter were based on the notion of requiring a "just cause", which Christian states supposedly had to conquer so-called "heathen" adversaries.[4]

Around 1500–1600, scholarly writings on international law proliferated, including the writing of Hugo Grotius (1583–1645) of The Netherlands, known in Dutch as *Hugo de Groot*.[5] Renowned as a proponent of natural law,[6] Grotius held theories on just war that were far different than those that exist today. They were significantly more permissive in accepting reasons for a state to have recourse to war. Grotius took the view that war "is good for defending lives and territory, of course. But it is also good for collecting debts . . . . War is also good for restitution: [i]f property is taken without permission, it may be recovered by force of arms. War is also good for securing compensation . . . [and] for punishing criminals".[7] He thus concluded: "[a] war is said to be 'just' if it consists in the execution of a right".[8]

By the eighteenth and nineteenth centuries, there was "an almost complete abandonment of the distinction between legal and illegal wars".[9] The field of international law, historically, has also unfortunately justified colonial conquest (often achieved through extreme savagery), employing the fiction that land prior to occupation by a colonial power was *terra nullius*, or empty land.[10] International law was certainly also

---

[4] One of the first theologians to write on the subject was St. Augustine (354–430 CE), who wrote:

> Just wars are usually defined as those which avenge injuries, when the nation or city against which warlike action is to be directed has neglected either to punish wrongs committed by its own citizens or to restore what has been unjustly taken from it. Further, that kind of war is undoubtedly just which God Himself ordains.

Malanczuk 1997. See also Aquinas (1265–74); Reichberg 2017 (also discussing St. Thomas Aquinas).

[5] Early additional writers include: Francisco de Vitoria (1480–1546), Francisco Suárez (1548–1617), Alberico Gentili (1552–1608), Richard Zouche (1590–1660), and Samuel von Pufendorf (1632–1694). Subsequent writers include: Christian Wolff (1676–1756) and Emmerich de Vattel (1714–1767).

[6] Grotius "believed nations should be guided by natural law", which followed from the "nature of things" as "discovered by human reason", as opposed to religious origins. See Powell 2000.

[7] Hathaway and Shapiro 2017, pp. 9–10, citing Grotius 1950, pp. 102–04.

[8] Ibid., citing Grotius 1950, p. 50. "Theology prior to the 16th century, concentrated almost exclusively on the right to declare war, the *jus ad bellum*, insisting that war could only be fought, if declared by a competent authority, fought for a just cause, with proper intent, and a proportionality between provocation and response, and toward the end of reestablishing peace". Stacey 1994, p. 30.

[9] Malanczuk 1997, p. 306. Summarizing thinking on *jus ad bellum*, Hathaway and Shapiro write:

> The Old World Order [pre-1928] was defined first and foremost by the belief that war is a legitimate means of righting wrongs. The inhabitants of the Old World Order would have found the famous maxim from Carl von Clausewitz's *On War* to be incontrovertibly true: *War is simply the continuation of politics by other means.* Resorting to arms did not signal a failure in the system: it was how the system worked. War was an instrument of justice. *Might was Right.*

Hathaway and Shapiro 2017, p. xv, citing von Clausewitz 1832/1976, p. 87 (emphasis in original).

[10] Anghie 1999. The Spanish and Portuguese also claimed a right to extend the Catholic faith and dominion over the people of such lands; thus, an alternative to *terra nullius* was the argument that

Eurocentric in its development,[11] with the approach eventually starting to change due to the growing significance of non-European states as powerful trading partners.[12] Oona A. Hathaway and Scott J. Shapiro trace these and later related developments in their excellent book, *The Internationalists: How a Radical Plan to Outlaw War Remade the World.*[13] Thus, I will only briefly describe them here.

2.2.2 The Early Peace Movement

The early peace movement, also known as the "peace through law movement",[14] had as its goal the elimination of war, with a particular focus on establishing an international court for arbitration that would "enable states to solve disputes through nonviolent methods".[15] It was furthered in the late 1800s in Europe[16] by the writing of Austrian Baroness Bertha von Suttner. Her book, *Die Waffen Nieder!* (*Lay Down Your Arms!*), published in 1889, "became an international bestseller and propelled her to the forefront of the peace movement".[17] Her 1912 pamphlet entitled "*Die Barbarisierung der Luft*" ("The Barbarization of the Sky") followed, with an outcry against weaponization of the air and advocacy that the sky should be a weapons-free zone.[18] Von Suttner was the first woman to be awarded the Nobel Peace Prize, which

---

the land was occupied and the inhabitants needed to acknowledge the "one true faith" and the sovereigns who supposedly represented its authority on earth. See, e.g., Gilder Lehrman Institute of American History nd ("The Papal Bull, '*Inter Caetera*,' issued by Pope Alexander VI on 4 May 1493, played a central role in the Spanish conquest of the New World", as it "stated that any land not inhabited by Christians was available to be 'discovered' . . .".). "[I]n wars against outsiders, infidel, or [supposed] barbarians, the West had inherited a brutal legacy from the Romans, which they termed *bellum romanum*, or *guerre mortelle*, a conflict in which no holds were barred and all those designated as enemy, whether bearing arms or not, could be indiscriminately slaughtered". Howard 1994, p. 3.

[11] Pushing back against this notion, R. P. Anand writes: "when European adventurers arrived in Asia in the 15th century, 'they found themselves in the middle of a network of states and inter-state relation based on traditions which were more ancient than their own and in no way inferior to notions of European civilization'". Anand 1983.

[12] "[T]he Law of Nations" "originally arose between the States of Christendom only and for hundreds of years was confined to these States . . . . But from about the beginning of the 19th century matters gradually changed". Oppenheim 1905, p. 30, Sect. 26.

[13] Hathaway and Shapiro 2017.

[14] May 2019, p. 208.

[15] Ibid.

[16] There were also much earlier pacifist writers, such as Erasmus of Rotterdam (a/k/a Erasmus) (1466–1536) who was an early critic of the notion of "just war". See Fernández 1973.

[17] May 2019, p. 208, n 2.

[18] Von Suttner 1912/2016. At the time, the issue was the dropping of projectiles from uncontrollable air balloons. May 2016, p. xii. Science fiction writers such as H. G. Wells were simultaneously writing "frightening tales of aerial combat" in "his 1908 book, *The War in the Air*". See Davis Biddle 1994, p. 146. Bertha von Suttner was not alone in her thinking. In 1912, the International Arbitration League, based in London, published *A Memorial Against the Use of Armed Airships*. May 2016,

she received in 1905, having also inspired Alfred Nobel to create the prestigious award.[19]

In the United States and United Kingdom, a number of early peace societies were founded, including the American Peace Society and the London Peace Society.[20] The first organized peace society in the United States was the New York Peace Society founded in 1815.[21] The Universal Peace Union, founded in 1866 in Rhode Island (later chartered in Philadelphia), grew to have "membership in the tens of thousands" and "called for immediate disarmament and the non-violent resolution of disputes through arbitration".[22] Through a confluence of the peace movement and the women's rights movement, suffragist Jane Addams (later also a Nobel Peace Prize laureate) in 1919 founded the Women's International League for Peace and Freedom, a group that still exists today.

2.2.3 Development of Jus in Bello

Developments in the early peace movement occurred in parallel with those in the area of *jus in bello* (the law governing the conduct of war).[23] This law, also referred to as International Humanitarian Law ("IHL") or the laws of war, has as its goal the

---

p. xii. "The 1899 *Declaration on the Launching of Projectors and Explosives from Balloons* had placed a five-year ban on 'the launching of projectors and explosives from balloons, and by other new methods of similar nature'". Ibid., p. xi. Von Suttner's vision, of course, would not prevail. A member of the US delegation to the 1899 Hague Peace Commission put forward the contrary argument that "international law should allow for the possibility that steerable flying machines could someday help to wage war more efficiently . . .". Ibid., p. xiii.

[19] May 2019, p. 207.

[20] For background, see Brock 1994; Liddington 1989.

[21] May 2019, p. 209. Summarizing developments in the early peace movement, May writes:

> The (non-violent) "war against war" was the subject of international peace congresses that were held in Europe in the mid 1800s, but in the early 1800s English Quakers began to urge the formation of peace societies combating war. Even before that, in the US, David Low Dodge, a Christian but not a Quaker, recognized that scripture and the doctrine of (violent) self-defense were incompatible, and published in 1809 the peace pamphlet "The Mediator's Kingdom Not of This World". Lodge's idea that armed retaliation was incompatible with scripture eventually evolved into the first organized peace society in the United States, the New York Peace Society (NYPS). Formed in 1815, the NYPS encouraged states to solve their disputes through pacific means.

Ibid. (internal citations omitted). The US peace movement was later furthered through the writings of Boston attorney and future Massachusetts Senator Charles Sumner. Ibid.

[22] Ibid., p. 210.

[23] *Jus ad bellum* and *jus in bello* are separate areas of the law (i.e., they are not connected). "The reason for this lies in the cardinal principle that *jus in bello* applies in cases of armed conflict, whether or not the inception of the conflict is lawful under *jus ad bellum*". Roberts and Guelff 2000, p. 1.

mitigation of some of the more horrific aspects of war, protecting civilians and other noncombatants, and affording at least some protection to combatants.[24]

Early rules regarding armed conflict can be found as far back as the writings of Hammurabi (1792–1750 BCE)[25] and Chinese general Sun Tzu, writing in the fourth century BCE in "The Art of War".[26] One finds them also in Greek and Roman customs and the Chivalric Codes of the Middle Ages.[27] Momentum related to *jus in bello* was propelled in the nineteenth century[28] by the publication by Henri Dunant in 1862 of *A Memory of Solferino.*[29] The book chronicled the casualties after a battle in Solferino, Italy, in 1859, between Franco-Italian and Austrian troops, which resulted in 40,000 fatalities. Dunant worked with local townspeople to assist the wounded and dying.[30] The outcry that resulted from the attention brought by his writing led to the establishment of the International Committee of the Red Cross, and their work led to agreement on the 1864 Geneva Convention.[31] Dispatches from the Crimean War (1853–1856) and photographs from the American Civil War (1861–1865) also "brought the realities of mass military slaughter" to public attention.[32]

Progress to limit the methods of warfare was furthered in 1868[33] by a conference convened by Russian Czar Alexander II in St. Petersburg, resulting in the St. Petersburg Declaration. "The St. Petersburg Declaration set out three fundamental principles [that emerged from preexisting custom and which] are still valid today:

---

[24] The goals of IHL are explained as follows:

> Humanitarian law recognizes that states cannot generally be expected to refrain from using weapons or tactics necessary to achieve legitimate military aims . . . . Thus, international humanitarian law attempts to shield individuals from all harm that cannot be justified as necessary and proportionate to the successful pursuit of military objectives, and from some types of harm, such as torture, whatever their military utility.

Dunoff et al. 2010, p. 489.

[25] See Hammurabi 1754 BCE/1903.

[26] For an English translation, see Giles 1910.

[27] Roberts and Guelff 2000, p. 3. There were "constraints as they applied in classical antiquity, in the High Middle Ages when war in Western Europe was specifically constrained by codes of chivalry and the dictates of Christendom, in the Europe of the Renaissance and Napoleonic eras, and in the frontier wars of North America". Howard 1994, p. 1. For constraints on war in classical Greece, see Ober 1994. For the "age of chivalry", see Stacey 1994.

[28] There existed intervening developments. For example, the King of Sweden in 1621 decreed various articles of war. Roberts and Guelff 2000, p. 3.

[29] Dunant 1862.

[30] Dunoff et al. 2010, p. 499.

[31] Ibid. Its full title was The Convention for the Amelioration of the Condition of the Wounded Armies in the Field.

[32] Howard et al. 1994, p. 5.

[33] An earlier important conference was held in 1856, the Congress of Paris, "which attempted to set limits to naval warfare" and did a great deal to end privateering. Ibid., p. 7.

the principle of distinction, the principle of proportionality, the prohibition of unnecessary suffering. It also proclaimed that at some point military necessity must yield to requirements of humanity".[34]

Important early peace conferences were held in The Hague in 1899 and 1907. The First Hague Peace Conference in 1899 resulted in three conventions and three declarations, and the Second Hague Peace Conference led to the conclusion of 13 conventions.[35] The first Hague Peace Conference saw the conclusion of the first multilateral treaty on the laws of land warfare,[36] which importantly also acknowledged the continuing significance of unwritten customary principles governing hostilities, known as the "Martens Clause".[37] One of the conventions concluded, the 1899 Hague Convention for the Pacific Settlement of International Disputes, contained provisions establishing 'good offices' as one of the peaceful methods of dispute settlements", and the 1907 Hague Convention for the Pacific Settlement of Disputes "enumerates the various forms of non-violent dispute settlement . . . ".[38]

Meanwhile, in the United States, Columbia University Professor Francis Lieber drafted a code, issued in 1863, to govern the conduct of hostilities during the US Civil War, commonly referred to as the Lieber Code.[39] Developed on the basis of pre-existing custom, it was "the first comprehensive codification of the regulations for the conduct of war by land",[40] and became the model for other national codes.[41]

The proliferation of laws on the conduct of war can be explained by the fact that during "the latter half of the 19th century, . . . the growing range and destructive power of weapons were beginning exponentially to increase the lethality of warfare,

[34] International Committee of the Red Cross nd. The principle of distinction goes back to the writing of Emer de Vattel, who explained in 1758, "the people, the peasants, the citizens, take no part in war, and generally have nothing to fear from the sword of the enemy". Hathaway and Shapiro 2017, p. 75, citing de Vattel 1797/2008.

[35] For details, see Roberts and Guelff 2000, p. 5. The Third Hague Peace Conference planned for 1915 never came to pass due to the advent of the First World War. May 2016, p. xvi.

[36] Roberts 1994, p. 121.

[37] The Martens Clause stated:

> Until a more complete code of the laws of war is issued, the High Contracting Parties think it right to declare that in cases not included in the Regulations adopted by them, populations and belligerents remain under the protection and empire of the principles of international law, as they result from the usages established between civilized nations, from the laws of humanity and the requirements of the public conscience.

Roberts and Guelff 2000, p. 8. The clause was "introduced for the first time in the preamble of the 1899 Hague Convention (Convention with Respect to the Laws and Customs of War on Land), on the proposal of Fyodor Fyodorovich Martens, a Russian lawyer and member of the Russian delegation to the 1899 International Peace Conference". Ibid.

[38] May 2019, p. 213, n 4.

[39] Its full title is "Instructions for the Government of the Armies of the United States in the Field". It was issued on 24 April 1963, as General Orders No. 100 by US President Abraham Lincoln. Gesley 2018.

[40] Howard et al. 1994, p. 6.

[41] Roberts and Guelff 2000, pp. 12–13. For background, see Witt 2012.

both on the battlefield and beyond it".[42] Thus, constraints on the conduct of war were seen as "all the more desirable as the weapons of war became increasingly destructive".[43]

2.2.4 *Continued Activism in the Peace Movement*

In addition to the 1899 and 1907 Hague Peace Conferences, momentum in the peace movement or "peace through law" movement[44] continued in 1913 with the opening of the Peace Palace (*Vredespaleis*) in The Hague, The Netherlands. The building was paid for by Scottish-American industrialist and philanthropist Andrew Carnegie.[45] Based on earlier ideas,[46] the concept behind it was a bold one: that states should arbitrate, and later, litigate, instead of going to war. It was designed as a forum where states could work through their grievances without recourse to force. It initially housed the Permanent Court of Arbitration (1913 to the present) and later the Permanent Court of International Justice (1922–1946), as well as its successor, the International Court of Justice ("ICJ") (1946 to the present).

These legal developments and aspirations for states to resolve their disputes peacefully (or with restraint, should states go to war) catastrophically failed to prevent World War I (1914–1918). The war left a cataclysmic 20 million dead.[47] The horrific number of fatalities and level of destruction throughout Europe, however, brought something of a "sea change" in thinking about war, a vision that built on earlier precedent. No longer could war be viewed as simply a method by which states resolved their disputes; rather, many came to consider it an appalling evil that must be avoided.[48]

---

[42] Witt 2012.

[43] Roberts and Guelff 2000, pp. 29–31.

[44] The phrase "peace through law" is also the title of an influential book by Hans Kelsen, first published in 1944. See Kelsen 1944.

[45] Carnegie (nd) Peace Palace. https://www.vredespaleis.nl/carnegie/?lang=en. Accessed 4 May 2025.

[46] Creation of a Permanent Court of Arbitration was actually agreed on earlier at the 1899 Hague Peace Conference and is described as a "watershed moment" in the "Peace through Law" movement. May 2019, p. 214.

[47] "The total number of military and civilian casualties in World War I, was around 40 million. There were 20 million deaths and 21 million wounded. The total number of deaths includes 9.7 million military personnel and about 10 million civilians". *Reperes, Partenariat Educatif Grundtvig* 2009–2011. https://www.census.gov/history/pdf/reperes112018.pdf. Accessed 4 May 2025.

[48] For violations of the laws of war during World War I, see Roberts 1994, pp. 123–25.

2.3 Bold Visions to Prevent War—The Covenant of the League of Nations and the Kellogg-Briand Pact

International law initially responded to the horrors of World War I boldly with US President Woodrow Wilson's vision for a League of Nations, but also somewhat tepidly in trying to rein in war. President Wilson, in drafting plans for a new world order, "committed himself to creating a new international order with a League of Nations at its center that would peacefully manage conflicts between states, great and small and put an end to senseless warfare".[49] Indeed, the preamble to the Covenant of the League of Nations (signed in 1919), states that the "high contracting parties, [i]n order to promote international co-operation and to achieve international peace and security *by the acceptance of obligations not to resort to war* . . . [a]gree to this Covenant of the League of Nations".[50] Yet, in the body of the Covenant, states were not prohibited from going to war, but were mandated first to pursue arbitration or litigation or to submit the matter to the Council of the League of Nations, and to utilize a "three months cooling off" period.[51] This provision was seemingly drafted as a reaction to the way in which World War I commenced; one can only wonder, had cooler heads prevailed, whether the war—not based on ideological reasons, but regional alliances[52]—possibly could have been averted. People also commonly viewed the proliferation of more complex, expensive, and deadly weapons systems as one of the factors that led to World War I; hence, there was also an increased focus on limiting arms in both the Covenant as well as specific arms control regimes during the interwar era.[53]

---

[49] Conway-Lanz 2017; see also Knock 1992.

[50] The Covenant of the League of Nations. https://www.ungeneva.org/en/about/league-of-nations/covenant. Accessed 4 May 2025, preamble (emphasis added) ("United Nations nd-b").

[51] Article 12 (1) provided:

> The Members of the League agree that, if there should arise between them any dispute likely to lead to a rupture, they will submit the matter either to arbitration or judicial settlement or to inquiry by the Council, and they agree in no case to resort to war until three months after the award by the arbitrators or the judicial decision, or the report by the Council.

Ibid., Article 12(1).

[52] See Hathaway and Shapiro 2017, p. 102 (describing the "chain reaction" that resulted in World War I).

[53] United Nations nd-b, note 50, Article 8. Conventions and agreements to regulate armed conflict concluded in the intervening years include: the 1919 Treaty of Versailles, which prohibited certain methods of warfare; the 1922 Treaty of Washington on submarine and gas warfare (signed, but not in force); the 1925 Geneva Protocol on gas and bacteriological warfare; the 1929 Geneva Convention on wounded and sick; the 1929 Geneva Convention on prisoners of war; the 1930 London Treaty on naval armaments and warfare; and the 1936 London *Procès-Verbal* on submarine warfare (which were all signed and entered into force). Roberts and Guelff 2000, p. 6. The 1923 Rules of Air Warfare were agreed on but never ratified. Davis Biddle 1994, p. 148. The Washington Naval Conference, 1921–1922, was seen as particularly significant:

It was not until the Kellogg-Briand Pact (a/k/a Pact of Paris or The General Treaty for the Renunciation of War as National Policy) was signed in 1928 that states clearly undertook to renounce aggressive war.[54] The Pact, named after US Secretary of State Frank B. Kellogg and French Minister of Foreign Affairs Aristide Briand, was based on the ideas of writers such as Chicago lawyer Salmon O. Levinson. In an article in *The New Republic,* he wrote that "[t]he only real way to bring an end to war was . . . [t]he outlawry of war'".[55] In 1921, Levinson formed the Committee for the Outlawry of War to promote the idea; he was later asked by Secretary of State Kellogg to prepare a draft of what became the Kellogg-Briand Pact.[56] In the Pact, states "condemn[ed] recourse to war for the solution of international controversies, and renounc[ed] [war] as an instrument of national policy in their relations with one another".[57] States also agreed that "the settlement or solution of all disputes or conflicts of whatever nature or of whatever origin they may be, which may arise among [states], shall never be sought except by pacific means".[58]

These commitments represented a hugely significant milestone: states finally entered into a multilateral treaty agreeing not to utilize war to solve their differences. Hathaway and Shapiro explain:

> The Peace Pact quite plainly did not create world peace. Yet it was among the most transformative events of human history, one that has, ultimately, made our world far more peaceful.

> Senator William E. Borah (R–Idaho) led a congressional effort to demand that the United States engage its two principal competitors in the naval arms race, Japan and the United Kingdom, in negotiations for disarmament . . . . Three major treaties emerged out of the Washington Naval Conference: the Five-Power Treaty, the Four-Power Treaty, and the Nine-Power Treaty.

United States Department of State Office of the Historian nd. The Washington Naval Conference was particularly notable because of the arms limitations as well as the Nine-Power Treaty that dealt with other root causes by trying to address the power vacuum of weak imperial China. Trahan 2024c.

[54] Treaty Between the United States and Other Powers Providing for the Renunciation of War as an Instrument of National Policy (1928) (Kellogg-Briand Pact). For the drafting history of the Pact, see Hathaway and Shapiro 2017, pp. 120–30. The Kellogg-Briand Pact passed the US Senate 85 to 1, after strong support by Senator William Borah. Ibid., p. 129.

[55] Ibid., p. 109, citing Levinson 1918, p. 172. This was followed in 1919 by Levinson and Senator Philander C. Knox (Pennsylvania) writing a pamphlet entitled *Plan to Outlaw War*. Hathaway and Shapiro 2017, p. 112, citing Levinson 1921. "Levinson's outlawry plan included a general treaty with civilized nations to abolish war by making it a criminal offense; establishing a code of international law based on equality of nations and justice; and an international court with independence and affirmative jurisdiction". Gillespie 2018, p. 20, citing Levinson nd. "Although Levinson had advocated just such a treaty for years, including in correspondence with Kellogg, Kellogg later claimed the idea as his own". Hathaway and Shapiro 2017, p. 124. Senator Borah became a key ally of Levinson, see Gillespie 2018, p. 31, with James T. Shotwell also playing a significant role in the negotiations of the Pact. Hathaway and Shapiro 2017, pp. 116–18.

[56] Gillespie 2018, pp. 34, 37, citing Ferrell 1952, p. 100.

[57] League of Nations Treaty Series, Vol. XCIV (1929). https://treaties.un.org/doc/Publication/UNTS/LON/Volume%2094/v94.pdf. Accessed 4 May 2025.

[58] Ibid.

> It did not end war between states, but it marked the beginning of the end—and, with it, the replacement of one international order with another.[59]

A weakness of the Pact, however, was that it lacked any enforcement mechanism.[60] The Pact, as well as the League of Nations, were ultimately completely ineffective in preventing World War II.[61] It did not help that the United States had been kept from joining the League of Nations by an isolationist US Senate that refused to ratify the treaty.[62]

After millions of deaths and the horrific atrocities of World War II[63]—including the unimaginable crimes of the Holocaust—the international community responded

---

[59] Hathaway and Shapiro 2017, p. xiii. See also Kreß 2018, pp. 2–3 ("the 1928 Kellogg-Briand Pact . . . marked the transition in positive international law from a *ius ad bellum* to a *ius contra bellum*".). By 1934, the following countries had become parties to the Pact: Afghanistan, Albania, Australia, Austria, Belgium, Brazil, Bulgaria, Canada, Chile, China, Columbia, Costa Rica, Cuba, Czechoslovakia, Danzig (later part of Poland), Denmark, Dominican Republic, Ecuador, Egypt, Estonia, Ethiopia, Finland, France, Germany, Greece, Guatemala, Haiti, Hejaz (later part of Saudi Arabia and Jordan), Honduras, Hungary, Iceland, India, Iraq, Irish Free State, Italy, Japan, Latvia, Liberia, Lithuania, Luxembourg, Mexico, The Netherlands, New Zealand, Nicaragua, Norway, Panama, Paraguay, Persia, Peru, Poland, Portugal, Romania, Siam, South Africa, Soviet Union, Spain, Sweden, Switzerland, Turkey, the United Kingdom, the United States, Venezuela, and Yugoslavia. Ibid., p. xii.

[60] Hathaway and Shapiro 2017, p. 127 ("Unlike the [Covenant of the League of Nations], the proposed [Kellogg-Briand Pact] did not allow states to go to war to enforce the peace. And unlike the Geneva protocol [of 1925], it did not provide for severe financial sanctions".).

[61] Summing up the failure of the Pact, Hathaway and Shapiro write:

> Three years after the grand pronouncement [to renounce war], Japan invaded China. Four years after that, Italy invaded Ethiopia. Four years later, Germany invaded Poland and then most of Europe. With the exception of Ireland, every one of the states that had gathered in Paris to renounce war was *at war*.

Hathaway and Shapiro 2017, p. xi (emphasis in original).

[62] United States Department of State 1920. Another impediment to the functioning of the League of Nations was that "unanimity among all members [present] was required" to reach decisions in both the Assembly and Council of the League of Nations. See Wouters and Ruys 2005, p. 5. For additional analysis of weaknesses of the League, see Mazower 2012, p. 136. Yet, the structure of the League was a direct precursor to the structure of the United Nations:

> The League of Nations consisted of three main organs. The Assembly, where all member states were represented on equal footing; the Council which was composed of permanent and non-permanent members; and the Secretariat which performed the day-to-day work at the League's headquarters in Geneva, Switzerland.

United Nations (nd-a). Main Organs of the League of Nations. https://www.ungeneva.org/en/about/league-of-nations/organs. Accessed 4 May 2025.

[63] See United States Department of Defense nd ("Official casualty sources estimate battle deaths at nearly 15 million military personnel and civilian deaths at over 38 million".). For analysis of the conduct of war during World War II, see Roberts 1994, pp. 128–33. Atrocities included infamous attacks on London, Coventry, Hamburg, and Dresden, the firebombing of Japanese cities, and, of course, use of nuclear weapons at Hiroshima and Nagasaki. Davis Biddle 1994, pp. 151, 154, 157. World War II "was the deadliest conflict in over a thousand years", Hathaway and Shapiro 2017, p. xi, citing Human Security Report 2013, p. 37. *Compare* Roberts 1994, p. 128 ("The nonuse

to threats to peace (fomenting aggressive war) through two principal legal avenues. The victorious allies decided to prosecute "crimes against peace" (now termed the crime of aggression) before the Nuremberg Tribunal, with the same approach pursued before the Tokyo Tribunal. States also tried to prevent future recourse to aggressive war through the founding of the United Nations, with a central focus of the UN Charter being the prohibition of aggressive force.[64]

2.4 The Nuremberg Tribunal—Prosecuting Crimes Against Peace

Contrary to popular perceptions that the trials before the Nuremberg Tribunal focused on the Holocaust, the key focus of the main trial, reflected in counts one and two of the Indictment, was in fact on crimes against peace.[65] One scholar explains this focus: it was through aggressive war, on both the European and Asian fronts, that the United States was forced to enter World War II; saving European Jews was not the key motivating factor animating the Americans.[66] The other counts in the Indictment were for war crimes and crimes against humanity; genocide was not even charged in the Indictment.[67]

The London Charter that established the Nuremberg Tribunal is significant for the proposition that there needed to be individual criminal responsibility.[68] No longer

of gas in land war in the Second World War can be seen as one worthwhile success for the laws of war".).

64 Charter of the United Nations (1945) 33 UNTS 933 ("UN Charter (1945)"), Article 2(4) (prohibition of the use of force), Article 51 (allowing self-defense). Parallel significant legal developments after the end of World War II included the birth of the modern human rights movement with the 1948 Universal Declaration of Human Rights, and advancements in the laws of war with the conclusion of the four 1949 Geneva Conventions. See Universal Declaration of Human Rights (1948) UN General Assembly Resolution 217A; Geneva Convention I for the Amelioration of the Condition of the Wounded and Sick in Armed Forces in the Field (1949); Geneva Convention II for the Amelioration of the Condition of Wounded, Sick and Shipwrecked Members of Armed Forces at Sea (1949); Geneva Convention III Relative to the Treatment of Prisoners of War (1949). The 1949 Geneva Conventions "focused entirely on the protection of victims of war and not to any significant extent with limitations on weaponry or fighting". Roberts 1994, pp. 136–37.

65 Indictment (1946) International Military Tribunal, The United States of America, et al. v. Hermann Wilhelm Goering et al. https://avalon.law.yale.edu/imt/count.asp. Accessed 4 May 2025 (count 1 covered the common plan or conspiracy; count 2 covered crimes against peace). For a comprehensive analysis of the Nuremberg Judgment on "crimes against peace", see McDougall 2017.

66 Bass 2000, p. 173.

67 For an explanation, see Sands 2016.

68 Agreement for the Prosecution and Punishment of the Major War Criminals of the European Axis, 8 August 1945, 82 UNTS 280, Article 6 (imposing individual responsibility). Individual criminal responsibility was also called for in the 1919 Treaty of Versailles. See Treaty of Peace Between the Allied and Associated Powers and Germany and Protocol (1919), sects. 227–30. While there had been plans for an allied tribunal after World War I—with judges from the United States, England, France, Italy, and Japan—no such tribunal was established; instead, prosecutions were held before

was it seen as sufficient to conclude that a state (Germany) had violated international law. The tribunal was to go beyond state responsibility to punish key individual actors (high-level German leaders).[69] The Judgment of the Nuremberg Tribunal famously explains that "[c]rimes against international law are committed by men, not by abstract entities, and only by punishing individuals who commit such crimes can the provisions of international law be enforced".[70] The Nuremberg Tribunal would later gain additional significance for leading to the establishment of the field of international justice and the subsequent international and hybrid criminal tribunals that followed.[71]

The Nuremberg Judgment also famously proclaimed crimes against peace (i.e., a war of aggression), to be "*the supreme international crime*" "differing only from other war crimes in that it contains within itself the accumulated evil of the whole".[72] The sentiment was that, had it not been for the initial aggression, none of the war crimes, crimes against humanity, or (in the case of the Holocaust), genocide[73] would have followed. (This was of course not entirely true; Germany was fully capable of committing atrocities against its own Jewish population without war. Yet, absent the initial aggression, including annexations, crimes beyond Germany's borders either would not have occurred or would not have occurred on the scale in which they did.)

---

a German court, the Supreme Court (*Reichsgericht*) at Leipzig, and were a failure. See Bass 2000, chap. 3. Pursuing individual criminal responsibility for what might be considered international crimes had also taken place earlier before national courts. See, e.g., Dunoff et al. 2010, p. 496 (war crimes trials in 15th century France); Bass 2000, chap. 4 (the failure of trials in Turkish courts in 1915 for the Armenian genocide).

[69] "Twenty-two defendants were indicted on seventy-four counts". Lippman 1991, p. 27.

[70] International Military Tribunal, Judgment of 1 October 1946, in The Trial of German Major War Criminals. Proceedings of the International Military Tribunal Sitting at Nuremberg, Germany, Part 22, p. 447 (22 August 1946 to 1 October 1946) ("IMT Judgment 1946"). For background on the trial, see, e.g., Hafetz 2018.

[71] For a book on the establishment of several of the criminal tribunals, see Scheffer 2013.

[72] IMT Judgment 1946, note 70, p. 421 (emphasis added). While charging crimes against peace has often been critiqued for violating the prohibition on retroactivity (*nullum crimen sine lege*), there were intervening international agreements and resolutions that referred to aggression *as a crime*, and not only conduct states were obligated to avoid. See ibid., pp. 445–46 (citing Draft Treaty of Mutual Assistance 1923, Article 1, sponsored by the League of Nations ("aggressive war is an international crime"); preamble to the League of Nations Protocol on the Pacific Settlement of International Disputes (1924) ("a war of aggression constitutes . . . an international crime"); Declaration of the Assembly of the League of Nations (1927) ("a war of aggression . . . is . . . an international crime"); Resolution of 18 February 1928, Sixth (Havana) Pan-African Conference (a "war of aggression constitutes an international crime").

[73] While the Nuremberg Tribunal did not adjudicate the crime of genocide, genocide most certainly was committed during the Holocaust. In fact, jurist and scholar Raphael Lemkin coined the term "genocide" to describe the Nazis' attempted extermination of Europe's Jewish populations. See United States Holocaust Memorial Museum nd. Lemkin used the word genocide in his 1944 book Axis Rule in Occupied Europe. See Lemkin 1944.

The Tokyo Tribunal[74] has fared less well in the eyes of history for a variety of reasons. While neither tribunal examined Allied atrocities,[75] the use of the atomic bomb at Hiroshima and Nagasaki, as well as other aspects of the Tribunal's work, have cast more of a shadow on its proceedings.[76]

Yet, both tribunals set hugely significant precedent not only for the prosecution of crimes against peace (i.e., the crime of aggression), but also for the need, at times, to prosecute grave international crimes before international or internationalized tribunals[77] and thereby ensure individual criminal responsibility.

2.5 The UN Charter—Advancing the Goals of International Peace

The negotiation and conclusion of the Charter of the United Nations, signed on 26 June 1945, was a parallel and extremely important development in the quest to rein in aggressive use of force. Finalized at San Francisco's War Memorial Opera House, the Charter was signed by the representatives of 50 states.[78] These included, significantly, the victorious allies, or "great powers" of the time, which became the permanent members of the UN Security Council—the United States, the United Kingdom, France, the USSR, and the Republic of China.[79] The drafters of the UN Charter envisioned creating a new world order, attempting to succeed where the League of Nations had failed.

US President Harry S. Truman made clear at the San Francisco Conference that the central focus of the United Nations was to guarantee international peace and security, stating:

---

[74] International Military Tribunal for the Far East (1946) Special Proclamation by the Supreme Commander to the Allied Powers at Tokyo, 19 January 1946, amended 26 April 1946 ("Tokyo Charter").

[75] For an account of Allied atrocities, see Becker 2013.

[76] Other shadows include failing to prosecute Emperor Hirohito; the dominance of the United States in establishing the tribunal; and the omission of various crimes, such as Japanese biochemical experimentation on Chinese prisoners of war, and the holding of women in sexual slavery to service the Japanese military (so-called "comfort women"). See Chang and Baker 2002. Additionally, the only judge to have background in international law, Indian Justice Radhabinod Pal, dissented. See Kopelman 1991. For the argument that the dissents were particularly important in relation to crimes against peace charges, see Sellars 2017.

[77] For what constitutes an "international" tribunal, see Chap. 5, Sect. 5.3.4.3. For features of "hybrid tribunals", see Chap. 6, note 11.

[78] It was primarily the United States, the United Kingdom, and the USSR that were responsible for drafting the Charter, with key negotiations occurring at the Dumbarton Oaks Conference, held in Washington D.C. (21 August–7 October 1944) and the Yalta Conference (4–11 February 1945).

[79] The USSR's seat is now held by the Russian Federation, and the Republic of China's seat is now held by the People's Republic of China.

> You members of the Conference are to be the architects of [a] better world. In your hands rest our future. By your labors at this Conference, we shall know if suffering humanity is to achieve a just and lasting peace.
>
> Let us labor to achieve a peace which is really worthy of their great sacrifice. We must make certain, by your work here, that another war will be impossible.
>
> We, who have lived through the torture and the tragedy of two world conflicts, realize the magnitude of the problem before us. We do not need far-sighted vision to understand the trend in recent history. Its significance is all too clear.
>
> With ever-increasing brutality and destruction, modern warfare, if unchecked, would ultimately crush all civilization. We still have a choice between the alternatives: the continuation of international chaos – or the establishment of a world organization for the enforcement of peace.[80]

Similarly powerful words are found in the 11 February 1945 Joint Statement by Winston S. Churchill, Franklin D. Roosevelt, and Joseph Stalin from the Yalta Conference.[81] In explaining the need for a United Nations, then-President Roosevelt also spoke extraordinarily eloquently to the US Congress about the importance of guaranteeing peace.[82] His famous "Four Freedoms speech" additionally made clear the linkage between the accelerating arms race and the risk of war.[83]

---

[80] Truman 1945/2014, p. 11.

[81] They affirmed:

> Our meeting here in the Crimea has reaffirmed our common determination to maintain and strengthen in the peace to come that unity of purpose, and of action which has made victory possible, and certain for the United Nations in this war. We believe that this is a sacred obligation which our Governments owe to our peoples and to all the peoples of the world.
>
> Victory in this war and establishment of the proposed international organization will provide the greatest opportunity in all history to create in the years to come the essential conditions of such a peace.
>
> With the continuing cooperation and understanding among our three countries and among all the peace-loving Nations can the highest aspirations of humanity be realized—a secure and lasting peace which will, in the words of the Atlantic Charter, "afford assurance that all the men in all the land may live out their lives in freedom from fear and want".
>
> Churchill WS et al. 1945/2014, p. 4.

[82] He stated:

> Never before have the major Allies been more closely united—not only in their war aims, but also in their peace aims. And they are determined to continue to be united with each other—and with all peace–loving Nations—so that the ideal of lasting peace will become a reality . . . .
>
> The structure of world peace cannot be the work of one man, or one party, or one Nation. It cannot be just an American peace, or a British peace, or a Russian, a French, or a Chinese peace. It cannot be a peace of large Nations—or of small Nations. It must be a peace which rests on the cooperative efforts of the whole world.
>
> Roosevelt 1945/2014, pp. 6–7.

[83] President Roosevelt stated: "The fourth [freedom] is freedom from fear—which, translated into world terms, means a world-wide reduction of armaments to such a point and in such a thorough

Achieving international peace and security—that is, avoiding war—is thus reflected centrally in the UN Charter. The Charter's preamble states that the Charter is concluded with the determination "to save succeeding generations from the scourge of war . . . ".[84] The first of the Charter's "Purposes" in Article 1(1), is "[t]o maintain international peace and security, and to that end: to take effective collective measures for the prevention and removal of threats to the peace, and for the suppression of acts of aggression, or other breaches of the peace, . . . and to bring about by peaceful means, . . . the settlement of international disputes or situations which might lead to a breach of the peace".[85] The Charter further emphasizes, as one of the UN's "Principles" in Article 2(3), the importance of the peaceful settlement of disputes, a topic expanded on in Chapter VI of the Charter.[86]

The Charter's non-aggression provision is contained in Article 2(4), and also framed as one of the UN's Principles. It provides: "All Member[] [States] shall refrain in their international relations from the threat or use of force against the territorial integrity or political independence of any state, or in any other manner inconsistent with the Purposes of the United Nations".[87] It is complemented by Article 51, which permits states to utilize individual and/or collective self-defense,[88] as well as by the ability of the UN Security Council to act under its Chapter VII enforcement powers.[89] Through this framework, the drafters of the Charter sought to introduce a collective mechanism for maintaining global peace and security (the UN Security Council) rather than allowing states to make unilateral decisions about going to war, a power states retained only for purposes of self-defense.[90]

The Charter system worked poorly in the initial years because the world fell into the Cold War (c. 1947–1991). During that period, offsetting vetoes (i.e., negative votes)[91] by the United States and Soviets meant that agreement on Chapter VII

fashion that no nation will be in a position to commit an act of physical aggression against any neighbor—anywhere in the world". Roosevelt 1941.

[84] UN Charter (1945), note 64, preamble.

[85] Ibid., Article 1(1).

[86] Ibid., Article 2(3); chap. VI.

[87] Ibid., Article 2(4).

[88] It states: "Nothing in the present Charter shall impair the inherent right of individual or collective self-defense if an armed attack occurs against a Member of the United Nations, until the Security Council has taken the measures necessary to maintain international peace and security . . . ". Ibid., Article 51.

[89] See ibid., chap. VII, Article 39 (trigger); Article 40 (provisional measures); Article 41 (non-forceful measures); Article 42 (forceful measures).

[90] "The Charter sought to fortify [the] prohibition [on the use of force] through a system of collective security, which aimed higher than its forerunner in the 1919 Covenant of the League of Nations". Kreß 2018, p. 4. Under the Charter, a state's right to use self-defense lasts only "until the Security Council has taken measures necessary to maintain international peace and security". See UN Charter 1945, note 64, Article 51.

[91] See ibid., Article 27(3) (voting provisions).

enforcement measures within the Security Council was an exceedingly rare occurrence.[92] The only Security Council resolution approving a force deployment that passed during this time period concerned the Korean War,[93] with the vote made possible only because the Soviet Union was boycotting the Council at the time over the question of Chinese representation.[94]

The United Nations, as we know, has not achieved the lofty goal of ensuring world peace. By empowering the UN Security Council to decide on peace enforcement, the Charter system has built-in limitations: each of the five permanent members has the ability to block the Council from passing resolutions by exercising its veto. The permanent members that drafted the Charter insisted on the veto—or there would have been no United Nations.[95] "[P]art of the rationale for the veto power . . . was to allow for greater enforcement power in security matters than the League [of Nation's] unanimity rule permitted . . .".[96]

The existence of the veto means that if a permanent member or its ally is the aggressor state, the Charter's enforcement system is likely to be paralyzed. Furthermore, the Charter provides for no override of the veto. Moreover, the permanent members essentially have veto power over Charter amendments, so that the veto cannot be eliminated.[97] And turning to the UN General Assembly is no substitute. The General Assembly has different competence than the Security Council, as it can, with very limited exceptions, only recommend measures in the face of a breach of the peace; it has no compulsory enforcement powers.[98] Another limitation of the

---

[92] The veto was used a total of 155 times during the Cold War. Security Council Veto List 2018.

[93] UN Security Council Resolution 84 (1950).

[94] Krasno and Das 2008, p. 178.

[95] A US delegate famously threatened that without the veto power, other states could forget about having a United Nations, and dramatically tore up his draft of the Charter. Connally 1954, p. 283, cited in Luck 2006, p. 14.

[96] Shapiro and Lampert 2014, Introduction, p. xv. Shapiro and Lampert write:

> At [the founding conference in San Francisco], small nations and outside groups, got the chance to enter the conversation, though the imperative to keep the US, the USSR, Great Britain, China, and France in the organization resulted in significant pressure to reach and maintain consensus, and to accede to the prerogatives the great powers reserved for themselves in the Security Council.

Ibid., p. viii. "[T]he Charter linked the lofty principles articulated in the Preamble and elsewhere in its text with realist considerations of great power affiliation and cooperation". Ibid., p. xv.

[97] UN Charter (1945), note 64, Article 108 (amendments to be ratified by all permanent members). One of the sticking points in the negotiations of the Charter was the veto (then referred to as the "principle of unanimity"—the requirement that decisions by permanent members should be unanimous). The United States and the United Kingdom took the view that a state involved in a situation should not have the veto power, whereas Joseph Stalin (on behalf of the USSR) insisted that there be no such exclusion. See Trahan 2020, pp. 10–21 (compiling negotiating history). A compromise was reached such that a party to a dispute is obligated to abstain from voting on a resolution under Chapter VI, but not a resolution under Chapter VII. See UN Charter (1945), note 64, Article 27(3). On the need to make more use of obligatory abstention when the Council is voting on a Chapter VI resolution, see Trahan 2024a.

[98] See UN Charter (1945), note 64, Article 10–14 (UNGA powers).

Charter system is that states make expansive invocations of "self-defense", which are not necessarily even discussed within the Security Council or otherwise at the UN, and are infrequently the subject of cases before the ICJ.[99] Still, despite its flaws, the Charter system is part of a global system that partly explains how a third world war has been averted, although massive bloodshed during other wars (both civil and interstate) have not been prevented, nor have other mass atrocities.[100]

2.6 Legal Developments During the Cold War to the 1998 Rome Conference

While the world fell into the Cold War (1947–1991), which cast a shadow over much of the work of the United Nations, additional developments continued after 1945 related to the prohibition of aggression and the crime of aggression.

In 1946, the United Nations General Assembly affirmed "the principles of international law" recognized by the Charter of the Nuremberg Tribunal and the Tribunal's Judgment.[101] Judge Antonio Cassese explained the significance:

> By "affirming" those principles, the General Assembly . . . clearly intended to express its approval of and support for the general concepts and legal constructs of criminal law that could be derived from the IMT Charter and had been set out . . . by the IMT. Translated into law-making terms, this approval and support meant that the world community had robustly set in motion the process for turning the principles at issue into general principles of customary law binding on member States of the whole international community.[102]

After the prosecutions before the Nuremberg Tribunal, a number of states incorporated the crime of aggression into their domestic criminal codes.[103] Additionally, by 1947, the UN General Assembly requested the International Law Commission ("ILC") to formulate "the principles of international law recognized in the Charter

---

[99] Some cases concerning the principle of non-intervention and issues of self-defense do reach the ICJ. See, e.g., International Court of Justice, *Oil Platforms (Iran v. United States of America)*, Judgment, 2003 ICJ Rep. 161; International Court of Justice, *Armed Activities on the Territory of the Congo (Democratic Republic of Congo v. Uganda)*, Judgment, 2005 ICJ Rep. 168; International Court of Justice, *Military and Paramilitary Activities in and Against Nicaragua (Nicaragua v. United States of America)*, Judgment, 1986 ICJ Rep. 14.

[100] For mortality figures, see Our World in Data nd. The veto is even used where its use appears to aid the commission of genocide, war crimes, and crimes against humanity. For extensive analysis of the problem and a proposed solution, see Trahan 2020. On veto use aiding aggression, see Trahan 2023.

[101] UN General Assembly Resolution 95(I) (1946).

[102] Cassese 2009.

[103] For legislation, see Coracini 2017, pp. 1038–78. Years later, after the crime was included in the ICC's Rome Statute, additional states incorporated the crime into domestic law on the basis of the Rome Statute's definition of the crime. For domestic legislation following the 2010 Review Conference, see Hartig 2023, chap. 6.

of the Nuremberg Tribunal and in the judgment of the Tribunal . . .",[104] which the ILC did in 1948–1950.[105]

In the same 1947 resolution, the General Assembly also requested the ILC to prepare a code of offenses against the peace and security of mankind, which it did, publishing a draft in 1954 that included an "act of aggression" as a crime.[106] Due to Cold War politics, the draft was never adopted by the General Assembly. Many years later, the General Assembly requested that the ILC resume its work;[107] the resulting ILC draft code of 1996 included the crime of aggression.[108]

The General Assembly additionally took up the topic of aggression in several resolutions. In its Friendly Relations Declaration of 1970, the General Assembly reiterated that "[a] war of aggression constitutes a crime against the peace, for which there is responsibility under international law".[109] It went on to define "act of aggression" in its Resolution 3314 of 1974 (discussed further in Chap. 3), as guidance for the UN Security Council.[110]

After the conclusion of the Cold War, work accelerated to develop a statute for an international criminal court, with the ILC including the crime of aggression in its 1994 draft statute.[111] The ILC also recognized the prohibition of aggression as

---

[104] UN General Assembly Resolution 177(II) (1947).

[105] International Law Commission (1950) Principles of International Law Recognized in the Charter of the Nuremberg Tribunal and in the Judgment of the Tribunal, Principle VI(a) (including "crimes against peace" as a crime under international law).

[106] International Law Commission (1954) Draft Code of Offences Against the Peace and Security of Mankind, Article 2.1–2.2.

[107] UN General Assembly Resolution 36/106 (1981).

[108] International Law Commission (1996) Draft Code of Crimes against the Peace and Security of Mankind, Report of the International Law Commission on its Forty-Eighth Session, UN GAOR, 51st Sess., Supp. No. 10, UN Doc. A/51/10, p. 9. Earlier versions of the ILC's work also encompassed the "threat" of aggression, but that approach dropped to the wayside in the negotiations of the Special Working Group on the Crime of Aggression. Trahan 2024b.

[109] UN General Assembly Resolution 2625(XXV), Annex (1970). The full title is Declaration on Principles of International Law concerning Friendly Relations and Cooperation Among States in accordance with the Charter of the United Nations. In 1965, the UN General Assembly also issued its Declaration on the Inadmissibility of Intervention in the Domestic Affairs of States and the Protection of their Independence and Sovereignty, deeming "armed intervention [to be] synonymous with aggression". See UN General Assembly Resolution 2131(XX) (1965).

[110] See Chap. 3, Sect. 3.2.2; UN General Assembly Resolution 3314(XXIX) (1974). The General Assembly's "primary purpose [was to] guide . . . the Security Council in determining aggression by States". See Wilmshurst 2008. "From 1973 to 1990, the Security Council adopted thirty-four resolutions in which it made express reference to the concept of 'act of aggression', primarily against apartheid South Africa and 'the illegal regime in Southern Rhodesia' for acts of aggression against neighbouring states; and two against Israel . . . ". Strapatsas 2017, p. 178.

[111] International Law Commission (1994) Draft Statute for an International Criminal Court, Report of the International Law Commission on Its Forty-Sixth Session, UN GAOR, 49th Sess., Supp. No. 10, UN Doc. A/49/10, p. 43.

a peremptory norm of international law (*jus cogens*)[112]—the highest level of international law, from which no derogations are permitted.[113] From 1995–1998, negotiations on a draft statute for an international criminal court continued before the Preparatory Committee on the Establishment of an International Criminal Court,[114] with its draft also including the crime of aggression.[115] Parallel significant developments also continued in the area of IHL[116] and the field of international justice, with the latter including the establishment of the International Criminal Tribunal for the former Yugoslavia and the International Criminal Tribunal for Rwanda.[117]

All of these developments set the foundation for eventual inclusion of the crime of aggression as one of the four core crimes contained in the Rome Statute of the ICC,[118] which will be discussed in the next chapter.

---

[112] See, e.g., International Law Commission (2019) Report on the Work of the Seventy-First Session, UN Doc. A/74/10, Conclusion 23 and Annex (providing a non-exhaustive list of peremptory norms).

[113] "*Jus cogens*" or "peremptory norms" are defined in the Vienna Convention on the Law of Treaties as norms of "general international law . . . accepted and recognized by the international community of States as a whole . . . from which no derogation is permitted and which can be modified only by a subsequent norm of general international law having the same character". Vienna Convention on the Law of Treaties (1969) 1155 UNTS 331, 8 ILM 6, Article 53. As a peremptory norm, there are obligations of states that arise regarding it. See International Law Commission (2001) Draft Articles on the Responsibility of States for Internationally Wrongful Acts, with Commentaries (adopted), UN Doc. A/56/10.

[114] See United Nations General Assembly Resolution 50/46 on the Establishment of an International Criminal Court (1995) (establishing the Preparatory Committee).

[115] United Nations Diplomatic Conference of Plenipotentiaries on the Establishment of an International Criminal Court, Summary Records of the Plenary and Committee of the Whole Meetings (1998) UN Docs A/CONF.183/SR.1-A/CONF.183/SR.9, A/CONF.183/C.1/SR.1-A/CONF.183/C.1/SR.42, pp. 12–14.

[116] Developments in IHL include conclusion of the two 1977 Geneva Convention Protocols, as well as treaties to limit the testing and proliferation of nuclear weapons, and the recent agreement to ban them entirely. See Protocol Additional to the Geneva Conventions of 12 August 1949, and Relating to the Protection of Victims of International Armed Conflicts (Protocol I) (1977) 1125 UNTS 3; Protocol Additional to the Geneva Conventions of 12 August 1949, and Relating to the Protection of Victims of Non-International Armed Conflicts (Protocol II) (1977) 1125 UNTS 609; Treaty Banning Nuclear Weapon Tests in the Atmosphere, in Outer Space and Under Water (Partial Test Ban Treaty) (1963) 480 UNTS 43; Comprehensive Nuclear-Test-Ban Treaty (1966). https://treaties.un.org/doc/Treaties/1997/09/19970910%2007-37%20AM/Ch_XXVI_04p.pdf. Accessed 4 May 2025 (not in force); Treaty on the Non-Proliferation of Nuclear Weapons (1968) 729 UNTS 161.

[117] See UN Security Council Resolution 827 (1993) (establishing the International Criminal Tribunal for the former Yugoslavia); UN Security Council Resolution 955 (1994) (establishing the International Criminal Tribunal for Rwanda). Since the establishment of the ad hoc tribunals, a number of hybrid and regional criminal tribunals have additionally been established. For an overview, see Scheffer 2013; see also Chap. 1, Sect. 1.3.2 (International Justice).

[118] Rome Statute (1998), note 1 (as amended).

2.7 Conclusion

States and prominent individuals have had the noble intentions of reining in the conduct of war and war itself for at least the last two hundred years. The crime of aggression is the present incarnation of this long and historic legacy. The laws related to the conduct of war (*jus in bello*) do not seek to prohibit war itself, but are complementary to the peace movement in that they aim to mitigate some of the more horrific aspects of war. The peace, or peace through law, movement seeks to curb recourse to war entirely, replacing it with the rule of law.

Preventing aggressive war was the central motivating factor behind the 1920 founding of the League of Nations, the 1928 conclusion of the Kellogg-Briand Pact, and the 1945 founding of the United Nations.[119] Yet, the League of Nations proved incapable of enforcement, and already in 1928 the negotiators of the Kellogg-Briand Pact were well aware that it lacked an enforcement provision.[120] That enforcement was essentially created with the decision to impose individual criminal responsibility for crimes against peace through the prosecutions before the Nuremberg and Tokyo Tribunals.

Enforcement was also created (to varying degrees) at the level of state responsibility within the UN Charter system. Yet, as discussed above, violations of the prohibition of the use of force do not always result in consequences. The Charter's enforcement system is essentially ineffective at reining in aggression by permanent members of the UN Security Council or their allies, because permanent members of the Security Council can block Security Council resolutions through their veto power.[121] Thus, a permanent member or its ally is unlikely to be condemned by the Security Council for committing aggression, and even more unlikely to face other consequences imposed by that body. Furthermore, only states that have consented to the ICJ's jurisdiction may be the subject of cases before it;[122] thus, it is not always possible for a state to bring a case against another state for violating the prohibition of the use of force or the principle of non-intervention, or exceeding what is permissible as self-defense.[123]

Thus, while the prohibition of the unlawful use of force is recognized at the highest level of the law—as a peremptory norm of international law (*jus cogens*),[124] enforcement at the level of state responsibility under the UN Charter system is sporadic and dependent on politics. Individual criminal responsibility for aggression has not been

[119] See Sect. 2.3 and Sect. 2.5.

[120] See Hathaway and Shapiro 2017 (absence of means to enforce the Kellogg-Briand Pact).

[121] For the argument that more use needs to be made of Security Council resolutions under Chapter VI, where a party to the dispute is obligated to abstain from voting, see Trahan 2024a.

[122] International Court of Justice (nd) Contentious Jurisdiction. https://www.icj-cij.org/index.php/contentious-jurisdiction. Accessed 4 May 2025 ("The Court can only deal with a dispute when the States concerned have recognized its jurisdiction. No State can therefore be a party to proceedings before the Court unless it has in some manner or other consented thereto".).

[123] For some cases the ICJ has adjudicated, see note 99.

[124] See notes 112–113 and accompanying text.

pursued at the international level since the prosecutions before the Nuremberg and Tokyo Tribunals. Yet, there is ample need for the crime to be enforced. Including the crime in the 1998 Rome Statute of the ICC (a topic discussed in the next chapter) is the most recent attempt to build on this long and historic legacy of trying to ensure that states do not resort to the unlawful use of force.

References

Anand R P (1983) The Influence of History on the Literature of International Law. In: St. John MacDonald R, Johnston DM (eds) The Structure and Process of International Law. Brill, The Hague

Anghie A (1999) Finding the Peripheries: Sovereignty and Colonialism in Nineteenth-Century International Law. Harvard International Law Journal 40: 1–80

Aquinas T (1265–74) *Summa Theologica*. Christian Classics Ethereal Library. https://ccel.org/ccel/aquinas/summa/summa. Accessed 4 May 2025

Aristotle (350 BCE) Politics, Book 1. Perseus Digital Library

Atkins J W (2023) Cicero on the Justice of War. In: Gilbert N, Graver M, McConnell S (eds) Power and Persuasion in Cicero's Philosophy. Cambridge University Press, Cambridge

Bass G (2000) Stay The Hand of Vengeance: The Politics of International War Crimes Tribunals. Princeton University Press, Princeton

Bassiouni M C et al. (eds) (2013) The Global Community Yearbook of International Law and Jurisprudence: Global Trends: Law, Policy & Justice Essays in Honour of Professor Giuliana Ziccardi Capaldo. Oxford University Press, Oxford

Becker S W (2013) The Inequality of Harm: Unpunished Allied Atrocities, the Nuremberg Fallacy, and Why Global Criminal Justice Remains a Mirage. In: Bassiouni M C et al. (eds) The Global Community Yearbook of International Law and Jurisprudence: Global Trends: Law, Policy & Justice Essays in Honour of Professor Giuliana Ziccardi Capaldo. Oxford University Press, Oxford

Boister N, Cryer R (eds) (2008) Documents on the Tokyo International Military Tribunal: Charter, Indictment and Judgments. Oxford University Press, Oxford

Brock P (1994) Pacifism in Europe to 1914. Thistle Printing, Toronto

Cassese A (2009) Affirmation of the Principles of International Law Recognized by the Charter of the Nürnberg Tribunal General Assembly Resolution 95 (I). https://legal.un.org/avl/ha/ga_95-I/ga_95-I.html. Accessed 4 May 2025

Chang M H, Baker R B (2002) Victor's Justice & Japan's Amnesia: The Tokyo War Crimes Trial Reconsidered. In: Li P (ed) The Search for Justice: Japanese War Crimes. Transaction Publishers, New Brunswick

Churchill W S, Roosevelt F D, Stalin J (1945/2014) Joint Statement of Winston S. Churchill, Franklin D. Roosevelt, and Joseph Stalin at the Yalta Conference. In: Shapiro I, Lampert J (eds) Charter of the United Nations: Together with Scholarly Commentaries and Essential Historical Documents. Yale University Press, New Haven

Connally T (1954) My Name is Tom Connally. Crowell, New York

Conway-Lanz S (2017) World War I: A New World Order—Woodrow Wilson's First Draft of the League of Nations Covenant. Library of Congress. https://blogs.loc.gov/loc/2017/04/world-war-i-a-new-world-order-woodrow-wilsons-first-draft-of-the-league-of-nations-covenant/. Accessed 4 May 2025

Coracini A R (2017) (Extended) Synopsis: The Crime of Aggression under Domestic Criminal Law. In: Kreβ C, Barriga S (eds) The Crime of Aggression: A Commentary. Cambridge University Press, Cambridge

Cox R (2017) Expanding the History of the Just War: The Ethics of War in Ancient Egypt. International Studies Quarterly 61: 371–384
Cronin B, Hurd I (eds) (2008) The UN Security Council and the Politics of International Authority. Taylor & Francis, Abingdon
Davis Biddle T (1994) Air Power. In: Howard M, Andreopoulos GJ, Shulman M R (eds) The Laws of War: Constraints on Warfare in the Western World. Yale University Press, New Haven
de Vattel E (1797/2008) The Law of Nations. Liberty Fund, Indianapolis.
Dunant J H (1862) A Memory of Solferino: *Un Souvenir de Solferino*
Dunoff J, Ratner S, Wippman D (eds) (2010) International Law Norms, Actors, Process: A Problem-Oriented Approach, 3rd edn. Aspen Publishers
Grotius H (1950) *De Jure Praedae Commentarius*, Commentary on the Law of Prize and Booty (Williams G (transl)). Clarendon Press, Oxford
Fernández J A (1973) Erasmus on the Just War. Journal of the History of Ideas 34: 209–226
Ferrell R (1952) Peace in Their Time: The Origins of the Kellogg-Briand Pact. Yale University Press, New Haven
Gesley J (2018) The "Lieber Code"—The First Modern Codification of the Laws of War. Library of Congress. https://blogs.loc.gov/law/2018/04/the-lieber-code-the-first-modern-codification-of-the-laws-of-war/#:~:text=The%20Lieber%20Code%20set%20out%20rules%20of%20conduct,the%20Department%20of%20Defense%20Laws%20of%20War%20Manual. Accessed 4 May 2025
Gilder Lehrman Institute of American History (nd) History Resources. The Doctrine of Discovery, 1493. https://www.gilderlehrman.org/history-resources/spotlight-primary-source/doctrine-discovery-1493. Accessed 4 May 2025
Giles L (transl) (1910) Sun Tzu on the Art of War. Luzac and Company, London
Gillespie A I (2018) "The Path to Peace Is Paved with Laws": Salmon Levinson and Outlawry. https://thekeep.eiu.edu/cgi/viewcontent.cgi?article=1129&context=honors_theses. Accessed 4 May 2025
Hafetz J (2018) Punishing Atrocities Through a Fair Trial: International Criminal Law from Nuremberg to the Age of Global Terrorism. Cambridge University Press, Cambridge
Hammurabi 1754 BCE/1903 The Laws of Hammurabi, King of Babylonia (Sommer H O (transl)) (1903). In: Records of the Past, Volume II, Part III
Hartig A (2023) Making Aggression a Crime under Domestic Law. T.M.C. Asser Press, The Netherlands
Hathaway O A, Shapiro S J (2017) The Internationalists: How a Radical Plan to Outlaw War Remade the World. Simon & Schuster, New York
Howard M (1994) Constraints on Warfare. In: Howard M, Andreopoulos GJ, Shulman M R (eds) The Laws of War: Constraints on Warfare in the Western World. Yale University Press, New Haven
Howard M, Andreopoulos G J, Shulman M R (eds) (1994) The Laws of War: Constraints on Warfare in the Western World. Yale University Press, New Haven
Human Security Report (2013) The Decline in Global Violence: Evidence, Explanation and Contestation
International Committee of the Red Cross (nd) St. Petersburg Declaration: Victory of Humanity in War. https://www.icrc.org/en/document/st-petersburg-declaration-victory-humanity-war#:~:text=150%20years%20ago%2C%20the%20St.%20Petersburg%20Declaration%20was,the%20use%20of%20inhumane%20weapon%20was%20officially%20renounced. Accessed 4 May 2025.
Kelsen H (1944) Peace Through Law. University of North Carolina Press, Chapel Hill.
Kopelman E S (1991) Ideology and International Law: The Dissent of the Indian Justice at the Tokyo War Crimes Trial. N.Y.U. Journal of International Law and Politics 23: 373–444
Knock T (1992) To End All Wars: Woodrow Wilson and the Quest for a New World Order. Princeton University Press, Princeton

Krasno J, Das M (2008) The Uniting for Peace Resolution and Other Ways of Circumventing the Authority of the Security Council. In: Cronin B, Hurd I (eds) The UN Security Council and the Politics of International Authority. Taylor & Francis, Abingdon

Kreβ C (2018) On the Activation of ICC Jurisdiction over the Crime of Aggression. Journal of International Criminal Justice 16: 1–17

Kwon D (2023) A Confucian Contribution to the Catholic Just War Tradition. Journal of Interreligious Studies 38: 62–77

Lemkin R (1944) Axis Rule in Occupied Europe: Laws of Occupation, Analysis of Government, Proposals for Redress. The Lawbook Exchange, Ltd., Clark

Levinson S O (nd) Definition of Outlawry, Box 29, Folder 6, Levinson Papers

Levinson S O (1918) The Legal Status of War. The New Republic

Levinson S O (1921) Outlawing of War. Chicago American Committee for the Outlawry of War

Li P (ed) (2002) The Search for Justice: Japanese War Crimes. Transaction Publishers, New Brunswick

Liddington J (1989) The Long Road to Greenham: Feminism and Anti-Militarism in Britain since 1820. Virago, London

Lippman M (1991) Nuremberg: Forty-Five Years Later. Connecticut Journal of International Law 7: 1

Luck E C (2006) UN Security Council: Practice and Promise. Taylor & Francis, Abingdon

Malanczuk P (1997) Akehurst's Modern Introduction to International Law, 7th edn. Routledge, London

May H E (2016) Introduction. In: May H E (ed) The Barbarization of the Sky, von Suttner B (reprint 2016) (Cooper B (transl)). Bertha von Suttner Project

May H E (2019) The March 1st Movement and the Red Thread of International Peace History. Korea Observer 50: 207–233

Mazower M (2012) Governing The World: The History of an Idea. Penguin Press, New York

McDougall C (2017) The Crimes against Peace Precedent. In: Kreβ C, Barriga S (eds) The Crime of Aggression: A Commentary. Cambridge University Press, Cambridge

Ober J (1994) Classical Greek Times. In: Howard M, Andreopoulos G J, Shulman M R (eds) The Laws of War: Constraints on Warfare in the Western World. Yale University Press, New Haven

Oppenheim L (1905) International Law, Vol. 1, Peace. Longmans, Green, and Company, London.

Our World in Data (nd) Deaths in Armed Conflict, World. https://ourworldindata.org/grapher/deaths-in-armed-conflicts-by-type. Accessed 4 May 2025

Powell J (2000) Libertarianism, "Natural Law and Peace: A Biography of Hugo Grotius". https://www.libertarianism.org/publications/essays/natural-law-peace-biography-hugo-grotius. Accessed 4 May 2025

Reichberg G (2017) Thomas Aquinas on War and Peace. Cambridge University Press, New York

Roberts A (1994) Land Warfare: From the Hague to Nuremberg. In: Howard M, Andreopoulos G J, Shulman M R (eds) The Laws of War: Constraints on Warfare in the Western World. Yale University Press, New Haven

Roberts A, Guelff R (eds) (2000) Documents on the Laws of War, 3rd edn. Oxford University Press, Oxford

Robinson P (2017) Just War in Comparative Perspective. Routledge, London

Roosevelt F D (1941) President Franklin Roosevelt's Annual Message (Four Freedoms) to Congress (1941). National Archives. https://www.archives.gov/milestone-documents/president-franklin-roosevelts-annual-message-to-congress. Accessed 4 May 2025

Roosevelt F D (1945/2014) Address to Congress, Reporting on the Yalta Conference. In: Shapiro I, Lampert J (eds) Charter of the United Nations: Together with Scholarly Commentaries and Essential Historical Documents. Yale University Press, New Haven

Sands P (2016) East West Street: On the Origins of "Genocide" and "Crimes Against Humanity". Alfred A. Knopf, New York

Scheffer D J (2013) All the Missing Souls: A Personal History of the War Crimes Tribunals. Princeton University Press, Princeton

Sellars K (2017) The Legacy of the Tokyo Dissents on "Crimes against Peace". In: Kreβ C, Barriga S (eds) The Crime of Aggression: A Commentary. Cambridge University Press, Cambridge
Shapiro I, Lampert J (eds) (2014) Charter of the United Nations: Together with Scholarly Commentaries and Essential Historical Documents. Yale University Press, New Haven
St. John MacDonald R, Johnston D M (eds) (1983) The Structure and Process of International Law. Brill, The Hague
Stacey R (1994) The Age of Chivalry. In: Howard M, Andreopoulos GJ, Shulman M R (eds) The Laws of War: Constraints on Warfare in the Western World. Yale University Press, New Haven
Strapatsas N (2017) The Practice of the Security Council Regarding the Concept of Aggression. In: Kreβ C, Barriga S (eds) The Crime of Aggression: A Commentary. Cambridge University Press, Cambridge
Trahan J (2020) Existing Legal Limits to Security Council Veto Power in the Face of Atrocity Crimes. Cambridge University Press, Cambridge
Trahan J (2023) Legal Issues Surrounding Veto Use and Aggression. Case Western Reserve Journal of International Law 55: 93–146
Trahan J (2024a) The Role of the UN Security Council and General Assembly In Responding to the Invasion of Ukraine. Polish Review of International and European Law 12: 23–64
Trahan J (2024b) Email with Roger Clark, 14 August 2024
Trahan J (2024c) Email with Mark R. Shulman, 19 August 2024
Truman H (1945/2014) Address to the United Nations Conference on International Organization at San Francisco. In: Shapiro I, Lampert J (eds) Charter of the United Nations: Together with Scholarly Commentaries and Essential Historical Documents. Yale University Press, New Haven
United States Department of Defense (nd) Defense Casualty Analysis System, World War II Conflict Casualties. https://dcas.dmdc.osd.mil/dcas/app/conflictCasualties/ww2. Accessed 4 May 2025
United States Department of State (1920) Archive, The League of Nations. https://2001-2009.state.gov/r/pa/ho/time/wwi/99150.htm#:~:text=Wilson%20and%20Lodge's%20personal%20dislike,a%2049%2D35%20Senate%20vote. Accessed 4 May 2025
United States Holocaust Memorial Museum (nd) Coining the Word and Championing a Cause: The Story of Raphael Lemkin. https://encyclopedia.ushmm.org/content/en/article/coining-a-word-and-championing-a-cause-the-story-of-raphael-lemkin. Accessed 4 May 2025
von Clausewitz C (1832/1976) On War. In: Howard M, Paret P (eds/transl). Princeton University Press, Princeton
von Suttner B (1912/2016) The Barbarization of the Sky (reprint 2016). In: May HE (ed) Cooper B (transl). Bertha von Suttner Project
Wilmshurst E (2008) Definition of Aggression General Assembly Resolution 3314(XXIX). https://legal.un.org/avl/ha/da/da.html. Accessed 4 May 2025
Witt J F (2012) Lincoln's Code: The Laws of War in American History. Simon and Schuster, New York
Wouters J, Ruys T (2005) Security Council Reform: A New Veto for a New Century? Royal Institute for International Relations, Egmont Paper 9

Other Documents

Agreement for the Prosecution and Punishment of the Major War Criminals of the European Axis, 8 August 1945, 82 UNTS 280
Carnegie (nd) Peace Palace. https://www.vredespaleis.nl/carnegie/?lang=en. Accessed 4 May 2025
Charter of the United Nations (1945) 33 UNTS 933
Comprehensive Nuclear-Test-Ban Treaty (1966). https://treaties.un.org/doc/Treaties/1997/09/19970910%2007-37%20AM/Ch_XXVI_04p.pdf. Accessed 4 May 2025
Declaration of the Assembly of the League of Nations (1927)

Geneva Convention I for the Amelioration of the Condition of the Wounded and Sick in Armed Forces in the Field (1949)

Geneva Convention II for the Amelioration of the Condition of Wounded, Sick and Shipwrecked Members of Armed Forces at Sea (1949)

Geneva Convention III Relative to the Treatment of Prisoners of War (1949)

Geneva Convention IV Relative to the Protection of Civilian Persons in Time of War (1949)

Indictment (1946) International Military Tribunal, The United States of America, et al. v. Hermann Wilhelm Goering et al. https://avalon.law.yale.edu/imt/count.asp. Accessed 4 May 2025

International Court of Justice, *Armed Activities on the Territory of the Congo (Democratic Republic of Congo v. Uganda)*, Judgment, 2005 ICJ Rep. 168

International Court of Justice (nd) Contentious Jurisdiction. https://www.icj-cij.org/index.php/contentious-jurisdiction. Accessed 4 May 2025

International Court of Justice, *Military and Paramilitary Activities in and Against Nicaragua (Nicaragua v. United States of America)*, Judgment, 1986 ICJ Rep. 14

International Court of Justice, *Oil Platforms (Iran v. United States of America)*, Judgment, 2003 ICJ Rep. 161

International Law Commission (2001) Draft Articles on the Responsibility of States for Internationally Wrongful Acts, with Commentaries (adopted), UN Doc. A/56/10

International Law Commission (1996) Draft Code of Crimes against the Peace and Security of Mankind, Report of the International Law Commission on its Forty-Eighth Session, UN GAOR, 51st Sess., Supp. No. 10, UN Doc. A/51/10

International Law Commission (1954) Draft Code of Offences against the Peace and Security of Mankind

International Law Commission (1994) Draft Statute for an International Criminal Court, Report of the International Law Commission on Its Forty-Sixth Session, UN GAOR, 49th Sess., Supp. No. 10, UN Doc. A/49/10

International Law Commission (1950) Principles of International Law Recognized in the Charter of the Nürnberg Tribunal and in the Judgment of the Tribunal

International Law Commission (2019) Report on the Work of the Seventy-First Session, UN Doc. A/74/10

International Military Tribunal, Judgment of 1 October 1946, in The Trial of German Major War Criminals. Proceedings of the International Military Tribunal Sitting at Nuremberg, Germany, Part 22 (22 August 1946 to 1 October 1946)

International Military Tribunal for the Far East (1946) Special Proclamation by the Supreme Commander to the Allied Powers at Tokyo, 19 January 1946, amended 26 April 1946

League of Nations Protocol on the Pacific Settlement of International Disputes (1924)

League of Nations Treaty Series, Vol. XCIV (1929). https://treaties.un.org/doc/Publication/UNTS/LON/Volume%2094/v94.pdf. Accessed 4 May 2025

Protocol Additional to the Geneva Conventions of 12 August 1949, and Relating to the Protection of Victims of International Armed Conflicts (Protocol I) (1977) 1125 UNTS 3

Protocol Additional to the Geneva Conventions of 12 August 1949, and Relating to the Protection of Victims of Non-International Armed Conflicts (Protocol II) (1977) 1125 UNTS 609

Reperes, Partenariat Educatif Grundtvig 2009–2011. https://www.census.gov/history/pdf/reperes112018.pdf. Accessed 4 May 2025

Resolution of 18 February 1928, Sixth (Havana) Pan-African Conference

Rome Statute of the International Criminal Court (1998) 2187 UNTS 3

Security Council Veto List (2018). http://research.un.org/en/docs/sc/quick. Accessed 4 May 2025

Treaty Banning Nuclear Weapon Tests in the Atmosphere, in Outer Space and Under Water (Partial Test Ban Treaty) (1963) 480 UNTS 43

Treaty Between the United States and Other Powers Providing for the Renunciation of War as an Instrument of National Policy (1928) (Kellogg-Briand Pact)

Treaty of Mutual Assistance (1923) (draft)

Treaty on the Non-Proliferation of Nuclear Weapons (1968) 729 UNTS 161

Treaty of Peace between the Allied and Associated Powers and Germany and Protocol (1919)
Treaty on the Prohibition of Nuclear Weapons (2017) 3379 UNTS
United Nations Diplomatic Conference of Plenipotentiaries on the Establishment of an International Criminal Court Report of the Preparatory Committee on the Establishment of an International Criminal Court (1998) UN Doc. A/CONF.183/2/Add.1
United Nations Diplomatic Conference of Plenipotentiaries on the Establishment of an International Criminal Court, Summary Records of the Plenary and Committee of the Whole Meetings (1998) UN Docs A/CONF.183/SR.1-A/CONF.183/SR.9, A/CONF.183/C.1/SR.1-A/CONF.183/C.1/SR.42
United Nations, Final Act of the United Nations Diplomatic Conference of Plenipotentiaries on the Establishment of an International Criminal Court (1998) UN Doc. A/CONF.183/10*
United Nations General Assembly Resolution 36/106 on the Draft Code of Offences Against the Peace and Security of Mankind (1981)
United Nations General Assembly Resolution 50/46 on the Establishment of an International Criminal Court (1995)
United Nations General Assembly Resolution 95(I) (1946)
United Nations General Assembly Resolution 177(II) (1947)
United Nations General Assembly Resolution 2131(XX), Declaration on the Inadmissibility of Intervention in the Domestic Affairs of States and the Protection of Their Independence and Sovereignty (1965)
United Nations General Assembly Resolution 2625(XXV) (1970)
United Nations General Assembly Resolution 3314(XXIX) (1974)
United Nations (nd-a) Main Organs of the League of Nations. https://www.ungeneva.org/en/about/league-of-nations/organs. Accessed 4 May 2025
United Nations (nd-b) The Covenant of the League of Nations. https://www.ungeneva.org/en/about/league-of-nations/covenant. Accessed 4 May 2025
United Nations Security Council Resolution 84 (1950)
United Nations Security Council Resolution 827 (1993)
United Nations Security Council Resolution 955 (1994)
Universal Declaration of Human Rights (1948) UN General Assembly Resolution 217A
Vienna Convention on the Law of Treaties (1969) 1155 UNTS 331, 8 ILM 679

Chapter 3
The Development of the Crime of Aggression: From the Rome Statute to the Present

Contents

Abstract This chapter traces the development of the definition of the crime of aggression found in the Rome Statute of the International Criminal Court ("ICC"). It explores the negotiations that resulted in agreement on the definition of the crime and the ICC's jurisdictional regime over the crime. It specifically examines the content of the definition, and how and why the jurisdictional regime before the ICC became so limited, unlike the ICC's jurisdictional regime as to genocide, war crimes, and crimes against humanity. It ultimately makes the case that jurisdiction should not be so limited regarding this "supreme" international crime and suggests ways to remedy this jurisdictional gap both in the situation of Ukraine and more broadly.

Keywords Crime of aggression · Rome Statute · Kampala Review Conference · Activation of jurisdiction · Leadership clause · Manifest threshold · Act of aggression · UN General Assembly Resolution 3314

J. Trahan, *The Crime of Aggression and Russia's Invasion of Ukraine*,
https://doi.org/10.1007/978-94-6265-763-2_3

3.1 Introduction

This chapter continues to discuss the development of the crime of aggression, covering the years 1998 through the present. The chapter starts by focusing on the decision by states—following the precedent of the Nuremberg and Tokyo Tribunals and development of the field of international justice more generally—to include the crime of aggression as one of the four core crimes within the Rome Statute of the International Criminal Court ("ICC") in 1998.[1] Yet, as will be explained, the definition of the crime, as well as conditions for the ICC's exercise of jurisdiction over it, needed to be agreed upon through later negotiations. The chapter traces these developments, and examines both the content of the definition of the crime contained in the Rome Statute and the ICC's jurisdictional regime over the crime. As to the latter, the chapter examines the agreements reached by States Parties to the Rome Statute at the 2010 Review Conference held in Kampala, Uganda, and the 2017 meeting of the ICC's Assembly of States Parties ("ASP") at which states activated the ICC's jurisdiction over the crime, effective on 17 July 2018. With this background, the chapter turns back to the situation of Ukraine and explains why the ICC cannot exercise jurisdiction over the crime of aggression in the situation, despite the fact that Ukraine had earlier accepted the ICC's jurisdiction, and, on 1 January 2025, became a State Party to the Rome Statute. The chapter concludes by exhorting states to create additional jurisdiction over the crime of aggression, both by establishing a special tribunal on the crime of aggression for the situation of Ukraine (a topic explored in Chaps. 5–7) and by amending the Rome Statute to cover future similar situations (a topic explored in Chap. 8).

3.2 Inclusion of the Crime of Aggression in the Rome Statute of the International Criminal Court

3.2.1 The Rome Negotiations

The next major development related to the crime of aggression was the decision by states, during negotiations held in Rome, Italy, during the summer of 1998, to include the crime as one of the four crimes in the Rome Statute.[2] The Rome Statute established the ICC as the first permanent international criminal court, created to prosecute "the most serious crimes of concern to the international community", in recognition that "such grave crimes threaten the peace and security and well-being

[1] Rome Statute of the International Criminal Court (1998) 2187 UNTS 3 ("Rome Statute (1998) (as amended)").

[2] Ibid., Article 5.1. For documentation of the discussion and proposals submitted between 1995 and 1998, see Kreß and Barriga 2017, pp. 201–331.

of the world".[3] The ICC would have jurisdiction over four crimes—genocide, crimes against humanity, war crimes, and the crime of aggression.[4]

By one tabulation, 119 states expressed support for including the crime of aggression in the Rome Statute, in one form or another, during the Rome Conference.[5] Only four states spoke against its inclusion,[6] with a few states expressing the concern that there would not be enough time during the Conference to reach agreement on a definition of the crime and conditions for the ICC's exercise of jurisdiction over it.[7] Ultimately, "a majority of Conference participants (led by Germany and the Non-Aligned Movement) were unwilling to adopt a statute that omitted the crime",[8] and a compromise was reached.[9]

Rome Statute Article 5(1) provides that the crime of aggression is one of the four crimes within the ICC's jurisdiction; however, Article 5(2) provided something of a "placeholder" regarding the crime. First, agreement on a definition of the crime—which had not been concluded at Rome—would need to be reached, as well as agreement on the conditions for the ICC's exercise of jurisdiction over the crime.[10] Negotiations on these items occurred through a separate process: first, in meetings of the Preparatory Commission for the International Criminal Court between 1999 and

[3] Rome Statute (1998) (as amended), note 1, preamble.

[4] Ibid., Article 5.1.

[5] McDougall 2021, p. 9 ("The summary records of the Plenary and Committee of the Whole meetings at the Rome Conference reveal that of the 134 States that made statements in relation to the crime of aggression, only 15 failed to indicate that they supported the crime's inclusion in the ICC's statute".).

[6] Ibid. ("Only Morocco, Pakistan, Turkey, and the USA questioned the idea that at least some State acts of aggression entail, or should entail, individual criminal responsibility".).

[7] Ibid., pp. 9–10 ("The remaining eleven States expressed only a fear that, in the limited time allowed for the Conference, participants would be unable to overcome their differences in relation to the definitional and jurisdictional issues associated with the crime".), citing United Nations Diplomatic Conference of Plenipotentiaries on the Establishment of an International Criminal Court, Summary Records of the Plenary and Committee of the Whole Meetings (1998) UN Docs A/CONF.183/SR.1-A/CONF.183/SR.9, A/CONF.183/C.1/SR.1-A/CONF.183/C.1/SR.42.

[8] McDougall 2021, p. 11. See also Trahan 2024a (Germany led the negotiations on the crime of aggression and insisted on having the crime included in the Statute, supported primarily by Greece and Italy in the group of "like-minded" states (approximately 80 states)); Trahan 2024b (the states in the Non-Aligned Movement also played a crucial role in lending support, both as a group as well as on an individual basis). On the contributions of Germany and Italy, see Kreβ 2018, nn 49, 51. For a compilation of the views of states, see also Clark 2017, p. 244, esp. pp. 260–68; Barriga and Kreß 2012, pp. 201–332 (state practice from the ad hoc Committee 1995 to the Rome Conference (15 June–17 July 1998)), and pp. 333–818 (state practice after the Rome Conference: Preparatory Commission (February 1999) to the Kampala Conference (31 May–11 June 2010)).

[9] Claus Kreß credits "a last-minute compromise resulting from a proposal submitted by the Movement of Non-Aligned countries" and recalls that Arab States "have been particularly active in support of this last minute, and very important, diplomatic activity". See Kreβ 2018, p. 4, n 9.

[10] Rome Statute (1998) (as amended), note 1, Article 5.2, since agreed to be deleted.

2002,[11] and, later, before the Special Working Group on the Crime of Aggression ("SWGCA") from 2003 through 2009.[12]

The latter process culminated by February 2009 in agreement on the definition of the crime.[13] The Nuremberg Tribunal's definition of crimes against peace was not utilized, as it was quite minimal and circular.[14] Furthermore, the Nuremberg definition only covered a full-scale "war" of aggression,[15] whereas states chose to encompass an "act" of aggression in the ICC's definition—thereby aligning more with the UN Charter, which bans "use of force"[16] (a lower threshold than war) and with the definition of "act of aggression" that had been agreed on by the General Assembly in Resolution 3314.[17]

3.2.2 The Definition of the Crime

Ultimately, both the definition of the crime and conditions for the ICC's exercise of jurisdiction over it were adopted by consensus of all States Parties at a Review Conference on the Rome Statute that took place from 31 May through 11 June 2010

---

[11] United Nations, Final Act of the United Nations Diplomatic Conference of Plenipotentiaries on the Establishment of an International Criminal Court (1998) UN Doc. A/CONF.183/10*, Resolution F, p. 424, para 7. For background on the Preparatory Commission, see Kirsch and Oosterveld 2001; for its drafting work on the crime of aggression, see Clark 2002, and as documented in Barriga and Kreβ 2012, pp. 334–419.

[12] International Criminal Court, Assembly of States Parties 2002; Permanent Mission of Liechtenstein to the United Nations 2013 (the SWGCA from 2003–2009 "continued negotiations on the outstanding issues regarding the crime of aggression"). The meetings were open to both Rome Statute States Parties and states not parties to the Rome Statute ("non-States Parties"). See Barriga et al. 2009, p. 5. Claus Kreβ, a member of the German delegation, credited much of the progress in the SWGCA negotiations to Liechtenstein Ambassador Christian Wenaweser, supported by his chief legal advisor Stefan Barriga, Nuremberg Prosecutor Benjamin Ferencz, and Jordanian Ambassador Zeid Ra'ad Al Hussein. See Kreβ 2018, p. 5. For more on the negotiation of the definition of the crime, see Coracini 2010a.

[13] Permanent Mission of Liechtenstein to the United Nations 2013, p. 3 ("In February 2009, the SWGCA found a consensus agreement on the definition of the crime of aggression".).

[14] See Agreement for the Prosecution and Punishment of the Major War Criminals of the European Axis (1945) 82 UNTS 279, Article 6(a) ("London Charter 1945") ("Crimes against peace" defined as "planning, preparation, initiation or waging of a war of aggression, or a war in violation of international treaties, agreements or assurances, or participation in a common plan or conspiracy for the accomplishment of any of the foregoing . . .".). There is no definition included of "war of aggression", although in the context of World War II this may have appeared fairly obvious. See also International Military Tribunal for the Far East (1946) Special Proclamation by the Supreme Commander to the Allied Powers at Tokyo, 19 January 1946, amended 26 April 1946, Article 5(a) ("Tokyo Charter 1946") (similar with the addition that the war could be "declared or undeclared" and that a war in violation of "international law" would be covered).

[15] Ibid.

[16] Charter of the United Nations (1945) 33 UNTS 933, Article 2(4) ("UN Charter (1945)").

[17] See United Nations General Assembly Resolution 3314(XXIX) 1974. See also Chap. 2, Sect. 2.6.

in Kampala, Uganda.[18] While much has been written on both the negotiating process and the definition of the crime,[19] a few aspects of both will be highlighted.

The definition of the crime, now found in Rome Statute Article 8*bis*, commences in paragraph 1 with the following:

> For the purpose of this Statute, "crime of aggression" means the planning, preparation, initiation or execution, by a person in a position effectively to exercise control over or to direct the political or military action of a State, of an act of aggression which, by its character, gravity and scale, constitutes a manifest violation of the Charter of the United Nations.[20]

The language, "planning, preparation, initiation or execution", is derived from the London Charter of the Nuremberg Tribunal (as well as the Charter of the Tokyo Tribunal), which encompassed "planning, preparation, initiation and waging".[21]

The requirement that the crime applies to "a person in a position effectively to exercise control over or to direct the political or military action of a [s]tate" is referred to as the "leadership clause". This language is in line with the Rome Statute's mandate to prosecute the most serious crimes of concern to the international community,[22] as well as the work of the Nuremberg and Tokyo Tribunals, which prosecuted only high-level leaders.[23] The definition thereby narrows the group of potential defendants. This language is based on the reasoning that it is a state's leaders who decide whether a state will go to war or commit an act of aggression, not its soldiers or even its mid-level commanders.[24]

---

18 See International Criminal Court, Assembly of States Parties 2010.

19 For a comprehensive analysis, see Kreβ and Barriga 2017; McDougall 2021. For a detailed account of the Kampala negotiations, see Kreβ and von Holtzendorff 2010; Coracini 2010b; Trahan 2011. For an account of the negotiations from 1998 to 2010, see Kreβ and Barriga 2017. For the documents that detail the negotiating history, see ibid.

20 Rome Statute (1998) (as amended), note 1, Article 8*bis*(1).

21 See London Charter (1945), note 14, Article 6(a); Tokyo Charter 1946, note 14, Article 5(a) (same).

22 Rome Statute (1998) (as amended), note 1, preamble, Article 5.1.

23 See Lippman 1991, p. 27 (22 prosecuted in the main trial at Nuremberg); see also Boister and Cryer 2008 (28 military and political leaders indicted).

24 The leadership clause "highlights the nature of the crime, and implies that it is not up to the individual soldier to determine whether the State's use of force is legal or not". Permanent Mission of Liechtenstein to the United Nations 2013, p. 16. The clause is akin to the approach taken in the High Command Case, although it uses a somewhat different standard. See High Command Case (1949) Trials of War Criminals Before the Nuremberg Military Tribunal Under Control Council Law No. 10, October 1946–April 1949, Vol. XI, p. 488 ("the perpetrator of a crime against peace must be 'in a position to shape or influence the policy that brings about [a crime against peace's] initiation or its continuance after initiation, either by furthering, or by hindering or preventing it'"); see Heller 2007 (discussing the difference).

The text next specifies that the definition covers a state's act of aggression where that act constitutes a "manifest" violation of the UN Charter, measured by its "character, gravity and scale".[25] This language was employed to make clear that it was not *any* act of aggression (or UN Charter violation) that would be covered, but only those that are neither *de minimis* in scale nor in a "grey area" in terms of legality.[26] The words "'gravity' and 'scale' were intended to exclude border skirmishes and the like".[27] As to "character", it is here that "genuinely legally controversial cases" are excluded.[28] There must be "an incontrovertible breach of Article 2(4)".[29] While the definition thus covers more than full-scale war (i.e., does not require "war" before it is triggered), the "manifest" requirement raises the threshold as to the "acts of aggression" that are encompassed.

Two Understandings agreed on at the Kampala Review Conference[30] reinforce the "manifest" threshold. Understanding 6 provides:

> It is understood that aggression is the *most serious and dangerous form* of the illegal use of force; and that a determination whether an act of aggression has been committed requires consideration of all the circumstances of each particular case, including the gravity of the acts concerned and their consequences, in accordance with the Charter of the United Nations.[31]

---

[25] Rome Statute (1998) (as amended), note 1, Article 8*bis*(1).

[26] This threshold clause "appropriately limit[s] the Court's jurisdiction to the most serious acts of aggression under customary international law, thus excluding cases of insufficient gravity and falling within a grey area". International Criminal Court 2008, Annex II, para 68. The SWGCA negotiations contributed to the finalization of the text and therefore constitute part of its negotiating history.

[27] Kreß 2009, p. 1138.

[28] Ibid. As to "character", Claus Kreß writes:

> It reflects the fact that the undisputed core of the prohibition of the use of force is surrounded by certain grey areas which are characterized by both sophisticated legal debate and deep legal policy divide. These areas, which unfortunately are of significant practical relevance, remain outside the scope of the definition of the crime of aggression. The threshold requirement provides the definition with its necessary anchor in customary international law and, at the same time, it ensures that the ICC will not have to deal with questions, which are not only legally but also politically highly controversial.

Kreβ 2018, p. 6.

[29] McDougall 2021, p. 158.

[30] The US delegation had attempted to reopen negotiations on the definition of the crime, but they had already been concluded through the SWGCA, meetings which the United States failed to attend despite their being open to all states (not only States Parties) and held primarily in Princeton, New Jersey. Thus, at the Review Conference, the US delegation had to content itself with the addition of various Understandings. See Kreβ 2018, p. 6 (noting that the United States returned to the negotiating table in 2009).

[31] Understanding 6 (emphasis added).

Understanding 7 adds that "the three components of character, gravity and scale must be sufficient to justify a 'manifest' determination. No one component can be significant enough to satisfy the manifest standard by itself".[32]

Returning to the definition of the crime, as to the state's act of aggression (the context in which an individual acts), the second paragraph of Article 8*bis* states:

> For the purpose of paragraph 1, "act of aggression" means the use of armed force by a State against the sovereignty, territorial integrity or political independence of another State, or in any other manner inconsistent with the Charter of the United Nations. Any of the following acts, regardless of a declaration of war, shall, in accordance with United Nations General Assembly resolution 3314 (XXIX) of 14 December 1974, qualify as an act of aggression . . . .[33]

The definition then provides a list of acts of aggression, quoting directly from General Assembly Resolution 3314.[34] "[R]esolution [3314], the culmination of some twenty years of negotiations, was seen by most delegations in the SWGCA as the appropriate basis for the definition of aggression in the Statute, given the fact that it constituted a consensual and time-tested document adopted by the General Assembly . . .".[35]

The language in Article 8*bis* is thus almost entirely based on pre-existing texts. Article 8*bis*(1) takes its "conduct" words from the Nuremberg and Tokyo Charters.[36] Article 8*bis*(2) first tracks the language of Article 2(4) of the UN Charter[37] and

---

[32] Understanding 7. The United States also insisted on the addition of further Understandings. For the text of all Understandings, see International Criminal Court, Assembly of States Parties 2010.

[33] Rome Statute (1998) (as amended), note 1, Article 8*bis*(2).

[34] Ibid. The list is as follows:

> (a) The invasion or attack by the armed forces of a State of the territory of another State, or any military occupation, however temporary, resulting from such invasion or attack, or any annexation by the use of force of the territory of another State or part thereof;
> (b) Bombardment by the armed forces of a State against the territory of another State or the use of any weapons by a State against the territory of another State;
> (c) The blockade of the ports or coasts of a State by the armed forces of another State;
> (d) An attack by the armed forces of a State on the land, sea or air forces, or marine and air fleets of another State;
> (e) The use of armed forces of one State which are within the territory of another State with the agreement of the receiving State, in contravention of the conditions provided for in the agreement or any extension of their presence in such territory beyond the termination of the agreement;
> (f) The action of a State in allowing its territory, which it has placed at the disposal of another State, to be used by that other State for perpetrating an act of aggression against a third State;
> (g) The sending by or on behalf of a State of armed bands, groups, irregulars or mercenaries, which carry out acts of armed force against another State of such gravity as to amount to the acts listed above, or its substantial involvement therein.

Ibid.

[35] Barriga et al. 2009, p. 9, citing June 2006 Princeton Report, paras 32–35.

[36] See note 14 and accompanying text.

[37] There are slight wording differences. Article 8*bis* adds the word "sovereignty" and refers to the Charter of the United Nations, whereas the UN Charter refers to the "Purposes" of the United

then incorporates the list of acts of aggression enumerated in General Assembly Resolution 3314.[38] The two new features are the leadership clause and the manifest threshold, both of which narrow the types of cases that may be brought before the ICC. In this regard, the definition is relatively conservative.

3.2.3 Conditions for the ICC's Exercise of Jurisdiction

Negotiations on the conditions for the ICC's exercise of jurisdiction over the crime were far more complicated. A few states—basically, the permanent members of the UN Security Council—believed that, by virtue of Article 39 of the UN Charter,[39] only the Security Council could determine if a state had committed aggression. Those states therefore argued that the Security Council's role in making such a determination should be an essential precondition before the ICC could undertake an investigation or prosecution.[40] Other states believed strongly that the ICC could make such a determination for itself.[41] Indeed, it would be critical for it to do so, because determining whether aggression was committed would constitute one of the elements of the crime.[42]

Nations. Additionally, the UN Charter prohibits the "threat" of the use of force, which is not included in Article 8*bis*.

[38] The list of acts of aggression is illustrative, but not necessarily a "closed list". The text states that the listed acts "qualify" as acts of aggression but does not preclude other comparable acts from being considered; however, any additional act would still need to constitute a "manifest" UN Charter violation to be covered by the crime. See Permanent Mission of Liechtenstein to the United Nations 2021, p. 10, para 3. https://crimeofaggression.info/wp-content/uploads/GIPA_The-Council-of-Advisers-Report-on-the-Application-of-the-Rome-Statute-of-the-International-Criminal-Court-to-Cyberwarfare.pdf. Accessed 6 May 2025. ("the list is not exhaustive").

[39] See UN Charter (1945), note 16, Article 39 ("The Security Council shall determine the existence of any threat to the peace, breach of the peace, or act of aggression and shall make recommendations, or decide what measures shall be taken in accordance with Articles 41 and 42, to maintain or restore international peace and security".). The UN Charter addresses only state responsibility, not individual criminal responsibility. In the negotiations, delegates agreed that "[t]he Court and the Security Council thus had autonomous, but complementary roles". Barriga et al. 2009, p. 103. Because the United States failed to attend the meetings of the SWGCA, the views on Article 39 were primarily expressed by other permanent members.

[40] Wenaweser 2024. See also Barriga et al. 2009, p. 11. Early proposals had suggested such a role might be played by the UN General Assembly or the International Court of Justice ("ICJ"). See Coracini 2010b, p. 751 ("Negotiations on the conditions [for the exercise of jurisdiction] have been dominated by defining an appropriate filter for the exercise of jurisdiction over the crime of aggression with a view to the determination of a State act of aggression".).

[41] Wenaweser 2024; Barriga et al. 2009, p. 11.

[42] See International Criminal Court (nd-a) Elements of Crimes, Article 8*bis*, Crime of Aggression. https://www.icc-cpi.int/sites/default/files/NR/rdonlyres/336923D8-A6AD-40EC-AD7B-45BF9DE73D56/0/ElementsOfCrimesEng.pdf. Accessed 6 May 2025 (requiring proof of an act of aggression as an element of the crime).

Agreement on the issue of jurisdiction was not reached until the 2010 Review Conference. While the issue is somewhat more complex,[43] states essentially decided that the ICC could exercise jurisdiction over the crime in two ways. The exercise of jurisdiction based on a UN Security Council referral is addressed in Rome Statute Article 15*ter*.[44] The exercise of jurisdiction based on referral by a State Party or the ICC Prosecutor acting *proprio motu* (on his or her own initiative) is addressed in Rome Statute Article 15*bis*.[45] These are also the routes by which cases involving genocide, crimes against humanity, and war crimes are initiated.[46]

Article 15*ter* is relatively straightforward. It provides for the Security Council to make referrals of situations concerning the crime to the ICC[47] and thus parallels Rome Statute Article 13(b), which governs the Security Council's referrals as to the crimes of genocide, war crimes, and crimes against humanity.[48] An additional feature of Article 15*ter* is the language of paragraph 4, which states that "[a] determination of an act of aggression by an organ outside the Court shall be without prejudice to the Court's own findings under this Statute".[49] Thus, were the Security Council to weigh in on whether a state has committed aggression, its determination would not bind the ICC. This provision was seen as critical to guarantee the ICC's independence.[50] It is also required to ensure that all elements of the crime are proven and to safeguard the rights of the accused.[51]

Rome Statute Article 15*bis,* however, alters the jurisdictional regime related to the crime of aggression significantly from the Rome Statute's general jurisdictional regime. Article 12—the *lex generalis* regime that pertains to genocide, crimes against

43 There were also issues as to how the amendment would enter into force—whether following the amendment regime in Rome Statute Article 121(4) or 121(5) (with the latter chosen). Additionally, a question arose as to which States Parties would need to ratify the amendments for the ICC to be able to exercise jurisdiction based on a State Party referral or the Prosecutor acting *proprio motu*—the aggressor State Party, the victim State Party, or both. See notes 62–64 (discussing the broad and narrow interpretations); for additional discussion of entry into force of an amendment, see Chap. 8, Sect. 8.4.2.

44 See Rome Statute (1998) (as amended), note 1, Article 15*ter*. This differed from the method that the permanent members had advocated; they had wanted the UN Security Council to decide whether an act of aggression had been committed before the crime of aggression could reach the ICC, and would have preferred that the Security Council be the only path whereby a situation involving aggression could reach the ICC.

45 See ibid., Article 15*bis*.

46 See ibid., Article 13(b) (Security Council referrals); Article 14 (State Party referrals); Article 15 (the Prosecutor acting *proprio motu*).

47 See ibid., Article 15*ter*. The Security Council's power to act derives from the UN Charter. The Rome Statute is not granting the Security Council referral powers, but accommodating the power that the Council holds, which emanate from the UN Charter.

48 See ibid., Article 13(b). The Security Council has made two such referrals, in the situations of Darfur, Sudan, and Libya. See United Nations Security Council Resolution 1593 (2005) (Darfur referral); United Nations Security Council Resolution 1970 (2011) (Libya referral).

49 See Rome Statute (1998) (as amended), note 1, Article 15*ter*(4).

50 Trahan 2024b; Trahan 2024d.

51 Ibid.

humanity, and war crimes—allows the ICC to exercise jurisdiction where a Rome Statute crime is committed (1) on the territory of a State Party or (2) by nationals of a State Party.[52] In this way, the ICC's jurisdiction also encompasses a crime committed by *nationals of a non-State Party* if the conduct occurs on the territory of a State Party.[53] Article 12(3) additionally provides that a state may accept the ICC's jurisdiction on an ad hoc basis, without becoming a State Party.[54] The only other way in which the ICC may exercise jurisdiction is through a Security Council referral, as discussed above.

However, in Kampala, states agreed to two novel features—a *lex specialis* regime—regarding the ICC's jurisdiction over the crime of aggression when the ICC's investigation is initiated *proprio motu* or by State Party referral of the situation. First, crimes committed by nationals, or on the territory, of non-States Parties would be *completely excluded* from the ICC's crime of aggression jurisdiction. This is memorialized in Article 15*bis*(5).[55] Furthermore, States Parties agreed that even a State Party may "opt out" of crime of aggression jurisdiction by lodging an "opt out" declaration. This is memorialized in Article 15*bis*(4).[56] It was primarily the United

---

[52] See Rome Statute (1998) (as amended), note 1, Article 12(2)(a)–(b).

[53] The United States has long objected to this reading of the Rome Statute. See, e.g., United States Department of State Press Statement 2021. Inconsistently, the United States appears to have accepted the reading with respect to the situation of Ukraine and the ICC's jurisdiction over Russian nationals. See, e.g., United States Consolidated Appropriations Act (2022) Public Law No: 117-328, Sec. 7073(b) (amending the Dodd Amendment by adding permission for the United States to "render[] assistance to the International Criminal Court to assist with investigations and prosecutions of foreign nationals related to the Situation in Ukraine, including to support victims and witnesses").

[54] See International Criminal Court (nd-c) Situation in Ukraine. https://www.icc-cpi.int/situations/ukraine. Accessed 6 May 2025 ("International Criminal Court (nd-c)") (Ukraine's Article 12(3) declarations). Rome Statute Article 12(3) states: "If the acceptance of a State which is not a Party to this Statute is required under paragraph 2, that State may, by declaration lodged with the Registrar, accept the exercise of jurisdiction by the Court with respect to the crime in question. . . ". Rome Statute (1998) (as amended), note 1, Article 12(3).

[55] Rome Statute Article 15*bis,* para 5, states: "In respect of a State that is not a party to this Statute, the Court shall not exercise its jurisdiction over the crime of aggression when committed by that State's nationals or on its territory". Ibid., Article 15*bis*(5).

[56] Rome Statute Article 15*bis,* para 4, states:

> The Court may, in accordance with Article 12, exercise jurisdiction over a crime of aggression, arising from an act of aggression committed by a State Party, unless that State Party has previously declared that it does not accept such jurisdiction by lodging a declaration with the Registrar. The withdrawal of such a declaration may be effected at any time and shall be considered by the State Party within three years.

Ibid., Article 15*bis*(4). The opt out procedure has hardly been used; to date, only Kenya and Guatemala have opted out. See International Criminal Court (nd-b) Declarations Lodged Under Article 15*bis*(4). https://www.icc-cpi.int/resource-library. Accessed 6 May 2025. For the argument that the "opt out" could amount to a reservation—with reservations being prohibited in Rome Statute Article 120, see Coracini 2010b, p. 778.

States (supported by some additional states) that insisted on the exemption for non-States Parties.[57] It is that exemption that has excluded Russian nationals and crimes committed on Russian territory from the ICC's jurisdiction regarding the crime of aggression, as will be discussed below.[58]

The crime of aggression amendments agreed on in Kampala also contained a delay feature. The ICC's jurisdiction was not activated immediately after the 2010 Review Conference, but was put off for several years, until certain preconditions could be met.[59] The decision to activate the ICC's jurisdiction over the crime occurred at a December 2017 meeting of the ICC's ASP,[60] with jurisdiction activated effective 17 July 2018.[61]

3.2.4 Activation of the ICC's Jurisdiction

Unfortunately, States Parties did not merely endorse what had been agreed on in Kampala when they activated jurisdiction. After Kampala, a dispute developed as to how to read the Kampala crime of aggression amendments. Most states believed that the proper reading of Rome Statute Article 15*bis*(4)—that States Parties could *opt out* of crime of aggression jurisdiction—meant that all States Parties were "in" the jurisdictional regime, unless they exercised such an opt-out; it would suffice that *either* the aggressor State Party *or* the victim State Party ratify the amendments to create jurisdiction in the absence of a Security Council referral, as long as the

[57] According to Carrie McDougall, "the US was the prime mover, but the exclusion of non-States Parties was a unanimous position of the P5 and some of their closest allies. While the exact formulation was only arrived at in Kampala, it was reflected in earlier SWGCA discussions—e.g., that the regime must be consent based, that Article 121(5) of the Rome Statute applied including its second sentence, that that second sentence has a negative interpretation, and that non-States Parties and non-ratifying States Parties should be in the same position". Trahan 2024c. For discussion of the second sentence of Article 121(5), see Chap. 8, note 97.

[58] See Sect. 3.2.5. There are three additional differences between the crime of aggression's jurisdictional regime agreed on in Kampala where there is a State Party referral or the Prosecutor acts *proprio motu,* and the Rome Statute's general Article 12 jurisdiction. First, under Article 15*bis*, there is no mention of the ability of a state to file an ad hoc declaration accepting the ICC's jurisdiction; thus, the procedure of Article 12(3) appears not to be preserved. See note 54 (Article 12(3)). Second, under Article 15*bis*, there is a waiting period of six months to ascertain whether the Security Council has made a determination of an act of aggression. Rome Statute (1998) (as amended), note 1, Article 15*bis*(6)–(8). Third, if no Security Council determination has been made, there is an additional requirement that the full Pre-Trial Division must authorize the commencement of the investigation. Ibid., Article 15*bis*(8).

[59] Ibid., Article 15*bis*(1)–(3); Article 15*ter*(1)–(3). Activation required the ratification or acceptance of the amendments by 30 States Parties and a decision to be taken, after 1 January 2017, by the ASP. Kreβ 2018, p. 7.

[60] The ASP is the management, oversight, and legislative body of the ICC; it consists of representatives of all States Parties to the Rome Statute. For background, see Trahan 2020.

[61] See International Criminal Court, Assembly of States Parties 2017.

aggressor State Party had not opted out of jurisdiction.[62] This became known as the "broad interpretation". However, the United Kingdom and France (and a few aligned states) developed a different reading.[63] They interpreted the amendments to mean that *both* the victim State Party *and* the aggressor State Party had to have ratified the amendments in order for the ICC to exercise jurisdiction absent a Security Council referral, as long as the aggressor State Party had not opted out of jurisdiction.[64] This became known as the "narrow interpretation".

During the December 2017 ASP meeting, the United Kingdom and France insisted on this latter reading.[65] Because of a concern that there might not be two-thirds of States Parties present who would vote on the activation, agreement had to be reached by consensus (i.e., agreement of all States Parties present, accomplished without voting).[66] Had France or the United Kingdom blocked consensus because of this issue, there would have been *no activation*; thus, their narrow interpretation appears to have prevailed. It is reflected in the text of paragraph two of the Activating Resolution.[67] However, many States Parties believed that this was not the agreement reached in Kampala and insisted on adding language to the resolution suggesting that the ICC judges would be the final arbiters of the ICC's jurisdiction.[68] This was intended to leave open the question of whether the Activating Resolution had improperly modified the text of the Kampala Amendments, preserving the broad interpretation.[69] Thus, something of an unresolved question remains as to whether the

---

[62] See Permanent Mission of Liechtenstein to the United Nations 2013, p. 10 ("Passive consent in the form of the abstention from opting-out of the Court's exercise of jurisdiction suffices [for there to be jurisdiction]".); ibid., p. 9 ("the amendments must have been ratified by and entered into force for at least one of the States Parties involved—be it the presumed aggressor or the victim State").

[63] See Kreβ 2018, p. 9 (citing Canada, Columbia, Japan, and Norway joining the French/UK reading, and Liechtenstein, Argentina, Botswana, Samoa, Slovenia, and Switzerland opposing it). Claus Kreβ explains the dynamics: "It turned out that France and the UK were not prepared to cross any. . . bridge. Their demand remained unchanged: all States Parties should accept the 'restrictive position' as part of the ASP resolution accompanying the activation decision". Ibid., p. 11.

[64] Ibid. The UK/French reading made little sense because it would require a State Party to ratify the Kampala amendments in order to be able to opt out of jurisdiction. But if that were the correct reading, why have the "opt-out" language? The State Party could simply decline to ratify the amendments.

[65] Ibid. For an account of the activation negotiations, see ibid., pp. 11–13.

[66] See Rome Statute (1998) (as amended), note 1, Article 121(3) (adoption of amendments by two-thirds or consensus).

[67] International Criminal Court, Assembly of States Parties 2017, para 2.

[68] Ibid., para 3.

[69] See Trahan 2018; see also McDougall 2024 (arguing that the Activating Resolution does not amount to a "subsequent agreement" under the Vienna Convention on the Law of Treaties and that if the resolution is only a "supplementary means of interpretation", it would be of lesser weight when interpreting the Kampala amendments); McDougall 2021 (setting forth the arguments in detail). Compare Kreβ 2018, p. 12 ("This language is no more than a statement of the obvious fact that the ASP cannot replace the Court as the judicial body charged with applying the law in complete independence".). For the Vienna Convention on the Law of Treaties, see Vienna Convention on the Law of Treaties (1969) 1155 UNTS 331, 8 ILM 679.

Activating Resolution was effective or not in modifying jurisdiction.[70] If effective, it would drastically curtail jurisdiction where Rome Statute States Parties are involved. As of late 2025, 49 States Parties have ratified the crime of aggression amendments.[71] Thus, if effective, jurisdiction would exist before the ICC only if one of those 49 States Parties commits an act of aggression against another of the 49 States Parties, where the aggressor State Party has not opted out of jurisdiction.

All in all, the compromises reached in 2010 and 2017 have created a weak jurisdictional regime before the ICC. Jurisdiction over nationals and crimes committed on the territory of non-State Parties was eliminated entirely in 2010, primarily at the behest of the United States. States Parties were then largely exempted in 2017, primarily at the behest of the United Kingdom and France—if one accepts that this was achieved by the Activating Resolution.

It is extremely ironic that three of the victorious allies of 1945 that established the Nuremberg Tribunal and supplied its judges and prosecutors,[72] have worked to truncate the ICC's jurisdiction over the crime of aggression. Thus, the ICC now cannot exercise jurisdiction when leaders of the successor state (the Russian Federation) to what was a significant part of the fourth ally (the USSR) appear to be implicated in the crime of aggression.[73] The same would be true if, for example, the conduct of the People's Republic of China or that of any other non-State Party were at issue.

The actions taken by the United States, the United Kingdom, and France[74]—most likely aimed at insulating their leaders were those states to commit aggression—betray a commitment made by Robert H. Jackson in his Opening Statement at Nuremberg. As lead Prosecutor for the United States, Jackson eloquently stated: "Let me make clear that while this law is first applied against German aggressors, the law includes, and if it is to serve a useful purpose it must condemn, aggression by any other nations, including those which now sit here in judgment".[75] As will be explored further in subsequent chapters, the negotiating tactics of the United States, the United Kingdom, and France raise serious questions about whether those states are committed to upholding the rule of law, particularly the UN Charter's use of force provisions (on which the crime of aggression is based), when it comes

---

70 For an article explaining, see Trahan 2018.

71 See Global Institute for the Prevention of Aggression (nd) Status of Ratification and Implementation. https://crimeofaggression.info/the-role-of-states/status-of-ratification-and-implementation/. Accessed 8 October 2025.

72 See Lippmann 1991, p. 37 ("The International Military Tribunal at Nuremberg was composed of judges from the Allied Powers".); ibid., p. 27 ("The Chief Prosecutors [were] appointed by each of the four States represented on the Tribunal".).

73 International criminal law incorporates the presumption of innocence and the requirement of proof beyond a reasonable doubt. Thus, whether Russia has committed an act of aggression and whether there are individuals who, as a result, have committed the crime of aggression would need to be adjudicated.

74 The author does not fully group these states into the same category. The United Kingdom and France are States Parties to the Rome Statute, while the United States, like Russia and China, is not. See United Nations Treaty Collection nd.

75 Jackson 1945.

to the conduct of their leaders. Of course, only German nationals were prosecuted before the Nuremberg Tribunal and only Japanese nationals were prosecuted before the Tokyo Tribunal—hence the historic claim that those tribunals imposed "victor's justice".[76] Unfortunately, support for international justice can become more tepid when a country's own nationals could face accountability.[77]

3.2.5 *The Lack of ICC Jurisdiction Over the Crime of Aggression Committed Against Ukraine*

Regardless of how or why this outcome was reached, it is clear that the crime of aggression cannot be prosecuted before the ICC where nationals of a non-State Party are implicated. This exempts Russian nationals as well as crimes committed on Russian territory. It also exempts nationals of the Republic of Belarus and crimes committed on its territory, which was utilized as a staging ground for Russia's invasion,[78] as well as nationals of North Korea, which has also sent troops to assist Russia.[79]

Thus, although Ukraine accepted the ICC's jurisdiction in 2014 and 2015 by executing two Article 12(3) declarations,[80] that only created jurisdiction before the

---

[76] See, e.g., Minear 1971.

[77] Clearly not all states are equally tepid in their support for international justice. One hundred and twenty-five States Parties to the Rome Statute have accepted the ICC's jurisdiction over genocide, crimes against humanity, and war crimes, which jurisdiction would cover their own nationals. See United Nations Treaty Collection nd (125 States Parties as of late 2025). Additionally, 49 States Parties appear to have no hesitation about accepting jurisdiction over the crime of aggression even when it could create jurisdiction over their own leaders. See note 71 and accompanying text (49 ratifications of the Kampala amendments).

Some of the United States' concerns may stem from the argument that the crime of aggression would inadvertently criminalize "humanitarian intervention". Another concern may be the imprecision that exists in the law as to what is covered by a state's right to self-defense under Article 51 of the UN Charter. See, e.g., Kreβ 2017, p. 459 ("While the existence of the right of self-defence is as uncontroversial as the core of its conditions and scope, significant grey areas surround this core".) (discussing some of the grey areas that exist as to self-defense). Yet, by requiring a "manifest" UN Charter violation, the definition rules out jurisdiction over conduct in any "grey area" of legality. See notes 26–29 and accompanying text. There is a strong argument that "humanitarian intervention" would fall in such a "grey area". See Trahan 2015; see also Kreβ 2018, pp. 15–16 (discussing humanitarian intervention as a grey area of legality). Where a state exercises self-defense that is based on a plausible legal theory, or where there is a split in the views of states, it also would not make a good case for prosecution. See, e.g., Haque 2021 (evaluating the split in the views of states as to the permissibility of self-defense against the attack of a non-state actor). Again, we see that the definition of the crime is a conservative one.

[78] Kłysiński and Żochowski 2023; see Rome Statute (1998) (as amended), note 1, Article 8*bis*(f) (including as an act of aggression, "[t]he action of a State in allowing its territory, which it has placed at the disposal of another State, to be used by that other State for perpetrating an act of aggression against a third State"). For discussion of the role of Belarus, see Chap. 4, Sect. 4.2.3.

[79] CBS News 2024. For discussion of the role of North Korea, see Chap. 4, Sect. 4.2.4.

[80] International Criminal Court (nd-c), note 54 (two declarations).

ICC over the crimes of genocide, crimes against humanity, and war crimes committed on the territory of Ukraine. Indeed, as of late 2025, the ICC has issued several warrants against Russian nationals on charges of war crimes and crimes against humanity.[81] Yet, Ukraine's acceptance of jurisdiction did not create jurisdiction over the crime of aggression in the situation of Ukraine due to the carve-out for the nationals of non-States Parties in Article 15*bis*(5).[82] This is equally true now that Ukraine has ratified the Rome Statute *including* the crime of aggression amendments.[83] The ratification does not alter the way in which jurisdiction operates related to the crime of aggression.[84]

Ukraine does have a domestic statute criminalizing aggression that will be discussed in subsequent chapters.[85] Thus, aggression prosecutions in Ukraine are possible and have been started.[86] Yet, for a variety of reasons, there is no substitute for prosecutions before an international tribunal, particularly as to those at the leadership level, for what is a "leadership crime". Moreover, as will be explained in later chapters, certain high-level leaders (i.e., heads of state, heads of government, and ministers of foreign affairs, referred to as the "troika") could not be tried through domestic proceedings due to immunities before national courts. Chapter 5 will explain why the best approach for achieving accountability for the invasion of Ukraine would have been before a fully international criminal tribunal created through the United Nations, which could have indicted and prosecuted such top-level leaders. Chapter 7 will explain why only a second best approach is being pursued—a tribunal that cannot prosecute the troika, although it will be able to prosecute other leaders and indict the troika.

---

[81] See ibid. (list of suspects).

[82] See note 55 and accompanying text.

[83] International Criminal Court Press Release 2025.

[84] See Law of Ukraine (nd) On the Ratification of the Rome Statute of the International Criminal Court and Its Amendments. Mischa Gureghian Hall on X: "An English translation (albeit unofficial and Google Translate): https://t.co/tnkgvAhb0k"/X. Accessed 6 May 2025 (unofficial translation). This is the case due to the carve-out of the nationals of non-States Parties contained in Article 15*bis*(5). Ukraine has also purported to invoke Article 124 (permitting an opt out before the ICC of jurisdiction over war crimes for seven years), but only insofar as Ukrainian nationals are concerned (i.e., it is attempting to leave in place the ICC's jurisdiction regarding war crimes committed by Russian nationals). It is unclear whether such a one-sided opt out would be effective.

[85] See Chap. 6, Sect. 6.3.2, especially n 26 (leadership clause read into the Ukrainian definition of the crime); Chap. 5, Sect. 5.3.3 (trials *in absentia* allowed under Ukrainian law).

[86] The website of Ukraine's Office of the Prosecutor General states that Ukraine has 437 registered crimes of aggression involving 736 suspects. Prosecutor General's Office, Crimes Committed during the Full-Scale Invasion of the RF. https://gp.gov.ua/en. Accessed 17 September 2025.

3.3 The Need to Remedy the Gap in Crime of Aggression Jurisdiction

While gaps in Rome Statute jurisdiction over the crime of aggression had arisen by 2010, Russia's invasion of Ukraine has highlighted their deleterious consequences—most significantly, impunity before the ICC. Prior to the invasion, it might have seemed that the practice of states invading other states was a thing of the past—that the main threats to international peace were civil wars and terrorism. The events of February 2022 showed how wrong this was. There is clearly a need for enforcing the crime of aggression.

States and experts have responded to the lacuna in jurisdiction in two ways. First, shortly after the invasion, states and others began exploring how to create a special tribunal on the crime of aggression for the situation of Ukraine. The different proposals, including the proposal for a fully international tribunal established through the United Nations, as well as the competing proposal of utilizing a Ukrainian chamber with some international elements, are explored in Chaps. 5 and 6. Chapter 7 explores the agreement that has been reached through negotiations within a Core Group of approximately 40 states,[87] to establish a new freestanding tribunal created by agreement between the Council of Europe and Ukraine.

Second, because accountability for the crime of aggression should not exist only for Ukraine but more broadly, a parallel initiative has emerged. It involves amending the Rome Statute (the Kampala crime of aggression amendments) to eliminate the exceptional jurisdictional regime related to the crime of aggression and harmonize the ICC's jurisdiction over all four of its crimes. This would significantly expand the ICC's jurisdiction over the crime.[88] In early 2025, five states, supported by a Group of Friends of approximately 38 states, formally tabled such an amendment proposal[89] to harmonize the ICC's jurisdiction over all four of its core crimes. However, during negotiations held in July 2025 during a Special Session of the ICC's ASP, the amendment proposal was deferred to future negotiations to be held in 2029. The amendment proposal and July Special Session will be discussed in Chap. 8.

---

[87] Representatives of the European Union and Council of Europe were also part of the Core Group.

[88] If an amendment were to pass such that the ICC's jurisdiction over the crime of aggression is the same as the Rome Statute's general Article 12 regime, subject to entry into force issues, the ICC would have jurisdiction whenever a crime of aggression is committed on the territory, or by a national, of a State Party, regardless of whether the other State (or States) involved in the act of aggression are ICC States Parties. The proposed amendment would additionally clarify that an Article 12(3) declaration could cover the crime of aggression. See note 54 (Article 12(3) declarations); see Costa Rica, Germany, Sierra Leone, Slovenia, and Vanuatu (2025) Proposal of Amendment. https://treaties.un.org/doc/Publication/CN/2025/CN.162.2025-Eng.pdf. Accessed 7 August 2025 ("Amendment Proposal 2025").

[89] Amendment Proposal 2025.

3.4 Conclusion

In incorporating the crime of aggression in the Rome Statute, defining the crime, and activating the ICC's jurisdiction over it, states not only built on the historic legacy of the Nuremberg and Tokyo Tribunals (as well as other developments discussed in Chap. 2), but essentially provided another route to reinforce the UN Charter's use of force provisions. The hope thereby is to deter political and military leaders from committing the crime of aggression and for the ICC to be in a position to prosecute should deterrence fail. Yet, the ICC cannot serve as a deterrent or conduct prosecutions where it cannot exercise jurisdiction.

The February 2022 invasion of Ukraine (and earlier 2014 illegal annexation of Crimea)[90] amply illustrate that the ICC *entirely failed to deter* high-level Russian political and military leaders. Nor was the ICC even anticipated to serve as a deterrent, since nationals of non-States Parties were carved out of the ICC's jurisdictional regime over the crime of aggression in 2010. Arguably, the US-led negotiation of the jurisdictional carve-out[91] may have delivered a dangerous message: that aggression by leaders of a non-State Party would be tolerated, at least at the level of individual criminal responsibility.[92] Furthermore, Russia sits as a permanent member of the UN Security Council, and therefore has neither been condemned nor had other punitive measures in response to its invasion imposed upon it there. In fact, Russia vetoed a resolution that would have done so.[93] It also vetoed a subsequent Security Council resolution that would have condemned its attempts at holding referenda in occupied territories in the East of Ukraine.[94] While the UN General Assembly was able to adopt several resolutions condemning Russia's actions and endorsing related measures, in most instances, the General Assembly has no enforcement power; typically, its resolutions are only recommendations.[95]

---

[90] For the illegal annexation of Crimea, see Chap. 4, Sect. 4.2.1.

[91] See note 57.

[92] It is not tolerated under the UN Charter. See UN Charter (1945), note 16, Article 2(4). Yet, enforcement against a permanent member of the UN Security Council or its ally remains a challenge.

[93] See United Nations Security Council Resolution 155 2022a (vetoed by the Russian Federation).

[94] United Nations Security Council Resolution 720 2022b (vetoed by the Russian Federation).

[95] For example, the General Assembly issued:

- two resolutions condemning Russia's invasion, United Nations General Assembly Resolution ES-11/1 2022a and United Nations General Assembly Resolution ES-11/2 2022b;
- a resolution expelling Russia from the Human Rights Council, United Nations General Assembly Resolution ES-11/3 2022c;
- a resolution condemning Russian attempts at annexing territory in the East of Ukraine and holding illegal referenda there, United Nations General Assembly Resolution ES-11/4 2022d;
- a call for the establishment of a compensation mechanism, United Nations General Assembly Resolution ES-11/5 2022e;
- a call for a just and lasting peace as well as accountability, United Nations General Assembly Resolution ES-11/6 2023b;

Thus, as also discussed in Chap. 2, at the level of state responsibility, states are effectively not protected by the UN Security Council from war or other aggression being waged against them if a permanent member or its ally is the aggressor state.[96] Due to compromises made in Kampala, they also are not protected by the ICC at the level of individual criminal responsibility from aggression being committed against them by nationals of non-States Parties. Furthermore, if the 2017 Activating Resolution was effective at modifying the statutory provisions agreed on in Kampala, in most situations they are also not protected before the ICC in the event of aggression being committed against them by States Parties.

International law and international institutions designed to enforce it develop gradually and imperfectly—full of bold vision but also vulnerable to setbacks in implementation. The work to criminalize aggression is only one aspect of the multi-faceted quest to prevent the scourge of war. Many more efforts beyond criminalization also have been marshalled to prevent or limit the horrors of armed conflict, including attempts to address the root causes of war, such as the arms race (including the nuclear arms race) and global arms trade, attempts to enforce International Humanitarian Law, and attempts to utilize alternative means for resolving disputes. Yet a critical component of the endeavor to move to a world governed by law, not force, remains absent. One of our key tools to attempt to limit the scourge of war (and other uses of force) is the crime of aggression, waiting to be utilized.

Adopting the definition of the crime of aggression in Kampala in 2010 was a historic achievement, as was the decision in 2017 to activate the ICC's jurisdiction over the crime.[97] Yet, the tepid approach to jurisdiction that resulted from compromises reached in 2010 and 2017 casts a pall on these accomplishments. Aggression is the act that sets off all the subsequent harm that ensues in the victim state. Despite some states' wariness to enforce the crime of aggression,[98] if it is "the supreme

- a resolution on the safety and security of nuclear facilities in Ukraine, United Nations General Assembly Resolution 78/L.90 2024; and
- a resolution on the situation of human rights in the temporarily occupied territories of Ukraine, including the Autonomous Republic of Crimea and the city of Sevastopol, United Nations General Assembly Resolution 78/221 2023a.

The March 2006 resolution that established the Human Rights Council stated that the General Assembly may suspend membership rights of a country "that commits gross and systematic violations of human rights". United Nations General Assembly Resolution 60/251 2006. Thus, the resolution expelling Russia from the Human Rights Council was treated as binding.

[96] For an argument that there are legality issues that arise when a veto is used to protect a state's own aggression, see Trahan 2023.

[97] For an explanation of the historic significance of activating jurisdiction, see Liechtenstein Ambassador Christian Wenaweser and Swiss delegate, Nikolas Stürchler, quoted in Kreβ 2018, p. 14, n 48.

[98] Some states have resisted the march toward the ICC and the crime of aggression, cautious not to lose the prerogative to use force in support of what they see as essential national interests, cognizant of sometimes difficult judgments related to what falls within self-defense, and perhaps concerned that the international order is inadequate to ensure peace and security. Yet, as explained, if there is even a plausible legal theory, use of force is likely excluded from being the crime of aggression due to the "manifest" threshold, see notes 26–29. States should be fully willing to accept that they must

international crime"—as it was proclaimed to be in the Judgment of the Nuremberg Tribunal[99]—the ICC must have more jurisdiction over it.[100] Only then can one hope to start achieving effective deterrence and begin to ensure that the promises made with the founding of the United Nations—preventing the scourge of war—can be kept. In the meantime, the conduct of Russian political and military leaders implicated in aggression against Ukraine should not remain entirely insulated from the rule of law.

References

Barriga S (2017) Negotiating the Amendments on the Crime of Aggression. In: Kreβ C, Barriga S (eds) The Crime of Aggression: A Commentary. Cambridge University Press, Cambridge

Barriga S, Kreß C (2012) The *Travaux Préparatoires* of the Crime of Aggression. Cambridge University Press, Cambridge

Barriga S, Danspeckgruber W, Wenaweser C (eds) (2009) The Princeton Process on the Crime of Aggression, Materials of the Special Working Group on the Crime of Aggression, 2003–2009. Liechtenstein Institute on Self-Determination, Princeton University, Princeton

Boister N, Cryer R (eds) (2008) Tokyo Tribunal Indictment. In: Boister N, Cryer R (eds) Documents on the Tokyo International Military Tribunal: Charter, Indictment and Judgments. Oxford University Press, Oxford

CBS News (2024) Over 1,000 North Korean Casualties in Russia-Ukraine War, South Korea Says. https://www.cbsnews.com/news/over-1000-north-korean-casualties-in-russia-ukraine-war-seoul-says. Accessed 5 May 2025

Clark R S (2002) Rethinking Aggression as a Crime and Formulating Its Elements: The Final Work-Product of the Preparatory Commission for the International Criminal Court. Leiden Journal of International Law 15: 859–90

Clark R S (2017) Negotiations on the Rome Statute, 1985–98. In: Kreβ C, Barriga S (eds) The Crime of Aggression: A Commentary. Cambridge University Press, Cambridge

Coracini A R (2010a) Defining the Crime of Aggression for the Rome Statute of the International Criminal Court. In: Stahn C, van den Herik L (eds) Future Perspectives on International Criminal Justice. T.C.M. Asser Press, The Hague

Coracini A R (2010b) The International Criminal Court's Exercise of Jurisdiction Over the Crime of Aggression – at Last ... in Reach ... Over Some. Göttingen Journal of International Law 2: 745–89

Haque A A (2021) Self-Defense Against Non-State Actors: All Over the Map. Just Security. https://www.justsecurity.org/75487/self-defense-against-non-state-actors-all-over-the-map/. Accessed 6 May 2025

not commit a manifest UN Charter violation—after all, states are already obligated not to violate the UN Charter's use of force provisions—or have their leaders face responsibility should they do so.

[99] See International Military Tribunal, Judgment of 1 October 1946, in The Trial of German Major War Criminals. Proceedings of the International Military Tribunal Sitting at Nuremberg, Germany, Part 22 (22 August 1946 to 1 October 1946), p. 421.

[100] In parallel, if more jurisdiction existed before the ICJ, more states could bring cases related to use of force issues also to that court. See United Nations, Meetings Coverage, Security Council (2023) Greater Acceptance, Participation in International Court of Justice's Compulsory Jurisdiction Key for Improving Global Dispute Settlement, Security Council Hears. https://press.un.org/en/2023/sc15171.doc.htm. Accessed 6 May 2025.

Heller K (2007) Retreat from Nuremberg: The Leadership Requirement in the Crime of Aggression. European Journal of International Law 18: 477–97
International Criminal Court (2008) Report of the Special Working Group on the Crime of Aggression (2008) ICC-ASP/6/20/Add.1
International Criminal Court, Assembly of States Parties (2002) Resolution on Continuity of Work in Respect of the Crime of Aggression, ICC-ASP/1/Res.1
International Criminal Court, Assembly of States Parties (2010) Review Conference, The Crime of Aggression, ICC Doc. RC/Res.6
International Criminal Court, Assembly of States Parties (2017) Activation of the Jurisdiction of the Court Over the Crime of Aggression, Res. ICC-ASP/16/Res.5
International Criminal Court Press Release (2025) ICC Welcomes Ukraine as New State Party. https://www.icc-cpi.int/news/icc-welcomes-ukraine-new-state-party. Accessed 5 May 2025
Jackson R H (1945) Opening Statement, Robert H. Jackson, Chief of Counsel for the United States (1945) International Military Tribunal. https://www.roberthjackson.org/speech-and-writing/opening-statement-before-the-international-military-tribunal/. Accessed 6 May 2025
Kirsch P, Oosterveld V (2001) The Preparatory Commission for the International Criminal Court. Fordham International Law Journal 25: 563–588
Kłysiński K, Żochowski P (2023) The Reluctant Co-Aggressor. Minsk's Complicity in the War Against Ukraine. OSW Centre for Eastern Studies. https://www.osw.waw.pl/en/publikacje/osw-commentary/2023-02-10/reluctant-co-aggressor-minsks-complicity-war-against-ukraine. Accessed 6 May 2025
Kreß C (2009) Time for Decision: Some Thoughts on the Immediate Future of the Crime of Aggression: A Reply to Andreas Paulus. European Journal of International Law 20: 1129–1146
Kreβ C (2017) The State Conduct Element. In: Kreβ C, Barriga S (eds) (2017) The Crime of Aggression: A Commentary. Cambridge University Press, Cambridge
Kreβ C (2018) On the Activation of ICC Jurisdiction Over the Crime of Aggression. Journal of International Criminal Justice 16: 1–17
Kreβ C, Barriga S (eds) (2017) The Crime of Aggression: A Commentary. Cambridge University Press, Cambridge
Kreβ C, von Holtzendorff L (2010) The Kampala Compromise on the Crime of Aggression. Journal of International Criminal Justice 8: 1179–1217
Lippman M (1991) Nuremberg: Forty Five Years Later. Connecticut Journal of International Law 7: 1
McDougall C (2021) The Crime of Aggression Under the Rome Statute of the International Criminal Court, 2nd edn. Cambridge University Press, Cambridge
McDougall C (2024) Expanding the ICC's Jurisdiction Over the Crime of Aggression. Journal of International Criminal Justice 22: 534–564
Minear R H (1971) Victors' Justice: Tokyo War Crimes Trials. Princeton University Press, Princeton
Oosterveld V, deGuzman M M (eds) (2020) The Elgar Companion to the International Criminal Court. Edward Elgar Publishing, Cheltenham
Permanent Mission of Liechtenstein to the United Nations (2013) Handbook: Ratification and Implementation of the Kampala Amendments to the Rome Statute of the ICC
Permanent Mission of Liechtenstein to the United Nations (2021) The Council of Advisers' Report on the Application of the Rome Statute of the International Criminal Court to Cyberwarfare. https://crimeofaggression.info/wp-content/uploads/GIPA_The-Council-of-Advisers-Report-on-the-Application-of-the-Rome-Statute-of-the-International-Criminal-Court-to-Cyberwarfare.pdf. Accessed 6 May 2025
Trahan J (2011) Negotiating the Amendment on the Crime of Aggression: Proceedings at the Kampala Review Conference on the International Criminal Court. International Criminal Law Review 11: 49–104
Trahan J (2015) Defining The "Grey Area" Where Humanitarian Intervention May Not Be Fully Legal, But is Not The Crime of Aggression. Journal on the Use of Force and International Law 2: 42–80

Trahan J (2018) From Kampala to New York—The Final Negotiations to Activate the Jurisdiction of the International Criminal Court Over the Crime of Aggression. International Criminal Law Review 18: 197–243

Trahan J (2020) The Assembly of States Parties. In: Oosterveld V, deGuzman M M (eds) The Elgar Companion to the International Criminal Court. Edward Elgar Publishing, Cheltenham

Trahan J (2023) Amending the Kampala Amendments: Proposal to Harmonize the ICC's Jurisdiction Over the Crime of Aggression with Its Jurisdiction Over Its Other Core Crimes. Opinio Juris. https://opiniojuris.org/2023/10/02/amending-the-kampala-amendments-a-proposal-to-harmonize-the-iccs-jurisdiction/. Accessed 6 May 2025

Trahan J (2024a) Interview with David Donat-Cattin, 5 August 2024

Trahan J (2024b) Interview with Roger Clark, 14 August 2024

Trahan J (2024c) Interview with Carrie McDougall, 17 August 2024

Trahan J (2024d) Interview with Jutta Bertram-Nothnagel, 4 September 2024

United States Department of State Press Statement (2021) Antony J. Blinken, Secretary of State, The United States Opposes the ICC Investigation into the Palestine Situation. https://2021-2025.state.gov/the-united-states-opposes-the-icc-investigation-into-the-palestinian-situation/. Accessed 6 May 2025

United Nations Treaty Collection (nd) Status, Rome Statute of the International Criminal Court. https://treaties.un.org/Pages/ViewDetails.aspx?src=TREATY&mtdsg_no=XVIII-10&chapter=18&clang=_en. Accessed 6 May 2025

Wenaweser C (2024) Remarks of Ambassador Christian Wenaweser, Permanent Representative of Liechtenstein to the United Nations, 18 July 2024

Other Documents

Agreement for the Prosecution and Punishment of the Major War Criminals of the European Axis (1945) 82 UNTS 279

Charter of the United Nations (1945) 33 UNTS 933

Costa Rica, Germany, Sierra Leone, Slovenia, and Vanuatu (2025) Proposal of Amendment. https://treaties.un.org/doc/Publication/CN/2025/CN.162.2025-Eng.pdf. Accessed 7 August 2025

Global Institute for the Prevention of Aggression (nd) Status of Ratification and Implementation. https://crimeofaggression.info/the-role-of-states/status-of-ratification-and-implementation/. Accessed 8 October 2025

High Command Case (1949) Trials of War Criminals Before the Nuremberg Military Tribunal Under Control Council Law No. 10, October 1946–April 1949, Vol. XI

International Criminal Court (nd-a) Elements of Crimes, Article 8*bis*, Crime of Aggression. https://www.icc-cpi.int/sites/default/files/NR/rdonlyres/336923D8-A6AD-40EC-AD7B-45BF9DE73D56/0/ElementsOfCrimesEng.pdf. Accessed 6 May 2025

International Criminal Court (nd-b) Declarations Lodged Under Article 15*bis*(4). https://www.icc-cpi.int/resource-library. Accessed 6 May 2025

International Criminal Court (nd-c) Situation in Ukraine. https://www.icc-cpi.int/situations/ukraine. Accessed 6 May 2025

International Military Tribunal, Judgment of 1 October 1946, in The Trial of German Major War Criminals. Proceedings of the International Military Tribunal Sitting at Nuremberg, Germany, Part 22 (22 August 1946 to 1 October 1946)

International Military Tribunal for the Far East (1946) Special Proclamation by the Supreme Commander to the Allied Powers at Tokyo, 19 January 1946, amended 26 April 1946

Law of Ukraine (nd) On the Ratification of the Rome Statute of the International Criminal Court and Its Amendments. https://zakon.rada.gov.ua/laws/show/3909-20/print. Accessed 6 May 2025

Prosecutor General's Office, Crimes Committed during the Full-Scale Invasion of the RF. https://gp.gov.ua/en. Accessed 17 September 2025.

Rome Statute of the International Criminal Court (1998) 2187 UNTS 3
United Nations Diplomatic Conference of Plenipotentiaries on the Establishment of an International Criminal Court, Summary Records of the Plenary and Committee of the Whole Meetings (1998) UN Docs A/CONF.183/SR.1-A/CONF.183/SR.9, A/CONF.183/C.1/SR.1-A/CONF.183/C.1/SR.42
United Nations, Final Act of the United Nations Diplomatic Conference of Plenipotentiaries on the Establishment of an International Criminal Court (1998) UN Doc. A/CONF.183/10*
United Nations General Assembly Resolution 3314(XXIX) (1974)
United Nations General Assembly Resolution 60/251 (2006)
United Nations General Assembly Resolution ES-11/1 (2022a)
United Nations General Assembly Resolution ES-11/2 (2022b)
United Nations General Assembly Resolution ES-11/3 (2022c)
United Nations General Assembly Resolution ES-11/4 (2022d)
United Nations General Assembly Resolution ES-11/5 (2022e)
United Nations General Assembly Resolution 78/221 (2023a)
United Nations General Assembly Resolution ES-11/6 (2023b)
United Nations General Assembly Resolution 78/L.90 (2024)
United Nations, Meetings Coverage, Security Council (2023) Greater Acceptance, Participation in International Court of Justice's Compulsory Jurisdiction Key for Improving Global Dispute Settlement, Security Council Hears. https://press.un.org/en/2023/sc15171.doc.htm. Accessed 6 May 2025
United Nations Security Council Resolution 1593 (2005)
United Nations Security Council Resolution 1970 (2011)
United Nations Security Council Resolution 155 (2022a)
United Nations Security Council Resolution 720 (2022b)
United States Consolidated Appropriations Act (2022) Public Law No: 117–328
Vienna Convention on the Law of Treaties (1969) 1155 UNTS 331, 8 ILM 679

Chapter 4
The Russian Federation's Invasion of Ukraine: The Crimes Committed and Why the Elements of the Crime of Aggression Are Likely Satisfied

Contents

Abstract The chapter traces the events leading up to and including the invasion of Ukraine, while acknowledging the illegal annexation of Crimea and fomenting of insurgency in the Donbas as the start of Russia's aggression. The chapter also surveys the crimes alleged to have been committed, mostly by Russian forces, during the course of the invasion—none of which would have occurred absent the decision to invade. The chapter ends with a discussion of the elements of the crime of aggression and why they are likely satisfied in the instant situation—by both Russia's invasion and annexation of Crimea and its invasion of Ukraine. The chapter also discusses some of the political and military leaders potentially implicated in committing the crime of aggression.

J. Trahan, *The Crime of Aggression and Russia's Invasion of Ukraine*,
https://doi.org/10.1007/978-94-6265-763-2_4

Keywords Invasion of Ukraine · Planning the invasion · Maidan protests · Annexation of Crimea · Separatists in the Donbas · Cyber operations · Role of Belarus · North Korean troops · Wagner Group · Russian military command structure · Targeting of civilians and civilian objects · Torture · Mistreatment of POWs · Rape and other sexual violence · Cultural heritage destruction · Destruction of the Kakhovka Dam · Deportation of Ukrainian children · Population transfers · Crimes committed in Bucha · Siege of Mariupol · Act of aggression · Crime of aggression

4.1 Introduction

This chapter chronologically traces the events leading up to and including the Russian Federation's 2022 invasion of Ukraine. It addresses key actors, the composition of forces, command structures, and the number of civilians and military personnel killed. While focusing on the 2022 invasion, the chapter acknowledges Russia's 2014 illegal annexation of Crimea as the start of the aggression. The chapter also discusses Belarus' actions in placing its territory at Russia's disposal for launching the invasion, the role of North Korean forces, and the role that cyberattacks have played as an additional modality by which Russia's invasion has been perpetrated. The chapter also surveys the war crimes and crimes against humanity allegedly committed since the invasion, as well as other harms suffered, none of which would have occurred without the original crime, the crime of aggression. The chapter culminates in a preliminary analysis of how the invasion, as well as the earlier illegal annexation of Crimea, falls within the definition of act of aggression contained in the Rome Statute[1] of the International Criminal Court ("ICC"), and suggests some of the Russian and other political and military leaders who might potentially be implicated in the crime of aggression.

4.2 The Commencement and Course of the Invasion

The invasion of Ukraine that commenced on 24 February 2022, was a "surprise and shock to the 'West'".[2] If states were operating under the belief that today's wars would primarily consist of internal armed conflicts and cyber operations by state and non-state actors, they were proven dramatically wrong.[3] This was a full-scale invasion of a neighboring state—by a permanent member of the UN Security Council, no less,

[1] Rome Statute of the International Criminal Court (1998) 2187 UNTS 90 (as amended), ("Rome Statute (1998) (as amended)").

[2] Osinga 2024, p. 124.

[3] One author writes:

the organ charged under the UN Charter with the maintenance of international peace and security.[4]

The war was predicted by US intelligence as early as October 2021.[5] In an essay written in July 2021, Russian President Putin articulated the central idea that an independent Ukraine can only exist in "partnership" with Russia (as he understands it), and that "Russians and Ukrainians were one people".[6] Putin took the view that "the people of Ukraine viewed Russians favorably and believe they were part of a shared civilization, cruelly divided by historical political mistakes".[7] "The barrier, in his view, to correct[ing] these mistakes was the government in Kyiv, which he accused of being a puppet to external powers hostile to Russia".[8] Gleb Bogush explains:

> Although the wording was much more restrained and vague than often alleged, it can be inferred from Putin's text that he regarded Ukraine's sovereignty as conditional and did not believe in a separate Ukrainian national identity. Russian state media widely disseminated the piece. It was also included in the mandatory reading list for the armed forces. Putin's rhetoric gradually radicalized following this piece. In his 2022 speeches, he referred to Russians as an "artificially divided people" and Ukrainian territories as "gifts from the Russian people"—according to him, apparently, gifts can be taken back.[9]

After the essay's publication, the tentative movement of military units to the Ukrainian border began to accelerate.[10]

By 24 February 2022, President Putin announced a "special military operation", which he claimed would defend Russian-speaking territories in the east of Ukraine, protect the Russian-speaking population from genocide, and counter neo-Nazis in the

---

> many subscribed to the prediction that war in the future would be conducted primarily by non-state actors, or wear the face of hybrid conflict in which state actors used all kinds of non-military instruments (including cyber attacks) . . . . But instead, Russia reminded the West that conventional military power and even nuclear sabre-rattling are still major currencies in international politics.

Ibid., p. 137.

[4] United Nations Charter (1945) ("UN Charter (1945)"), Article 24.1.

[5] Osinga 2024, p. 124.

[6] Putin 2021.

[7] Zabrodskyi et al. 2022, p. 7.

[8] Ibid.

[9] Trahan 2025b. See also Bogush 2025.

[10] Freedman 2022, p. 391.

Ukrainian government.[11] Russia also invoked Article 51 of the UN Charter,[12] which allows for the use of self-defense, but only *if* an armed attack is committed against a state.[13] One scholar describes the goals of the Russian invasion as: "'denazification'" ("the destruction of national sovereignty and the banning of Ukrainian identity"); "'demilitarisation'" ("the destruction and banning of the [Ukrainian Armed Forces] and export to Russia of enterprises of the defence industrial complex of Ukraine"); and "'denuclearisation'" ("the capture of nuclear power plants and their transfer to the direct management of [Russia's State Atomic Energy Corporation,] Rosatom").[14]

The months prior to February 2022 saw a "steady build-up of forces along Ukraine's border that remained on station there for months . . .".[15] Russia's military buildup commenced in March 2021, with large numbers of conventional troops added to existing forces along Ukraine's borders.[16] Assessments of the buildup estimate that it involved as many as 190,000 troops.[17] Yet, warnings by US and Baltic leaders to European capitals were essentially ignored.[18] Europe was divided—"it felt no political obligation to militarily help defend Ukraine (not being a NATO member), and it allowed its energy dependence on Russia to prevail over security considerations".[19] Meanwhile, the Kremlin was denying any intent to start a war.[20]

---

[11] In announcing the invasion, Putin stated: "we will seek to demilitarise and denazify Ukraine, as well as to bring to trial those who perpetrated numerous bloody crimes against civilians, including against citizens of the Russian Federation". Ibid., p. 393, citing Transcript: Bloomberg News 2022. When Putin "ordered the invasion of Ukraine on February 24, 2022, he cited the vulnerable position of the separatists [in the Donbas] as the pretext, although his underlying objective was to bring all of Ukraine back into Russia's sphere of influence". Freedman 2022, p. 366. Another source explains:

> Russia has just issued a genocide handbook for its war on Ukraine. The Russian official press agency "RIA Novosti" published . . . an explicit program for the complete elimination of the Ukrainian nation as such . . . . "[D]enazification" in official Russian usage just means the destruction of the Ukrainian state and nation. A "Nazi", as the genocide manual explains, is simply a human being who self-identifies as Ukrainian. According to the handbook, the establishment of a Ukrainian state thirty years ago was the "nazification of Ukraine". Indeed "any attempt to build such a state" has to be a "Nazi" act. Ukrainians are "Nazis" because they fail to accept "the necessity that the people support Russia".
>
> Snyder 2022.

[12] Permanent Representative of the Russian Federation 2022.

[13] See UN Charter, note 4, Article 51.

[14] Zabrodskyi et al. 2022, p. 11.

[15] Osinga 2024, p. 124.

[16] Zabrodskyi et al. 2022, p. 7.

[17] Freedman 2022, p. 391. In early February 2022, British and American intelligence publicly confirmed these assessments. Ibid., citing Herszenhorn 2022. "The main reason why there were doubts about the Russian intentions was that it seems self-evidently foolish for Russia to attempt to conquer a country the size of France with a population of 44 million". Ibid.

[18] Osinga 2024, p. 125.

[19] Ibid.

[20] Ibid. In his address on 24 February 2022, Putin claimed that Russia did not aim at occupation of Ukrainian territories; meanwhile there were obvious preparations to establish a puppet or pro-Putin government in Ukraine. Trahan 2025b.

According to some, the Kremlin planned for a rapid ten to fifteen day campaign[21] to invade Ukraine, occupy it, and annex the country by August 2022.[22] Others describe the goal as setting up a puppet government in Kyiv and probably annexing two "peoples' republics".[23] In a report by the United Kingdom's Royal United Services Institute for Defense and Security Studies ("RUSI"), the outlines of Russia's invasion plan are detailed in captured copies of orders issued to Russian units.[24] Russian forces sent to the Ukrainian border in autumn 2021 "received orders to the effect that they would be away from their barracks for nine months".[25] According to the RUSI report, it was the 9th Section of the 5th Service of Russia's Federal Security Service ("FSB") that was tasked, as of July 2021, with planning the occupation.[26] The RUSI report states that Chief of the General Staff of the Russian Armed Forces Valery Gerasimov had assured Putin of Russia's military capabilities.[27] The Russian military "[e]njoyed superiority in numbers . . . and [the] prevailing doctrine [among Russian political and military elite] led to expectations that Russia would be able to overrun Ukraine".[28]

The decision to invade can largely be laid at the feet of one individual: "Russian president Vladimir Putin [had] systematically consolidated his power by eliminating other forms of authority, and all rivals, arriving at a one man dictatorship".[29] According to RUSI, it was the FSB, Minister of Defense Sergei Shoigu, General Gerasimov, and "elements within the presidential administration" who developed the plan for the invasion.[30] Thus, the invasion plans "were drawn up by a very

---

[21] Osinga 2024 (claiming the plan was for a 10 day campaign); compare Freedman 2022, p. 392, citing Roblin 2022 ("Captured Russian documents, stamped 18 January 2022, show preparations then being made for operations for 15 days between 20 February and 6 March".).

[22] Zabrodskyi et al. 2022, p. 1.

[23] See, e.g., Cordon 2024; Trahan 2025a.

[24] Zabrodskyi et al. 2022, p. 2.

[25] Ibid., p. 12.

[26] Ibid., p. 7. The FSB (*Federalnaja Sluzhba Bezopasnosti*, which translates to Federal Security Service) is one of the successor agencies to the Soviet KGB. It conducts counterintelligence, antiterrorism, and surveillance of the military. Britannica nd-b.

[27] Zabrodskyi et al. 2022, p. 7. "Gerasimov had control of the military's main intelligence agency, the GRU and had established a special operations forces command". Freedman 2022, p. 365. The GRU is Russia's military intelligence agency. Faulconbridge 2018.

[28] Osinga 2024, p. 125. These views proved largely erroneous:

> Clearly, the Kremlin had based its initial invasion plans on faulty assumptions. Politically, it had not anticipated the swift Western reaction in the shape of massive sanctions and military support for Ukraine. It also assumed a divided Ukrainian population, a weak regime, and a weak military. It discovered a stiff military resistance instead and found the invasion unified the nation, fueled a remarkable societal resilience, and energized its leadership. Zelensky became what Churchill was for Great Britain in 1940. Putin had also overestimated Russia's own military capabilities . . . .

Ibid., p. 130.

[29] Merkx 2023, p. 14. See also Bogush 2023a, p. 94 (referring to the "total consolidation of power in Russia by Vladimir Putin").

[30] Zabrodskyi et al. 2022, p. 8.

small group of officials, and the intent was directed by Putin"; many other officials, including even deputy heads of branches within the Russian general staff, were apparently unaware of the invasion plans until days before it commenced.[31] Thus:

> Russian decision-making prior to the invasion [was] almost entirely top down. Putin's obsession with secrecy meant that consultations were limited to a small circle of trusted military advisors. Not even Russia's foreign minister, Sergey Lavrov, was included in this group. He was informed of the invasion on [24 February], the day it took place. Russian field commanders on the ground in Belarus for military exercises had no idea that they would be leading an invasion.[32]

In deciding whether to launch the invasion, according to one source, the voices Putin listened to "were from his closest advisers, old comrades from the Russian security apparatus and his days in St[.] Petersburg . . . . These included Nikolai Patrushev, the hawkish chairman of his [Russian] Security Council and former head of the FSB; security service chief Alexander Bortnikov; and foreign intelligence head Sergey Naryshkin".[33] "Putin's own background was in intelligence operations. So were those closest to him in the decision-making process".[34]

The invasion began with a massive military campaign across Ukraine.[35] Russia invaded "by land, air, and sea from the north, east, and south".[36] The invasion launched from six different axes:

> from the Black Sea in the southeast; from Crimea in the south; from Donbas in the east; from Belgorod in the northeast (toward Kharkiv); from Kursk in the northeast (toward Kyiv); and from Gomel, Belarus, in the north (toward Kyiv). The Russians thought that they had planned an invasion of sufficient scale, speed, and pressure to cause a catastrophic breakdown of the Ukrainian state.[37]

The initial phase of the invasion seemed to go "according to plan. Ukraine's transport and communications infrastructure suffered massive cyberattacks".[38] The units advancing from Belarus were under orders to reach Kyiv.[39] Russian forces quickly seized "the entire Kherson and much of the Zaporizhia regions as well as the eastern part of the Kharkiv region and the southern part of the Donetsk region".[40]

By the third day of the invasion, however, it was apparent that plans had gone "seriously wrong"—those aimed at "neutralising Ukraine's political leadership . . . were failing as the Security Service of Ukraine identified, isolated, and destroyed

---

[31] Ibid., p. 12.

[32] Merkx 2023, p. 15. Compare Open Society Justice Initiative 2022 (OSJI Model Indictment suggesting Lavrov was involved in planning the invasion).

[33] Freedman 2022, p. 392, citing Stanovaya 2022; Kirby 2022a.

[34] Freedman 2022, p. 399.

[35] Zabrodskyi et al. 2022, p. 24.

[36] Armed Conflict Location & Event Data Project (ACLED) 2023, p. 1.

[37] Merkx 2023, p. 16. For details of the initial phase of the invasion, see ibid., pp. 19–21.

[38] Osinga 2024, p. 125. For more on cyberattacks, see Sect. 4.2.5.

[39] ACLED 2023, p. 3.

[40] Ibid., p. 1.

their infiltrated groups".[41] Within weeks, Russia's campaign was "losing momentum . . . . Ukraine had put up a surprisingly effective resistance".[42] After the initial push to take Kyiv failed, "Putin, on April 9, declared units would retreat from Kyiv and instead focus on the Donbas, the complete conquest of Ukraine, clearly [by then] out of reach".[43]

With Russian units causing "horrific numbers of civilian casualties and committing war crimes in Bucha and Irpin",[44] and adopting siege tactics in its battle for Mariupol,[45] by the summer of 2022, a coalition of states from Western countries emerged willing to offer military support to Ukraine.[46] Notwithstanding, the period from early April through the end of August 2022 saw the Russian-Ukrainian fronts "marked by a relative stalemate".[47] By August and September 2022, Ukrainian troops had staged a counteroffensive, reconquering Kharkiv province and liberating Kherson by 9 November.[48]

Russia struck back with an air offensive over the winter of 2022–2023, with the "intended strategic goal to demoralize the population in cities and undermine their resolve".[49] "But when, in November 2022, Russia bombed Ukrainian electricity plants[,] public support for Ukraine across Europe rose to 74%".[50] According to

---

[41] Zabrodskyi et al. 2022, p. 29. The plan was to eliminate Zelenskyy and Ukraine's political leadership. Sky News 2022 ("Russian special services were tasked with killing the Ukrainian leadership").

[42] Osinga 2024, p. 126.

[43] Ibid., p. 127. After Russia's retreat from Kyiv, days 38 through 91 of the invasion focused on the destruction of the Ukrainian Armed Force in the Donbas and the "seizure and annexation of Luhansk and Donetsk". Zabrodskyi et al. 2022, p. 35; see also ACLED 2023, p. 1 (after setbacks in northern Ukraine, Russian forces concentrated on securing the Donbas. "By mid-summer 2022 Russia had largely occupied the Luhansk region".).

[44] "When the Russian occupation of Bucha in the early days of Russia's full-scale invasion of Ukraine ended in March 2022, widespread destruction was revealed, and a UN commission concluded that war crimes had been committed against the civilian population". UN News 2024. For discussion of crimes in Bucha, see Sect. 4.3.2.8.

[45] For discussion of the siege of Mariupol, see Sect. 4.3.2.9.

[46] Osinga 2024, p. 130. Since 2022, the Armed Forces of Ukraine have received significant assistance from Western countries. An alliance of 54 states that were part of the Ukraine Defense Contact Group provided military assistance to Ukraine. Merkx 2023, p. 25. "To ensure that NATO countries did not get directly involved in the fight, early in the war Putin invoked the nuclear deterrent"—threatening to utilize nuclear weapons should they do so. Freedman 2022, p. 395. For US military assistance, see Gady and Kofman 2023, p. 15. For British military assistance see ibid., p. 16. In October 2022, the European Union set up the EU Military Assistance Mission Ukraine—EUMAM Ukraine—"in part to provide training for an initial tranche of 15,000 Ukrainian soldiers . . .". Ibid. For US and NATO contributions, see also Economist Intelligence Unit 2022.

[47] Merkx 2023, p. 22.

[48] Osinga 2024, p. 129. "Ukraine's lightning counter-offensive in early September [2022] in Kharkiv *oblast* in northeastern Ukraine was a spectacular tactical victory". Gady and Kofman 2023, p. 9. For the Kherson offensive, see ibid., pp. 12–13. See also ACLED 2023, p. 1 ("In early September 2022, Ukrainian forces broke through thinly manned Russian defenses and liberated most of the Kharkiv region").

[49] Osinga 2024, p. 129.

[50] Ibid., p. 131, citing European Commission (2022) Eurobarometer 98.1, Brussels.

British intelligence, "Russia was losing 500–800 men a day in February [2023]. By mid-2023 th[e] war already ranked among the 10% bloodiest wars of the past 100 years, not counting the civilian casualties".[51] A second period of stalemate occurred from November 2022 through the end of May 2023, when Russian ground forces conducted a largely unsuccessful winter/spring offensive.[52]

In June 2023, Ukraine began an anticipated counteroffensive.[53] However, by the summer of 2023, "most analysts and Western politicians had become convinced that the war might well last for years".[54] There was "[n]o end in sight".[55] Ukraine's Armed Forces made "little territorial progress", with "high human and materiel losses and struggling in a few directions of the counter-offensive with gaps in equipment and training of troops who were facing well-prepared Russian defense lines".[56]

Russia has been gradually gaining territory since December 2023.[57] In November 2024, "more than 720 square kilometers of Ukrainian territory came under Russian control, the biggest gain since the start of the full-scale invasion on February 24, 2022".[58] As of August 2025, Russia controlled about 19 percent of Ukrainian territory, down from just over a quarter of the territory in March 2022.[59] Meanwhile, Ukraine also struck back with cross-border incursions into Russia's Kursk *oblast*[60] commencing in summer 2024 and controls some Russian territory.[61]

As of late 2025, the war continues, with "the main challenges [for Ukraine being] the uncertainty in the US Congress for financing assistance to Ukraine and the possible change of American policy" under the administration of US President Trump,[62] as well as enormous problems with manpower.[63] As to the Trump

---

[51] Ibid., p. 132.

[52] Merkx 2023, p. 23.

[53] Osinga 2024, p. 132. This included the use of cluster munitions. Ibid. Cluster munitions are a problematic weapon due to their wide dispersal radius and high dud rate. Gardner 2023. Neither Russia nor Ukraine are parties to the Convention on Cluster Mines. See Convention on Cluster Munitions (2008) 2688 UNTS 39; see also Convention on Cluster Munitions, States Parties and Signatories by Region (nd) https://www.clusterconvention.org/states-parties/. Accessed 20 October 2025.

[54] Osinga 2024, p. 133.

[55] Ibid. "[T]here was never a chance in 2022 and 2023 that an agreement could be reached. There was no trust that the other side would honour a diplomatic agreement and neither side had political space to start negotiating in the first place". Ibid. "Moreover, 85% of the Ukrainian population considered concessions unacceptable . . .". Ibid., p. 134.

[56] Piotrowski 2024.

[57] Breteau 2024.

[58] Ibid.

[59] Ibid.; Faulconbridge 2025.

[60] An *oblast* can be thought of as a region or province. For background, see Merriam-Webster Dictionary nd.

[61] Kottasová 2024; Spencer 2024.

[62] Piotrowski 2024.

[63] See, e.g., Mirovalev 2025.

administration, there is concern that the United States could withdraw military assistance, forcing Ukraine into territorial concessions[64] and a disadvantageous peace agreement.

4.2.1 The Earlier Illegal Annexation of Crimea and the Role of Russian Proxy Forces in the Donbas

The war in Ukraine, however, did not commence with the 2022 invasion, but with Russia's 2014 illegal annexation of Crimea.[65] The decision for Russia to take Crimea was made in February 2014 by Putin himself.[66] He apparently "told senior aides that events had 'unfolded in such a manner that we had to start planning how to return Crimea to Russia. We could not leave the region and its people to the whim of fate and the nationalist steamroller'".[67]

The illegal annexation came at a time when Ukraine was seen as politically weak. In late 2013, protests (known as the Maidan protests or revolution) erupted in Kyiv's central square, Maidan, in response to Ukraine's President Viktor Yanukovych's decision not to sign an Association Agreement with the European Union, opting instead to form closer ties with Russia.[68] When the protest movement turned violent, Yanukovych was ousted and fled to Russia, and a pro-Western government formed from opposition parties in Ukraine's parliament.[69] This set the stage for a perceived power vacuum that paved the way for Russian actions.[70]

The attempt to re-exert Russia's influence over Ukraine at that time took the form of two military operations—the invasion and annexation of Crimea in late February through early March 2014, and fomenting insurgency in eastern Ukraine between February and May 2014[71] and thereafter.[72]

As to Crimea, on 25 February 2014, Russia launched a ship carrying 200 Russian special operations forces that landed in Sevastopol.[73] "On the morning of February 27, government institutions in Crimea, including the parliament in Simferopol, were

---

64 "Advisers to Donald Trump publicly and privately are floating proposals to end the Ukraine war that would cede large parts of the country to Russia for the foreseeable future". Euractiv and Reuters 2024.

65 The origins of the war also trace back to the dissolution of the Soviet Union. Freedman 2022, p. 361. One might also include Russia's intervention in Georgia. See Labuda 2024, p. 286 (discussing "violations of other countries' territorial integrity, most recently in Georgia in 2008").

66 Freedman 2022, p. 369.

67 Ibid., citing Zygar 2016.

68 Kofman et al. 2017, p. 1; Merkx 2023, p. 17.

69 Kofman et al. 2017, p. 1; Freedman 2022, p. 364; Merkx 2023, p. 17.

70 Indeed, Ukraine "did not react to the Russian operation when launched". Kofman et al. 2017 pp. 19–20.

71 Zabrodskyi et al. 2022, p. 13.

72 There have been years of war in the Donbas. Ibid., p. 17.

73 Kofman et al. 2017, pp. 7–8. For a detailed timeline of the invasion, see ibid., pp. 85 et seq.

taken over by notably well-armed men, who claimed to be members of Crimea's 'self-defense force'".[74] On 28 February, Russian forces seized Simferopol airport and subsequently blockaded Ukraine's Navy.[75] After Ukrainian forces lost effective command and control over their units on the Crimean Peninsula, the Crimean Parliament declared that a referendum on independence would be held on 16 March.[76] Meanwhile, in a press conference on 4 March, Putin claimed that Russia had no plans to annex Crimea and there were no Russian soldiers on Crimean soil.[77] From 6 March onward, Russia began a conventional troop buildup[78] and ultimately seized full control of Crimea, with no significant resistance from Ukraine.[79] On 16 March, the population purportedly voted to become part of Russia, although the election results are contested.[80] In what has been referred to as "passportisation", citizens of Crimea have since been forced to obtain Russian passports.[81]

Crimea's strategic significance stems from Russia's Black Sea Fleet having historically been based there,[82] as well as its economic significance.[83] Nikita Khrushchev made the decision to transfer Crimea from Russia to Ukraine at a time when both were part of the USSR, making the move "largely symbolic and [then] of little political consequence".[84] After the dissolution of the USSR and Ukraine's independence, Russia maintained its naval base at Sevastopol under a treaty with Ukraine.[85]

While the United States and the European Union imposed sanctions on Russia after its seizure of Crimea,[86] there was no dramatic response by the international

---

[74] Freedman 2022, p. 370. The Russian troops entering Crimea came to be known as "'little green men'". Ibid., p. 370. They were Russian soldiers who were masked and wore unmarked uniforms. Schreck 2019.

[75] Kofman et al. 2017, p. 9.

[76] Ibid., p. 10; Freedman 2022, p. 371.

[77] Kofman et al. 2017, p. 14.

[78] Ibid., p. 9.

[79] Ibid., p. 16; Merkx 2023, p. 15.

[80] See Samuel 2025 ("The results of the referendum alleged that 96.7 percent of voters were in favor of Crimea's accession to the Russian Federation. In May [2014] it was discovered that actual voter turnout was around 30 percent, and only half of those voters voted for annexation".).

[81] The European Court of Human Rights has since ruled that this practice violates the European Convention on Human Rights. See Fripp 2025 (discussing the case *Ukraine v. Russia (Re Crimea)*, App. Nos. 20958/14 and 38334/18 [2024] ECHR 569). See also Green 2014.

[82] Kofman et al. 2017, p. 16.

[83] Pineda 2025 (discussing Crimea's strategic economic importance).

[84] Kofman et al. 2017, p. 16.

[85] "Under the Treaty on Friendship, Cooperation and Partnership signed by Moscow and [Ukraine] in 1997, Russia recognized Sevastopol's Ukrainian status and the inviolability of Ukraine's borders, while Ukraine granted Russia the right to retain the Sevastopol naval base and to keep its Black Sea Fleet in Crimea until 2017". Litovkin 2014. "A second agreement, signed in Kharkiv in 2010, extended the duration of the Russian Black Sea Fleet's presence in Sevastopol till 2042". Ibid.

[86] See BBC 2017 ("After Russia annexed Crimea and backed separatists in eastern Ukraine, in 2014, the Obama administration in tandem with the European Union introduced an array of economic sanctions on Russian individuals and businesses".).

community.[87] This lackluster reaction is thought to have emboldened Putin in his eventual plan to invade Ukraine in 2022.[88] In the words of one scholar, "Europe had responded timidly to the annexation of Crimea, communicating weakness and a divided Europe instead of strength and unity".[89] Another report concludes: "Events in Crimea may have strengthened long-held Russian views about the weakness and incompetence of the Ukrainian state".[90]

Along with Russia's seizure of Crimea, Russian proxy forces in the Donbas (consisting of the Donetsk and Luhansk regions in eastern Ukraine) mobilized and seized control of those territories, igniting years of simmering conflict there.[91] Protests in Eastern Ukraine began after Yanukovych's flight from power and the decision by the Ukrainian Parliament on 23 February 2014, to repeal a language law (later quickly reversed) that permitted the speaking of Russian in government institutions in certain areas.[92] The language law was an issue in the east where most of the population speaks Russian. This triggered the mobilization of "leftist and right-wing organizations in Eastern Ukraine".[93] While protesters portrayed their actions as "spontaneous and self-initiated", the Ukrainian government attributed the outbreak to "pro-Russian agitators and intelligence operators".[94] By April, armed separatists had seized government buildings.[95] On 11 May, after referenda were held in Donetsk and Luhansk, the breakaway republics proclaimed themselves to be "people's republics" and declared their independence.[96] This sparked war in the Donbas. From late April to late May 2014, the Ukrainians mounted a campaign to contain the pro-Russian rebellion, while the separatists obtained short-range air-defense weaponry from either Russia or old Ukrainian stockpiles.[97] Separatist forces

[87] The UN General Assembly condemned the annexation, but Russia vetoed a resolution by the UN Security Council that would have expressed condemnation. See United Nations General Assembly Resolution 11493 (2014); United Nations Security Council Resolution S/2014/189 (2014) (vetoed by the Russian Federation).

[88] "The successful Russian invasion of Crimea in 2014 had not led to major interventions by other countries, and after 2014 Western Europe had grown increasingly dependent on flows of Russian natural gas. Russian intelligence [incorrectly] predicted that European objections to an invasion of Ukraine [in 2022] would be pro forma rather than substantive". Merkx 2023, p. 16.

[89] Osinga 2024, p. 124.

[90] Kofman et al. 2017, p. 31.

[91] There were years of war in the Donbas. Zabrodskyi et al. 2022, p. 17.

[92] Kofman et al. 2017 p. 33. Kudriavtseva 2016 ("In 2014, in the aftermath of Euromaidan, the Ukrainian parliament, the Verkhovna Rada, passed a law to repeal the 'language law' of 2012, which had enabled the expansion of Russian at the regional level".) (footnote omitted). The earlier 2012 law had allowed use of minority (non-Ukrainian) languages in courts, schools and other government institutions in areas where the minority exceeded 10% of the population. For background on the language laws, see Riabchuk 2012.

[93] Kofman et al. 2017, p. 33.

[94] Ibid.

[95] Pitchford 2022.

[96] Freedman 2022, p. 375. "Russian recognition of the breakaway republics was widely condemned as violating international law". Pitchford 2022.

[97] Kofman et al. 2017, p. 42.

thereafter consolidated into more of a conventional army, "equipped by Russia and supported by a capable contingent of Russian troops . . .".[98] The enclaves of Donetsk and Luhansk came under separatist control, sustained by Russian subsidies, but formally still part of Ukraine.[99] Russia has "never acknowledged the Russian Armed Forces' participation in the Donbas conflict",[100] although it is reported that the 8th CAA (part of Russia's Combined Arms Armies) commands the separatist units in Donetsk and Luhansk.[101] On 21 February 2022, President Putin announced that Russia would recognize the separatist republics as independent states.[102] On 30 September 2022, Russia purported to annex Donetsk and Luhansk as well as Kherson and Zaporizhzhia as part of Russia.[103] As of late 2025, large parts of the four areas remain under Russian military control.

4.2.2 *Russian Military Hierarchy and Military Units Involved*

In the Russian military hierarchy, the Supreme Commander of the Armed Forces is President Vladimir Putin.[104] The next person in the military hierarchy is the Minister of Defense, Sergey Shoigu.[105] The Chief of the General Staff of the Armed Forces is Valery Gerasimov, who is in charge of the Main Directorate of the General Staff of the Armed Forces.[106] The Minister of Defense is in charge of the United Group of Forces, with the commanders of the various groups of forces below him.[107] Separately, there are commanders of the military branches for ground forces, aerospace forces, and the navy.[108] The following chart (see Fig. 4.1)[109] summarizes the Russian military command structure.

---

[98] Ibid., p. 45.

[99] Freedman 2022, p. 364. See Bogush 2023a, p. 100 (referring to Donetsk and Luhansk as "puppet 'peoples' republics").

[100] Whisler 2020, p. 250. See ibid. (detailing the Russian military units thought to have been involved).

[101] Bowen 2022, p. 1.

[102] Putin 2022.

[103] Kirby 2022b.

[104] Truth Hounds and Project Expedite Justice 2023/2024, p. 43.

[105] Ibid.

[106] Ibid.

[107] Ibid.

[108] Ibid.

[109] Ibid.

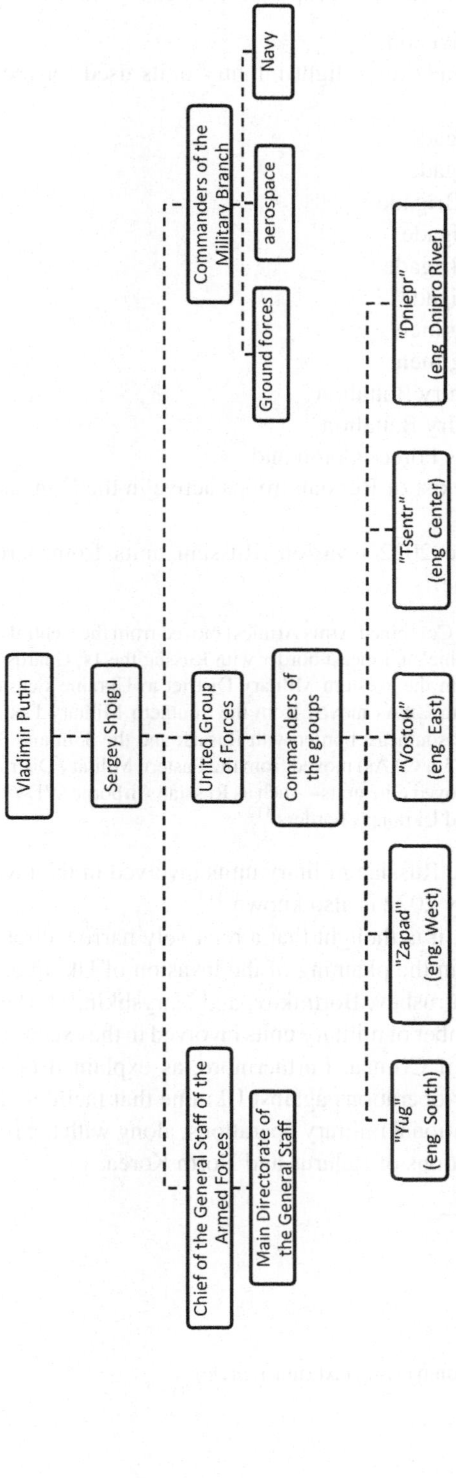

Fig. 4.1 Visual summary of the Russian military command structure. *Source* Truth Hounds and Project Expedite Justice 2023/2024, p. 43

According to one source,[110] elements from the following Russian army and airborne units entered Ukraine to occupy the Crimean Peninsula:

- 7th Air Assault Division
- 3rd Spetsnaz Brigade (elite light infantry units used for reconnaissance and direct action)
- 10th Spetsnaz Brigade
- 16th Spetsnaz Brigade
- 18th Motor Rifle Brigade
- 22nd Spetsnaz Brigade
- 31st Air Assault Brigade
- 291st Artillery Brigade
- 25th Spetsnaz Regiment
- 45th Spetsnaz Regiment
- 382nd Naval Infantry Battalion
- 727th Naval Infantry Battalion
- Special Operations Forces Command

Detailed accounts also exist of Russian troops active in the Donbas commencing in 2014.[111]

In the lead-up to the 2022 invasion, Russian units from across Russia were deployed toward Ukraine:

> The 41st and 2nd CAAs [Combined Arms Armies] moved from the Central Military District into Belarus and to Ukraine's northeast border with Russia; the 1st Guards Tank Army and the 6th CAA moved from the Western Military District to Ukraine's eastern border with Russia; the 49th and 58th CAAs moved from the Southern Military District to occupied Crimea and to Ukraine's southeast border with Russia; and the 35th and 36th CAAs (and elements of the 29th and 5th CAAs) moved from the Eastern Military District to Belarus . . . . In addition, Russia deployed elite units—such as Russian Airborne (VDV), Naval Infantry, and *spetsnaz* . . .—around Ukraine's borders.[112]

A complete listing of the Russian military units involved in the invasion of Ukraine commencing in February 2022 is also known.[113]

As mentioned above, it is thought that a relatively narrow circle of military and civilians were involved in the planning of the invasion of Ukraine, including Putin, Shoigu, Gerasminov, Patrushev, Bortnikov, and Naryshkin.[114] The same cannot be said, however, of the number of military units involved in the execution of the invasion and illegal annexation of Crimea. Furthermore, as explained below, the invasion also encompassed cyber-operations against Ukraine that facilitated and operated in conjunction with conventional military operations, along with the role of the Wagner Group, and the contributions of Belarus and North Korea.

---

[110] Galeotti 2019a, p. 11.

[111] Sutyagin 2015.

[112] Bowen 2022, p. 2.

[113] Proekt Media nd.

[114] See notes 29–34 and accompanying text (inner circle).

4.2.3 The Role of Belarus in Allowing Its Territory to Be Utilized in the Invasion

Belarus, a close ally of Russia, was also involved in Russia's invasion of Ukraine. In January and February 2022, Russian forces entered Belarus, purportedly to conduct joint military drills.[115] Thirty thousand Russian troops were then well-positioned to invade Ukraine, with Belarus providing Russian forces their closest land route to Kyiv.[116] Belarus thus permitted its territory to be used as a staging ground for the launch of Russian forces.[117] President Alexander Lukashenko is the commander-in-chief of the Armed Forces of Belarus.[118] The Minister of Defense is Lieutenant General Victor Khrenin.[119] Lukashenko later also "ordered the passage of a constitutional referendum that allowed Russian troops and nuclear weapons to be permanently stationed on Belarusian territory".[120] On 17 June 2023, Putin confirmed that nuclear weapons had arrived in Belarus.[121]

4.2.4 North Korean Involvement, Russian Recruitment, and Wagner Forces

While Belarus did not commit its forces to fight in Ukraine, North Korea sent approximately 14,000 soldiers as well as weaponry to join Russia's invasion.[122] Russian President Putin and North Korean leader Kim Jong-un signed a pact that includes the obligation to come to each other's aid if either country is attacked.[123] US intelligence officials have expressed concerns about Putin providing North Korea with nuclear

---

[115] BBC 2023b.

[116] Coakley 2022. Compare note 327 and accompanying text (estimate of 70,000).

[117] Ibid. The invasion was mounted from Russia, Crimea and Belarus. Freedman 2022, pp. 393–94. A report further details the role of Belarus:

> Over the course of Russia's 2022 invasion of Ukraine, Belarus has permitted Russian forces to use Belarusian infrastructure for military purposes. At the outset of the invasion, Belarus made its air defense and traffic control systems and fueling stations available to Russian forces. Belarus also allowed Russia to use Belarusian territory to provide logistical support and to station Russian aircraft, in addition to supplying ammunition, tanks and armored vehicles. As of April 2024, Russian troops were still using Belarusian "military infrastructure, including bases, supply chains, and railroads".

Global Accountability Network 2024.

[118] Muzyka 2021, p. 3.

[119] Ibid. For the structure of the Armed Forces of Belarus, see ibid.

[120] Global Accountability Network 2024, p. 7, citing Reuters 2022.

[121] Ibid., citing BBC 2023a.

[122] Yeung 2026.

[123] Tong-Hyung and Ghosal 2024.

submarine and ballistic missile technology.[124] According to one report, North Korean troops were treated as if they were "expendable" and tasked with undertaking "hopeless assaults against Ukrainian defenses".[125] As of February 2025, North Korean troops were being withdrawn from combat operations due to heavy losses.[126]

Russia reportedly has also made efforts to recruit foreign fighters, including from Cuba, Syria, and India, and successfully did so, with estimates of a few thousand to 15,000 Nepali men signing up to fight in Ukraine and an estimated 5,000 Cubans.[127] The Russian regime also allegedly targeted vulnerable populations. Recruitment efforts have taken place in Russian immigration detention centers, mainly holding migrant workers from Central Asia.[128] For example, 30,000 migrants with Russian citizenship were rounded up when they failed to register for military service.[129] Another report suggests that Russian officials made prison conditions unbearable in an effort to pressure inmates to join the fighting.[130]

Forces of the Wagner Group,[131] a private military company linked to the Russian state,[132] founded by Russian mercenary and oligarch Yevgeny Prigozhin, also played a role in the invasion.[133] An estimated 2,000 to 4,000 members of the Wagner Group

---

[124] Earle 2024.

[125] Aggarwal 2024.

[126] Nazarenko 2025.

[127] Spencer 2024; Pokharel et al. 2024; Lubold et al. 2022; Pamuk 2025 (up to 5,000 Cubans are thought to be fighting on the Russian side). For discussion of Russian recruitment in Africa, see Ostrovsky et al. 2025.

[128] Spencer 2024. See also Pannier 2024 (noting a particular focus of detaining Tajik nationals).

[129] Spencer 2024.

[130] Najibullah 2024.

[131] The Wagner Group

> was essentially formed in 2014, arising from Russia's desire to have armed forces in Ukraine that it could plausibly deny were its forces. The firm was subsequently used in Syria to assist Russian forces, playing an important role in the second battle in Palmyra in 2016, helping the Syrian government recapture the city from the Islamic State. Wagner has also been used in Mali, the Central African Republic, Libya, Sudan . . . , and Mozambique . . . . [I]t was also reported by US intelligence to be working with Chadian rebels . . . .

Pattison 2024, p. 18 (footnotes omitted).

[132] According to one post:

> On June 27, 2023, Russian President Vladimir Putin made a remarkable announcement. After years of denying any links between the Wagner Group and the Russian State, Putin stated, "I want to point out and I want everyone to know about it: The maintenance of the entire Wagner Group was fully provided for by the State". President Putin added that from May 2022 to May 2023, the Russian State paid more than 86 billion rubles to the Wagner Group.

Maddocks 2023.

[133] Pattison 2024, p. 17. Wagner forces were also involved in the illegal annexation of Crimea and fighting in the Donbas. Sparks 2016.

were involved at the start of the invasion,[134] with the number growing to as many as 50,000.[135] Prigozhin was also known for recruiting fighters from Russian prisons,[136] with 40,000 of the 50,000 estimated to have been former convicts.[137] The Wagner Group suffered approximately 30,000 fatalities, of which ninety percent are estimated to have been former convicts.[138]

In one of the odder aspects of the war, after Prigozhin became a "vocal critic of the Russian military hierarchy", Wagner Group forces mutinied in June 2023, captured the Russian city of Rostov-on-Don, and started marching towards Moscow.[139] After the forces halted partway, Belarus' President Lukashenko helped broker an agreement for Prigozhin and his forces to relocate to Belarus in exile.[140] Two months later, Prigozhin and some of the Wagner Group's senior leadership died in a suspicious plane crash, thought to have been caused by a bomb planted on board.[141] Approximately 500 members of the Wagner Group are believed to have returned to fight in eastern Ukraine.[142]

4.2.5 The Role of Cyber Operations as Part of Russia's Invasion

In addition to Russia's kinetic (i.e., conventional military) attack, Russian-aligned actors have launched a massive number of cyber operations against Ukraine. Tom Burt, a Vice President of Microsoft, writes that: "Starting just before the invasion, we have seen at least six separate Russia-aligned nation-state actors launch more than

---

134 Bostock 2022. Approximately 400 were initially deployed to Kyiv, tasked with killing 23 senior figures in Ukraine's government, including President Zelenskyy. Ibid.

135 Luna et al. 2023.

136 For Wagner's prison recruitment, see Pattison 2024. "Since summer 2022, Wagner forces in Ukraine have been largely comprised of recruits from prisons". Ibid., p. 17. "The war in Ukraine is the first time that a mercenary army/ [private military and security company] has used prisoners to fight on a very large scale, with an estimated fifty thousand prisoners having been deployed by Wagner in Ukraine". Ibid., citing Romanova in Ostrovsky 2023.

137 Luna et al. 2023.

138 AlJazeera 2023.

139 Compare Pattison 2024, p. 17 (the Russian military failed to provide Wagner Forces with necessary ammunition); with Luna et al. 2023 ("Prigozhin sent out an audio message warning of an armed rebellion against Russia's military leadership after accusing it of deliberately shelling his forces".). See also Psaropoulos 2023 ("Prigozhin said his 25,000 armed men would 'march for justice' to 'stop the evil brought by the Russian military leadership'. He promised that after settling scores with Russian Defence Minister Sergei Shoigu and Chief of Staff General Valery Gerasimov, his troops would then return to the front lines in Ukraine".).

140 BBC 2023b.

141 Haworth et al. 2023; Associated Press 2023. "[M]any Western officials believe [the plane crash] was Putin's retribution for the uprising . . .". VOA News 2023.

142 Ibid.

237 operations against Ukraine—including destructive attacks that are ongoing and threaten civilian welfare".[143] He explained:

> Russia's use of cyberattacks appears to be strongly correlated and sometimes directly timed with its kinetic military operations targeting services and institutions crucial for civilians. For example, a Russian actor launched cyberattacks against a major broadcasting company on March 1st, the same day the Russian military announced its intention to destroy Ukrainian "disinformation" targets and directed a missile strike against a TV tower in Kyiv. On March 13th, during the third week of the invasion, a separate Russian actor stole data from a nuclear safety organization weeks after Russian military units began capturing nuclear power plants sparking concerns about radiation exposure and catastrophic accidents. While Russian forces besieged the city of Mariupol, Ukrainians began receiving an email from a Russian actor masquerading as a Mariupol resident, falsely accusing Ukraine's government of "abandoning" Ukrainian citizens.[144]

Russian cyber operations into Ukraine had been expected to have a "major impact" in the invasion, but most were surprised by their "overall ineffectiveness".[145] As then US Deputy Assistant Secretary of Defense for Cyber Policy Mieke Eoyang observed, "cyber 'did not have the strategic impact [the Russians] wanted'".[146] "Most observers attribute Ukraine's preparedness to the fact that Ukraine had been defending against Russian cyberattacks for years. So far, Ukraine, assisted by both Western governments and commercial firms, has demonstrated that collective cyber defense has 'proven stronger than offensive cyber capabilities'".[147]

Thus, the invasion of Ukraine was clearly a well-planned and deliberate operation, following on the heels of Russia's illegal annexation of Crimea and fomenting of insurgency in the Donbas. Belarusian territory was involved in the launch of the invasion, North Korea's leader sent forces, and conventional military operations were supplemented by cyber operations. While the elements of the crime will be discussed below,[148] the facts clearly point to Russian political and military leaders, as well as the leaders of Belarus and perhaps North Korea, being implicated in the crime of aggression. Of course, any accused deserves his or her day in court; thus, proof of the elements of the crime and roles of the key perpetrators would need to be established through admissible evidence that satisfies the requisite burden of proof before a tribunal that is independent and credible.[149]

---

[143] Burt 2022.

[144] Ibid. "[T]he Human Rights Center at UC Berkeley's School of Law sent a formal request to the ICC prosecutor's office urging it to consider war crime prosecutions of Russian hackers for their cyberattacks in Ukraine . . .". Ibid. That report focuses on cyber operations prior to the February 2022 invasion. The Human Rights Center later sent a second submission, focused on subsequent cyberattacks. Meeting at Liechtenstein Mission to the United Nations (2024).

[145] Hammes 2023, p. 5.

[146] Ibid., quoting Gill 2022.

[147] Ibid., quoting Beecroft 2022. "Microsoft security teams have worked closely with Ukrainian government officials and cybersecurity staff at government organizations and private enterprises to identify and remediate threat activity against Ukrainian networks". Burt 2022.

[148] See Sect. 4.4.

[149] See note 264 (reports are not evidence).

4.3 Key Atrocities and Harm Suffered During the Invasion

The next section discusses the harms inflicted during the 2022 invasion. It demonstrates why the crime of aggression is so significant—because the magnitude of the harm inflicted can be massive. The crime is additionally a threat to the global order. It is thus essential that leaders responsible for the crime be prosecuted.

4.3.1 Overall Harm

The harm resulting from Russia's invasion of Ukraine is staggering. The total number of dead and wounded exceeds one million.[150] As of February 2025, it is estimated that 45,000 Ukrainian soldiers have been killed and 390,000 more have been wounded.[151] While estimates vary, as many as 250,000 Russian soldiers may have been killed and more than 700,000 wounded.[152] There are unconfirmed reports that three thousand North Korean troops are thought to have been killed or wounded.[153] Civilian casualties in Ukraine are estimated to be in the range of 40,000 killed or wounded.[154]

The economic ramifications of the invasion have also been massive. The Government of Ukraine, the World Bank Group, the European Commission, and the United Nations estimate the cost of rebuilding Ukraine at $524 billion.[155] By some estimates, Ukraine has suffered a 40% decline in GDP.[156] An estimated 3.7 million people have been internally displaced, and an estimated 6.9 million refugees have fled, primarily to European countries.[157] An estimated 12.7 million people are in need of humanitarian assistance.[158] By one calculation, the United States has spent $118 billion on financial, military, and humanitarian aid to Ukraine;[159] the EU has spent 39 billion euros on financial and humanitarian aid, and many other countries have contributed

[150] Sauer 2025.

[151] Basmat 2025.

[152] Jones and McCabe 2025, p. 2.

[153] "Ukrainian President Volodymyr Zelenskyy said in a statement on Telegram [on 27 December 2024] that at least 3,000 North Korean soldiers have died or been wounded in Russia's Kursk region". Aggarwal 2024.

[154] According to the website Statista: "The Office of the United Nations High Commissioner for Human Rights (OHCHR) verified a total of 40,838 civilian casualties during Russia's invasion of Ukraine as of 31 December 2024. Of them, 28,382 people were reported to have been injured. However, OHCHR specified that the real numbers could be higher". Statista nd-a.

[155] World Bank Group, Press Release 2025. The estimate is as of 31 December 2024.

[156] Osinga 2024, p. 134.

[157] UNHCR 2025. See also Statista nd-b; Freedman 2022, p. 395 ("as the fighting became concentrated in the east, some 2 million [refugees] returned").

[158] UN OCHA 2025, p. A2.

[159] Global Conflict Tracker nd.

additional billions of euros.[160] Environmental destruction is also estimated to have resulted in billions of dollars in damage.[161]

In the words of one author, there have been "millions of Ukrainian refugees and internally displaced persons, livelihoods and futures destroyed, . . . thousands of civilian casualties and tens of thousands of military maimed, traumatized or killed".[162] Russia committed "forced deportation of families and abduction of children, and the obliteration of . . . society . . . . Mariupol fell after prolonged, almost mediaeval, siege tactics".[163] "The casual use of nuclear threats by Russian media personalities and senior politicians also echoes a previous era".[164]

One could additionally include as victims the thousands of Russians and Ukrainians jailed for political reasons in Russia. According to the human rights group Memorial: Russian authorities have detained approximately 7,000 Ukrainian civilians; several hundred Russians are being held for "high treason" or "sabotage" for their anti-war views; and the Russian authorities have brought "'thousands' of criminal cases for refusing to fight in Ukraine".[165]

4.3.2 *Key Atrocities*

Russian forces[166] have committed horrific atrocities during the invasion.[167] While criminal proceedings can be and are being instituted by various authorities—the

---

[160] Statista nd-c.

[161] Volokita 2024 (2024 estimate of approximately $71 billion). See also Sect. 4.3.2.10.

[162] Osinga 2024, p. 141.

[163] Ibid., p. 137.

[164] Ibid.

[165] The Guardian 2024 (discussing the Russian human rights group Memorial).

[166] Ukrainian forces have also been accused of a "'small number of violations'". Bowen and Weed 2023, p. 1, citing Independent International Commission of Inquiry on Ukraine 2023. See also Sect. 4.3.2.3.

[167] Multiple entities have been conducting investigations, including the Organization for Security and Cooperation in Europe ("OSCE"), acting under what is known as the "'Moscow Mechanism'". Bowen and Weed 2023, p. 1. The UN Human Rights Council also established the Independent International Commission of Inquiry on Ukraine. See Human Rights Council 2022. Additionally, the European Union Agency for Criminal Justice Cooperation ("Eurojust") on 3 July 2023, with cooperation from the United States and the International Criminal Court, launched the International Centre for the Prosecution of the Crime of Aggression ("ICPA"). See European Union, Press Release 2023. Ukraine, six EU countries (Lithuania, Poland, Estonia, Latvia, Slovakia, and Romania) and the ICC have also established a joint investigative team ("JIT") coordinated through and supported by Eurojust. Bowen and Weed 2023, p. 23, n 131, citing various sources. For reports on suspected war crimes and crimes against humanity by Russian nationals, see, e.g., OSCE 2022; OHCHR 2022; OHCHR 2023a; OHCHR 2023b; Independent International Commission of Inquiry on Ukraine 2023; Independent International Commission of Inquiry on Ukraine 2024.

ICC,[168] the Ukrainian authorities,[169] and prosecutors in third countries[170]—the crimes committed, as with the harms discussed above, all stem from Russia's aggression against Ukraine. The crime of aggression encompasses *all* of the harms of the invasion as well as the 2014 annexation of Crimea. Moreover, diligent as prosecutors may be, some or even many of the war crimes and crimes against humanity will inevitably go unaddressed by any judicial system. There are simply too many crimes for any single judicial institution, or even multiple institutions, to investigate and prosecute. Furthermore, even if investigations are undertaken, authorities will not always be able to locate the required evidence or ascertain the identities of the perpetrators. Yet, all of these harms are part of the harm of the crime of aggression.

It is for this reason that the crime of aggression (at the time, termed crimes against peace)[171] was deemed to be "the supreme international crime" in the Judgment of the International Military Tribunal at Nuremberg, "differing only from other war crimes in that it contains within itself the accumulated evil of the whole".[172] The crime encompasses all of the harm caused, including crimes committed as well as all other harms. For example, while combatants may be targeted during an international armed conflict (doing so is not a war crime),[173] they too are victims of the crime of

---

[168] The ICC has issued arrest warrants against Vladimir Putin, Maria Lvova-Belova, Sergei Kobylash, Viktor Sokolov, Sergei Shoigu, and Valery Gerasimov. See International Criminal Court nd-b. The ICC had jurisdiction over the crimes of genocide, war crimes and crimes against humanity committed in the territory of Ukraine initially because Ukraine executed two declarations under Article 12(3) of the Rome Statute, accepting jurisdiction. See ibid. An Article 12(3) declaration allows a state to accept the ICC's jurisdiction on an ad hoc basis without becoming a Rome Statute State Party. See Rome Statute (1998) (as amended), note 1, Article 12(3). Subsequently, Ukraine became a full State Party to the Rome Statute as of 1 January 2025. See International Criminal Court, Press Release 2025.

[169] Ukraine's Prosecutor General's Office is reportedly investigating tens of thousands of alleged atrocity crimes. Bowen and Weed 2023, p. 14, citing Office of the Prosecutor General of Ukraine nd. "As of September 29, 2023, Ukrainian authorities in the office of the prosecutor general of Ukraine stated that they [had] recorded 108,904 [cases of] potential war crimes committed by Russian forces". Ibid., p. 1, citing same.

[170] "At least 20 other countries have instituted investigations, within their respective national justice systems, of alleged atrocities committed in Ukraine". Ibid., p. 2. Countries that have opened investigations into crimes in Ukraine include Lithuania, Latvia, Estonia, Poland, Romania, and Slovakia, as well as Germany, Sweden, Spain, Switzerland, and Canada. Ibid., p. 15, citing Crawford and Cruvellier 2022.

[171] Charter of the International Military Tribunal (1945) 85 UNTS 251, Article 6(a) ("London Charter 1945") ("Crimes against peace" defined as "planning, preparation, initiation or waging of a war of aggression, or a war in violation of international treaties, agreements or assurances, or participation in a common plan or conspiracy for the accomplishment of any of the foregoing . . .".).

[172] International Military Tribunal (1946) Judgment of 1 October 1946 in The Trial of German Major War Criminals. Proceedings of the International Military Tribunal Sitting at Nuremberg, Germany, Part 22 (22 August 1946 to 1 October 1946), p. 421.

[173] The killing of combatants during armed conflict, with certain limitations, is not a war crime, as it is permitted under International Humanitarian Law. See, e.g., Rome Statute (1998) (as amended), note 1, Articles 8(2)(b)(i), 8(2)(e)(i) (war crime of intentionally directing attacks against the civilian population—but no war crime of targeting combatants).

aggression, as they should not have to fight or die in an illegal war, be they Ukrainian, Russian, North Korean, or any other nationality.[174] The same is true of those whose deaths are characterized as "collateral damage"; while their killing is allowed under International Humanitarian Law,[175] they too are victims of the crime of aggression.

Thus, while the crimes discussed below can be categorized as war crimes and crimes against humanity,[176] they are also part of the harm that resulted from the crime of aggression. Those who decided to launch the invasion against Ukraine have set in motion all of the harm that ensued. It is almost beyond comprehension that the decision of one person (with a small group of advisers)[177] was able to unleash such massive destruction and loss of life.

4.3.2.1 Targeting of Civilians and Civilian Objects, as Well as Indiscriminate Collateral Damage

During the invasion, Russia has bombed methodically, "often striking non-military sites, and killing or maiming civilians . . .".[178] Ukrainian cities and towns "suffered

---

[174] On the involvement of North Korean troops and Nepali nationals, see Sect. 4.2.4.

[175] Protocol Additional to the Geneva Conventions of 12 August 1949, and relating to the Protection of Victims of International Armed Conflicts (1977) ("Protocol I"), Article 51(5)(b) (only prohibiting "an attack which may be expected to cause incidental loss of civilian life, injury to civilians, damage to civilian objects, or a combination thereof, which would be excessive in relation to the concrete and direct military advantage anticipated").

[176] While the ICC has to date issued charges for war crimes and crimes against humanity, allegations of genocide in the context of Russia's war against Ukraine should not be automatically dismissed. Certain indicators of genocide exist. According to one source:

> In the context of Russia's war against Ukraine, the Russian military has been accused of many actions that might fall within the definition of genocide, including the forcible transfer of Ukrainian children to Russia. Putin's statements and the statements of other Russian officials have been characterized by some observers as reflecting genocidal intent and planning. News and opinion in Russian state-run media, which might be expected to include only government-approved information, have published statements that call for "liquidation", "concentration camps", and "reeducation" of the Ukrainian population, including children. These statements, if describing Russian military and government behavior, could be considered evidence of the intent to commit genocide in Ukraine.

Bowen and Weed 2023, p. 17, citing Maynard 2022; U.S. Congress, Senate Committee on Foreign Relations (2022) U.S. Efforts to Support Ukraine Against Russian Aggression. 117th Cong., 2nd Sess. (testimony of US Ambassador-at-Large for Global Criminal Justice Beth Van Schaack); Apt 2023 (collecting Russian officials' statements about "eliminating" Ukraine). On "Russification" through destruction of cultural heritage, see Sect. 4.3.2.5; on the deportation and indoctrination of Ukrainian children, see Sect. 4.3.2.6; on the eradication of Ukrainian identity, see the siege of Mariupol, Sect. 4.3.2.9.

[177] See notes 29–34 and accompanying text (Putin's inner circle).

[178] ACLED 2023, p. 2. It is a complex and painstaking process to ascertain which strikes that struck civilians or civilian objects were in fact *intended* to do so. The author does not suggest all strikes discussed in this section necessarily meet that threshold. Other strikes may constitute permissible or impermissible "collateral damage"—the euphemism for an attack launched "in the

collateral damage in civilian casualties due to the concentrated and often incriminate nature of Russian artillery [attacks]".[179] In addition to rocket and artillery strikes that "appear to be launched without regard to collateral damage, Russia continues to launch cruise missiles and other precision guided missiles (PGMs) to strike civilian targets across Ukraine, including a sustained strike campaign to damage and destroy Ukraine's critical infrastructure, such as key energy and transport centers".[180] The strikes have also hit hospitals, theaters, civilian railway stations, shopping centers, and civilian apartment blocks.[181]

For example, in over 800 strikes against civilians in Kharkiv, "about three-quarters constituted artillery, missile, and airstrike events . . .".[182] In one instance on 25 September 2022, over 50 civilians trying to flee from Kupiansk by car were killed.[183] Civilians in the city of Zaporizhzhia have also been the subject of direct attacks. "These include firing at vehicles carrying evacuating civilians, as well as torture and execution. In areas under Russian occupation, reports of the abduction of local officials, teachers, journalists, Ukrainian army veterans, and civil activists are common".[184] A report discussing these crimes also notes that the scale of the violence and intimidation is likely underreported in areas that are still occupied by Russia.[185]

The "Kyiv region experienced the heaviest civilian targeting by Russian forces in northern Ukraine, including targeting civilians fleeing affected areas".[186] "In some instances, Russian violence against Ukrainian civilians appears indiscriminate, such as reprisals for battlefield losses against the Ukrainian Armed Forces (UAF). In other instances, Russian forces appear to be using specific or calibrated violence against civilians perceived to pose a threat to Russian control".[187]

Mass graves containing both Ukrainian civilians and prisoners of war ("POWs") have been uncovered in areas liberated from Russian control, including Bucha, Irpin, Izyum, Lyman, Kherson, and Mariupol.[188] Mass burial sites were also discovered

---

knowledge that such attack will cause incidental loss of life or injury to civilians or damage to civilian objects or widespread, long-term and severe damage to the natural environment which would be clearly excessive in relation to the concrete and direct overall military advantage anticipated". See Rome Statute (1998) (as amended), note 1, Article 8(2)(b)(iv) (a war crime when perpetrated in international armed conflict).

[179] Bowen and Weed 2023, p. 8, citing Rust et al. 2022; Radio Free Europe and Radio Liberty 2023; Olearchyk 2023.

[180] Bowen and Weed 2023, p. 8, citing Williams 2023.

[181] Ibid., citing various sources. For strikes on a theater containing 300, an apartment building where 200 bodies were later found, and the bombing of a maternity and children's hospital, see the siege of Mariupol, Sect. 4.3.2.9.

[182] ACLED 2023, p. 7.

[183] Ibid., p. 8. For the siege of Mariupol, see Sect. 4.3.2.9.

[184] ACLED 2023, p. 14.

[185] Ibid.

[186] Ibid., p. 4.

[187] Bowen and Weed 2023, p. 4.

[188] Ibid., citing various sources.

"upon the retreat of Russian forces in April [2022] from the Kyiv suburbs".[189] The detonation of landmines and other explosives has also proven a significant danger to civilians following liberation from formerly Russian-occupied areas.[190]

Attacks on Energy Infrastructure

Ukraine's civilian energy infrastructure also became the target of "salvos of missiles and scores of Iranian-made suicide drones".[191] "Russia has blocked gas transit to Ukraine, seized assets, launched cyberattacks, and, since October 2022, systematically bombed Ukraine's energy infrastructure".[192] One report addresses the systematic targeting of energy infrastructure in autumn and winter.[193] Another report, issued by the Independent International Commission of Inquiry on Ukraine established by the UN Human Rights Council,[194] concludes that the Russian Federation has conducted "[c]ontinuous, massive waves of attacks" against Ukraine's energy-related infrastructure, which "have resulted in blackouts, at times affecting millions of civilians. The power cuts have, among other consequences, curtailed the enjoyment of the rights to health and education, with severe effects on children, older persons, persons living with disability or a medical condition".[195] By one estimate, attacks on Ukraine's energy infrastructure have caused available capacity to plummet by an estimated 85 percent.[196]

Attacks on Healthcare

The attacks on energy have additionally imperiled access to critical healthcare services. A study by Physicians for Human Rights and Truth Hounds documents how Russian attacks on Ukraine's energy infrastructure have had massive impacts on healthcare and led to suffering and fatalities.[197] Frequent power outages "jeopardized patient health by interrupting or delaying surgeries; forc[ed] surgeons to

---

[189] ACLED 2023, p. 5.

[190] Ibid., p. 13.

[191] Ibid., p. 2.

[192] Physicians for Human Rights and Truth Hounds 2024.

[193] ACLED 2023, p. 17.

[194] For establishment of the Commission, see note 167.

[195] OHCHR, Press Release 2024. For additional discussion, see Independent International Commission of Inquiry on Ukraine 2024, para 8.

[196] Physicians for Human Rights and Truth Hounds 2024, p. 3.

[197] Ibid. For additional discussion of the impact of attacks against Ukraine's energy-related infrastructure on the right to health, see Independent International Commission of Inquiry on Ukraine 2024, paras 12–18.

operate in darkness illuminated only by headlamps; discontinu[ed] flow of water to the hospital, creating unhygienic conditions; and render[ed] diagnostic and treatment equipment unusable".[198] A separate report "shows how Russia appears to be . . . deliberately and indiscriminately targeting Ukraine's health care system".[199] The report details attacks on health care facilities; attacks on ambulances; destruction of critical health infrastructure and theft of supplies; and assaults, torture, and ill-treatment of health workers, including doctors, nurses, and paramedics.[200] Research from 2022 alone documented 707 attacks against the health care system: 281 destroyed hospitals and clinics; 61 documented attacks on ambulances; 181 attacks on other health infrastructure (e.g., pharmacies, blood centers); and 86 attacks on health care workers.[201]

4.3.2.2 Torture

Ukrainian civilians and POWs have additionally been the victims of the widespread and systematic use of torture.[202] The Independent International Commission of Inquiry on Ukraine has found "cases of torture against Ukrainian civilians and [POWs, which show] the use of torture in all areas under Russian control in Ukraine and in the detention facilities it has investigated in the Russian Federation".[203] Former detainees described "consistently the same harsh practices designed to scare, break, humiliate, coerce, and punish".[204] The use of sexual violence as a form of torture was also employed, mostly against male detainees, including through electric shocks with TASERs.[205] Witnesses referred to the involvement of high-ranking detention

198 Physicians for Human Rights and Truth Hounds 2024, p. 3.

199 Ibid., p. 1.

200 Ibid.

201 Ibid., p. 3. For the impact of attacks against Ukraine's energy-related infrastructure on education, see Independent International Commission of Inquiry on Ukraine 2024, paras 19–22. The ICC has issued arrest warrants against Russian Minister of Defence Sergei Shoigu and Chief of the General Staff of the Armed Forces and First Deputy Minister of Defence Valery Gerasimov for the war crime of directing attacks at civilian objects, the war crime of causing excessive incidental harm to civilians or damage to civilian objects, and the crime against humanity of inhumane acts. International Criminal Court, Press Release 2024b. The ICC has also charged Russian Army Lieutenant General Sergei Kobylash and Navy Admiral Viktor Sokolov regarding "missile strikes carried out by the forces under their command against the Ukrainian electric infrastructure". Wright 2024. The specific charges are for the war crime of directing attacks at civilian objects, the war crime of causing excessive incidental harm to civilians or damage to civilian objects, and the crime against humanity of inhumane acts. International Criminal Court, Press Release 2024a.

202 Independent International Commission of Inquiry on Ukraine 2024, para 92 (the use of torture was "widespread and systematic").

203 OHCHR Press Release 2024. For the full report, see Independent International Commission of Inquiry on Ukraine 2024.

204 OHCHR Press Release 2024.

205 Ibid.

facility officials who appeared to operate with a sense of impunity.[206] The Chair of the Commission of Inquiry, Erik Møse, concluded: "Based on our evidence, we have found that the Russian authorities have acted pursuant to a coordinated state policy of torturing Ukrainian civilians and [POWs] . . .".[207]

The Commission also found a general absence or denial of medical assistance to detainees who were injured or required treatment after torture.[208] Their report states:

> According to testimonies, in some detention facilities, medical personnel had been involved in the violent treatment of detainees or negligent acts. In rare instances where medical assistance was provided, it often appeared insufficient or inadequate. Victims and witnesses reported deterioration of the health of those affected, at times coupled with severe complications, and even death.[209]

4.3.2.3 Mistreatment of Prisoners of War

Additionally (and overlapping somewhat with the above findings), both Russia and Ukraine have been accused of abuses towards POWs, including execution, torture, malnourishment, and other mistreatment.[210] The Independent International Commission of Inquiry on Ukraine found:

> a widespread pattern of torture and inhuman treatment committed by Russian authorities against people they detained in Chernihiv, Donetsk, Kharkiv, Kherson, Kyiv, Sumy, and Zaporizhzhia regions, in Ukraine, and in the Russian Federation. Torture has been prevalent against certain categories of people. Most victims were men; both civilians and [POWs] were tortured.[211]

Similarly, the Office of the High Commissioner for Human Rights ("OHCHR") has documented mistreatment of POWs by Russian Forces, including summary executions, torture and other forms of ill-treatment, pillage of belongings, exposure to public humiliation, sexual violence, and killing and injuring POWs.[212] It has also documented some of the same practices by Ukrainian forces as to POWs it has held, including summary execution, torture and other forms of ill-treatment, pillage of belongings, and exposure to public humiliation.[213]

---

206 Ibid.

207 Ibid.

208 Ibid.

209 Independent International Commission of Inquiry on Ukraine 2024, para 50. For additional discussion of the absence or denial of medical assistance during detention, see ibid., paras 50–57. An October 2024 report noted that "Ukrainian authorities have opened 872 investigations concerning cases of torture in the context of the ongoing armed conflict and issued indictments against 125 persons". Ibid., para 39.

210 Bowen and Weed 2023, p. 7, citing OHCHR 2023a.

211 Independent International Commission of Inquiry on Ukraine 2023.

212 OHCHR 2023a, pp. 9–22.

213 Ibid., pp. 23–31.

4.3.2.4 Rape and Other Sexual Violence

There are extensive reports of sexual violence, which is also a form of torture.[214] According to a report by the OHCHR: "From February 2022 to 31 January 2023, OHCHR documented 133 cases of [Confect-Related Sexual Violence ("CRSV")] (85 men, 45 women, [three] girls), the majority of which took place in territory occupied by the Russian Federation".[215] One hundred and nine cases are attributable to "Russian armed forces or Russian law enforcement and penitentiary staff".[216] The US State Department additionally describes "'a mountain of credible reports of sexual violence committed by Russia's forces against civilians'".[217] Ukraine's Prosecutor General Andriy Kostin described "how 'sexual violence has been used as a political and military tactic by Russian forces'".[218] The scale of sexual violence against civilians in occupied areas is also thought to be "severely underreported",[219] with more recent estimates that there are likely thousands of cases of rape.[220]

Sexual violence has additionally been prevalent in detention facilities operated by Russian authorities.[221] According to the Independent International Commission of Inquiry on Ukraine:

> Since its establishment, the Commission has collected testimonies concerning acts that amount to sexual violence as a form of torture committed in 41 detention facilities of various types, in the Russian Federation and areas under Russian control in Ukraine. Such acts included rape and attempted rape, sometimes with the use of objects, beatings, electric shocks, burns, or other attacks on genital organs, forced nudity going beyond possible security requirements, threats of sexual mutilation and castration, and intrusive body searches. According to testimonies, in each detention facility held by Russian authorities documented so far, perpetrators have used at least one or a combination of several above-mentioned methods. Some forms of sexual violence have been recurrent in certain detention facilities. The victims were men and women, civilians and prisoners of war; the majority were men. Most prisoners of war that have been detained by Russian authorities reported having been subjected to sexual violence.[222]

---

214 See, e.g., International Criminal Tribunal for the former Yugoslavia, Appeals Chamber (2022) *Prosecutor v. Kunarac, Kovac, and Vokovic*, Case No. IT-96-23 and IT-96-23/1, para 150 ("Sexual violence necessarily gives rise to severe pain or suffering, whether physical or mental, and in this way justifies its characterisation as an act of torture".).

215 OHCHR 2023b, p. 2.

216 Ibid., p. 2.

217 Bowen and Weed 2023, p. 6, citing US Department of State 2023.

218 Ibid., citing U.S. Congress, House Committee on Foreign Affairs (2023) Exposing Putin's Crimes: Evidence of Russian War Crimes and Other Atrocities in Ukraine, 118th Cong., 1st Sess. (testimony given to House Committee on Foreign Affairs).

219 ACLED 2023, p. 1.

220 Gall and Chubko 2025.

221 Independent International Commission of Inquiry on Ukraine 2024, para 47.

222 Ibid.

Sexual violence has also been committed in the context of forced house searches. According to the Independent International Commission of Inquiry on Ukraine:

> [V]ictims have been subjected to rape and sexual violence when Russian armed forces broke into their homes in areas under their control. In recent cases, the victims were women . . . . The perpetrators were Russian soldiers, who identified women in a vulnerable situation during one or several initial searches of their houses.[223]

4.3.2.5 Destruction of Cultural Heritage

Persons are not the only victims of the war. Russian forces have also targeted Ukraine's cultural heritage. Such practices started with the annexation of Crimea, as the Peninsula has an extremely rich archaeological heritage.[224] Objects taken from Crimean museums have been exhibited in leading Russian institutions.[225] The removal of architectural artifacts from Ukrainian museums and sites continued during the invasion.[226] In addition, many cultural heritage properties have been damaged or destroyed, both intentionally and as collateral damage, during Russia's invasion.[227] As of 22 January 2025, the United Nations Educational, Scientific and Cultural Organization ("UNESCO") had identified 476 damaged sites.[228] One author writes that these actions appear to be part of a broader strategy of trying to annihilate "Ukrainian national identity, historical memory, and language", as part of a "Russification" process in occupied territories, which includes the deportation of Ukrainian children and the "abusive control of education and school teaching".[229]

4.3.2.6 Deportation and Indoctrination of Ukrainian Children

Russia's federal government has "systematically relocated at least 6000 children from Ukraine to a network of re-education and adoption facilities in Russian-occupied Crimea and mainland Russia".[230] A total of 43 facilities are believed to have been involved in holding the children, with facilities as far away as Siberia and Russia's Far

---

[223] Ibid., para 86.

[224] Jakubowski 2023, p. 143.

[225] Ibid.

[226] Ibid., pp. 143–44.

[227] Ibid., p. 144.

[228] UNESCO 2025. These include: "149 religious sites, 241 buildings of historical and/or artistic interest, 32 museums, 33 monuments, 18 libraries, 1 archive and 2 archaeological sites". Ibid. See also Independent International Commission of Inquiry on Ukraine 2024, para 27 ("The Commission investigated attacks affecting cultural objects . . . . For instance, an explosive weapons attack carried out by Russian armed forces on 5 November 2023 hit Odesa in two locations and led to the damage of Odesa National Art Museum. According to Ukrainian authorities, a total of seven monuments of cultural heritage were damaged following attacks carried out on that day . . .".).

[229] Jakubowski 2023, p. 144.

[230] Conflict Observatory Report 2023. It is difficult to ascertain the full number of children abducted:

East.[231] The majority of camps have "engaged in pro-Russian reeducation efforts[,] and some camps have provided military training to children and/or suspended the children's return to their parents in Ukraine".[232] The children held have been reported to be between four months and 17 years in age.[233] The primary purpose of the camps appears to be political education, with children exposed to a "Russia-centric academic, cultural, patriotic, and military education".[234] Consent from Ukrainian parents is collected under duress and/or routinely violated, with all levels of Russia's government reported to be involved.[235]

4.3.2.7 Deportation and Forced Transfer of Adults

In addition to the transfer of children, Russian authorities are implicated in the large-scale deportation of Ukrainian adults to Russia. Reports exist of "filtration camps"; Russian authorities reportedly "have used these camps to document, process, and potentially remove Ukrainian civilians who may present a threat to Russian occupation".[236] While numbers are difficult to verify, one source estimated that

> about 33,000 residents of the city of Mariupol were forcibly taken across the border into Russia, and alleged more broadly that through March 25, "402,000 people, including 84,000 children, had been taken against their will to Russia". Ukrainians have reportedly been "taken to camps where Russian forces checked their phones and documents, then redirected some . . . to remote cities in Russia".[237]

> Ukraine estimates that 16,000 children have been forcibly removed from Ukraine since February 2022. As of 13 February 2023, the Yale University's Humanitarian Research Lab identified 6,000 children across a network of 43 facilities in Russia. A March 2023 Human Rights Watch report indicates it is difficult to verify the exact number, and it may be far higher.

Bowen and Weed 2023, p. 7, citing Yale Humanitarian Research Lab 2023; Human Rights Watch 2023. For added details on the abduction of children, see Netherlands Helsinki Committee 2024.

231 Conflict Observatory Report 2023, key finding 2.

232 Ibid., Introduction.

233 Ibid., key finding 1.

234 Ibid., key finding 4.

235 Ibid., key findings 6, 8. The illegal transfer of Ukrainian children into Russian territory is the subject of two ICC arrest warrants, one against President Putin and the other against the Russian Commissioner for Children's Rights Maria Lvova-Belova for the war crimes of unlawful deportation and unlawful transfer. International Criminal Court, Press Release 2023.

236 Bowen and Weed 2023, p. 6.

237 Eichensehr 2022, citing various sources. Liudmyla Denisova, Ukraine's ombudswoman for human rights, was fired for making unsupported statements to this effect, although multiple sources are cited. At the same time, one must exercise caution when dealing with figures related to the war as both Russian and Ukrainian sources can inflate figures.

4.3.2.8 Atrocities in Bucha

There have been many horrific crime scenes throughout Ukraine. One such site has been in the town and area surrounding Bucha, near Kyiv, where Russian forces engaged in the torture, unlawful killing, and summary execution of civilians. Estimates run to at least 422 civilians killed in Bucha and another 132 civilians in nearby Makariv.[238] A memorial wall installed in Bucha contains the names of 501 residents who were killed.[239] There are also multiple reports of "sexual violence, including the mass rape of women and girls in Bucha in March 2022".[240] According to Germany's Federal Intelligence Service, an airborne regiment and an army unit were initially responsible for the crimes, and the Wagner Group later played a leading role in the atrocities in Bucha.[241]

One account of the violence contains the following details:

> Reports of violence include "evidence of torture before death, beheading and dismemberment, and the intentional burning of corpses". The Ukrainian government released footage showing hundreds of corpses "strewn" around Bucha after Russia's retreat, with some victims clearly bound and shot in the head. French President Emmanuel Macron called the images from Bucha "unbearable".... When the images from Bucha were released, Russia's Ministry of Defense denied responsibility and suggested that they were staged, despite considerable video and satellite evidence to the contrary. Putin later "awarded honors . . . to an army brigade that Ukraine has accused of committing war crimes in Bucha".[242]

4.3.2.9 Siege Warfare: The Siege of Mariupol

Another particularly notorious crime scene has been the siege of the civilian city of Mariupol in Donetsk *oblast*. The siege lasted for almost three months until the end of May 2022. One author writes: "The symbol of Russian brutality and Ukrainian resistance was the city of Mariupol on the southern coast, which was rendered uninhabitable, with thousands of civilians trapped and then killed".[243] The city "was subjected to relentless artillery, missile, and air strikes".[244] In two particularly horrific incidents, "[o]n 16 March 2022, an airstrike on a theater reportedly killed an estimated 300 people [despite being clearly marked as containing children inside], while 200 bodies were found under the rubble of an apartment building believed to have been targeted in May 2022".[245] Another "notorious incident came only two weeks after

---

[238] ACLED 2023, p. 5.

[239] Meduza nd.

[240] ACLED 2023, p. 1.

[241] Amann et al. 2022.

[242] Eichensehr 2022, citing various sources.

[243] Freedman 2022, p. 395.

[244] ACLED 2023, p. 11.

[245] Ibid., p. 12. The Russian word for "children" had been written on the ground outside the theater. Bachega 2022 (with photo by Reuters).

the full-scale invasion began, when Russia's air force bombed a maternity and children's hospital in the city of Mariupol".[246] One author writes that traces of Ukrainian identity in the city have been eradicated.[247] There are an estimated 10,000 new graves in and around Mariupol; the death toll, originally underestimated at 25,000, is now believed to be closer to 75,000.[248] Russian forces are also reported to have used mobile crematoriums.[249]

4.3.2.10 Environmental Harm: Destruction of the Kakhovka Dam

The environment too has suffered, along with massive additional harm having been inflicted, by the destruction of the Kakhovka Hydroelectric Power Plant, located in the Kherson *oblast*. The dam was blown up on 6 June 2023.[250] According to a detailed report, evidence supports the conclusion that the dam's destruction "appears to have been a deliberate act by Russian forces who had control of the area at the time".[251] The report summarizes the massive extent of the harm caused by the destruction of the dam:

> The flood affected over 600 square kilometers, inundating over 80 settlements, displacing thousands of residents, and causing extensive damage to homes, infrastructure, and agricultural lands. The ecological impact was profound, with significant destruction to local habitats, contamination of water bodies, and long-term adverse effects on the region's flora and fauna. Economically, the destruction impaired agricultural production, disrupted local economies, and caused substantial financial losses due to the damage to infrastructure and the cost of reconstruction and relief efforts. The flooding also impacted numerous cultural sites located in the affected regions.[252]

The report goes on to explain the extraordinary breadth of the harm inflicted—from floodwaters dispersing disaster waste from "cemeteries, waste disposal sites, sewage treatment facilities, oil refineries, mines, chemical manufacturing sites, agricultural facilities, gas stations, and fuel depots", to floating landmines, and an exacerbated risk of infectious disease via the corpses of livestock, domestic, and zoo animals.[253] Broad damage to irrigation capacity amounted to an estimated 150–160 billion *hryvnias* ($4.1–4.3 billion 2023 USD), with 78 percent of Ukraine's cropland dependent on water from the Kakhovka reservoir.[254] As many as a million Ukrainians abruptly lost access to drinking water, while the groundwater of surrounding *oblasts* remains above potable salinity, contaminated with heavy metals,

---

[246] Physicians for Human Rights et al. 2023.

[247] Hinnant et al. 2022.

[248] Ibid.

[249] ACLED 2023, p. 13. For forced deportation of adults from Mariupol, see Sect. 4.3.2.7.

[250] Truth Hounds 2023/2024, p. 5.

[251] Ibid.

[252] Ibid., p. 6.

[253] Ibid., pp. 108, 88–89.

[254] Ibid., pp. 169, 175.

pesticides, and flame retardants, and, at depleted levels, is expected to remain for at least 33 years.[255]

Finally, while disaster has not yet struck, environmental and other harms have been at extreme risk with the Russian military operation and supervision of the Zaporizhzhia nuclear power plant, which is located in Russian-controlled southeastern Ukraine.[256] The International Atomic Energy Agency has sounded repeat warnings of the risk of the release of radiation and nuclear disaster.[257] A drone carrying a high-explosive warhead also struck the shuttered Chernobyl nuclear plant,[258] located approximately 130 kilometers outside Kyiv. It caused fires inside the still radioactive plant, with the strike predicted to cause a spike in radioactivity within Chernobyl's exclusion zone.[259]

A report summarizes the totality of the harm:

> [O]ne can be certain that the Russian aggression against Ukraine subjected millions of Ukrainians to violence and hardship. Thousands of civilians are believed to have been killed or injured . . . . [T]he discovery of mass graves in northern Ukraine and the Kharkiv region indicates that torture, rape, and summary executions may have also occurred . . . . Likewise, the experience of people allegedly abducted or disappeared in occupied southern and southeastern Ukraine – many of them former and current local administrators and cases of targeting of Russian appointed officials by suspected Ukrainian partisans active in occupied areas – is telling and warrants further exploration. Revelations of atrocities are not the sole side effect of liberation. Contamination of formerly occupied areas with mines and explosives poses and will continue to pose a serious risk to civilians returning to their homes and livelihoods, especially in rural areas. It will require one of the greatest demining efforts in human history and is likely to kill and maim civilians in the coming years, even if the war ended immediately.[260]

The description of harms and crimes inflicted in Ukraine and on the Ukrainian people[261] set forth above does not purport to be comprehensive.[262] Rather, it is illustrative of the types of harms suffered—*all* due to the initial decision to invade Ukraine and earlier decision to annex Crimea. It further demonstrates why the crime of aggression is so significant and must be prosecuted.

---

255 Ibid., pp. 90, 98.

256 Bowen and Weed 2023, p. 9, citing Reuters 2023.

257 Ibid.

258 Alsford and Kristeva 2025.

259 Ibid.

260 ACLED 2023, p. 18.

261 As mentioned, liberal Russia scholars, non-governmental organizations, and even ordinary citizens who have spoken out against the war have also suffered. See note 165 (Memorial) and accompanying text. There have also been Ukrainian abuses against Russian POWs. See Sect. 4.3.2.3.

262 For additional reports on the crimes, see note 167.

4.4 Application of the Elements of the Crime of Aggression

As explained in earlier chapters, the ICC cannot exercise jurisdiction to prosecute the crime of aggression in the situation of Ukraine.[263] Yet, the facts are quite suggestive that Russian (and other) political and military leaders have committed the crime. A prosecutor necessarily would make a far more comprehensive case based on admissible evidence.[264] Thus, the analysis below is merely suggestive of the basic parameters of such a case.

4.4.1 Elements of the Crime

Pursuant to the internationally accepted definition of the crime of aggression found in the ICC's Rome Statute,[265] the crime is committed if the following elements are present: (1) there is an act of aggression by a state; (2) the act constitutes a "manifest" violation of the Charter of the United Nations; (3) the perpetrator planned, prepared, initiated or executed the act; (4) the perpetrator is a person "in a position effectively to exercise control over or to direct the political or military action of a [s]tate";[266] and (5) the perpetrator acted with the required *mens rea.*[267] Because the ICC cannot exercise jurisdiction over the crime in the situation of Ukraine, the analysis below focuses on *whether/how* the crime was committed, not where it might be prosecuted—a topic that is taken up in later chapters.[268] The Ukrainian Criminal Code contains its own, more minimal, definition of the crime, which is similar to the 1945 definition

---

[263] See Chap. 3, Sect. 3.2.5.

[264] Factual information contained in reports does not constitute evidence. The evidence would need to be gathered. The ICPA and national authorities, whether Ukrainian or in third countries, no doubt have already compiled some of the evidence. See note 167 on the ICPA; see note 170 on investigations in third countries.

[265] Rome Statute (1998) (as amended), note 1.

[266] Ibid., Article 8*bis*.

[267] Ibid., Article 30(1). For the ICC to prosecute, jurisdiction would also need to exist—and it does not in the present case. The situation additionally would need to rise to the ICC's gravity threshold. See International Criminal Court, Office of the Prosecutor 2016, para 32 (gravity as a criterion for admissibility); paras 35–41 (gravity for case selection). These would no doubt be met in the present situation. This chapter does not delve into the gravity threshold, as the crime likely will not be prosecuted before the ICC. If, in the future, the Rome Statute amendment on the crime of aggression is further amended it is possible that the crime could be prosecuted before the ICC—if the aggression is continuing by the time the amendment enters into force, which seem unlikely as the negotiations to adopt the amendment have been delayed until 2029. For details, see Chap. 8. But this would not be true regarding any case that has already been investigated or prosecuted due to the prohibition on double jeopardy (*ne bis in idem*).

[268] See Chaps. 5–7.

contained in the London (Nuremberg) Charter.[269] The elements of the Ukrainian definition would likely be easier to prove, at least vis-à-vis the invasion;[270] thus, the proof would be subsumed in the analysis below (that is, if the definition below is met, the Ukrainian definition likely would be as well).

The analysis below uses the Rome Statute's definition of the crime of aggression. The definition of the crime that has been agreed on by the Council of Europe and Ukraine for use by the Special Tribunal for the Crime of Aggression against Ukraine ("Special Tribunal"), which will be discussed in Chap. 7, contains minor variances from the Rome Statute definition, which will be described in that chapter.

4.4.2 Act of Aggression

The first requirement is that an "act of aggression" occurred.[271] As discussed in Chap. 3,[272] act of aggression is defined in Rome Statute Article 8*bis*, paragraph 2, as the use of armed force by a State "against the sovereignty, territorial integrity or political independence of another state, or in any other manner inconsistent with the Charter of the United Nations".[273] Article 8*bis*, paragraph 2, provides a list of acts that qualify as acts of aggression based on United Nations General Assembly Resolution 3314 (XXIX) of 14 December 1974.[274] The list includes:

(a) The invasion or attack by the armed forces of a State of the territory of another State, or any military occupation, however temporary, resulting from such invasion or attack, or any annexation by the use of force of the territory of another State or part thereof;

---

[269] See Ukraine: Law No. 2341-III, Criminal Code (2021), Article 437 (criminalizing planning, preparation or initiation of an aggressive war or an armed conflict, conspiring for any such purpose or waging of an aggressive war or aggressive hostilities); see London Charter (1945), note 171.

[270] Because the Ukrainian definition covers "aggressive war" and "armed conflict", it is not fully clear whether it would encompass the annexation of Crimea—achieved without resistance by Ukrainian forces. On the lack of resistance, see text accompanying note 79. The same concern, whether the annexation of Crimea could be prosecuted before the Special Tribunal, is discussed in Chap. 7, Sect. 7.4.1 (the temporal start date).

[271] While "attempt" is encompassed within Rome Statute Article 25(3)(f), it should be thought of as covering attempts to plan, prepare, initiate or execute the crime of aggression. However, as discussed below, if there is no manifest UN Charter violation, there is no crime. Attempted aggression that never occurs is not covered by the definition of the crime. McDougall 2021; Kreß and Barriga 2016. But see Clark 2016 (General Principles of International Criminal Law), in Kreß and Barriga 2016.

[272] See Chap. 3, Sect. 3.2.2.

[273] Rome Statute (1998) (as amended), note 1, Article 8*bis*, para 2.

[274] Ibid.

(b) Bombardment by the armed forces of a State against the territory of another State or the use of any weapons by a State against the territory of another State;
(c) The blockade of the ports or coasts of a State by the armed forces of another State;
(d) An attack by the armed forces of a State on the land, sea or air forces, or marine and air fleets of another State;
(e) The use of armed forces of one State which are within the territory of another State with the agreement of the receiving State, in contravention of the conditions provided for in the agreement or any extension of their presence in such territory beyond the termination of the agreement;
(f) The action of a State in allowing its territory, which it has placed at the disposal of another State, to be used by that other State for perpetrating an act of aggression against a third State; [and]
(g) The sending by or on behalf of a State of armed bands, groups, irregulars or mercenaries, which carry out acts of armed force against another State of such gravity as to amount to the acts listed above, or its substantial involvement therein.[275]

While the UN General Assembly[276] and other bodies[277] have denounced Russia's actions as "aggression", the determinations of such political bodies would not bind a

[275] Ibid.

[276] See, e.g., United Nations General Assembly Resolution ES-11/1 (2022) (the General Assembly "condemn[ed] the 24 February 2022 declaration by the Russian Federation of a 'special military operation' in Ukraine", and "recogniz[ed] that the military operations of the Russian Federation inside the sovereign territory of Ukraine [were] on a scale that the international community has not seen in Europe in decades and that urgent action is needed to save this generation from the scourge of war". It went on to "deplore[] in the strongest terms the aggression by the Russian Federation against Ukraine in violation of Article 2(4) of the Charter"); United Nations General Assembly Resolution ES-11/2 (2022) (condemning the invasion, demanding unconditional withdrawal, and demanding "an immediate cessation of the hostilities"); United Nations General Assembly Resolution ES-11/4 (2022) (condemning Russia's illegal attempts at annexation, noting "that the Donetsk, Kherson, Luhansk and Zaporizhzhia regions of Ukraine . . . have been under the temporary military control of the Russian Federation, as a result of aggression, in violation of the sovereignty, political independence and territorial integrity of Ukraine".); United Nations General Assembly Resolution ES-11/L.10 (2025) (recalling "the need for full implementation of its relevant resolutions adopted in response to the aggression against Ukraine"). A significant change occurred with the United States' failure, under the Trump Administration, to vote in favor of a February 2025 General Assembly resolution condemning Russia's aggression. Hansler 2025.

[277] See, e.g., NATO Parliamentary Assembly 2025; Parliamentary Assembly of the Council of Europe, Resolution 2433 (2022) Consequences of the Russian Federation's Continued Aggression Against Ukraine: Role and Response of the Council of Europe; Organization for Security and Cooperation in Europe 2024; European Union (2023) Joint Motion for a Resolution 2022/3017 (RSP) of 18 January 2023 on the Establishment of a Tribunal on the Crime of Aggression Against Ukraine. For statements by The African Union, The Economic Cooperation Organisation of Western African States, The Pacific Islands Forum, The Organization of American States, The Caribbean Community, and The Nordic Council condemning the invasion, see Corten and Koutroulis 2022, p. 4, nn 22–27. See also ibid., p. 4, nn 28–29 (individuals and academic societies condemning the invasions as illegal).

judicial institution, which must independently examine the question. This conclusion is made clear, at least for ICC purposes, in Rome Statute Article 15*bis*(9) and Article 15*ter*(4), which state that "[a] determination of an act of aggression by an organ outside the Court shall be without prejudice to the Court's own findings under this Statute".[278] Whether aggression was committed would thus be part of the elements of the crime and need to be proven.

Scholarly consensus supports the conclusion that Russia's invasion constitutes the crime of aggression.[279] On its face, Russia's invasion appears to qualify as the use of armed force by a state "against the sovereignty, territorial integrity or political independence of another State, or in any other manner inconsistent with the Charter of the United Nations".[280] Specifically, Russia's invasion of Ukraine and earlier annexation of Crimea appear to meet several of the enumerated acts of aggression:

- Subsection (a) would appear violated because there was:
  - an "invasion" "by the armed forces of a State [Russia] of the territory of another State [Ukraine]";
  - "military occupation" of Crimea[281] and areas in the south and east of Ukraine; and
  - illegal "annexation" of Crimea[282] and attempted illegal "annexation" of Donetsk, Kherson, Luhansk, and Zaporizhzhia.[283]

---

278 Rome Statute (1998) (as amended), note 1, Article 15*bis*, para 9; Article 15*ter*, para 4.

279 Bogush 2023b, p. 2.

280 Rome Statute (1998) (as amended), note 1, Article 8*bis*, para 2.

281 Some Russian troops were permitted to be stationed in Crimea prior to 2014 by virtue of a treaty between Russia and Ukraine permitting Russia to operate its Naval Base at Sevastopol. See note 85. Thus, an alternative reading is that rather than violating subsection (a), Russia's occupation and annexation of Crimea violated subsection (e). That is, there was "[t]he use of armed forces of one State [Russia] which are within the territory of another State [the Crimean Peninsula in Ukraine] with the agreement of the receiving State [Ukraine], in contravention of the conditions provided for in the agreement [which did not permit Russian forces to seize the Crimean Peninsula]. See Green et al. 2022, p. 6, note 13 (making this argument).

282 See Sect. 4.2.1.

283 See notes 43, 276. See also McDougall 2023, p. 205, n 8 ("Russia's purported annexation of the Ukrainian regions of Donetsk, Kherson, Luhansk and Zaporizhzhia in September 2022 is a separate, archetypal, act of aggression . . ."; noting that "[a]nnexation is expressly referred to in Article 8*bis* (2)(a) of the Rome Statute"); Kreβ 2022, p. 4 ("The so-called Donetsk and [Luhansk] People's Republics owe their existence to this Russian violation of the prohibition of the use of force, and without Russia's continued military intervention in violation of international law, these entities would not have become and remained viable; they are puppet regimes".). For additional arguments that Russia's actions violate subsection (a), see Open Society Justice Initiative 2022, pp. 17–18, paras 38–41.

- Subsection (b) would appear violated as "[b]ombardment" by Russian armed forces occurred "against the territory of another State".[284]
- Subsection (c) would appear violated as Russia imposed a blockade on Ukrainian ports in the spring of 2022.[285]
- Subsection (d) would appear violated as there was "[a]n attack by the armed forces of a State [Russia] on the land, sea or air forces, or marine and air fleets of another State [Ukraine]".[286]
- Subsection (g) would appear violated by Russia sending "armed bands, groups, irregulars or mercenaries" in that Wagner Group forces were deployed to Ukraine at the behest of Russia.[287]

Moreover, a prosecutor would only need to prove one of these acts of aggression to make the case.[288] Additionally, the list is illustrative (not exhaustive), such that comparable other acts not specifically enumerated could also be encompassed.[289]

Cyberattacks fit into the above-listed acts of aggression, as they are a modality/means of perpetrating Russia's acts of aggression, along with Russia's use of kinetic (conventional) military force.[290] As with much of International Humanitarian Law, the Rome Statute is weapons-neutral;[291] that is, it does not specify the means by which any of the crimes are committed. Cyberattacks can involve the "use of force" because cyber operations can result in deaths and destruction just as conventional (kinetic) attacks do. As the International Court of Justice ("ICJ") explains in its Nuclear Weapons advisory opinion, "use of force" may be accomplished "regardless of the

[284] For additional arguments that Russia's actions violate subsection (b), see ibid., pp. 18–20, paras 42–46.

[285] De Luce and Williams 2022. For additional arguments that Russia's actions violate subsection (c), see Open Society Justice Initiative 2022, p. 20, paras 47–48.

[286] For additional arguments that Russia's actions violate subsection (d), see ibid., p. 20, paras 449–451.

[287] Marten 2022 ("The Wagner Group always serves at the behest of the Russian state . . ."; "the Russian Defense Ministry appears to have paid for the 2022 contracts of Wagner Group fighters in Ukraine"); Razek and Barabanov 2022 ("The serving mercenary who spoke to the BBC said new [Wagner Group] recruits are being placed in units under the command of officers from the GRU, the Russian military intelligence unit of the ministry of defence"). For additional arguments that Russia's actions violate subsection (g), see Open Society Justice Initiative 2022, pp. 20–21, paras 52–53. See also Green et al. 2022, p. 6 (arguing that Russia's action implicates subsections (a), (b), (c), (d), and (g)).

[288] That is, one could prove (a), (b), (c), (d), *or* (g). Furthermore, subsection (a) encompasses three different acts—invasion, military occupation, and annexation—proof of only one of which would suffice to establish an act of aggression.

[289] Permanent Mission of Liechtenstein to the United Nations 2021, p. 10, para 3 ("the list is not exhaustive"). The list is open-ended (e.g., illustrative) but "closed" by the need to meet the requirements in Article 8*bis,* paragraph 1—including that the act of aggression rise to the level of a "manifest" violation of the UN Charter. Where an act enumerated on the list can be proven, that would be preferable, in order that questions about the application of the principle of legality (*nullum crimen sine lege*) do not arise.

[290] For discussion of cyberattacks against Ukraine, see Sect. 4.2.5.

[291] International Criminal Court, Office of the Prosecutor 2025 (the Rome Statute is "technology-neutral").

weapons employed".[292] In addition to contributing to Russia's acts of aggression in subsections (a), (b), (c), and (d), cyberattacks additionally appear to fall directly within subsection (b)—"the use of *any weapons* by a State against the territory of another State".[293] Because attribution of cyberattacks can be complex, the source of the attacks would need to be attributable to Russia before the case could be made that the cyberattacks were part of the aggression.[294] Russia has denied responsibility for various cyberattacks,[295] although the United States and the United Kingdom attribute some of the cyberattacks directly to the Russian GRU.[296]

As to the conduct of Belarus, that would appear to fall within subsection (f)—"[t]he action of a State in allowing its territory [the territory of Belarus], which it has placed at the disposal of another State [Russia], to be used by that other State for perpetrating an act of aggression against a third State".[297] As detailed above, part of

---

[292] International Court of Justice (1996), *Legality of the Threat or Use of Nuclear Weapons*, Advisory Opinion, 1996 ICJ Rep. 226, para 39 ("International Court of Justice (1996), *Legality of the Threat or Use of Nuclear Weapons*, Advisory Opinion"). The Tallinn Manual 2.0 further states:

> [T]he mere fact that a computer (rather than a more traditional weapon, weapon system, or platform) is used during an operation has no bearing on whether that operation amounts to a 'use of force' .... In the cyber context, it is not the instrument used that determines whether the use of force threshold has been crossed, but rather ... the consequences of the operation and its surrounding circumstances.

Schmitt 2017, p. 328, para 1. The Council of Advisers' Report on the Application of the Rome Statute of the International Criminal Court to Cyberwarfare takes the view that cyber operations can qualify as use of armed force, stating "[t]here is no reason to treat the situation differently from equivalent attacks conducted through kinetic methods of warfare". Permanent Mission of Liechtenstein to the United Nations 2021, p. 10, para 2. Tallinn Manual 2.0 opines that "[a] cyber operation constitutes a use of force when its scale and effects are comparable to a non-cyber operation rising to the level of a use of force". Schmitt 2017, Rule 69.

[293] Rome Statute (1998) (as amended), note 1, Article 8*bis*, para 2 (b) (emphasis added). *See* International Court of Justice 1996, *Legality of the Threat or Use of Nuclear Weapons*, Advisory Opinion, note 292. For more extensive analysis of how cyberattacks fall within the crime of aggression, see Trahan 2024; Trahan 2025c.

[294] See International Law Commission 2001, Article 8 ("[t]he conduct of a person or group of persons shall be considered an act of a State under international law if the person or group of persons is in fact acting on the instructions of, or under the direction or control of, that State in carrying out the conduct"); ibid., Article 11 ("[c]onduct ... shall ... be considered an act of that State under international law if and to the extent that the State acknowledges and adopts the conduct in question as its own").

[295] McMillan and Volz 2022.

[296] See, e.g., UK Government 2022 (attributing a 15 February 2022 attack to the GRU); Vazquez et al. 2022 (the United States doing the same).

[297] Rome Statute (1998) (as amended), note 1, Article 8*bis*, para 2(f). Lukashenko claims that Putin "did not ask him for authorisation to attack Ukraine from the territory of Belarus, as it was a routine 'withdrawal of troops after the exercises'". Balachuk 2024. Yet, in evaluating whether there was an act of aggression, the question is whether Belarus' territory was utilized to launch part of the invasion, which it undeniably was.

the invasion—specifically, the initial attack on Kyiv—was launched from Belarus' territory.[298]

The conduct of North Korea in sending forces and weapons to assist Russia, also discussed above,[299] might constitute aiding of Russian acts of aggression in subsections (a)-(d). It is less clear whether North Korea has committed its own act of aggression under subsection (g). That subsection covers "[t]he sending by or on behalf of a State [North Korea] of armed bands, groups [North Korean troops], irregulars or mercenaries, which carry out acts of armed force against another State [Ukraine] of such gravity as to amount to the acts listed above, or its substantial involvement therein".[300] A question might exist whether sending 14,000 troops[301] and weaponry[302] is of comparable gravity to the other enumerated acts, and whether North Korea was substantially involved in Russia's aggression. Furthermore, it might only be the North Korean troops fighting on Ukrainian territory or launching weapons into Ukrainian territory that would be considered. To the extent that North Korean forces are fighting on Russian territory occupied by Ukraine (the Kursk region), they would be on Russian territory with Russia's consent, so that arguably would not be evaluated as an act of aggression.

4.4.3 A "Manifest" UN Charter Violation

As also discussed in Chap. 3, a second requirement under Article 8*bis,* paragraph 1 is that the act of aggression "by its character, gravity and scale, constitutes a *manifest* violation of the Charter of the United Nations".[303] This threshold clause "appropriately limit[s] the Court's jurisdiction to the most serious acts of aggression under customary international law, thus excluding cases of insufficient gravity and falling within a grey area" in terms of their legality.[304] The components of character, gravity, and scale must be sufficient to justify a "manifest" determination.[305]

The ICC's Elements of Crimes further state that "[t]he term 'manifest' is an objective qualification",[306] meaning it is not dependent on the subjective belief of

---

298 See Sect. 4.2.3.

299 See Sect. 4.2.4.

300 Rome Statute (1998) (as amended), note 1, Article 8*bis*, para 2(g).

301 See Sect. 4.2.4.

302 Yeung 2026.

303 See Chap. 3, Sect. 3.2.2; Rome Statute (1998) (as amended), note 1, Article 8*bis*, para 1 (emphasis added).

304 Special Working Group on the Crime of Aggression 2008, para 68. The negotiations in the Special Working Group on the Crime of Aggression ("SWGCA") fed into the finalization of the crime of aggression, and therefore constitute negotiating history.

305 International Criminal Court, Assembly of States Parties 2010, Annex III, Understanding 7.

306 International Criminal Court nd-a, p. 43, Introductory Note 3.

the actors involved.[307] The words "'gravity' and 'scale' were intended to exclude border skirmishes and the like".[308] As to "character", it is here that genuinely legally controversial cases are excluded.[309] Thus, there must be "an incontrovertible breach of Article 2(4)" of the UN Charter.[310] As mentioned in Chap. 3, Understanding 6 agreed on at the 2010 Review Conference on the Rome Statute[311] additionally provides:

> It is understood that aggression is the most serious and dangerous form of the illegal use of force; and that a determination whether an act of aggression has been committed requires consideration of all the circumstances of each particular case, including the gravity of the acts concerned and their consequences, in accordance with the Charter of the United Nations.[312]

Furthermore, Understanding 7, also agreed on at the 2010 Review Conference, adds that "the three components of character, gravity and scale must be sufficient to justify a 'manifest' determination. No one component can be significant enough to satisfy the manifest standard by itself".[313] This leaves it open to interpretation whether all three terms must collectively satisfy the threshold, or whether two may suffice.[314]

While a defendant would of course be entitled to put on a contrary case, the invasion and annexation of Crimea suggest that Russia, in both instances, committed not only a violation of the UN Charter, but a *manifest* violation of the Charter.[315] As to satisfying "gravity and scale", the enormous size of the invasion clearly would meet those requirements. The gravity and scale of annexing Crimea would presumably be met as well—Crimea's territory is 27,000 square kilometers[316] (about the size of the US state of Massachusetts). Furthermore, one might argue that the 2014 annexation of Crimea and the 2022 invasion were part and parcel of the same aggression (with insurgency in the Donbas fomented in the intervening years).[317] Thus, under the

[307] Heinsch 2010, p. 727 ("This [Introductory Note] tries to illustrate that the interpretation of the term is independent from subjective opinions and not dependent on the opinion of the actors involved".).

[308] Kreß 2009, p. 1138.

[309] Ibid.; Kreß and Barriga 2016, pp. 1138, 1142.

[310] McDougall 2021, p. 158.

[311] The Review Conference on the Rome Statute was held 31 May–11 June 2010, in Kampala, Uganda, at the Munyonyo Conference Center on the shores of Lake Victoria. See International Criminal Court, Press Release 2010.

[312] International Criminal Court, Assembly of States Parties 2010, Annex III, Understanding 6.

[313] Ibid., Understanding 7.

[314] Heinsch 2010, p. 728 (Understanding 6 "begs the question whether two of those components can already be enough to constitute a manifest violation".); ibid. at 729 ("one would . . . be inclined to conclude that two of th[e] components are already sufficient".). Cases of unclear legality were intended to be excluded, and that should be the case even if the incident is one having sufficient "gravity and scale". In that instance, satisfying the two criteria of gravity and scale would not suffice.

[315] "Russia's use of force against Ukraine constitutes an act of aggression which, by its character, gravity, and scale, constitutes a manifest violation of the UN Charter within the meaning of Article 8 *bis*(1) of the Statute of the ICC". Kreβ 2022, p. 22.

[316] Britannica nd-a.

[317] The invasion and illegal annexation of Crimea played a crucial role in the 2022 invasion of the South of Ukraine. Crimea served as a staging ground for the southern offensive, facilitating the rapid

"accumulation of events" theory or otherwise, one might evaluate them together in considering whether there was a manifest Charter violation.[318]

As to the word "character", it is here that incursions of questionable legality would be excluded. Again, while an accused would need to be given his or her day in court (e.g., to present arguments regarding saving Russian speakers in the East of Ukraine, or other theories),[319] Russia's actions do not appear to satisfy any accepted grounds under the *jus ad bellum.*[320] James Green, Christian Henderson, and Tom Ruys, for example, write:

> [A] lawful justification for Russia's military invasion of – or 'special military operation' in – Ukraine does not exist; the various claims advanced by Russia not only all fail, but most of them fail on multiple grounds. The invasion of Ukraine constitutes an unlawful use of force, an act of aggression and an egregious violation of a rule of *jus cogens*.[321]

Neither Russian speakers being required to speak Ukrainian,[322] nor the supposed "de-Nazification" of Ukraine, nor possible NATO expansion constitutes an "armed attack" that could trigger Russia's right to self-defense.[323] Russia's invasion was

occupation of key areas and cities. For example, the eastern thrust from Crimea proved decisive in the encirclement and fall of Mariupol. One of the goals of the 2022 invasion was the establishment of a so-called "land bridge" to Crimea. Trahan 2025a and 2025b.

[318] Cf. Permanent Mission of Liechtenstein to the United Nations 2021, p. 15, para 18 (the accumulation of events theory), citing various sources including ICJ cases.

[319] For Putin's rationales for the invasion, see Sect. 4.2.

[320] See, e.g., Green et al. 2022 (examining in detail the legal justifications advanced by President Putin for Russia's use of military force and subjecting them to scrutiny); see also Corten and Koutroulis 2023 (examining Russia's arguments for invading Ukraine and concluding they have found little acceptance outside Russia).

[321] Green et al. 2022, p. 27. For additional arguments that the manifest threshold is satisfied, see Open Society Justice Initiative 2022, pp. 21–27, paras 54–67.

[322] For the Ukrainian law passed regarding the Russian language, see note 92. Ukraine instituted proceedings before the ICJ to argue that Russia falsely invoked claims of genocide as a pretext for its invasion. See International Court of Justice (2022) *Allegations of Genocide under the Convention on the Prevention and Punishment of the Crime of Genocide (Ukraine v. Russian Federation)*, Application Instituting Proceedings, para 16. In its 16 March 2022 Provisional Measures Order, the ICJ recognized Ukraine's "plausible right not to be subjected to military operations" by Russia on the basis of alleged genocide. For background, see Lopez and Worthington 2022.

[323] See Green et al. 2022, pp. 7–21 (explaining why none of Russia's arguments reveal any "armed attack" that could have triggered the right to self-defense, notwithstanding Russia's invocation of UN Charter article 51); see, e.g., ibid., pp. 8–13 (perceived threat of NATO expansion does not constitute an armed attack or imminent threat thereof), relying on International Court of Justice (2005) *Armed Activities on the Territory of the Congo (Democratic Republic of the Congo v. Uganda)*, Judgment, 2005 ICJ Rep. 168, para 143 ("International Court of Justice (2005), *Armed Activities on the Territory of the Congo (Democratic Republic of the Congo v. Uganda)*, Judgment") ("'security needs [that are] essentially preventative'" cannot sustain a self-defense claim). For Russia's letter invoking self-defense, see Permanent Representative of the Russian Federation 2022.

certainly not authorized by the UN Security Council.[324] Furthermore, Ukraine obviously never consented to Russia's invasion (or earlier annexation of Crimea).[325] Even if one were to consider Donetsk and Luhansk to be independent states (which most agree they were not), any consent they could have given would have been limited to their territory and not the whole territory of Ukraine.[326]

Belarus, in allowing, by one estimate, 70,000 Russian soldiers and 7,000 vehicles to launch from its territory,[327] and North Korea, in committing approximately 14,000 troops as well as weapons,[328] arguably both contributed to Russia's manifest violations of the UN Charter. Furthermore, at least Belarus' actions did so in a manner of sufficient gravity and scale to separately constitute a manifest Charter violation.[329]

4.4.4 Planning, Preparation, Initiation, and Execution

As noted in Chap. 3, a third requirement under Article 8*bis*, paragraph 1, is that the individual accused was involved in the "planning, preparation, initiation or execution" of the act of aggression.[330] This describes the perpetrator's contribution to the state's act of aggression. Under the Rome Statute, the individual conduct is additionally subject to the modes of individual criminal responsibility enumerated in Rome Statute Article 25 and superior responsibility in Article 28.[331] As to the interaction of Article 8*bis* and Articles 25 and 28, Articles 25 and 28 essentially broaden the

324 See UN Charter (1945), note 4, Chap. VII, Article 42 (UN Security Council's ability to authorize forceful measures).

325 "The notion that military intervention can be lawful if it is undertaken at the request of the governing authorities of a third state is well established". Green et al. 2022, p. 21, citing International Court of Justice (1986) *Military and Paramilitary Activities in and Against Nicaragua (Nicaragua v. United States of America)*, Merits, 1986 ICJ Rep. 14, para 246; International Court of Justice (2005), *Armed Activities on the Territory of the Congo (Democratic Republic of the Congo v. Uganda)*, Judgment, note 323, paras 39–54. For further discussion of the doctrine, also known as military assistance on request or intervention by invitation, see, e.g., De Wet 2020.

326 Green et al. 2022, p. 22 (making both arguments). Additionally, even if one were to accept the much-disputed theory of "humanitarian intervention", it also would not apply. For a comprehensive discussion of the origins and dispute regarding the legality of humanitarian intervention, see Trahan 2020, chap. 2. As to why the theory, even if accepted, would not apply, see Green et al. 2022, pp. 23–27.

327 Ukrinform 2023. Other sources estimate 30,000 Russian soldiers. See note 116 and accompanying text.

328 See Sect. 4.2.4.

329 Allowing Belarus' territory to be used to launch the invasion fits directly into an enumerated "act of aggression" under Rome Statute article 8*bis*(2)(f). See notes 299–302 (the deployment of North Korean troops on Russian territory would arguably *not* be evaluated as an independent act of aggression absent their launching attacks into Ukrainian territory).

330 Rome Statute (1998) (as amended), note 1, Article 8*bis*, para 1.

331 Ibid. Articles 25, 28. The Special Tribunal uses different modes of responsibility, as will be discussed in Chap. 7. See Chap. 7, Sect. 7.4.1. But the requirement of being involved in the "planning, preparation, initiation or execution" remains the same. Ibid.

field of who may be accused. Thereby, responsibility would extend to those who *aid* in the planning, or *order* the execution, of an act of aggression or have superior responsibility over such individuals—as no single person does all of the planning, preparation, initiation or execution of an act of aggression. Yet, the requirement of involvement in "planning, preparation, initiation or execution" contained in the definition of the crime is required for any accused.[332]

As discussed above, it is believed that a fairly small circle of individuals was involved in ***planning*** the invasion.[333] The names Putin, Shoigu, Gerasminov, Patrushev, Bortnikov, and Naryshkin have surfaced.[334] A "Model Indictment for the Crime of Aggression Committed against Ukraine" prepared by the Open Society Justice Initiative (OSJI) details the roles of Putin, Patrushev, and Shoigu in the planning of the invasion, as well as those of Sergei Naryshkin, Valentina Matviyenko, and Sergei Lavrov.[335]

As to the ***preparation*** of the invasion, large numbers of individuals, including high-level Russian military commanders, were no doubt involved, as at least 130,000 Russian troops were mobilized from the Russian-Ukrainian border or Belarus.[336] In particular, the Model OSJI Indictment makes the case that Putin, Patrushev, Shoigu, Naryshkin, Matviyenko, Lavrov, Gerasimov, and Sergey Beseda are implicated in the preparation of the invasion.[337]

---

[332] Under ICC case law, there appears to be some debate as to whether a "significant" contribution to the commission of the crime is required. According to ICC Pre-Trial Chamber II:

> Of the cases said to comprise the "more recent" jurisprudence, *Ongwen* and *Al Mahdi* held that an accused's contribution need not be significant. The Prosecution also cites to *Ntaganda*, and to *Blé Goudé*, which did not specify the level of contribution required. In *Ruto et al.*, not cited by the Prosecution, the Pre-Trial Chamber said that the contribution "is satisfied by a less than 'substantial' contribution", but did not define what it should be. Academic commentaries endorse the "significant" standard as being "beyond any reasonable doubt", and a "valid interpretation" which "best fits with the phrasing of the other *actus reus* criteria". Regardless of the term, the jurisprudence is consistent on the need for a **causal effect** between the contribution and the crime: the suspect's contribution must influence, or have a bearing on, if and how the crime is committed, and minimal contributions from a suspect "should be exempted from criminal responsibility".

International Criminal Court, Pre-Trial Chamber II (2023) *Prosecutor v. Maxime Jeoffroy Eli Mokom Gawaka*, ICC-01/14-01/22-274-Conf., Public Redacted Version of "Defence Response to 'Prosecution's Additional Submissions Following the Confirmation of Charges Hearing'", paras 17–18 (emphasis in original).

[333] See Sect. 4.2.

[334] See notes 29–34 and accompanying text.

[335] Open Society Justice Initiative 2022, pp. 28–31, paras 70–75. For discussion of the positions held by Naryshkin, Matviyenko, and Lavrov, see Sect. 4.4.5. But see text accompanying note 32 (suggesting Lavrov was not involved in the planning). For a second model indictment, see Goodman and Hamilton 2022.

[336] Kingsley 2022. Another source puts the total number of those mobilized on Russia's border with Ukraine, in Belarus, and in the occupied Crimea region at 150,000–190,000. Bowen 2022, p. 1.

[337] Open Society Justice Initiative 2022, pp. 31–58, paras 76–102. For discussion of the positions held by Beseda, see Sect. 4.4.5.

As to the ***initiation*** of the invasion, the Russian military units involved are known;[338] accordingly, the commanders of those units were certainly involved in the initiation of Russia's actions. Cyberattacks that took place prior to and during the initial invasion[339] might also constitute part of the initiation of Russia's actions. The OSJI Model Indictment, however, construes the word "initiation" narrowly and makes the case that only Putin is implicated in the decision to initiate the invasion.[340] Such a narrow construction of the word is arguably unwarranted. The OSJI defines initiation as "the decision taken immediately before the first use of force to commit the act of aggression . . . *and the first actual use of force*";[341] thus, its own definition is broad enough to encompass those involved in the first uses of force.

In terms of the ***execution*** of the invasion, many military units were involved, as well as Wagner Group forces.[342] Cyberattacks that occurred during or leading into the invasion could also be considered part of the execution of the crime.[343] Yet, as will be discussed below, not all commanders of military (or cyber) units would necessarily be implicated because the next criterion, known as the "leadership clause", would additionally need to be satisfied.[344] The OSJI Model Indictment makes the case that Putin, Shoigu, Matviyenko, and Lavrov are implicated in the execution of the invasion.[345] Further investigation might reveal others who are implicated in all four categories (i.e., those involved in the planning, preparation, initiation, and execution of the invasion).[346]

Belarus' President Alexander Lukashenko, who is also the commander-in-chief of the Armed Forces of Belarus, and Belarus' Minister of Defense, Lieutenant General Victor Khrenin, could have been involved in planning and preparation of the invasion—this would need to be ascertained. A clearer case would probably focus on their involvement in the initiation of the invasion (providing Belarus' territory for the attack of Russian forces from Belarus towards Kyiv) and thus their involvement in part of the execution of the crime.[347]

The leader of North Korea, Kim Jong-un, might be potentially implicated in part of (e.g., aiding or co-perpetration of) the execution of the crime by sending

---

338 See Sect. 4.2.2 (military units involved).

339 See Sect. 4.2.5.

340 Open Society Justice Initiative 2022, pp. 58–59, paras 103–06.

341 Ibid., p. 58, para 103 (emphasis added).

342 See Sect. 4.2.2 (military units involved); Sect. 4.2.4 (involvement of the Wagner Group).

343 See note 296 (attributing at least some of the cyberattacks to the GRU).

344 See Rome Statute (1998) (as amended), note 1, Article 25(3*bis*) ("In respect of the crime of aggression, the provisions of this article shall apply only to persons in a position effectively to exercise control over or to direct the political or military action of a State".).

345 Open Society Justice Initiative 2022, pp. 59–81, paras 107–12.

346 According to Gleb Bogush, it is undeniable that "many Russian and Belarusian state officials, military, and non-state actors associated with them were directly involved" in the planning, preparing for, initiating, and executing the act of aggression. Bogush 2023a, p. 100.

347 For the role of Belarus, see Sect. 4.2.3.

North Korean forces.[348] However, as will be discussed in Chap. 7, the Statute for the Special Tribunal on the Crime of Aggression against Ukraine ("Tribunal Statute")[349] that has been agreed on may not permit prosecution of those who aided or were co-perpetrators, as those modes of responsibility are omitted from the Tribunal Statute.[350]

4.4.5 The Leadership Clause and Who Might Fit Within It

The above analysis, however, needs to factor in the fourth requirement in Article 8*bis*, paragraph 1, that, irrespective of whether an individual played a role in the "planning, preparation, initiation, or execution" of an act of aggression, the ICC's definition of the crime only pertains to a person "in a position effectively to exercise control over or to direct the political or military action of a State".[351] This is referred to as the leadership clause.[352]

Carrie McDougall explains that "[t]he definition applies to de facto 'leaders' who are in a position to have a decisive say over, govern, instruct, or command the deeds of the political or military establishments of a State aimed at achieving particular objectives".[353] From the language itself, what matters is the leader's *effective* control, and the leader could be either political or military. The "leadership clause" is intended to cover a fairly narrow group of senior leadership, most certainly excluding ordinary soldiers and probably mid-level commanders as well.[354] Claus Kreβ explains the leadership clause as follows:

---

[348] For the role of North Korean troops, see Sect. 4.2.4. It is less clear whether North Korea has committed an independent act of aggression. See notes 299–302.

[349] Statute of the Special Tribunal for the Crime of Aggression against Ukraine (2025). https://search.coe.int/cm?i=0900001680b678ca. Accessed 28 September 2025 ("Tribunal Statute").

[350] See Chap. 7, Sect. 7.4.1 (Modes of responsibility).

[351] Rome Statute (1998) (as amended), note 1, Article 8*bis*, para 1; Article 25, para 3*bis*. The leadership clause is also contained in the Tribunal Statute. Tribunal Statute, note 349, Articles 2(1), 4(1).

[352] While Ukraine's definition of the crime of aggression, see note 269, does not contain the equivalent of a leadership clause, the Grand Chamber of Ukraine's Supreme Court interprets their law to contain a comparable requirement. See Masol 2024.

[353] McDougall 2021, p. 257 ("this definition excludes business and religious leaders (unless they otherwise meet the leadership definition)", resulting in a "narrowing of the class of potential perpetrators").

[354] One source interprets the clause this way:

> [T]he following individuals can, in any event, be regarded as leaders: heads of government, heads of state, ministers of foreign affairs, ministers of defense, heads and deputy heads of a national security council and (senior) officers in the armed forces who are involved in planning, preparing and coordinating the act of aggression.

Advisory Committee on Public International Law 2022, p. 15.

> [The] [l]eadership requirement shields the ordinary soldier, who fights on the side of the aggressor and kills an enemy combatant, from the threat of being punished for a crime of aggression. By contrast, the executioner in a concentration camp may be responsible for genocide or for a crime against humanity. Several justifications have been offered in order to explain this difference. The best among them would appear to be the desire to preserve the existence of as strong a legal incentive as possible for the "unjust warrior" to comply with the law of international armed conflict.[355]

Evaluating whether an individual satisfies the leadership clause will certainly be fact-dependent in terms of how much control an individual actually exerts over the political or military action of a state.[356]

In terms of Russian leadership, the OSJI Model Indictment suggests the following individuals were in positions to exercise control over or to direct Russia's political or military actions:

- **Vladimir Putin** is the Head of State and constitutionally tasked with determining the main course of Russia's domestic and foreign policy.[357] He is also Supreme Commander-in-Chief of the Armed Forces of Russia.[358] As to Putin's role, Gleb Bogush writes:

  > There is no doubt that Vladimir Putin should personally be a primary target of any investigation into the crime of aggression. His fingerprints are on everything related to the Ukraine war: Putin personally oversaw the occupation of Crimea and the war in [the] Donbas and directed the full-scale invasion of Ukraine. His countless statements and actions reveal his premeditation to wage a war against Ukraine. He personally conceded that the purported territorial expansion resulted from the use of force. By virtue of his role, Putin effectively exercises control over Russia's political and military actions.[359]

355 Kreß 2016, p. 9. Gleb Bogush explains it differently. He writes:

> Many hundred thousand military and security personnel engaged in the act of aggression... however... it is crucial to avoid extremes and refrain from labeling the entire aggressor army or officer core as criminal .... [M]any soldiers and officers of the aggressor side can be seen as victims of the crime of aggression rather than responsible perpetrators.

Bogush 2023a, pp. 105–06.

356 For further discussion of the "leadership clause", see, e.g., McDougall 2021, p. 214 et seq.; Reisinger Coracini and Wrange 2016, pp. 309–12; Clark 2016, pp. 583 et seq. "The 'control or direct' standard [contained in the Rome Statute] differs from the one of 'shape or influence', outlined by the post-WW II jurisprudence". Bogush 2023a, pp. 96–97, citing Heller 2007.

357 Open Society Justice Initiative 2022, p. 2, para 2, citing Constitution of the Russian Federation (1993) (amended 2020), Article 80(3) ("Constitution of the Russian Federation 1993 (as amended)").

358 Ibid., p. 3, para 2, citing Constitution of the Russian Federation (1993) (as amended), note 357, Article 87.

359 Bogush 2023a, p. 101 (internal citations omitted).

- **Nikolai Patrushev** has served as Secretary of the Russian Security Council since 2008.[360] Each Member of the Russian Security Council,[361] especially its Permanent Members, is believed to have the ability to influence the conduct of its main tasks and functions.[362] Patrushev previously served as the Director of the Russian Federal Security Service ("FSB").[363] He is thought to be one of Putin's most trusted advisors.[364]
- **Sergei Shoigu** has served as Russia's Minister of Defense since 2012,[365] and is thought to hold decision-making power by virtue of his relationship with Putin, as he is considered among Putin's strongest supporters.[366] He is believed to have been one of the "two architects" of the annexation of Crimea and support for armed groups in the Donbas,[367] and the invasion of Ukraine.[368] He is second in the chain of command after Putin.[369]
- **Sergei Naryshkin** has served as Director of the Russian Foreign Intelligence Service ("SVR") since 2016.[370] He is thought to hold decision-making power by virtue of his relationship with Putin[371] and is believed to hold "significant sway over security decisions", including those in relation to the invasion of Ukraine.[372]
- **Valentina Matviyenko** has served as Chairwoman and Speaker of the Federation Council (one of the two chambers of Russia's parliament) since 2011.[373] She is also a Permanent Member of the Russian Security Council and therefore has a vote on state security decisions.[374]

---

360 Open Society Justice Initiative 2022, p. 4, para 6, citing Security Council of the Russian Federation nd-a. *Compare* Bogush 2023a, p. 102 (suggesting that experts tend to exaggerate the Russian Security Council's powers and real influence, but "membership indicates influence and closeness to Putin").

361 "The [Russian] Security Council, an autonomous element of the wider Russian Presidential Administration, is the central body responsible for managing the formulation and execution of security-related policies". Galeotti 2019b.

362 Open Society Justice Initiative 2022, p. 4, para 6.

363 Ibid., p. 5, para 8, citing Database of Free Russia Forum nd.

364 Ibid., p. 6, para 9.

365 Ibid., p. 7, para 11 (citation omitted).

366 Ibid., p. 7, para 12, citing Langton 2022; United Russia nd.

367 Ibid., para 15, citing Seibt 2022.

368 Ibid., p. 8, para 16.

369 Ibid., p. 15, para 31 (citation omitted).

370 Ibid., p. 9, para 18, citing Foreign Intelligence Service of the Russian Federation nd.

371 Ibid., p. 10, para 19.

372 Ibid., p. 10, para 20.

373 Ibid., p. 11, para 22. See Bogush 2023a, p. 104 ("The chairpersons of the Russian parliament . . . organized and oversaw 'parliamentary approval' of the war and the territorial grab and can be characterized as 'leaders' for the purposes of the crimes of aggression".). On the powers of the Russian parliament, see ibid., p. 103.

374 Open Society Justice Initiative 2022, p. 12, para 23.

- **Sergey Beseda** heads the 5th Service of the FSB, the FSB's foreign intelligence and espionage branch.[375] It is believed that he has been overseeing the FSB's foreign intelligence work in relation to Ukraine.[376]
- **Sergei Lavrov** has served as Foreign Minister since 2004[377] and is a Permanent Member of the Security Council.[378]
- **Valery Gerasminov** has served as Chief of the General Staff of the Russian Armed Forces and First Deputy Minister of Defense since 2012.[379] He oversees command of the armed forces under the Ministry of Defense.[380] He is third in the chain of command after Putin and Shoigu.[381] He is a Member of the Security Council[382] and is believed to have been another of the "two architects" of the annexation of Crimea and support for armed groups in the Donbas.[383]

In his analysis of the leadership clause, Gleb Bogush takes the view that **Sergei Kiriyenko**, the Deputy Head of the Presidential Administration, should also be included. Bogush writes that:

> [He] previously served as prime minister under Boris Yeltsin, [and] is responsible for the "integration" of occupied Ukrainian territories. His activity includes overseeing the implementation of the sham annexation referenda and associated ideological campaigns. Additionally, the presidential administration is primarily responsible for quelling internal dissent . . . .[384]

Bogush also considers the responsibility of **Valery Zorkin**, chairman of the Russian Constitutional Court.[385]

The leadership clause would not necessarily be limited only to the individuals listed above.[386] For example, "[i]n Russia, strings were pulled by businessmen and political associates of Putin, as well as the FSB and the GRU".[387] Bogush also examines the role of the media, noting that their role has been "particularly significant".[388]

---

[375] Ibid., p. 13, para 25, citing Harding 2022.

[376] Ibid., p. 13, para 26, citing R. Politik 2022.

[377] Ibid., p. 14, para 29, citing Security Council of the Russian Federation nd-b.

[378] Ibid., p. 14, para 29, citing Kremlin nd.

[379] Ibid., p. 15, para 31, citing Ministry of Defense of the Russian Federation nd.

[380] Ibid., p. 15, para 31.

[381] Ibid., p. 15, para 31 (citation omitted).

[382] Ibid., p. 15, para 3, citing Kremlin nd.

[383] Ibid., p. 15, para 33, citing Seibt 2022.

[384] Bogush 2023a, p. 102.

[385] The court provided legal opinions on the legality of the annexation of Crimea and the four other Ukrainian regions purportedly annexed; ultimately, however, Bogush expresses doubt as to whether Zorkin satisfies the leadership clause. See ibid., pp. 104–05.

[386] See, e.g., ibid., p. 102 (suggesting that additional individuals, including in the Office of the President and Russian Security Council, should be investigated).

[387] Freedman 2022, p. 365.

[388] He writes:

Belarusian President Lukashenko[389] and Minister of Defense Khrenin would certainly fall within the leadership clause, as would North Korean President Kim Jong-un. President Lukashenko is potentially implicated in Belarus allowing its territory to be used to launch the invasion. He also could be complicit as a co-perpetrator in the entire invasion, if, as explored in Chap. 7, "co-perpetration" is read into the Special Tribunal's Statute, as it is not expressly listed as a mode of responsibility.[390] It is also possible that President Kim Jong-un could be implicated as an aider and abettor and/or a co-perpetrator[391]—again, if those forms of responsibility are read into the Tribunal's Statute, as they are not expressly listed.[392]

4.4.6 Intent and Knowledge

Finally, for any accused, Rome Statute Article 30(1) also requires proof of "intent" to commit the crime as well as "knowledge" of the circumstances.[393] Because the definition of the crime of aggression in Rome Statute Article 8*bis* contains no intent requirement, it is necessary to look to the general requirements in the Rome Statute for the definition of intent.[394] Article 30(2) specifies that intent exists when (1) a "person means to engage in the conduct" or (2) "means to cause th[e] consequences or is aware that [the consequences] will occur in the ordinary course of events".[395]

> The media have been complicit in creating and maintaining an aggressive imperialistic mindset for years, if not decades, and particularly since 2014 toward Ukraine. Specifically, propaganda presented Ukraine as "not a real state" and repeatedly accused the Ukrainian government of being "Nazi" filled with "Nazi collaborators," effectively waging a war of extermination against [the] Donbas' "predominantly Russian" population. The Russian state media, especially television, were dominated by extreme statements based on pure emotions, exploiting racism and homophobia . . . . In the weeks and months leading up to Russia's full-scale invasion, pro-Kremlin media employed false and misleading narratives to justify military action against Ukraine, mask the Kremlin's operational planning, and deny any responsibility for the coming attack.

Bogush 2023a, pp. 107–08 (internal citations omitted). Yet, Bogush also acknowledges that "[t]he Russian regime *has had absolute control over the media* since Putin's rise to power", ibid., p. 108 (emphasis added), which suggest that those in the media would not meet the leadership clause.

389 See ibid., pp. 109–10 (arguing that Lukashenko was complicit and meets the leadership requirement; also suggesting that additional Belarusian military commanders should be investigated).

390 See Tribunal Statute, note 349; Chap. 7, Sect. 7.4.1.

391 For whether the North Korean leader is implicated in North Korea's own act of aggression, see notes 299–302 and accompanying text.

392 See Chap. 7, Sect. 7.4.1.

393 Rome Statute (1998) (as amended), note 1, Article 30(1).

394 McDougall 2021, p. 239.

395 Rome Statute (1998) (as amended), note 1, Article 30(2)(a)–(b).

Intent may be inferred through circumstantial evidence.[396] Knowledge is defined as awareness that a "circumstance exists" or "a consequence will occur in the ordinary course of events".[397] Thus, for any accused, these requirements would also need to be met, at least before the ICC. The Special Tribunal, which will be discussed in detail in Chap. 7, is silent on its intent requirement; thus, the judges likely would be guided by the Rome Statute and/or Ukrainian law and no doubt would also require a showing of intent.

Duress excludes criminal responsibility, at least under the Rome Statute, although under very limited circumstances.[398] Further investigation might focus on whether Belarus' President Lukashenko knew why Russian forces were being stationed on Belarus' territory (as they were purportedly being deployed to conduct training exercises),[399] and whether he was in a position of duress such that he could not have refused the troop deployment to Belarus' territory by a much larger neighboring state that possesses nuclear weapons.[400] Yet, the standard for showing duress, at least under the Rome Statute, is difficult to meet.[401] Moreover, Lukashenko also appears to have engaged in a variety of related actions that facilitated the Russian invasion.[402]

---

[396] See, e.g., International Criminal Tribunal for Rwanda (2006) *Gacumbitsi v. Prosecutor*, Case No. ICTR-2001-64-A, Judgment, para 40 ("By its nature, intent is not usually susceptible to direct proof. Only the accused himself has first-hand knowledge of his own mental state, and he is unlikely to testify to his own genocidal intent. Intent thus must usually be inferred".); International Criminal Court, Appeals Chamber (2009) *Prosecutor v. Omar Hassan Ahmad al Bashir ("Omar al Bashir")*, ICC-02/05-01/09 OA, Prosecution Document in Support of Appeal against the "Decision on the Prosecution's Application for a Warrant of Arrest against Omar Hassan Ahmad Al Bashir", para 40 ("the intent and knowledge of suspects before this Court will often be proved by inference established through circumstantial evidence").

[397] Rome Statute (1998) (as amended), note 1, Article 30(3).

[398] Ibid., Article 31(1)(d).

[399] See note 32 and accompanying text.

[400] See, e.g., Balachuk 2024 (Lukashenko claims Putin did not ask him for authorization to attack Ukraine from Belarus).

[401] The Rome Statute requires the following showing:

> The conduct which is alleged to constitute a crime within the jurisdiction of the Court has been caused by duress resulting from *a threat of imminent death or of continuing or imminent serious bodily harm against that person or another person*, and the person acts necessarily and reasonably to avoid this threat, provided that the person does not intend to cause a greater harm than the one sought to be avoided.

Rome Statute (1998) (as amended), note 1, Article 31(1)(d) (emphasis added).

[402] See Global Accountability Network 2024, note 117.

4.5 Conclusion

Russia's invasion of Ukraine was a shock to the global order and unleashed a host of horrors on the people of Ukraine. Russia's aggression dates to at least 2014 and the illegal annexation of Crimea, followed by years of fomenting of insurgency in the Donbas. It is difficult to comprehend that the massive harms and crimes inflicted during the invasion—with an estimated 1 million people killed or wounded[403]—followed from the decision of one individual, acting in consultation with a relatively small inner circle of advisers, at least in the planning of the invasion. A more comprehensive case would need to be made to prove all the elements of the crime of aggression and thoroughly investigate all leaders who should be held responsible for their roles in its planning, preparation, initiation, or execution. However, this chapter provides at least a preliminary analysis, suggesting that the elements of the crime likely could be proven and indicating some of the key political and military leaders who might be implicated.

The real challenge has been determining where this case could be prosecuted, a topic taken up in the next three chapters. Those chapters explore: what had been a proposal for an ad hoc international criminal tribunal to be established through the United Nations to prosecute the crime of aggression in the situation of Ukraine (Chap. 5); the counter-proposal of using a hybrid Ukrainian chamber for the prosecutions (Chap. 6); and what has been ultimately agreed on, the Special Tribunal, to be established (if sufficient funding and support is obtained) pursuant to an agreement between the Council of Europe and Ukraine (Chap. 7). For anyone who believes in the importance of international law and the preservation of world peace and security, it would be incomprehensible to leave such a clear crime of aggression unredressed. The author fully concurs with Gleb Bogush that "[i]dentifying and prosecuting the individuals responsible for the most egregious aggression committed since World War II is essential for delivering justice to millions of victims and is a necessary precondition for any sustainable peace and reconciliation once the conflict comes to an end".[404]

References

Advisory Committee on Public International Law (2022) Challenges in Prosecuting the Crime of Aggression: Jurisdiction and Immunities, Advisory Report No. 40

---

[403] Pancevski 2024.

[404] Bogush 2023a, p. 111.

Aggarwal M (2024) North Korean Soldiers Kill Themselves to Avoid Capture in Ukraine, U.S. Says. NBC News. https://www.nbcnews.com/news/world/north-korean-soldiers-suicide-avoid-capture-ukraine-russia-rcna185625. Accessed 28 May 2025

AlJazeera (2023) Russia's Wagner Fighters Suffer 30,000 Casualties in Ukraine: US. https://www.aljazeera.com/news/2023/2/18/russias-wagner-forces-suffered-30000-casualties-in-ukraine-us. Accessed 28 May 2025

Alsford L, Kristeva G (2025) Nuclear expert issues Chernobyl update after it emerges fires are still burning. MSN. https://www.msn.com/en-us/news/world/nuclear-expert-issues-chernobyl-update-after-it-emerges-fires-are-still-burning/ar-AA1z9gBi?ocid=msedgntp&pc=U531&cvid=23073563ced647e3dd86ed3704f89ca1&ei=18. Accessed 28 May 2025

Amann M, Gebauer M, Schmid F (2022) Possible Evidence of Russian Atrocities: German Intelligence Intercepts Radio Traffic Discussing the Murder of Civilians in Bucha. Der Spiegel. https://www.spiegel.de/international/germany/possible-evidence-of-russian-atrocities-german-intelligence-intercepts-radio-traffic-discussing-the-murder-of-civilians-in-bucha-a-0a191c96-634f-4d07-8c5c-c4a772315b0d. Accessed 28 May 2025

Apt C (2023) Russia's Eliminationist Rhetoric against Ukraine: A Collection. Just Security. https://www.justsecurity.org/81789/russias-eliminationist-rhetoric-against-ukraine-a-collection/. Accessed 28 May 2025

Armed Conflict Location & Event Data Project (ACLED) (2023) War in Ukraine One Year On, Nowhere Safe

Associated Press (2023) Russia Officially Confirms Wagner Leader Yevgeny Prigozhin Died in Plane Crash. PBS News. https://www.pbs.org/newshour/world/russia-officially-confirms-wagner-leader-yevgeny-prigozhin-died-in-plane-crash. Accessed 28 May 2025

Bachega H (2022) Russia's Attack on Mariupol Theatre a Clear War Crime, Amnesty Says. BBC News. https://www.bbc.com/news/world-europe-61979873. Accessed 28 May 2025

Balachuk I (2024) Belarusian Leader Claims Putin Did Not Ask Him for Authorisation to Attack Ukraine from Belarus. Ukrainska Pravda. https://www.pravda.com.ua/eng/news/2024/10/25/7481302/. Accessed 28 May 2025

Basmat D (2025) Over 45,000 Ukrainian Soldiers Killed since Start of War, Zelensky Says. The Kyiv Independent. https://kyivindependent.com/over-45-000-ukrainian-soldiers-killed-since-start-of-war-zelensky-says/. Accessed 28 May 2025

BBC (2017) US-Russia Sanctions: How Did We Get Here? https://www.bbc.com/news/world-us-canada-40720673. Accessed 28 May 2025

BBC (2023a) Ukraine War: Putin Confirms First Nuclear Weapons Moved to Belarus. https://www.bbc.com/news/world-europe-65932700. Accessed 28 May 2025

BBC (2023b) Why Is Belarus Admitting Wagner Leader and Backing Russia against Ukraine? https://www.bbc.com/news/world-65964623. Accessed 28 May 2025

Beecroft N (2022) Evaluating the International Support to Ukrainian Cyber Defense. Carnegie Endowment for International Peace https://carnegieendowment.org/2022/11/03/evaluating-international-support-to-ukrainian-cyber-defense-pub-88322. Accessed 28 May 2025

Bloomberg News (2022) Transcript: Vladimir Putin's Televised Address on Ukraine. https://www.bloomberg.com/news/articles/2022-02-24/full-transcript-vladimir-putin-s-televised-address-to-russia-on-ukraine-feb-24. Accessed 4 November 2025

Bogush G (2023a) "Committed by Men": Individual Criminal Responsibility for Aggression Against Ukraine Polish Review of International & European Law 12: 93–114

Bogush G (2023b) Taking Russia to Court: Prosecution of International Crimes. Russian Analytical Digest 307: 2–8 https://doi.org/10.3929/ethz-b-000648037. Accessed 27 June 2025

Bogush G (2025) Putin's Memory Policies in the Context of Military Aggression in Ukraine. In: Gliszczynska-Grabias A, Nußberger A, Mälksoo M, Belavusau U (eds) (2025) The Politics of Memory Laws: Russia, Ukraine and Beyond. Bloomsbury Academic, London

Bostock B (2022) The Kremlin Ordered 400 Russian Mercenaries in Kyiv to Hunt and Kill Ukraine's President, Report Says. Business Insider. https://www.businessinsider.com/russia-orders-mercenaries-assassinate-ukraine-president-report-2022-2. Accessed 28 May 2025

Bowen A (2022) Russia's War in Ukraine: Military and Intelligence Aspects. R47069, Congressional Research Service. https://crsreports.congress.gov/product/pdf/R/R47068/2. Accessed 28 May 2025

Bowen A, Weed M (2023) War Crimes in Ukraine. R47762, Congressional Research Service. https://crsreports.congress.gov/product/pdf/R/R47762. Accessed 28 May 2025

Breteau P (2024) War in Ukraine: In November 2024, Russia Made Its Largest Gains in Two Years and a Half. Le Monde

Britannica (nd-a) Crimea. https://www.britannica.com/place/Crimea

Britannica (nd-b) Federal Security Service. https://www.britannica.com/topic/Federal-Security-Service. Accessed 28 May 2025

Burt T (2022) The Hybrid War in Ukraine. Microsoft on the Issues. https://blogs.microsoft.com/on-the-issues/2022/04/27/hybrid-war-ukraine-russia-cyberattacks/. Accessed 28 May 2025

Clark R (2016) Individual Conduct. In: Kreß C, Barriga S (eds) (2016) The Crime of Aggression: A Commentary. Cambridge University Press, Cambridge

Coakley A (2022) Lukashenko Is Letting Putin Use Belarus to Attack Ukraine. Foreign Policy. https://foreignpolicy.com/2022/02/24/russia-ukraine-war-belarus-chernobyl-lukashenko/. Accessed 28 May 2025

Conflict Observatory Report (2023) Russia's Systematic Program for the Re-education and Adoption of Ukraine's Children. https://unpublished.ca/opinion/conflict-observatory-report-russia%E2%80%99s-systematic-program-of-re-education-and-adoption-of. Accessed 28 May 2025

Cordon G (2024) West Fears Vladimir Putin Wants to Install Puppet Regime in Ukraine. The Independent. https://www.independent.co.uk/news/uk/vladimir-putin-kyiv-ukraine-belarus-russia-b2022409.html. Accessed 27 June 2025

Corten O, Koutroulis V (2022) In-Depth Analysis: Tribunal for the Crime of Aggression Against Ukraine: A Legal Assessment. European Parliament. https://www.europarl.europa.eu/RegData/etudes/IDAN/2022/702574/EXPO_IDA(2022)702574_EN.pdf. Accessed 15 May 2025

Corten O, Koutroulis V (2023) The 2022 Russian Intervention in Ukraine: What Is Its Impact on the Interpretation of *Jus Contra Bellum*? Leiden Journal of International Law 36: 997–1022

Crawford J, Cruvellier T (2022) Ukraine Responds to Warfare with "Lawfare". Justice-Info.net https://www.justiceinfo.net/en/89266-ukraine-responds-to-warfare-with-lawfare.html. Accessed 28 May 2025

Database of Free Russia Forum (nd) Putin's List – Patrushev Nikolai. https://www.spisok-putina.org/en/personas/patrushev-2/. Accessed 28 May 2025

De Luce D, Williams A (2022) Russia Agreed to Lift Blockade on Ukraine Grain Due to Growing Global Condemnation, Senior U.S. Diplomat Says. NBC News. https://www.nbcnews.com/politics/national-security/russia-agreed-lift-blockade-ukraine-grain-due-growing-global-condemnat-rcna37624. Accessed 28 May 2025

De Wet E (2020) Military Assistance on Request and the Use of Force. Oxford University Press, Oxford

Earle G (2024) U.S. Fears Putin and Kim Jong-Un Are Planning a Military October Surprise to Spark Chaos Before the Election . . . as Russia Supplies North Korea with Nuclear Technology. Daily Mail, https://www.dailymail.co.uk/news/article-13456507/U-S-fears-Putin-Kim-Jong-planning-military-October-surprise-spark-chaos-election-Russia-supplies-North-Korea-nuclear-weapons.html. Accessed 28 May 2025

Economist Intelligence Unit (2022) Reaction to NATO Troop Deployment in Eastern Europe Diverge

Eichensehr K (2022) International Institutions Mobilize to Impose Accountability on Russia and Individual Perpetrators of War Crimes and Other Abuses. American Journal of International Law 116: 631–642

Euractiv/Reuters (2024) Trump's Plan for Ukraine: Territorial Concessions but NATO Off the Table. https://www.euractiv.com/section/global-europe/news/trumps-plan-for-ukraine-territorial-concessions-but-nato-off-the-table/. Accessed 28 May 2025

European Union, Press Release (2023) Ukraine: International Centre for the Prosecution of Russia's Crime of Aggression Against Ukraine Starts Operations Today

Faulconbridge G (2018) Factbox-What Is Russia's GRU Military Intelligence Agency? Reuters. https://www.reuters.com/article/us-britain-russia-gru-factbox/what-is-russias-gru-military-intelligence-agency-idUSKCN1MF1VK/. Accessed 28 May 2025

Faulconbridge G (2025) How Much Territory Does Russia Control in Ukraine? Reuters. https://www.reuters.com/world/americas/how-much-territory-does-russia-control-ukraine-2025-08-14/. Accessed 12 October 2025

Foreign Intelligence Service of the Russian Federation (nd) Director of the Foreign Intelligence Service of the Russian Federation. http://www.svr.gov.ru/svr_today/director.htm. Accessed 28 May 2025

Freedman L (2022) Command: The Politics of Military Operations from Korea to Ukraine. Oxford University Press, Oxford

Fripp E (2025) "Passportisation": ECtHR Finds Imposition of Russian Citizenship in Crimea a Breach of Article 8 ECHR. EJIL:*Talk!* https://www.ejiltalk.org/passportisation-ecthr-finds-imposition-of-russian-citizenship-in-crimea-a-breach-of-article-8-echr/. Accessed 28 May 2025

Gady F-S, Kofman M (2023) Ukraine's Strategy of Attrition, Survival: Global Politics and Strategy. IISS. https://www.iiss.org/online-analysis/survival-online/2023/04/ukraine-strategy-of-attrition/. Accessed 28 May 2025

Galeotti M (2019a) Armies of Russia's War in Ukraine. Osprey Publishing, Oxford

Galeotti M (2019b) Russia's Security Council: Where Policy, Personality, and Process Meet. George C. Marshall European Center for Security Studies. No. 041. https://www.marshallcenter.org/en/publications/security-insights/russias-security-council-where-policy-personality-and-process-meet-0. Accessed 28 May 2025

Gall C, Chubko O (2025) Overcoming Stigma, Women Unmask Rape in Ukraine War. NY Times

Gardner F (2023) What Are Cluster Bombs and Why Is US Sending Them to Ukraine? BBC. https://www.bbc.com/news/world-europe-66133527 Accessed 28 May 2025

Gill J (2022) DoD Must "Think Very Differently" About Armed Conflict, Cyber in the Light of Ukraine War: Official. Real Clear Defense. https://www.realcleardefense.com/2022/11/17/dod_must_think_very_differently_about_cyber_in_armed_conflict_865423.html. Accessed 28 May 2025

Global Accountability Network (2024) Holding Heads of State Accountable: The Case of President Lukashenko's Aiding and Abetting President Putin's Crime of Aggression against Ukraine. https://www.globalaccountabilitynetwork.org/_files/ugd/77bd37_a1d528f2db244637acca31818a7f530c.pdf. Accessed 4 November 2025

Global Conflict Tracker (nd) War in Ukraine. The Center for Preventive Action. https://www.cfr.org/global-conflict-tracker/conflict/conflict-ukraine#:~:text=Since%20January%202022%2C%20Ukraine%20has,6.8%20million%20have%20fled%20Ukraine. Accessed 28 May 2025

Goodman R, Hamilton R (2022) Model Indictment for Crime of Aggression against Ukraine: *Prosecutor v. President Vladimir Putin.* Just Security. https://www.justsecurity.org/80669/model-indictment-of-the-crime-of-aggression-against-ukraine-vladimir-putin/. Accessed 29 June 2025

Green J A (2014) The Annexation of Crimea: Russia, Passportisation and the Protection of National Revisited. Journal on the Use of Force and International Law 1: 3–10

Green J, Henderson C, Ruys T (2022) Russia's Attack on Ukraine and the *Jus ad Bellum*. Journal on the Use of Force and International Law 9: 4–30

Hammes T X (2023) Game-Changers: Implications of the Russo-Ukraine War for the Future of Ground Warfare. Atlantic Council

Hansler J (2025) US Joins Russia to Vote Against UN Resolution Condemning Russia's War Against Ukraine. CNN. https://www.cnn.com/2025/02/24/politics/us-joins-russia-ukraine-un-vote/index.html. Accessed 28 May 2025

Harding T (2022) Russian General Killed and Clutch of Spy Chiefs Arrested. The National News. https://www.thenationalnews.com/world/uk-news/2022/03/11/russian-general-killed-and-clutch-of-spy-chiefs-arrested/. Accessed 28 May 2025

Haworth J, Martinez L, Chile P, Winsor M, Margolin J (2023) Bomb Likely The Cause of Explosion that Downed Wagner Leader Prigozhin's Plane, US Officials Say. ABC News. https://abcnews.go.com/International/prigozhins-body-medical-examiners-office-kremlin-remains-silent/story?id=102525074. Accessed 28 May 2025

Heinsch R (2010 The Crime of Aggression after Kampala: Success or Burden for the Future. Göttingen Journal of International Law 2: 713–743

Heller K J (2007) Retreat from Nuremberg: The Leadership Requirement in the Crime of Aggression. European Journal of International Law 18: 477–497

Herszenhorn D M (2022) US Warns War Could Be "Imminent" in Ukraine. Politico. https://www.politico.eu/article/ukraine-russia-european-union-diplomats-leave/. Accessed 28 May 2025

Hinnant L, Stepanenko V, El Deeb S, Tilna E (2022) Russia Scrub's Mariupol's Ukraine Identity, Builds on Death. AP. https://apnews.com/article/russia-ukraine-war-erasing-mariupol-499dceae43ed77f2ebfe750ea99b9ad9. Accessed 20 May 2025

Human Rights Council (2022) Situation of Human Rights in Ukraine Stemming from the Russian Aggression. UN Doc. A/HRC/RES/49/1

Human Rights Watch (2023) Ukraine: Perils of War for Children in Institutions. "We Must Provide a Family, Not Rebuild Orphanages": The Consequences of Russia's Invasion of Ukraine for Children in Ukrainian Residential Institutions | HRW. Accessed 3 November 2025

Independent International Commission of Inquiry on Ukraine (2023) Report, UN Doc. A/HRC/52/62

Independent International Commission of Inquiry on Ukraine (2024) Report, UN Doc. A/79/549

International Criminal Court (nd-a) Elements of Crimes, Article 8*bis*, Crime of Aggression. https://www.icc-cpi.int/sites/default/files/NR/rdonlyres/336923D8-A6AD-40EC-AD7B-45BF9DE73D56/0/ElementsOfCrimesEng.pdf. Accessed 28 May 2025

International Criminal Court (nd-b) Ukraine, Situation in Ukraine. https://www.icc-cpi.int/situations/ukraine. Accessed 28 May 2025

International Criminal Court, Assembly of States Parties (2010) Review Conference, The Crime of Aggression, ICC Doc. RC/Res.6

International Criminal Court, Office of the Prosecutor (2016) OTP Policy Paper on Case Selection and Prioritization

International Criminal Court, Office of the Prosecutor (2025) Draft Policy on Cyber-Enabled Crimes Under the Rome Statute. https://www.icc-cpi.int/sites/default/files/2025-03/250306-OTP-Policy-on-Cyber-Enabled-Crimes-for-public-consultation.pdf. Accessed 28 May 2025

International Criminal Court, Press Release (2010) Review Conference of the Rome Statute Opened in Kampala. https://www.icc-cpi.int/news/review-conference-rome-statute-opened-kampala. Accessed 28 May 2025

International Criminal Court, Press Release (2023) Situation in Ukraine: ICC Judges Issue Arrest Warrants Against Vladimir Vladimirovich Putin and Maria Alekseyevna Lvova-Belova

International Criminal Court, Press Release (2024a) Situation in Ukraine: ICC Judges Issue Arrest Warrants Against Sergei Ivanovich Kobylash and Viktor Nikolayevich Sokolov

International Criminal Court, Press Release (2024b) Situation in Ukraine: ICC Judges Issue Arrest Warrants Against Sergei Kuzhugetovich Shoigu and Valery Vasilyevich Gerasimov

International Criminal Court, Press Release (2025) ICC Welcomes Ukraine as a New State Party. https://www.icc-cpi.int/news/icc-welcomes-ukraine-new-state-party. Accessed 28 May 2025

International Law Commission (2001) Draft Articles on the Responsibility of States for Internationally Wrongful Acts, with Commentaries (adopted), UN Doc. A/56/10

Jakubowski A (2023) Safeguarding Ukraine's Cultural Heritage in War: Identifying the Obligations of Non-Parties to the Conflict, with Special Focus on the European Union. Polish Review of International and European Law 12: 141–165

Jones S, McCabe R (2025) Russia's Battlefield Woes in Ukraine. Center for Strategic and International Studies (CSIS). https://www.csis.org/analysis/russias-battlefield-woes-ukraine. Accessed 27 October 2025

Kingsley T (2022) New Satellite Images Show Russian Military Activity as "130,000" Troops Now On Ukraine Border. The Independent. www.independent.co.uk/news/world/europe/russia-ukraine-satellite-images-b2015354.html. Accessed 28 May 2025

Kirby P (2022a) Ukraine Conflict: Who's in Putin's Inner Circle and Running the War? BBC. https://www.bbc.com/news/world-europe-60573261. Accessed 28 May 2025

Kirby P (2022b) Russia to Formally Annex Four More Areas of Ukraine. BBC. https://www.bbc.com/news/world-europe-63072113. Accessed 28 May 2025

Kofman M, Migacheva K, Nichiporuk B, Radin A, Tkacheva O, Oberholtzer J (2017) Lessons from Russia's Operations in Crimea and Eastern Ukraine. RAND Corporation

Kottasová I (2024) Ukraine Claims Control of Hundreds of Square Miles of Russian Territory as Operation Forces Tens of Thousands to Flee. CNN. https://edition.cnn.com/2024/08/12/europe/russia-ukraine-incursion-belgorod-intl/index.html. Accessed 28 May 2025

Kremlin (nd) Security Council Structure – Members. http://www.en.kremlin.ru/structure/security-council/members. Accessed 28 May 2025

Kreß C (2009) Time for Decision: Some Thoughts on the Immediate Future of the Crime of Aggression: A Reply to Andreas Paulus. European Journal of International Law 20: 1129–1146

Kreß C (2016) Introduction. In: Kreß C, Barriga S (eds) (2016) The Crime of Aggression: A Commentary. Cambridge University Press, Cambridge

Kreβ C (2022) The Ukraine War and the Prohibition of the Use of Force in International Law. Occasional Paper Series No. 12

Kreß C, Barriga S (eds) (2016) The Crime of Aggression: A Commentary. Cambridge University Press, Cambridge

Kudriavtseva N (2016) Kennan Cable No. 15: Ukraine: What's a Language for? Wilson Center. https://www.wilsoncenter.org/publication/kennan-cable-no15-ukraine-whats-language-for. Accessed 28 May 2025

Labuda P (2024) Countering Imperialism in International Law: Examining the Special Tribunal for Aggression against Ukraine through a Post-Colonial Eastern European Lens. Yale Journal of International Law 49: 271–310

Langton J (2022) Meet Russia's *Siloviki* – Putin's Inner Circle. The National News. https://www.thenationalnews.com/world/europe/2022/03/15/meet-russias-siloviki-putins-inner-circle/. Accessed 28 May 2025

Litovkin V (2014) The Importance of Sebastopol for Russia. Russia Beyond, Rossiyskaya Gazeta. https://www.rbth.com/world/2014/03/04/the_importance_of_sevastapol_for_russia_33479. Accessed 28 May 2025

Lopez J, Worthington B (2022) What's the Status of Ukraine's Case Against Russia at the ICJ? Lawfare. https://www.lawfaremedia.org/article/whats-status-ukraines-case-against-russia-icj#:~:text=In%20its%20initiation%20of%20formal%20proceedings%20against%20Russia,an%20insufficient%20rationale%20for%20the%20use%20of%20force. Accessed 28 May 2025

Lubold G, Youssef N A, Cullison A (2022) Russia Recruiting Syrians for Urban Combat in Ukraine, U.S. Officials Say. Wall St. Journal. https://www.wsj.com/articles/russia-recruiting-syrians-for-urban-combat-in-ukraine-u-s-officials-say-11646606234?msockid=0671e85760f5627530dce108617263c3. Accessed 28 May 2025

Luna N, Vredenbregt L, Pereira I (2023) What Is The Wagner Group? The "Brutal" Russian Military Unit in Ukraine. ABC News. https://abcnews.go.com/International/International/wagner-group-brutal-russian-military-group-fighting-ukraine/story?id=96665326. Accessed 28 May 2025

Maddocks J (2023) Putin Admits to Funding The Wagner Group: Implications for Russia's State Responsibility. Lieber Institute. https://lieber.westpoint.edu/putin-admits-funding-wagner-group-implications-russias-state-responsibility/. Accessed 28 May 2025

Marten K (2022) Testimony before the Committee on Oversight and Reform Subcommittee on National Security, United States House of Representatives, Russia's Use of the Wagner Group: Definitions, Strategic Objectives, and Accountability. https://www.congress.gov/117/meeting/house/115113/witnesses/HHRG-117-GO06-Wstate-MartenK-20220921.pdf. Accessed 28 May 2025

Masol S (2024) Are You a Leader? Ukraine's Supreme Court Clarifies the Definition of the Crime of Aggression. EJIL:*Talk!* https://www.ejiltalk.org/are-you-a-leader-ukraines-supreme-court-clarifies-the-definition-of-the-crime-of-aggression/. Accessed 28 May 2025

Maynard J L (2022) Is Genocide Occurring in Ukraine? An Expert Explainer on Indicators and Assessments. Just Security. https://www.justsecurity.org/80998/is-genocide-occurring-in-ukraine-an-expert-explainer-on-indicators-and-assessments/. Accessed 28 May 2025

McDougall C (2021) The Crime of Aggression under the Rome Statute of the International Criminal Court, 2nd edn. Cambridge University Press, The Hague

McDougall C (2023) The Imperative of Prosecuting Crimes of Aggression Committed Against Ukraine. Journal of Conflict and Security Law 28: 203–230

McMillan R, Volz D (2022) Ukraine Hacks Signal Broad Risks of Cyberwar Even as Limited Scope Confounds Experts. Wall St. Journal. https://www.wsj.com/articles/ukraine-hacks-signal-broad-risks-of-cyberwar-even-as-limited-scope-confounds-experts-11642683723. Accessed 28 May 2025

Meduza (nd) В Буче открыли инсталляцию в память о жителях, убитых во время российской оккупации. Фотография. https://meduza.io/short/2023/07/02/v-buche-otkryli-installyatsiyu-v-pamyat-o-zhitelyah-ubityh-vo-vremya-rossiyskoy-okkupatsii-fotografiya. Accessed 28 May 2025

Merkx G W (2023) Russia's War in Ukraine: Two Decisive Factors. Journal of Advanced Military Studies. 14: 13–33

Merriam-Webster Dictionary (nd) s.v. "oblast". https://www.merriam-webster.com/dictionary/oblast. Accessed 28 May 2025

Ministry of Defense of the Russian Federation (nd) https://eng.mil.ru/en/management/leader.htm?id=10330475@SD_Employee. Accessed 28 May 2025

Mirovalev M (2025) Is Russia Running Out of Weapons and Manpower for its War in Ukraine? AlJazeera. https://www.aljazeera.com/news/2025/2/14/is-russia-running-out-of-weapons-and-manpower-for-its-war-in-ukraine. Accessed 27 June 2025

Muzyka K (2021) The Belarusian Armed Forces: Structures, Capabilities, and Defense Relations with Russia. International Center for Defense and Security (ICDS)

Najibullah F, RFE/RL's Kyrgyz Service (2024) Russia Pressures Central Asian Prisoners to Fight in Ukraine as "Expendable Force". https://www.rferl.org/a/russia-central-asian-prisoners-war-ukraine-expendable/33162689.html. Accessed 4 November 2025

NATO Parliamentary Assembly (2025) Bureau Statement on the Third Anniversary of Russia's Full-Scale Invasion of Ukraine. https://www.nato-pa.int/news/bureau-statement-third-anniversary-russias-full-scale-invasion-ukraine. Accessed 28 May 2025

Nazarenko V (2025) South Korean Intelligence Confirms North Korean Troops Withdrawal from Kursk Region. MSN. https://www.msn.com/en-us/news/world/south-korean-intelligence-confirms-north-korean-troops-withdrawal-from-kursk-region/ar-AA1ynK28?ocid=msedgntp&pc=U531&cvid=e7bf6309c1054614a883c64d2f2a0f48&ei=13. Accessed 28 May 2025

Netherlands Helsinki Committee (2024) Towards Justice for Victims: A Case of Deportation and Forcible Transfer Against the Russian Authorities. https://www.nhc.nl/assets/uploads/2024/09/Towards-Justice-for-Victims_ENG.pdf. Accessed 27 June 2025

Office of the Prosecutor General of Ukraine (nd) https://gp.gov.ua/. Accessed 28 May 2025

OHCHR (2023b) Report on the Human Rights Situation in Ukraine: August 1, 2022–January 31, 2023, March 24, 2023

OHCHR, Press Release (2024) Ukraine: Torture by Russian Authorities Amounts to Crimes Against Humanity, Says UN Commission of Inquiry. https://www.statista.cohtthttps//www.ohchr.org/en/press-releases/2024/10/ukraine-torture-russian-authorities-amounts-crimes-against-humanity-says-0. Accessed 28 May 2025

Olearchyk R (2023) Ukraine's Civilian Death Toll Mounts as Russia Strikes Kherson. FT https://www.ft.com/content/a6910b36-8122-4803-b7bc-40e477c5d5b0. Accessed 28 May 2025

Open Society Justice Initiative (2022) Model Indictment for the Crime of Aggression Committed Against Ukraine. https://www.justiceinitiative.org/publications/model-indictment-for-the-crime-of-aggression-committed-against-ukraine. Accessed 28 May 2025

Organization for Security and Cooperation in Europe (2024) 31st Meeting of the OSCE Ministerial Council I Joint Statement on Malicious Activities Conducted by the Russian Federation in the OSCE Area. https://osce.usmission.gov/31st-meeting-of-the-osce-ministerial-council-i-joint-statement-on-malicious-activities-conducted-by-the-russian-federation-in-the-osce-area/. Accessed 28 May 2025

OSCE (2022) Report on Violations of International Humanitarian and Human Rights Law, War Crimes, and Crimes Against Humanity, Committed in Ukraine Since 24 February 2022

Osinga F (2024) Putin's War, a European Tragedy: Why Russia's War Failed and What It Means for NATO. In: Rothman M et al. (eds) (2024) Reflections on the Russia-Ukraine War. Leiden University Press, Leiden

Ostrovsky S (2023) From Prison to the Frontlines: Thousands of Russian Convicts Sent to Fight in Ukraine. PBS NewsHour

Ostrovsky S, Putin K, Kopelev S (2025) Ukraine Says Russia is Recruiting African Mercenaries to Fight in Its War. PBS NewsHour. https://www.pbs.org/newshour/show/ukraine-says-russia-is-recruiting-african-mercenaries-to-fight-in-its-war. Accessed 22 November 2025

Pamuk H (2025) Citing Cuban Fighters in Ukraine, U.S. Urges Allies to Shun Havana at U.N. The Japan Times, https://www.japantimes.co.jp/news/2025/10/06/world/politics/cuban-fighters-ukraine-us-un/. Accessed 10 October 2025.

Pannier B (2024) Central Asia in Focus: Russia Continues Sending Central Asians to Ukraine. Radio Free Europe/Radio Liberty. https://about.rferl.org/article/central-asia-in-focus-russia-continues-sending-central-asians-to-ukraine/. Accessed 4 November 2025

Pancevski B (2024) One Million Are Now Dead or Injured in the Russia-Ukraine War. Wall St. Journal. https://www.wsj.com/world/one-million-are-now-dead-or-injured-in-the-russia-ukraine-war-b09d04e5?msockid=0671e85760f5627530dce108617263c3. Accessed 28 May 2025

Pattison J (2024) Ukraine, Wagner, and Russia's Convict-Soldiers. Ethics & International Affairs 38: 17–30

Permanent Mission of Liechtenstein to the United Nations (2021) The Council of Advisers' Report on the Application of the Rome Statute of the International Criminal Court to Cyberwarfare. The Council of Advisers' Report on the Application of the Rome Statute of the International Criminal Court to Cyberwarfare.docx (crimeofaggression.info). Accessed 28 May 2025

Permanent Representative of the Russian Federation (2022) Letter Dated 24 February 2022 from the Permanent Representative of the Russian Federation to the United Nations Addressed to the Secretary-General (2022) UN Doc. S/2022/154

Physicians for Human Rights et al. (2023) Destruction and Devastation: One Year of Russia's Assault on Ukraine's Health Care System

Physicians for Human Rights, Truth Hounds (2024) Health Care in the Dark: The Impacts of Russian Attacks on Energy in Ukraine. https://reliefweb.int/report/ukraine/health-care-dark-impacts-russian-attacks-energy-ukraine-enuk. Accessed 4 November 2025

Pineda M (2025) The Strategic Importance of Crimea. Profolus. https://www.profolus.com/topics/the-strategic-importance-of-crimea/. Accessed 27 June 2025

Piotrowski M A (2024) Ukraine Focuses on "Active Defence" Strategy. The Polish Institute of International Affairs, Bulletin No. 30

Pitchford S (2022) Russian Recognition of Donetsk and Luhansk: Legal Analysis. Human Rights Pulse. https://www.humanrightspulse.com/mastercontentblog/russian-recognition-of-donetsk-and-luhansk-legal-analysis. Accessed 28 May 2025

Pokharel S, Chance M, Melwani M, Khanal N (2024) Russia Has Recruited as Many as 15,000 Nepalis to Fight Its War. Many Returned Traumatized, Some Never Came Back. CNN. https://www.cnn.com/2024/02/10/asia/nepal-fighters-russia-ukraine-families-intl-cmd/index.html. Accessed 28 May 2025

Proekt Media (nd) Who Is Fighting in Ukraine. https://war-proekt.media/base/voiska/. Accessed 28 May 2025

Psaropoulos J T (2023) As Wagner Troops Marched on Moscow, Ukraine Made Further Gains. AlJazeera. https://www.aljazeera.com/news/2023/6/28/as-wagner-troops-marched-on-moscow-ukraine-made-further-gains. Accessed 28 May 2025

Putin V (2021) On the Historical Unity of Russians and Ukrainians. http://en.kremlin.ru/events/president/news/66181. Accessed 28 May 2025

Putin V (2022) Russian President Putin Statement on Ukraine. C-SPAN

R. Politik (2022) Bulletin No. 5 (91) – Analytical Report (on file with Gleb Bogush)

Radio Free Europe/Radio Liberty (2023) Bakhmut from the Air Reveals Devastation as Russia Pounds Ukrainian City into Dust

Razek H, Barabanov I (2022) War in Ukraine: How Russia is Recruiting Mercenaries. BBC News. https://www.bbc.com/news/world-europe-60711211. Accessed 28 May 2025

Reisinger Coracini A, Wrange P (2016) The Specificity of the Crime of Aggression. In: Kreß C, Barriga S (eds) (2016) The Crime of Aggression: A Commentary. Cambridge University Press, Cambridge

Reuters (2022) Belarus Referendum Approves Proposal to Renounce Non-Nuclear Status - Agencies. https://www.reuters.com/world/europe/launchpad-russias-assault-ukraine-belarus-holds-referendum-renounce%20-non-nuclear-2022-02-27/. Accessed 28 May 2025

Reuters (2023) IAEA "Very Concerned" Over Nuclear Plant's Safety as Ukraine Counterattacks—Grossi

Riabchuk M (2012) Playing with Ambiguities: Ukraine's Language Law. Open Democracy. https://www.opendemocracy.net/en/odr/playing-with-ambiguities-ukraines-language-law/. Accessed 28 May 2025

Roblin S (2022) Alleged Captured Documents Imply Ukraine Invasion Planned in January. Forbes. https://www.forbes.com/sites/sebastienroblin/2022/03/03/alleged-captured-documents-imply-ukraine-invasion-planned-in-january/. Accessed 28 May 2025

Rust M et al. (2022) Photos Chronicle the Devastation of Mariupol. Wall St. Journal. https://www.wsj.com/articles/photos-chronicle-the-devastation-of-mariupol-11648373400. Accessed 28 May 2025

Samuel J (2025) The Russian Constitutional Path to the Annexation of Crimea. Jurist News. https://www.jurist.org/commentary/2014/05/jason-samuel-russia-crimea/. Accessed 28 May 2025

Sauer P (2025) One Million and Counting: Russia's Casualties Hit Milestone in Ukraine War. The Guardian. https://www.theguardian.com/world/ng-interactive/2025/jun/22/one-million-and-counting-russian-casualties-hit-milestone-in-ukraine-war. Accessed 4 November 2025

Schmitt E (2022) More Russian Mercenaries Deploying to Ukraine to Take on Greater Role in War. NY Times. https://web.archive.org/web/20220327112928/https:/www.yahoo.com/news/more-russian-mercenaries-deploying-ukraine-143421204.html. Accessed 28 May 2025

Schmitt M (ed) (2017) Tallinn Manual 2.0 on the International Law Applicable to Cyber Operations, 2nd edn. Cambridge University Press, Cambridge

Schreck C (2019) From "Not Us" to "Why Hide It?": How Russia Denied Its Crimea Invasion, Then Admitted It. Radio Free Europe/ Radio Liberty. https://www.rferl.org/a/from-not-us-to-why-hide-it-how-russia-denied-its-crimea-invasion-then-admitted-it/29791806.html. Accessed 28 May 2025

Security Council of the Russian Federation (nd-a) Patrushev Nikolai Platonovich. http://www.scrf.gov.ru/about/leadership/person8/. Accessed 28 May 2025

Security Council of the Russian Federation (nd-b) Members of the Security Council of the Russian Federation Since Its Inception. http://www.scrf.gov.ru/about/all_time/. Accessed 28 May 2025

Seibt S (2022) Shoigu and Gerasimov: Masters of Putin's Wars. France 24. https://www.france24.com/en/europe/20220304-shoigu-and-gerasimov-masters-of-putin-s-wars Accessed 28 May 2025

Sky News (2022) Ukraine War: Captured Russian Documents Reveal Moscow's 10-Day Plan to Take over the Country and Kill Its Leaders. https://news.sky.com/story/ukraine-war-captured-russian-documents-reveal-moscows-10-day-plan-to-take-over-the-country-and-kill-its-leaders-12759836 Accessed 28 May 2025

Snyder T (2022) Russia's Genocide Handbook: The Evidence of Atrocity and of Intent Mounts. Mgrublian Center for Human Rights. https://human-rights.cmc.edu/2022/04/14/russias-genocide-handbook/. Accessed 28 May 2025

Sparks J (2016) Revealed: Russia's "Secret Syria Mercenaries". Sky News. https://news.sky.com/story/revealed-russias-secret-syria-mercenaries-10529248. Accessed 28 May 2025

Spencer K (2024) Foreign Troops Help Putin Avoid Pitfalls of another Russian Mobilization. Atlantic Council

Special Working Group on the Crime of Aggression (2008) Report of the Special Working Group on the Crime of Aggression, Annex II, ICC-ASP/6/20/Add.1

Stanovaya T (2022) 3 Things the World Should Know about Putin. Foreign Policy. https://foreignpolicy.com/2022/01/27/putin-russia-ukraine-crisis-invasion/. Accessed 28 May 2025

Statista (nd-a) Number of Civilian Casualties in Ukraine During Russia's Invasion Verified by OHCHR from February 24, 2022 to December 31, 2024. https://www.statista.com/statistics/1293492/ukraine-war-casualties/. Accessed 28 May 2025

Statista (nd-b) Estimated Number of Refugees from Ukraine Recorded in Europe and Asia Since February 2022 as of July 2024, by Selected Country. https://www.statista.com/statistics/1312584/ukrainian-refugees-by-country/. Accessed 28 May 2025

Statista (nd-c) Total Bilateral Aid Allocations to Ukraine between January 24, 2022 and June 30, 2024, by Donor and Type. https://www.statista.com/statistics/1303432/total-bilateral-aid-to-ukraine/. Accessed 28 May 2025

Sutyagin I (2015) Briefing Paper: Russian Forces in Ukraine. Royal United Services Institute (RUSI). https://web.archive.org/web/20210111112810/https://rusi.org/sites/default/files/201503_bp_russian_forces_in_ukraine.pdf. Accessed 28 May 2025

The Guardian (2024) Ukraine War Briefing: North Korea Ratifies Landmark Mutual Defence Pact with Russia. https://www.theguardian.com/world/2024/nov/12/ukraine-war-briefing-north-korea-ratifies-landmark-mutual-defence-pact-with-russia. Accessed 14 October 2025

Tong-Hyung K, Ghosal A (2024) Russia and North Korea Sign Partnership Deal That Appears to Be the Strongest since the Cold War. AP. https://apnews.com/article/vladimir-putin-kim-jong-un-russia-north-korea-summit-ukraine-a6b8d2c12de7ee2ab6716d4747c9850e. Accessed 28 May 2025

Trahan J (2020) Existing Legal Limits to Security Council Veto Power in the Face of Atrocity Crimes. Cambridge University Press, Cambridge

Trahan J (2024) Scenario 32: Crime of Aggression. Cooperative Cyber Defence Centre of Excellence, 2024. https://cyberlaw.ccdcoe.org/wiki/Scenario_32:_Crime_of_aggression. Accessed 28 May 2025

Trahan J (2025a) Email with Gleb Bogush, 7 April 2025

Trahan J (2025b) Email with Gleb Bogush, 3 July 2025

Trahan J (2025c) Cyber Operation and the Crime of Aggression. 57 Case Western Reserve Journal of International Law 77

Truth Hounds, Project Expedite Justice (2023/2024) Submerged: Study of the Destruction of the Kakhovka Dam and its Impacts on Ecosystems, Agrarian, Other Civilians, and International Justice

UK Government (2022) UK Assesses Russian Involvement in Cyber-Attacks on Ukraine. https://www.gov.uk/government/news/uk-assess-russian-involvement-in-cyber-attacks-on-ukraine. Accessed 28 May 2025

Ukrinform (2023) Defense Official Recalls 30 Ukrainian SOF Soldiers Hampering Russia's Advance Towards Kyiv. https://www.ukrinform.net/rubric-ato/3694293-defense-official-recalls-30-ukrainian-sof-soldiers-hampering-russias-advance-toward-kyiv.html. Accessed 28 May 2025

UN News (2024) Ukraine: Bucha and Irpin Rise from Ashes of Russian Military Occupation. https://news.un.org/en/story/2024/02/1146872. Accessed 28 May 2025

UNESCO (2025) Damaged Cultural Sites in Ukraine Verified by UNESCO. https://www.unesco.org/en/articles/damaged-cultural-sites-ukraine-verified-unesco. Accessed 28 May 2025

UNHCR (2025) Ukraine Emergency as of February 2025. https://www.unrefugees.org/emergencies/ukraine/. Accessed 28 May 2025

United Russia (nd) Shoigu Sergey Kuzhugetovich. https://er.ru/person/62a3fd77-d8e1-4663-8f45-36cf0679c905. Accessed 28 May 2025

US Department of State (2023) Supporting Justice and Accountability in Ukraine, Fact Sheet

Vazquez M, Liptak K, Klein B, Fossum S (2022) Biden Says He's Now Convinced Putin Has Decided to Invade Ukraine, but Leaves Door Open for Diplomacy. CNN. https://edition.cnn.com/2022/02/18/politics/joe-biden-russia-ukraine/index.html Accessed 28 May 2025

VOA News (2023) Some Wagner Troops Return to Ukraine to Resume Fighting, Kyiv Says. https://www.voanews.com/a/some-wagner-troops-return-to-ukraine-to-resume-fighting-kyiv-says/7288183.html Accessed 28 May 2025

Volokita V (2024) Ukraine Assesses Environmental Damage Caused in Thousand Days of Full-Scale Russian Invasion. Ukrainska Pravda 25. https://www.pravda.com.ua/eng/news/2024/11/19/7485374/. Accessed 27 June 2025

Whisler G (2020) Strategic Command and Control in the Russian Armed Forces: Untangling the General Staff, Military Districts, and Service Main Commands (Part Three). The Journal of Slavic Military Studies 33: 237–258

Williams I (2023) Putin's Missile War: Russia's Strike Campaign in Ukraine. CSIS. https://www.csis.org/analysis/putins-missile-war. Accessed 28 May 2025

World Bank Group, Press Release (2025) Updated Ukraine Recovery and Reconstruction Needs Assessment Released. http://worldbank.org/en/news/press-release/2025/02/25/updated-ukraine-recovery-and-reconstruction-needs-assessment-released. Accessed 28 May 2025

Wright G (2024) ICC Issues Arrest Warrants for Top Russian Commanders. BBC. https://www.bbc.com/news/world-europe-68483012. Accessed 28 May 2025

Yale Humanitarian Research Lab (2023) Russia's Systematic Program for the Re-Education and Adoption of Ukraine's Children

Yeung J (2026) 14,000 Troops, 100 Ballistic Missiles and Millions of Munitions: What North Korea Has Sent to Russia, Report Finds. CNN. https://edition.cnn.com/2025/05/30/asia/north-korea-russia-ukraine-weapons-report-intl-hnk. Accessed 27 June 2025

Zabrodskyi M, Watling J, Danylyu O V, Reynolds N (2022) Preliminary Lessons and Conventional War Fighting from Russia's Invasion of Ukraine: February–July 2022. Royal United Services Institute for Defense and Security Studies (RUSI)

Zygar M (2016) All the Kremlin's Men: Inside the Court of Vladimir Putin. Perseus, London

Other Documents

Charter of the International Military Tribunal (1945) 85 UNTS 251

Charter of the United Nations (1945) 1 UNTS XVI

Convention on Cluster Munitions (2008) 2688 UNTS 39

Convention on Cluster Munitions, States Parties and Signatories by Region (nd) https://www.clusterconvention.org/states-parties/. Accessed 20 October 2025

Constitution of the Russian Federation (1993) (amended 2020)

European Commission (2022) Eurobarometer 98.1, Brussels

European Union (2023) Joint Motion for a Resolution 2022/3017 (RSP) of 18 January 2023 on the Establishment of a Tribunal on the Crime of Aggression Against Ukraine

International Court of Justice (1986) *Military and Paramilitary Activities in and Against Nicaragua (Nicaragua v. United States of America)*, Merits, 1986 ICJ Rep. 14

International Court of Justice (1996) *Legality of the Threat or Use of Nuclear Weapons*, Advisory Opinion, 1996 ICJ Rep. 226

International Court of Justice (2005) *Armed Activities on the Territory of the Congo (Democratic Republic of the Congo v. Uganda)*, Judgment, 2005 ICJ Rep. 168

International Court of Justice (2022) *Allegations of Genocide under the Convention on the Prevention and Punishment of the Crime of Genocide (Ukraine v. Russian Federation)*, Application Instituting Proceedings

International Criminal Court, Appeals Chamber (2009) *Prosecutor v. Omar Hassan Ahmad al Bashir ("Omar al Bashir")*, ICC-02/05-01/09 OA, Prosecution Document in Support of Appeal against the "Decision on the Prosecution's Application for a Warrant of Arrest against Omar Hassan Ahmad Al Bashir"

International Criminal Court, Pre-Trial Chamber II (2023) *Prosecutor v. Maxime Jeoffroy Eli Mokom Gawaka,* ICC-01/14-01/22-274- Conf., Public Redacted Version of "Defence Response to 'Prosecution's Additional Submissions Following the Confirmation of Charges Hearing'"

International Criminal Tribunal for the former Yugoslavia, Appeals Chamber (2022) *Prosecutor v. Kunarac, Kovac, and Vokovic*, Case No. IT-96-23 and IT-96-23/1

International Criminal Tribunal for Rwanda (2006) *Gacumbitsi v. Prosecutor*, Case No. ICTR-2001-64-A, Judgment

International Military Tribunal (1946) Judgment of 1 October 1946 in The Trial of German Major War Criminals. Proceedings of the International Military Tribunal Sitting at Nuremberg, Germany, Part 22 (22 August 1946 to 1 October 1946)

Meeting at Liechtenstein Mission to the United Nations (2024)

OHCHR (2022) Killing of Civilians: Summary Executions and Attacks on Individual Civilians in Kyiv, Chernihiv, and Sumy Regions in the Context of the Russian Federation's Armed Attack Against Ukraine

OHCHR (2023a) Treatment of Prisoners of War and Persons *Hors De Combat* in the Context of the Armed Attack By the Russian Federation Against Ukraine: February 24 2022–February 23 2023

Parliamentary Assembly of the Council of Europe, Resolution 2433 (2022) Consequences of the Russian Federation's Continued Aggression Against Ukraine: Role and Response of the Council of Europe

Protocol Additional to the Geneva Conventions of 12 August 1949, and Relating to the Protection of Victims of International Armed Conflicts (1977)

Rome Statute of the International Criminal Court (1998) 2187 UNTS 90 (as amended)

Statute of the Special Tribunal for the Crime of Aggression against Ukraine (2025). https://search.coe.int/cm#{%22CoEIdentifier%22:[%220900001680b678ca%22],%22sort%22:[%22CoEValidationDate%20Descending%22]}. Accessed 28 September 2025

Ukraine: Law No. 2341-III, Criminal Code (2021)

United Nations Charter (1945) 1 UNTS XVI

UN Office for the Coordination of Humanitarian Affairs (UN OCHA) (2025) Ukraine Humanitarian Needs and Response Plan. Accessed 27 October 2025

United Nations General Assembly Resolution 11493 (2014)

United Nations General Assembly Resolution ES-11/1 (2022)

United Nations General Assembly Resolution ES-11/2 (2022)

United Nations General Assembly Resolution ES-11/4 (2022)

United Nations General Assembly Resolution ES-11/L.10 (2025)

United Nations Security Council Resolution S/2014/189 (2014) (vetoed by the Russian Fed.)

US Congress, Senate Committee on Foreign Relations (2022) U.S. Efforts to Support Ukraine Against Russian Aggression. 117th Cong., 2nd Sess.

US Congress, House Committee on Foreign Affairs (2023) Exposing Putin's Crimes: Evidence of Russian War Crimes and Other Atrocities in Ukraine, 118th Cong., 1st Sess. (testimony given to House Committee on Foreign Affairs)

Chapter 5
Calls to Establish an International Tribunal on the Crime of Aggression for the Situation of Ukraine

Contents

Abstract The invasion of Ukraine illuminated a glaring gap in the international judicial architecture regarding enforcement of the crime of aggression. Many voices, both from academia and states' representatives, spoke in favor of filling that gap by establishing an ad hoc international criminal tribunal through the United Nations to prosecute the crime of aggression in the situation of Ukraine. The sentiment was that when a powerful aggressor state, a permanent member of the UN Security Council no less, appears to be manifestly violating the UN Charter, the tribunal would need to be established in the most legitimate way possible, with the backing of the international community, through the United Nations. An international tribunal also could overcome the application of personal immunities that otherwise could shield top-level Russian leaders from prosecution. For the states and individuals who supported this position, it appeared to be clearly *the best way forward.* Such a tribunal would have the greatest legitimacy and appearance of legitimacy and its judgments could have stood the test of time, thereby establishing valuable precedent for the need to enforce the UN Charter, at least when manifestly violated, through the regime of individual criminal responsibility, reviving the precedent of the Nuremberg and Tokyo Tribunals. This chapter discusses the proposal to establish an international criminal tribunal through the United Nations to prosecute the crimes of aggression in the situation of Ukraine. Subsequent chapters explain why the tribunal that would

J. Trahan, *The Crime of Aggression and Russia's Invasion of Ukraine*,
https://doi.org/10.1007/978-94-6265-763-2_5

have presented the strongest and most legitimate response in the situation was not implemented and discuss the tribunal that has been agreed upon.

Keywords Crime of aggression · International tribunal · Special tribunal on the crime of aggression for the situation of Ukraine · Key features · Yale Club Roundtable · Personal immunities · Trials *in absentia* · General Assembly power · Definition of the crime of aggression · Relationship with the International Criminal Court · Selectivity · Views of states

5.1 Introduction

This chapter turns to efforts to establish a special tribunal on the crime of aggression for the situation of Ukraine. Shortly after Russia's full-scale invasion, calls began to mount for accountability for the invasion. Because the UN Security Council was essentially paralyzed from acting due to Russia's veto power, it became clear that the Security Council would neither be able to refer the situation to the International Criminal Court ("ICC") for prosecution of the crime of aggression nor be able to utilize any other of its typical enforcement measures under the UN Charter. Scholars, states' representatives, and non-governmental organizations began to call for the establishment of an aggression-specific tribunal for the situation and suggested various possible forms the tribunal might take. By June 2022, a group of scholars at the Yale Club in New York City put a concrete proposal on the table. The proposal was for a fully international tribunal to be created by agreement between the United Nations and Ukraine upon the recommendation of the UN General Assembly. For many reasons, including the powerful precedent it could set, and particularly due to the ability of an international tribunal to avoid the application of personal immunity that could otherwise prevent the prosecution of top Russian leaders, this was seen as by far the strongest method by which to create the tribunal. A tribunal established through the United Nations would also carry the greatest legitimacy and appropriately convey that aggression is a global threat—an offense against the international order. Yet, the proposal came not to be supported by the "G7" group of states,[1] and, absent such support, the concern arose that the tribunal might not garner a sufficiently persuasive number of votes within the UN General Assembly. Another reason for concern about the vote was that states from other regions had begun questioning (to some extent rightly) why so much focus was being put on creating a tribunal to address Russian aggression but not aggression in other regions.

[1] The Group of Seven (G7) consists of Canada, France, Germany, Italy, Japan, the United Kingdom, and the United States.

5.2 Early Calls for the Establishment of a Tribunal

Not long after Russia commenced its invasion of Ukraine, academics,[2] civil society organizations,[3] and representatives of states[4] began to focus on the issue of prosecuting the crime of aggression in the situation. A threshold question was whether any possibility existed of the ICC having jurisdiction over the crime of aggression related to Ukraine. Experts quickly concluded that it did not have such jurisdiction.[5] Calls then began to mount for the establishment of a separate crime of aggression tribunal to prosecute the crime in regard to the invasion of Ukraine.

5.2.1 The Proposal by Philippe Sands and Gordon Brown

The first model to be publicly floated was by UK barrister and international law expert Philippe Sands,[6] whose idea was subsequently endorsed by former UK Prime Minister Gordon Brown and a fair number of other proponents.[7] The proposal called for pooling the domestic jurisdictions of several European countries to establish the tribunal.[8] Specifically, the proposal stated:

> The Special Tribunal should be constituted—on the same principles that guided the allies in 1942—to investigate the acts of violence by Russia in Ukraine and whether they constitute a crime of aggression. Countries should agree to grant jurisdiction arising under national criminal codes and general international law to a dedicated criminal tribunal, and confer on such a tribunal jurisdiction to investigate both the perpetrators of the crime of aggression and those who have materially contributed to or shaped the commission of that crime.[9]

---

[2] See Sect. 5.3.2; notes 36–41 (academics).

[3] See, e.g., Global Institute for the Prevention of Aggression (2022) Statement by Members of the Council of Advisors on Russia's Invasion of Ukraine. https://crimeofaggression.info/wp-content/uploads/GIPA-Statement_24-March-2022-7.pdf. Accessed 19 August 2025 (calling for accountability); Goldston 2022 (Open Society Justice Initiative calling for "a special tribunal" supported by "one or more international organizations, such as the UN General Assembly, European Union, or the Council of Europe . . ."); The Elders 2022 (calling for an international or hybrid tribunal).

[4] See, e.g., Council of Europe, Newsroom 2022 (the Parliamentary Assembly of the Council of Europe calling on "all the organisation's member and observer states to urgently set up an ad hoc international criminal tribunal"); see also Sect. 5.4 (support of Ukraine and other states).

[5] For analysis of why the ICC cannot exercise jurisdiction in the situation, see Chap. 3, Sect. 3.2.5.

[6] Sands 2022. For his seminal book on the work of Raphael Lemkin and Hersch Lauterpacht, see Sands 2017.

[7] See Green 2022. The proposal was launched at an event at Chatham House. Dannenbaum 2022b, p. 873; Chatham House (2022) A Criminal Tribunal for Aggression in Ukraine. https://www.chathamhouse.org/events/all/research-event/criminal-tribunal-aggression-ukraine. Accessed 5 May 2025.

[8] Combined Statement and Declaration Calling for the Creation of a Special Tribunal for the Punishment of the Crime of Aggression against Ukraine (2002) Gordon & Sarah Brown. https://gordonandsarahbrown.com/wp-content/uploads/2022/03/Combined-Statement-and-Declaration.pdf. Accessed 19 August 2025 ("Combined Statement").

[9] Ibid.

Despite the initial enthusiasm that this model garnered, it raised several concerns. For one, issues existed about the feasibility of pooling domestic jurisdiction. Namely, would this only transfer to the tribunal the jurisdiction that existed before domestic courts? If so, that could potentially exempt high-level leaders from prosecution through the application of personal immunities that attach at the national level. Specifically, the International Court of Justice ("ICJ"), in the *Yerodia* (Arrest Warrant) case,[10] established the precedent that certain individuals, known as "the troika" (the Head of State, Head of Government, and Minister of Foreign Affairs), are exempt from prosecution before another state's national courts.[11] If a national court were only to transfer the jurisdiction it possessed, some would argue that such immunities could potentially transfer as well.[12] The tribunal likely would require further internationalization if it were to overcome personal immunities.[13]

Another difficulty with this model was that if a few European countries pooled their jurisdictions, particularly, for instance, countries located in Eastern Europe, would their judges and a tribunal formed by those states be seen as sufficiently neutral in the situation? Arguably, they would not. The famous adage is that "justice must not only be done, but must also be seen to be done".[14] The appearance of impartiality matters as well as actual impartiality.

---

[10] International Court of Justice (2002) *Arrest Warrant of 11 April 2000 (Democratic Republic of Congo v. Belgium)*, Judgment, 2002 ICJ Rep. 3 ("ICJ 2002, *Arrest Warrant*").

[11] Ibid., para 51.

[12] See Heller 2024, p. 11 ("a Special Tribunal created by a group of states would not have the power to set aside the personal immunity of Russian officials like Putin or Lavrov").

[13] During the Nuremberg trials, the accused were ex-Nazi officials (with ex-regime officials also tried by the Tokyo Tribunal). Thus, any issue of personal immunities—which apply during a person's term in office—did not arise. Additionally, the International Military Tribunal at Nuremberg ("the Nuremberg Tribunal") involved *more than* a few states agreeing to pool jurisdiction. The London Charter that established the Nuremberg Tribunal was initially agreed on by the four Allied Powers (the United States, the United Kingdom, the USSR, and France). See Agreement for the Prosecution and Punishment of the Major War Criminals of the European Axis, Charter of the International Military Tribunal (1945) 59 Stat. 1544, 82 UNTS 279 ("London Charter 1945"). The Allies exercised their combined legislative powers as Occupying Powers. Thus, the Judgment stated that "[t]he making of the Charter was the exercise of the sovereign legislative power by the countries to which the German Reich unconditionally surrendered; and the undoubted right of these countries to legislate for the occupied territories . . .". International Military Tribunal 1946) Judgment of 1 October 1946 in The Trial of German Major War Criminals. Proceedings of the International Military Tribunal Sitting at Nuremberg, Germany, Part 22 (22 August 1946 to 1 October 1946), p. 443. It continued: "The signatory Powers created this Tribunal, . . . and [i]n doing so, they have done together what any one of them might have done singly". Ibid. See also Lippman 1991, p. 28 (explaining the same). Nineteen states additionally adhered to, or acceded to, the London Charter. The states joining were from various regions, including Australia, Ethiopia, Haiti, Honduras, India, New Zealand, Panama, Paraguay, Uruguay. UNTS (nd). https://treaties.un.org/pages/showDetails.aspx?objid=08000002801572a2.

[14] The dictum is attributed to then Lord Chief Justice of England in the case of *Rex v. Sussex Justices,* [1924] 1 KB 256. Datar 2020.

Such pooling of jurisdiction additionally meant that the tribunal, absent more, might not be an international one.[15] As will be discussed further below, a strong argument existed that an offense against the international legal order should be addressed at the international level through the establishment of an international tribunal and that pooling a few states' domestic jurisdictions would be too tepid a response.[16]

Additionally, there was some irony that the proposal emanated from British nationals when the use of force by the United States and the United Kingdom in 2003 in Iraq posed considerable questions about adherence to international law and the UN Charter's regime related to the use of force.[17] A huge risk existed of the appearance of (and actual) hypocrisy in trying Russian leaders for the crime of aggression after US and UK leaders had faced no similar scrutiny. This risk would exist with any effort focused on only one situation (i.e., an ad hoc solution), hence the need to simultaneously fix the ICC's jurisdiction over the crime under the Rome Statute[18] so the crime may be prosecuted more broadly.[19] Having the effort to establish a tribunal led by two UK nationals presented overtly complicated optics, placing the question of selectivity front and center.

Credit, however, is due to Philippe Sands for putting the idea of forming a crime of aggression tribunal for the situation on the map. Even though the precise formulation suggested did not progress, he galvanized public attention on, and interest in, the issue, and thus paved the way for further efforts to establish a tribunal for the situation.

5.3 Calls to Establish an International Tribunal

While the Philippe Sands/Gordon Brown model was moving forward in the public discourse, others began to formulate plans to call for an international tribunal to be established through the United Nations.

---

[15] See note 13 (nineteen additional states endorsing the London Charter). If countries pooled jurisdiction, they could form the tribunal by an international agreement (a treaty), but it still would not represent the will of the international community.

[16] The Sands/Brown proposal was short on details. Perhaps they envisioned further internationalization of the tribunal, but such plans were not contained in their proposal. See Combined Statement, note 8.

[17] For additional discussion, see Chap. 1, Sect. 1.1; Sect. 5.3.4.6. Similar questions exist about the June 2025 Israeli and US military strikes against Iranian nuclear installations. Rosen et al. 2025. Concerns are now arising about US strikes against Venezuelan boats. See, e.g., Nevitt 2025.

[18] Rome Statute of the International Criminal Court (1998) 2187 UNTS 3 (as amended) ("Rome Statute (1998) (as amended)").

[19] For additional discussion of amending the Rome Statute to fix the ICC's jurisdiction over the crime of aggression, see Chap. 8.

5.3.1 Why Establish an International Tribunal

There were obvious reasons to support the establishment of an international tribunal through the United Nations. First, for an offense that was being committed simultaneously against the state of Ukraine and against the international order that protects the boundaries of all states, establishing such an international tribunal was seen as particularly appropriate. Aggression is a violation of the core norm found in the UN Charter against the use of force, Article 2(4),[20] and in this instance, the aggression had been vociferously condemned by a large number of states within the UN General Assembly.[21] Because of Russia's veto power as a permanent member of the UN Security Council, condemnation would not be able to be issued, nor any other action be able to be taken, by that body.[22]

Second, as mentioned above and will be discussed further below, was the issue of immunities. The ICJ in the *Yerodia* (Arrest Warrant) case gave examples of the International Criminal Tribunal for the former Yugoslavia ("ICTY"), the International Criminal Tribunal for Rwanda ("ICTR"), and ICC as tribunals before which personal immunities would not attach,[23] but it did not limit its holding to those courts. It thereby suggested personal immunities would not exist before *any international criminal tribunal*. For an offense that is particularly committed at the leadership

---

[20] Article 2(4) states: "All Members shall refrain in their international relations from the threat or use of force against the territorial integrity or political independence of any state, or in any other manner inconsistent with the Purposes of the United Nations". Charter of the United Nations (1945) 33 UNTS 933, Article 2(4) ("UN Charter (1945)"). It is complemented by the allowance of Security Council authorized interventions and the ability of a state to exercise individual or collective self-defense. See ibid., Chap. VII, Article 51.

[21] See, e.g., United Nations General Assembly Resolution ES-11/1 (2022) (141 votes in favor); United Nations General Assembly Resolution ES-11/2 (2022) (140 votes in favor); United Nations General Assembly Resolution ES-11/4 (2022) (143 votes in favor); United Nations General Assembly Resolution ES-11/L.10 (2025) (93 votes in favor).

[22] On 25 March, the Russian Federation vetoed a UN Security Council resolution that would have condemned the invasion and taken various additional steps. United Nations Security Council Resolution 155 (2022) vetoed by the Russ. Fed. (draft resolution co-sponsored by 81 member states). Thus, the best the Security Council could do was invoke "the 'Uniting for Peace' resolution of 1950 by which the Council, on a procedural vote not subject to the veto, requested that the General Assembly meet in emergency special session to consider the issue . . .". Johnson 2022; United Nations Security Council Resolution 623 (2022). The inability of the Security Council to act in the situation was particularly ironic because, under the UN Charter, the Security Council holds "primary responsibility for the maintenance of international peace and security". UN Charter, note 20, Article 24.1. For discussion of a permanent member shielding its own aggression through veto use and the legal questions raised, see Trahan 2023a.

[23] ICJ 2002, *Arrest Warrant*, note 10, paras 51, 61. By contrast, "[t]he ICJ agreed with the Democratic Republic of Congo that its incumbent foreign minister had immunity from arrest for international crimes with respect to Belgian judicial proceedings". Hamilton 2023, p. 45, citing ICJ 2002, *Arrest Warrant*, note 10, para 78.

level—by political and military leaders[24]—it appeared critical to avoid the application of such immunities.[25] One could not fully see justice done or hope to create deterrence unless the tribunal would be able to prosecute the top-level leaders who decided to initiate the invasion.

Third, creating an international tribunal through the United Nations would carry the greatest weight in terms of the legitimacy of the precedent it could set. The effort would not only be endorsed by states from a particular region, but ideally, endorsed multilaterally, by the full international community. The judgments of such an international tribunal could carry the greatest weight and legitimacy. Because the crime of aggression has not been prosecuted at the international level since the prosecutions before the Nuremberg[26] and Tokyo Tribunals,[27] the thinking was that the tribunal should be established in the most legitimate way possible. Furthermore, in the face of an invasion by a permanent member of the UN Security Council, precedent and legitimacy mattered. If one wished to potentially deter other future would-be aggressors from other regions[28] or additional Russian aggression in the future, nothing less than a fully legitimate tribunal, backed by the weight of the international community, would do.

Fourth, as also addressed in Chaps. 1 and 4, prosecuting only other crimes—such as crimes against humanity and war crimes committed in Ukraine—would leave the invasion itself and much of the harm it has caused unaddressed.[29] As Tom Dannenbaum writes:

> Aggression is not simply an aggregation of the war crimes that arise inevitably in war, such that the comprehensive prosecution of the latter would satisfy the accountability imperative associated with the former. Nor is it reducible to an interstate violation better left to noncriminal fora. The crux of aggression's criminality is the widespread death, suffering, destruction, and displacement it wreaks in *compliance* with international humanitarian law

[24] For discussion of the leadership clause, see Chap. 3, Sect. 3.2.2; Chap. 4, Sect. 4.4.5.

[25] For why functional immunity exists in proceedings before another state's domestic courts, see Hamilton 2023, p. 44, citing International Court of Justice (2012) *Jurisdictional Immunities of the State (Germany v. Italy)*, Judgment, 2012 ICJ Rep. 99, para 57; United Nations General Assembly 2011.

[26] See London Charter, note 13, Article 6(a) (jurisdiction over crimes against peace).

[27] See International Military Tribunal for the Far East (1946) Special Proclamation by the Supreme Commander for the Allied Powers at Tokyo, Article 5(a) ("Tokyo Charter") (jurisdiction over crimes against peace).

[28] For discussions of Rwandan incursions in the DRC, Israeli strikes into Syria, Chinese threats to invade Taiwan, Chinese incursions into the South China Sea, Venezuelan threats to invade Guyana, and the US President's threats to invade Greenland, Canada, and Panama, see Africa News 2022 (Rwandan intervention in DRC); Israeli Defense Forces 2024 (IDF strikes against Syrian military installations); Bodeen 2023 (Chinese threats against Taiwan); BBC News 2023 (China and the South China Sea); Cotovio and Goodwin 2024 (Venezuelan threats against Guyana); Collinson 2025 (Trump threats against Greenland, Canada, and Panama). See also Labuda 2024, p. 294 (listing "Ugandan or Rwandan interventions in the DRC, Turkey's involvement in Syria, China's expansion into the South China Sea, or Morocco's occupation of Western Sahara" as examples). For Israeli and US military strikes against Iran and Venezuelan boat strikes by the United States, see note 17.

[29] See Chap. 4, Sect. 4.3 (harm caused by the invasion).

> (IHL) . . . . An exclusive focus on the other core crimes would ignore the wrongfulness of much of the death, injury, terror, and displacement inflicted on Ukrainian troops in battle, on civilians considered proportionate collateral damage under IHL, or on persons or communities otherwise caused to suffer in ways that IHL does not prohibit.[30]

For example, as explained in Chap. 1, the killing of combatants is allowed under IHL in a state of international armed conflict, but they too are victims of the crime of aggression.[31] IHL also permits a certain level of "collateral damage"—the euphemism for civilian fatalities and destruction of civilian objects around a military target[32]—yet, these individuals also should not be killed or civilian objects destroyed. Thus, "the group of victims of the crime of aggression is by no means the same as that of victims of other international crimes".[33] Moreover, it will never be possible to prosecute all the war crimes and crimes against humanity that have been committed; inevitably, a significant number of crimes and a great deal of harm would go unaddressed if the crime of aggression is not prosecuted.[34] Nor would there necessarily be overlap in those prosecuted for war crimes and crimes against humanity, and those prosecuted for the crime of aggression.[35] Absent prosecuting the crime of aggression, key perpetrators could escape accountability as well.

---

[30] Dannenbaum 2022b, pp. 863–64.

[31] The targeting of combatants during international armed conflict, with certain limitations, is not a war crime, as it is permitted under IHL. See, e.g., Rome Statute (1998) (as amended), note 18, Article 8(2)(b)(i) (war crime of intentionally directing attacks against the civilian population—but no war crime of targeting combatants).

[32] Protocol I to the Geneva Conventions prohibits "an attack which may be expected to cause incidental loss of civilian life, injury to civilians, damage to civilian objects, or a combination thereof, which would be excessive in relation to the concrete and direct military advantage anticipated". Protocol Additional to the Geneva Conventions of 12 August 1949, and Relating to the Protection of Victims of International Armed Conflicts (1977), Article 51(5)(b). Thus, incidental loss of civilian life, injury to civilians, damage to civilian objects, or a combination thereof, which would *not be excessive* in relation to the concrete and direct military advantage anticipated is permitted.

[33] Korynevych et al. 2023, p. 373. Anton Korynevych and his colleagues write:

> The aggression destroys the entire human rights architecture of the country against which it is unleashed, causing direct, indirect and cascading damage in all spheres of life: thousands of Ukrainians, both combatants and civilians, have lost their lives and health—sometimes as a result of attacks that are lawful according to international humanitarian law or legitimate retaliatory attacks by the Ukrainian side (e.g. air defence)—and millions have lost and continue to lose their jobs, housing, education and other social, economic and environmental rights.
>
> Ibid.

[34] On the harm caused by the invasion, see Chap. 4, Sect. 4.3.

[35] See Korynevych et al. 2023, p. 372 ("The group of Russian leaders who committed the crime of aggression does not necessarily overlap with the circle of war criminals (allegedly, such Troika members as Putin, Lavrov and Mishustin who allegedly committed the crime of aggression but not the war crimes), which means that without a mechanism to prosecute the crime of aggression, its perpetrators may enjoy impunity indefinitely".); compare McDougall 2023a, p. 226 ("The idea that a prosecution for war crimes or crimes against humanity (possibly even genocide) would be a substitute for the crime of aggression overlooks the difficulty of establishing the criminal responsibility of those at the top table. President Putin will not himself have directly perpetrated

5.3.2 Advocates of an International Tribunal

In the spring of 2022, various academics expressed support for the establishment of an international tribunal or at least considered it as one of the potential options. They included Larry Johnson,[36] Tom Dannenbaum,[37] Carrie McDougall,[38] Oona Hathaway and Alexander Komarov,[39] myself,[40] Claus Kreβ, Astrid Reisinger Coracini, Ambassador David Scheffer, and a number of others.[41] David Crane, Hans Corell, and Irwin Cottler later developed a proposal for the establishment of an international tribunal closely modeled on the Statute of the Special Court for Sierra Leone[42] and became additional key proponents of such an approach.[43] Eventually, organizations such as "the North Atlantic Treaty Organization (NATO) Parliamentary Assembly, the Organisation for Security and Cooperation in Europe (OSCE) Parliamentary Assembly, as well as the Parliamentary Assembly and the Committee of Ministers of the Council of Europe" and the European Parliament did as well.[44] "In sum, the idea of creating a special international tribunal for the crime of aggression ... gained support from a wide range of observers, academics and institutions".[45] Only a few

any of the other three crimes. Thus, his liability would have to be established using complex theories of (indirect) co-perpetration still being developed by the ICC, or on the basis that he ordered the crimes, or command responsibility".). Putin has since been indicted by the ICC for the illegal transfer of Ukrainian children into Russian territory. See International Criminal Court, Press Release 2023 (arrest warrants issued against President Putin and Maria Lvova-Belova).

36 Johnson 2022 (setting forth various options).

37 Dannenbaum 2022a (blog); Dannenbaum 2022b (article).

38 McDougall 2022 (blog); McDougall 2023a (article); McDougall 2023b (article).

39 Komarov and Hathaway 2022. See also Hathaway 2022a.

40 Trahan 2022a.

41 For a comprehensive listing of blog posts in chronological order, see Corten and Koutroulis 2022, n 1; Just Security nd-a. See also International Crisis Group 2023 (discussing as one of the options); Corten and Koutroulis 2022 (discussing as one of the options).

42 Statute of the Special Court for Sierra Leone 2002 ("SCSL Statute").

43 See Global Accountability Network 2022a (proposal supported by David M. Crane, Hans Corell, and Irwin Cotler).

44 Corten and Koutroulis 2022, p. 2, citing NATO Parliamentary Assembly 2022, Plenary, § 18j (urging member governments and parliaments of the Alliance to support the initiatives aiming at establishing an ad hoc tribunal to investigate and prosecute the crime of aggression); OSCE Parliamentary Assembly (2022) Resolution on the Russian's Federation War of Aggression against Ukraine and Its People, and Its Threat to Security across the OSCE Region, pp. 22–27, §§ 35–36; Council of Europe Parliamentary Assembly (2022) The Russian's Federation's Aggression against Ukraine: Ensuring Accountability for Serious Violations of International Humanitarian Law and Other International Crimes, Resolution 2436 (2022); Council of Europe (2022) Consequences of the Aggression of Russian Federation against Ukraine—Accountability for International Crimes, Committee of Ministers, 1442nd meeting, CM/Del/Dec(2022)1442/2.3; European Parliament (2022) Resolution of 19 May 2022 on the Fight Against Impunity for War Crimes in Ukraine, P9_TA(2022)0218.

45 Corten and Koutroulis 2022, p. 2.

contrary voices emerged, such as that of Kevin Jon Heller, who argued against establishing an international tribunal for the situation.[46] Some of those who supported the establishment of an international tribunal adopted the nuanced stance that it *must* be established in conjunction with amending the Rome Statute to create broader jurisdiction over the crime before the ICC.[47] In other words, they would not support *only* selective justice in one situation, but insisted on it more broadly.

While many efforts were underway to promote the establishment of a tribunal (with considerable focus, at this point in time, on efforts to establish an international tribunal), I was privileged to be part of one set of efforts. It commenced when a small group of like-minded academics reached out to Ambassador Christian Wenaweser, who serves as Permanent Representative of Liechtenstein to the United Nation and had led many of the negotiations that resulted in the definition of the crime of aggression and conditions for the ICC's exercise of jurisdiction over it being adopted as part of the Rome Statute.[48] Our initial group consisted of Yale Law School Professor Oona Hathaway, former US Ambassador-at-Large for War Crimes David Scheffer,

[46] Heller 2022b (calling for "a hybrid tribunal established as part of the Ukrainian justice system"); Heller 2022a (similar); Heller 2024 (similar); see also text accompanying note 173 for some of his arguments. Heller serves as a Special Adviser to ICC Prosecutor Karim Khan, who also took a dim view of establishing an international tribunal. See Sect. 5.3.4.5. See also Public International Law and Policy Group (nd) Draft Law for a Ukrainian High War Crimes Court. https://static1.squarespace.com/static/5900b58e1b631bffa367167e/t/62d6c27baae10b6ca51cadb7/1658241661209/DRAFT+Ukraine+High+War+Crimes+Court.pdf. Accessed 19 August 2025 ("Public International Law and Policy Group") (calling for the establishment of a High War Crimes Court in Ukraine to prosecute, along with other crimes, the crime of aggression).

[47] A number fell in this camp. They included: Liechtenstein Ambassador Christian Wenaweser, Professor Claus Kreβ, Professor Astrid Reisinger Coracini, Professor Oona Hathaway, Professor Carrie McDougall, Ambassador-at-Large of the Foreign Ministry of Ukraine Professor Anton Korynevych, Professor Patrycja Grzebyk, and myself. See, e.g., Representatives of Latvia, Liechtenstein, and Ukraine to the UN 2022, p. 3 (support of Wenaweser, Kreβ, Reisinger Coracini, Hathaway, Trahan); Korynevych et al. 2023, p. 371 ("it is imperative to pursue in parallel with the amendments to the Rome Statute the creation of a functional accountability mechanism to address the crime of aggression committed by Putin and his entourage"); Sluiter 2023 ("The idea of establishment of an aggression tribunal for Putin would be more credible if it were accompanied by a campaign to lift the ICC's jurisdictional restrictions on aggression by means of an amendment to the Statute".); Corten and Koutroulis 2022, p. 40 ("Triggering an exceptional procedure for aggression committed in Ukraine without accepting a structural modification of the Statute in order to allow for similar future aggressions to be tried would obviously discredit the initiative, depriving it of much needed legitimacy. Thus, to appear credible, this initiative should be coupled with a long-term will to vest the main permanent criminal jurisdiction of the international community with the jurisdiction necessary to prosecute the crime of aggression in exactly the same way as for other international crimes".); Independent International Commission of Inquiry on Ukraine 2023, para 104 ("[d]iscussions about a new tribunal should be combined with efforts to amend the [Rome] Statute, so that the [ICC]'s jurisdiction over aggression is identical to the other three crimes").

[48] See International Criminal Court, Assembly of States Parties 2010. Ambassador Wenaweser played a key role in the crime of aggression negotiations, serving as Chair of the Special Working Group on the Crime of Aggression ("SWGCA") from 2003–2009 and from 2008–2010 as President of the Assembly of States Parties ("ASP"), including at the 2010 ICC Review Conference.

and myself.[49] As US nationals, we quickly realized that we had the same optics problem as British nationals. The group quickly enlarged to include international crime of aggression experts Professor Claus Kreβ of the University of Cologne[50] and Professor Astrid Reisinger Coracini of the University of Vienna.[51]

In addition to initial blog posts calling for the establishment of an international tribunal,[52] in spring 2022, the group commenced work on the design of a draft tribunal statute. By 22 June 2022, we presented the tribunal proposal to a group of states, academics and representatives of civil society at the invitation of the Permanent Missions of Latvia and Liechtenstein to the United Nations, at a meeting at the Yale Club in New York City.[53] The meeting was entitled "Yale Club Roundtable: A Special Tribunal for the Crime of Aggression Recommended by the UN General Assembly" ("the Yale Club meeting").[54] A summary of the presentations, described below, was subsequently sent to the UN Secretary-General, who, at the request of the Permanent Missions of Latvia, Liechtenstein, and Ukraine to the UN, distributed it to all UN Member States.[55]

5.3.3 *The Yale Club Meeting and Features of the Proposed Tribunal*

The Yale Club meeting focused on various features of the proposed tribunal. Our group later supplemented the presentations through a series of blog posts on the blog "Just Security",[56] with others blogging in a similar vein.[57] The Yale Club meeting was framed by introductory remarks from Ambassador Wenaweser, Ambassador Andrejs Pildegovičs of Latvia, and Ambassador Sergiy Kyslytsya of Ukraine on

---

[49] Oona Hathaway serves as the Gerard C. and Bernice Latrobe Smith Professor of International Law and Counselor to the Dean at Yale Law School. David Scheffer is former US Ambassador-at-Large for War Crimes Issues, US Department of State and Clinical Professor Emeritus and Director Emeritus, Center for International Human Rights, Northwestern University Pritzker School of Law.

[50] Professor Kreβ has represented Germany in the crime of aggression negotiations. He also serves as a judge *ad litem* on the ICJ's *Gambia v. Myanmar* case. See International Court of Justice (nd) *Application of the Convention on the Prevention and Punishment of the Crime of Genocide (The Gambia v. Myanmar)*. He also serves as Special Adviser to the Prosecutor of the ICC for the Crime of Aggression.

[51] Reisinger Coracini has represented Austria in the crime of aggression negotiations. She is now affiliated with the Law School of the University of Salzburg.

[52] For a compilation of blog posts on the topic, see Just Security nd-a.

[53] For a write-up of the content of the meeting, see Representatives of Latvia, Liechtenstein, and Ukraine to the UN 2022.

[54] Ibid.

[55] Ibid.

[56] See Hathaway 2022b; Reisinger Coracini 2022; Trahan 2022b; Scheffer 2022a,b; Reisinger Coracini and Trahan 2022; Kreβ 2022.

[57] For a compilation of blog posts on the topic, see Just Security nd-a.

the imperative need for a tribunal and the importance of prosecuting the crime of aggression in the situation of Ukraine.[58] They also highlighted the advantages of a UN-backed tribunal compared with other ideas under consideration.[59] Professor Hathaway framed the discussion in the context of the history of outlawing aggressive use of force, tracing the evolution from a permissive history on the acceptability of the use of force as justified in many situations, to the current UN Charter regime, established after two World Wars, that prohibits it.[60]

- **An International Tribunal**

First and foremost was the call to establish a freestanding international tribunal to adjudicate the crime of aggression in the situation of Ukraine. The proposal was for the tribunal to be formed by bilateral agreement between the United Nations and Ukraine, on the recommendation of the UN General Assembly.[61] The court was envisioned to resemble the Special Court for Sierra Leone in size; thus, the tribunal would be "a lean court with a narrow focus".[62] Because Russia, as previously mentioned, possesses veto power over Security Council decisions under Chapter VII of the UN Charter,[63] the ability of the Security Council to establish the tribunal under Chapter VII—the path used to establish the ICTY and ICTR (and Special Tribunal for Lebanon ("STL"))[64]—was seen as foreclosed. Having the UN Security Council refer the situation to the ICC, which referral could include the crime of aggression,[65] was seen as foreclosed for the same reason.

The presenters did not advocate that the General Assembly *create* the tribunal, but *recommend* the tribunal's creation, with the tribunal established by agreement between the United Nations and Ukraine.[66] Such an approach would fall squarely within the powers of the UN General Assembly, which, under the UN Charter, are, with a few exceptions, limited to recommendations.[67]

---

[58] Representatives of Latvia, Liechtenstein, and Ukraine to the UN 2022, p. 2.

[59] Ibid.

[60] Ibid. (remarks of Oona Hathaway). For background, see Hathaway and Shapiro 2017 (highlighting the significant change in 1928 with agreement on the Kellogg-Briand Pact, a/k/a the General Treaty for Renunciation of War as an Instrument of National Policy); Chap. 2, notes 87–89; note 20 (UN Charter regime).

[61] Representatives of Latvia, Liechtenstein, and Ukraine to the UN 2022, p. 3 (remarks of Oona Hathaway).

[62] Ibid.

[63] UN Charter (1945), note 20, Article 27.3.

[64] United Nations Security Council Resolution 827 (1993) (establishing the ICTY); United Nations Security Council Resolution 955 (1994) (establishing the ICTR); United Nations Security Council Resolution 1757 (2007) (establishing the STL with attached "STL Statute"). For discussion of the UN Security Council acting under Chapter VI of the UN Charter, see Chap. 7, Sect. 7.2.

[65] See Rome Statute (1998) (as amended), note 18, Article 15*ter* (UNSC referrals), activated as of 17 July 2018. See International Criminal Court, Assembly of States Parties 2017.

[66] Representatives of Latvia, Liechtenstein, and Ukraine to the UN 2022, p. 2.

[67] See UN Charter (1945), note 20, Articles 10–14 (UN General Assembly powers); Andrassy 1956, p. 571, n 27 (citing areas where the General Assembly can make binding decisions as:

- **Selection of Judges and the Prosecutor**

The proposal called for an internationally selected roster of judges and an internationally selected prosecutor. This was designed to ensure the highest degree of impartiality.[68] A tribunal focused on the crime of aggression would potentially face greater scrutiny than other tribunals because the crime of aggression necessarily is based on the commission of an act of aggression by one state against another; thereby state conduct is inherently at issue.[69]

- **The Definition of the Crime of Aggression**

Another aspect of the proposal was that the internationally accepted definition of the crime contained in Article 8*bis* of the ICC's Rome Statute be used as the definition of the crime.[70] As discussed more extensively below,[71] that definition was negotiated and consensually agreed to by all interested states, including the Russian Federation.[72] It was then adopted in 2010 by consensus by all States Parties to the ICC's Rome Statute.[73] The crime of aggression is part of customary international law,[74]

"[a]dmission, exclusion, suspension of Members, approval of trusteeship agreements and of agreements entered into with specialized agencies, approval of budgets, [and] apportionment of expenses among Members"). The General Assembly may also establish "such subsidiary organs as it deems necessary for the performance of its functions". UN Charter (1945), note 20, Article 22.

68 Representatives of Latvia, Liechtenstein, and Ukraine to the UN 2022, p. 4 (remarks of Astrid Reisinger Coracini). One of the great benefits of an international tribunal is that its roster of judges can hail from many countries, which helps ensure independence and insulate against any perception of partiality. For example, the ICC's roster of judges hail from eighteen countries. See International Criminal Court. International Criminal Court nd-a (listing the current roster of judges from Japan, Italy, Benin, Peru, Uganda, Canada, the United Kingdom, Georgia, Mexico, Costa Rica, Sierra Leone, Trinidad and Tobago, Republic of Korea, Mongolia, Romania, Tunisia, France, and Slovenia).

69 Representatives of Latvia, Liechtenstein, and Ukraine to the UN 2022, p. 4 (remarks of Astrid Reisinger Coracini). For discussion of the requirement contained in the definition of the crime that there must be an act of aggression by a state, see Chap. 3, Sect. 3.3.2; Chap. 4, Sect. 4.4.2.

70 Representatives of Latvia, Liechtenstein, and Ukraine to the UN 2022, p. 4 (remarks of Astrid Reisinger Coracini).

71 See Sect. 5.3.4.2.

72 Ibid. Delegates from both Russia and China participated in the negotiations of the SWGCA, with the Russian delegate in particular expressing his agreement with the definition reached. See Kuzmin and Panin in Kreß and Barriga 2017, p. 1264 ("Russia is satisfied with the outcome of the Review Conference with regard to the definition of the crime of aggression, which largely is in conformity with the relevant 1974 GA Resolution 3314".). The United States declined to attend the negotiations even though they were held in Princeton, New Jersey. Observations of the author who attended the SWGCA negotiations.

73 International Criminal Court, Assembly of States Parties 2010. A prior important step was agreement on the work of the SWGCA by consensus. Reisinger Coracini 2025.

74 Representatives of Latvia, Liechtenstein, and Ukraine to the UN 2022, p. 4 (remarks of Astrid Reisinger Coracini that it is customary international law). See also Sect. 5.3.4.2. But see McDougall

and the definition contains both a very high threshold (the "manifest threshold")[75] and a narrow scope (only leaders may be prosecuted).[76]

- **Location of the Tribunal**

Because war was, and, as of the date of this writing, still is, ongoing in Ukraine, it was envisioned that the tribunal would have its seat elsewhere, such as in The Hague, Netherlands.[77] Being located in The Hague would allow it to benefit from judicial synergies of being in the same town as other international justice mechanisms, including the ICC.[78]

- **Rights of the Accused**

The tribunal would need to have all of the internationally accepted due process/fair trial protections of present-day tribunals in order to protect the rights of the accused.[79] The tribunal would need to be a fair one, where an accused would have a full chance to be heard and represented in court.[80] Only through such an institution could one hope to set powerful precedent and potentially create deterrence. To have the desired impact, the tribunal could not be a "poisoned chalice".[81]

- **Territorial Jurisdiction**

The crime of aggression occurs in both an aggressor state and a victim state, with the crime at issue potentially occurring in Russia, Ukraine, and Belarus.[82] The tribunal's statute might also include a reference to jurisdiction extending to neighboring states,

2024, p. 563 (agreeing the crime is customary international law, but maintaining that it is the Nuremberg definition that represents customary international law).

[75] For discussion of the manifest threshold, see Chap. 3, Sect. 3.2.2; Chap. 4, Sect. 4.4.3.

[76] For discussion of the leadership clause, see Chap. 3, Sect. 3.2.2; Chap. 4, Sect. 4.4.5.

[77] Representatives of Latvia, Liechtenstein, and Ukraine to the UN 2022, p. 4 (remarks of Astrid Reisinger Coracini).

[78] Ibid.

[79] Ibid., p. 6 (remarks of Jennifer Trahan). See, e.g., Statute of the International Criminal Tribunal for the former Yugoslavia (1993) United Nations Security Council Resolution 827, Article 21 ("ICTY Statute"); Statute of the International Criminal Tribunal for Rwanda (1994) United Nations Security Council Resolution 955, Article 20 ("ICTR Statute"); SCSL Statute, note 42, Article 17; Rome Statute (1998) (as amended), note 18, Articles 55, 66, 67.

[80] By contrast, the accused before the Tokyo Tribunal were not permitted to introduce evidence of Japan's economic encirclement or present arguments on self-defense. See Kopelman 1991, p. 395 ("The Tribunal categorically refused to hear mitigating evidence touching on Japanese perceptions of economic encirclement or of the Chinese communist threat".).

[81] At Nuremberg, Justice Robert H. Jackson, in his Opening Statement for the United States, stated: "To pass to these defendants a poisoned chalice is to put it to our own lips as well". Jackson 1945, p. 101. It was a commitment that the Nuremberg Tribunal needed to have fair proceedings *and* proceedings that were seen to be fair. Of course, in 1945, the Nuremberg Tribunal's fair trial protections (see London Charter, note 13, Article 16) were a comparatively short list. Later, the list became significantly expanded. See International Covenant on Civil and Political Rights (1966) 999 UNTS 171, Article 14.

[82] Representatives of Latvia, Liechtenstein, and Ukraine to the UN 2022, p. 5 (remarks of Astrid Reisinger Coracini). Jurisdiction over events in Ukraine would suffice to establish the tribunal since

as the ICTR's Statute did.[83] This was suggested because at the time of the Yale Club meeting it was unclear whether other states in the region would be drawn into the war.

- **Temporal Jurisdiction**

The proposal was for temporal jurisdiction to commence in February 2014 with Russia's illegal annexation of Crimea.[84] Alternatively, jurisdiction might commence with the February 2022 invasion.[85] Here, financial considerations would come into play—whether the entirety of the potential aggression should be encompassed or the tribunal should be more narrowly focused, which could potentially help secure political and financial support.[86]

- **Organization of the Tribunal**

Given that the tribunal would only focus on one crime in one situation, the suggestion was that it could, as mentioned, be relatively small in size. It could have a pre-trial chamber, one trial chamber of three judges, and one appeals chamber of five judges,[87] as well as an office of the prosecutor and registry.[88] Three pre-trial chamber judges were suggested, although it was noted that the number could be reduced to one.[89]

- **Working Languages**

The suggestion was made to utilize English, French, Ukrainian, and Russian as working languages for the tribunal.[90]

---

part of the crime is occurring there. The grant of such jurisdiction to the tribunal clearly would be something to which Ukraine could agree.

[83] Ibid.; ICTR Statute, note 79, Article 1 (jurisdiction "to prosecute persons responsible for serious violations of international humanitarian law committed in the territory of Rwanda and Rwandan citizens responsible for such violations committed in the territory of neighbouring States between 1 January 1994 and 31 December 1994 . . .").

[84] For discussion of the illegal annexation of Crimea, see Chap. 4, Sect. 4.2.1.

[85] Representatives of Latvia, Liechtenstein, and Ukraine to the UN 2022, p. 5 (remarks of Astrid Reisinger Coracini). See Hamilton 2023, p. 43 ("A temporal jurisdiction clause that begins on February 24, 2022 will prevent a tribunal from considering acts short of full-scale invasion. This does not mean, of course, that Russia's acts of aggression prior to February 24, 2022 do not constitute aggression, however, it does set the bar very high for the future engagement of international criminal law with the crime of aggression".) (internal citations omitted).

[86] Representatives of Latvia, Liechtenstein, and Ukraine to the UN 2022, p. 6 (discussions about the proposal). Similar deliberations occurred about the start date of the temporal jurisdiction of the Special Court for Sierra Leone—namely, whether it should commence with the start of the Sierra Leone Civil War or a later date, with the latter being chosen. See United Nations Security Council 2000, paras 25–28.

[87] Representatives of Latvia, Liechtenstein, and Ukraine to the UN 2022, p. 4 (remarks of Astrid Reisinger Coracini).

[88] Ibid. One might also include a standing defense unit.

[89] Ibid.

[90] Ibid.

- **How Many to Prosecute**

As noted above, the crime of aggression covers a limited subset of potential perpetrators in that the Article 8*bis* definition contained in the Rome Statute only applies to "persons in a position effectively to exercise control over or to direct the political or military action of a State",[91] referred to as the "leadership clause". While the Special Court for Sierra Leone, for example, limited its jurisdiction to persons who bore the "greatest responsibility" for crimes committed during the Civil War in Sierra Leone,[92] that formulation was not suggested because there already is this built-in limitation contained in the definition of the crime. Large numbers would not fall within the leadership clause and they would necessarily be high-level leaders. The ultimate decision as to the number of individuals to be prosecuted would be left to the discretion of the prosecutor.[93]

- **Rules of Procedure and Evidence**

Rules of procedure and evidence would need to be drafted. It was noted that the drafting of such rules is often left to the judges.[94]

- **Judgment**

It was recommended that the statute specify the need for a reasoned opinion, rendered in writing, by a majority of judges of the trial or appeals chamber, respectively, with the possibility of dissenting and separate opinions.[95]

- ***Ne bis in Idem***

It was recommended that the tribunal statute specify that the accused may not be prosecuted twice for the same acts or conduct, a provision found in numerous tribunal statutes.[96]

---

[91] Ibid., p. 6 (remarks of Jennifer Trahan); Rome Statute (1998) (as amended), note 18, Article 8*bis*, para 1.

[92] SCSL Statute, note 42, Article 1.1. This focused mandate reflected a reaction by states to the size and cost of the ICTY and ICTR. See Skilbeck 2008, p. 10 (arguing that "[t]he huge budgets of the ICTY and ICTR have produced unsustainable and un-repeatable models . . .").

[93] Representatives of Latvia, Liechtenstein, and Ukraine to the UN 2022, p. 6 (remarks of Jennifer Trahan).

[94] Ibid. This was the case, for example, with the ICTY (ICTY Statute, note 79, Article 15), ICTR (ICTR Statute, note 79, Article 14), and the Special Court for Sierra Leone (SCSL Statute, note 42, Article 14). The States Parties to the ICC's Rome Statute negotiated its Rules of Procedure and Evidence. Rome Statute (1998) (as amended), note 18, Article 51.1.

[95] Representatives of Latvia, Liechtenstein, and Ukraine to the UN 2022, p. 6 (remarks of Jennifer Trahan). See, e.g., ICTY Statute, note 79, Article 23; ICTR Statute, note 79, Article 22; SCSL Statute, note 42, Article 18; *see also* Rome Statute (1998) (as amended), note 18, Article 76.

[96] Representatives of Latvia, Liechtenstein, and Ukraine to the UN 2022, p. 6 (remarks of Jennifer Trahan). See, e.g., ICTY Statute, note 79, Article 10; ICTR Statute, note 79, Article 9; SCSL Statute, note 42, Article 9; Rome Statute (1998) (as amended), note 18, Article 20. An exception applies where the acts at issue in the first trial were characterized as an ordinary crime, or where the

- **Amnesty**

It was recommended that the tribunal statute state: "An amnesty granted to any person falling within the jurisdiction of the [tribunal] in respect of the crimes defined in the Statute shall not be a bar prosecution".[97] The language mirrors that of Article 10 of the SCSL Statute.[98] The Special Court had to grapple with the fact that there had been an amnesty in Sierra Leone, the Lomé Peace Agreement,[99] and thus an issue arose as to whether the amnesty might impact on its proceedings.[100] As of late 2025, there is no amnesty for Russian leaders, but it was thought that the issue should be addressed.

- **Immunity**

It was stressed that immunity does not exist before international criminal tribunals, and, thus, it was critical that the tribunal be an international one to avoid the application of personal immunities. Personal immunity (i.e., immunity *ratione personae*), "provides immunity to certain high-level officials who represent the state, such as heads of state and foreign ministers, but only for the period in which they hold their official position".[101] Avoiding the application of personal immunities, as mentioned, was seen as particularly important because of the leadership nature of the crime.[102] Shielding top officials from prosecution could undermine the whole purpose of the endeavor.[103]

In this respect, it was recommended that the Statute replicate language from Rome Statute Article 27(1):

> This Statute shall apply equally to all persons without any distinction based on official capacity. In particular, official capacity as a Head of State or Government, a member of a Government or parliament, an elected representative or a government official shall in no case exempt a person from criminal responsibility under this Statute, nor shall it, in and of itself, constitute a ground for reduction of sentence.[104]

---

national court proceedings were not conducted impartially or independently, were designed to shield the accused from international criminal responsibility, or the case was not diligently prosecuted. See Rome Statute (1998) (as amended), note 18, Article 20(3).

[97] Representatives of Latvia, Liechtenstein, and Ukraine to the UN 2022, p. 6 (remarks of Jennifer Trahan).

[98] SCSL Statute, note 42, Article 10.

[99] Lomé Peace Agreement between the Government of Sierra Leone and the Revolutionary United Front of Sierra Leone (1999).

[100] See Special Court for Sierra Leone (2004) *Prosecutor v. Morris Kallon and Brima Buzzy Kamara*, SCSL-2004-15 AR72(E) and SCSL-2004-16-AR72(E), Decision on Challenge to Jurisdiction: Lomé Accord Amnesty (Appeals Chamber), para 88 (ruling that "whatever effect" an amnesty might have had in national courts it was "ineffective" to deprive an international court of jurisdiction).

[101] Hamilton 2023, p. 44. On immunity, see also Eboe-Osuji 2024.

[102] Representatives of Latvia, Liechtenstein, and Ukraine to the UN 2022, p. 6 (remarks of Jennifer Trahan).

[103] For more extensive discussion of the question of immunities, see Sect. 5.3.4.3.

[104] Representatives of Latvia, Liechtenstein, and Ukraine to the UN 2022, p. 6 (remarks of Jennifer Trahan), quoting Rome Statute (1998) (as amended), note 18, Article 27(1). See also London

- **Penalties**

The penalties would be limited to serving time in prison, thereby excluding the death penalty. The judges would be able to consider aggravating and mitigating factors as well as asset forfeiture.[105]

- **Trials *in Absentia***

The Ukrainian penal code permits trials *in absentia* in its domestic courts,[106] whereas the current and past international and hybrid tribunals do not, with the exception of the STL.[107] It was recommended not to permit trials *in absentia,* although it was noted that there could be something of a middle ground. Procedures exist that allow for the preservation of evidence without the presence of the accused, such as those found in rule 61 of the Rules of Procedure and Evidence of the ICTY.[108] Confirmation of charges proceedings can also occur in the absence of an accused and evidence can be presented during them as well.[109] Both processes can serve to preserve evidence and allow a limited amount of evidence to be presented in the absence of the accused.[110]

- **Additional Features**

The presentations included additional topics, such as the need for provisions on the sharing of classified information, witness protection, outreach, the establishment of a defense unit, victim participation, evidence collection, seizure and freezing of property, and a residual function.[111]

The Yale Club meeting concluded with discussion of the way forward provided by Ambassador Wenaweser, moderated by Prince Zeid Ra'ad Al Hussein (former

---

Charter (1945), note 13, Article 7 ("The official position of defendants, whether as Heads of State or responsible officials in Government Departments, shall not be considered as freeing them from responsibility or mitigating punishment".); ICTY Statute, note 79, Article 7.2; ICTR Statute, note 79, Article 6.2; SCSL Statute, note 42, Article 6.2.

105 Representatives of Latvia, Liechtenstein, and Ukraine to the UN 2022, p. 6 (remarks of Jennifer Trahan). See, e.g., ICTY Statute, note 79, Article 24; ICTR Statute, note 79, Article 23; SCSL Statute, note 42, Article 19; Rome Statute (1998) (as amended), note 18, Article 77.

106 See Code of Criminal Procedure of Ukraine 2012 (as amended), Article 262 ("Code of Criminal Procedure of Ukraine 2012 (as amended)").

107 The STL is something of an outlier in that it prosecuted the crime of terrorism. Its practice of holding trials *in absentia* has left lingering questions about the efficacy of the tribunal. See Wählisch 2017 ("Critics have commented that *in absentia* trials contradict the legitimacy basis of the tribunal, as the STL is supposed to be founded on the 'highest international standards of criminal justice'".).

108 Representatives of Latvia, Liechtenstein, and Ukraine to the UN 2022, p. 8 (remarks of David Scheffer). See Rules of Procedure and Evidence of the International Criminal Tribunal for the former Yugoslavia, as amended (1994), rule 61.

109 Rome Statute (1998) (as amended), note 18, Article 61.

110 For background on the ICC Office of the Prosecutor's request to confirm charges *in absentia* in the case of Joseph Kony, see Massimino 2024.

111 For details of these proposals, see Representatives of Latvia, Liechtenstein, and Ukraine to the UN 2022, pp. 7–8 (remarks of David Scheffer).

Permanent Representative of Jordan to the United Nations), and closing remarks by Ambassador Pildegovičs, Ambassador Wenaweser, and Professors Kreβ and Hathaway.[112] Closing remarks focused on the aggression against Ukraine as one of the most blatant violations of the prohibition of the use of force since the establishment of the UN Charter and stressed the imperative need to ensure justice.[113]

As mentioned, our group was by no means the only set of academics or government officials to call for the establishment of an international tribunal, and we were not the only ones to suggest the structure for a tribunal statute. David Crane, Hans Corell, and Irwin Cotler later produced a draft statute that shared many of the same features as our proposal, and credit should also be given to them for being vocal proponents of the establishment of an international tribunal.[114] Quite a number of additional individuals,[115] civil society organizations,[116] and states[117] were also thinking along the same lines—that the most legitimate and sound way to proceed was the establishment of an international tribunal.

As will be detailed in the next two chapters, this proposal for creating an international tribunal established through the United Nations did not prevail.[118] Those chapters detail the political considerations that came into play such that the strongest and most legitimate approach—in terms of ensuring accountability, pursuing the rule of law, and creating the strongest deterrence to protect the global order and stability of state boundaries—was not pursued.

5.3.4 Debate About Some of the Proposed Key Features

While, as will be discussed in Chap. 6, the G7 position developed into full-fledged political opposition to the establishment of an international tribunal,[119] questions of a technical variety about the proposal for an international tribunal meanwhile also arose. They included: (1) whether, or how, the tribunal could be established on the recommendation of the UN General Assembly; (2) the choice to utilize the Rome Statute's Article 8*bis* definition of the crime of aggression; (3) the question of immunities that could attach to high-level leaders absent the establishment of an international tribunal; (4) the issue of trials *in absentia*; and (5) the tribunal's

[112] For a summary of their remarks, see ibid., p. 10.

[113] Ibid.

[114] Global Accountability Network 2022a, pp. 7–14 (proposal for a Statute of a Special Tribunal for Ukraine on the Crime of Aggression).

[115] See notes 35–41 (academics); but see Heller 2022b (calling for "a hybrid tribunal established as part of the Ukrainian justice system"); Heller 2022a; Heller 2024.

[116] See note 3 (GIPA, Open Society Justice Initiative, The Elders); see also Global Accountability Network 2022a. But see Public International Law and Policy Group, note 46.

[117] See Sect. 5.4 (views of states).

[118] See Chaps. 6–7.

[119] See discussion, Chap. 6, Sect. 6.4.

relationship with the ICC. These topics, as well as the broader concern about pursuing selective (ad hoc) justice, are examined below.

5.3.4.1 Whether the Tribunal Could Be Established on the Recommendation of the UN General Assembly

One issue was whether the UN General Assembly could recommend the tribunal's establishment, with it formed by agreement between the UN and Ukraine. An important nuance of the proposal was that the UN General Assembly would not be *creating* or *establishing* the tribunal, but only *recommending* its establishment, with the power to make recommendations, as mentioned, firmly grounded in the UN Charter.[120] The tribunal would then be established by agreement between the UN and Ukraine.[121]

Two fairly close precedents existed. The first was the establishment of the Special Court for Sierra Leone. After a Chapter VI (not a Chapter VII) resolution of the UN Security Council,[122] the UN and the Government of Sierra Leone entered into an agreement to establish the Special Court. Specifically, UN Security Council Resolution 1315 "*[r]equest[ed]* the Secretary-General to negotiate an agreement with the Government of Sierra Leone to create an independent special court consistent with this resolution".[123] There is no reference to Chapter VII contained in the resolution.[124] The absence of a reference to Chapter VII means that by acting under Chapter VI, the Security Council was not using its Chapter VII powers. This distinction was important because the UN General Assembly has no equivalent to the Chapter VII powers. Subsequently, the UN and Government of Sierra Leone entered into such an agreement,[125] with the Special Court established after Sierra Leone's Parliament ratified the agreement.[126]

The second precedent was the establishment of the Extraordinary Chambers in the Courts of Cambodia ("ECCC"). The Tribunal was negotiated after the General Assembly requested that the Secretary-General establish a Group of Experts to explore the question of creating a tribunal to prosecute crimes committed in Cambodia.[127] The Group of Experts recommended that "the United Nations should establish an *ad hoc international tribunal* to try Khmer Rouge officials for crimes

---

[120] Corell 2023; note 67 (UN General Assembly powers).

[121] See Komarov and Hathaway 2022.

[122] "The Special Court for Sierra Leone (SCSL) was created by the Secretary-General based on a request by the Security Council acting under Chapter VI, not Chapter VII". Hathaway et al. 2023.

[123] United Nations Security Council Resolution 1315 (2000), para 1.

[124] Admittedly, there is sometimes ambiguity whether the Security Council is acting under Chapter VI or VII unless it expressly states or it is contextually obvious (e.g., the exercise of certain coercive powers necessarily mean it is acting under Chapter VII).

[125] Agreement between the United Nations and the Government of Sierra Leone on the Establishment of a Special Court for Sierra Leone (2002) 2178 UNTS 137.

[126] The Agreement was ratified by Sierra Leone's Parliament in March 2022. See Special Court for Sierra Leone, Outreach and Special Affairs Section 2011.

[127] United Nations General Assembly Resolution 52/135 (1998).

against humanity and genocide . . . [and] that the Security Council establish this tribunal under Chapter VI or VII of the Charter of the United Nations, or, should it not do so, that the General Assembly establish it".[128] After lengthy negotiations, by March 2003, the UN and Cambodia concluded an agreement to establish the tribunal,[129] with the General Assembly approving it.[130] The Agreement was signed on 6 June 2023 by the Government of Cambodia and the United Nations.[131] Cambodia's National Assembly ratified it the following year.[132] The ECCC ultimately was established within the Cambodian Court system,[133] but the Group of Experts certainly took the view that an international tribunal could have been established following a General Assembly resolution.[134]

A special tribunal on the crime of aggression for Ukraine would be mixing and matching the two precedents, taking the more international features of the Special Court, but following a resolution of the General Assembly, as occurred with the ECCC. The Yale Club meeting presenters, as well former Under-Secretary-General for Legal Affairs and the Legal Counsel of the United Nations, Ambassador (ret.) Hans Corell[135] and former Assistant Secretary-General for Legal Affairs at the United Nations Larry Johnson,[136] agreed that there was solid foundation for the General Assembly making such a recommendation and having the tribunal established by this route.

The General Assembly, can, of course, also create subsidiary bodies, as it did when it established an investigative mechanism that compiles evidence of atrocity crimes in the situation in Syria—the International, Impartial and Independent Mechanism

---

[128] United Nations General Assembly 1999 (emphasis added).

[129] Draft Agreement between the United Nations and the Royal Government of Cambodia Concerning the Prosecution under Cambodian Law of Crimes Committed During the Period of Democratic Kampuchea (2003).

[130] United Nations General Assembly Resolution 57/228B (2003).

[131] Corell 2020.

[132] Cambodia (2004) Law on the Establishment of the Extraordinary Chambers, with Inclusion of Amendments as Promulgated on 27 October 2004. NS/RKM/1004/006. https://www.eccc.gov.kh/sites/default/files/legal-documents/KR_Law_as_amended_27_Oct_2004_Eng.pdf. Accessed 19 August 2025.

[133] Ibid.

[134] See also Hathaway et al. 2023.

[135] See, e.g., Corell 2023; Hathaway et al. 2023.

[136] Johnson wrote:

> There are . . . tools that the General Assembly can utilize to facilitate accountability for the persons responsible for international crimes during the ongoing Russian invasion of Ukraine. This action would be legally on solid ground if requested by the Ukrainian Government . . . . What might be of interest to the Ukraine Government is to establish some form of . . . investigative mechanism or criminal tribunal which could deal specifically with the crime of aggression as this case presents a prima facie case for investigation and possible prosecution of that crime.
>
> Johnson 2022.

for Syria ("IIIM").[137] As Oona Hathaway, Maggie Mills, and Heather Zimmerman explain, the UN General Assembly also established the UN Administrative Tribunal in 1949.[138] "The tribunal was an independent organ that could hear and judge internal administrative matters, such as employment contract disputes".[139] In a 1954 Advisory Opinion, "the ICJ considered the legality of the Tribunal, which it described as 'an independent and truly judicial body pronouncing judgments without appeal within the limited field of its functions'".[140] Thus, precedent exists both for the UN General Assembly to establish a judicial body (on at least one occasion),[141] to establish an investigative mechanism (the IIIM), and to trigger a process that led to the establishment of an ad hoc hybrid criminal tribunal (the ECCC).[142]

5.3.4.2 Utilizing the Rome Statute's Definition of the Crime of Aggression

Another important feature of the proposal was utilizing the ICC's definition of the crime of aggression. There were sound reasons to use the Rome Statute Article 8*bis* definition. This definition represents the current definition of the crime, having been adopted by consensus of all States Parties to the ICC's Rome Statute after a process (the meetings of the SWGCA) that had been open to all states.[143] While Ukrainian (and Russian) law contains a more minimal and circular definition of the crime[144]

---

137 See United Nations General Assembly Resolution A/71/248 (2016) (establishing the IIIM); for the website of the IIIM, see International, Impartial and Independent Mechanism for Syria (nd). https://www.ungeneva.org/en/about/organizations/IIIM-Syria. Accessed 19 August 2025.

138 Hathaway et al. 2023; United Nations General Assembly Resolution 351 (IV) (1949) (establishing the UN Administrative Tribunal).

139 Hathaway et al. 2023.

140 Ibid., citing International Court of Justice (1954) *Effect of Awards of Compensation Made by the UN Administrative Tribunal*, Advisory Opinion, 1954 ICJ Rep. 47, p. 53.

141 Admittedly, the UN Administrative Tribunal is a "tribunal judging UN civil servants". Corten and Koutroulis 2022, p. 15.

142 See ibid., p. 18 ("it is clearly within the powers of UNGA to trigger the process of setting up a tribunal and request the UN Secretary-General to undertake the necessary steps to this effect"). Corten and Koutroulis go on to suggest that unless the UNGA creates the tribunal under binding powers (which they suggest is possible, p. 15, but was not our proposal), the tribunal would only be grounded in Ukraine's domestic criminal jurisdiction. Ibid., p. 19. Our proposal would be grounded in Ukraine's territorial jurisdiction as victim of the crime of aggression; yet, the recommendation or endorsement of the UN General Assembly would mean the tribunal would be endorsed by the international community, making it an international tribunal. For discussion of what makes a tribunal international, see Reisinger Coracini and Trahan 2022; text accompanying note 163.

143 International Criminal Court, Assembly of States Parties 2010. On the work of the SWGCA, see International Criminal Court nd-b.

144 "Article 437 of the Ukrainian Criminal Code outlaws planning, preparation or initiation of an aggressive war or an armed conflict, conspiring for any such purpose or waging of an aggressive war or aggressive hostilities". Masol 2024; Criminal Code of Ukraine 2011, Article 437; see also Criminal Code of the Russian Federation No. 63-Fz 1996, Article 353.

modeled on the definition found in the London Charter that established the Nuremberg Tribunal,[145] the 1945 definition of the crime is outdated. One difference is that the Nuremberg formulation only covered a war of aggression,[146] whereas the Article 8*bis* definition covers an act of aggression (a lower threshold than full-scale war); however, the act also needs to rise to the level of a manifest violation of the UN Charter.[147] The Article 8*bis* definition is also significantly more specific as to what it encompasses, containing two lengthy paragraphs,[148] while the Nuremberg definition contained one sentence.[149]

Additionally, as explained in Chap. 3, the Article 8*bis* definition of the crime is historically based on sound precedent.[150] The definition of *act of aggression* in Article 8*bis*(2) takes its text almost entirely from Article 2(4) of the UN Charter and UN General Assembly resolutions 3314 (which, in turn was based on text from 1933); the definition of the crime in Article 8*bis*(1) takes its conduct words from the London Charter of the Nuremberg Tribunal.[151]

In further support of utilizing the Article 8*bis* definition, Reisinger Coracini explains:

> The prohibition and criminalization of aggression involve rules that are beyond any doubt part of customary international law. This is true for the customary nature of the prohibition on the use of force, the principle of individual criminal responsibility for serious violations of international law, and the crime of aggression .... The elements of the crime of aggression as defined in Article 8*bis* are well established in statutory criminal definitions on national and international levels (the leadership element and individual conduct). The understanding of aggression, the collective act underlying the crime, has remained virtually unchanged in GA Resolution 3314 and Article 8*bis*(2) of the ICC Statute since it was first introduced by a Soviet diplomat in 1933 and was found to reflect customary law by the International Court of Justice (*Nicaragua v. United States* ...). Finally, and in order to codify a narrow definition of the crime, a threshold clause confines the scope of individual criminal responsibility vis-à-vis unlawful acts of aggression. The result is a particularly narrow definition that is difficult to meet.[152]

---

145 London Charter 1945, note 13, Article 6(a) (defining "crimes against peace" as "planning, preparation, initiation or waging of a war of aggression, or a war in violation of international treaties, agreements or assurances, or participation in a common plan or conspiracy for the accomplishment of any of the foregoing . . ."). The Charter contains no definition of "a war of aggression".

146 Ibid.

147 For details on the "manifest" threshold, see Chap. 3, Sect. 3.2.2; Chap. 4, Sect. 4.3.3.

148 See Rome Statute (1998) (as amended), note 18, Article 8*bis*.

149 London Charter (1945), note 13, Article 6(a).

150 See Chap. 3, Sect. 3.2.2.

151 See ibid.

152 Reisinger Coracini 2022, citing Stahn and van den Herik 2010, ch 18; Kreβ and Barriga 2016, ch. 14; Definition of "Aggressor" at the League of Nations Conference for the Reduction and Limitation of Armaments on the 6th February 1933 (nd). http://www.letton.ch/lvx_33sdn.htm. Accessed 19 August 2025; International Court of Justice (1986) *Case Concerning Military and Paramilitary Activities in and Against Nicaragua (Nicaragua v. United States)*, Merits, 1986 ICJ Rep. 14, para 195 (*a minore ad meius*). There is admittedly some disagreement whether it is the Nuremberg definition that is customary international law, or whether it is now the Article 8*bis* definition that is. See Heller 2024, p. 4 (examining the discrepancy in views). While the Nuremberg definition

Reisinger Coracini further explains that at the 2010 Review Conference where the definition was adopted: "Delegations voiced particular strong support for the definition and Elements of Crimes of the crime of aggression. The United States delegation's attempts to spread doubts about the existence of a consensus on issues of substantive law were unequivocally rejected".[153]

5.3.4.3 Avoiding the Application of Immunities

It came to be seen by various authorities,[154] including, importantly, Ukraine,[155] that a key feature of the tribunal needed to be the ability to overcome personal immunities that otherwise could attach to the so-called "troika"—the Head of State, Head of Government, and Minister of Foreign Affairs.[156] It is clear from the case law of the ICJ in its *Yerodia* (Arrest Warrant) decision,[157] as well as the Special Court for Sierra Leone's *Charles Taylor* decision,[158] and the ICC's decision regarding Jordan's failure to arrest then President Bashir of Sudan,[159] "that such immunities do not attach when prosecution of an international crime occurs before an international tribunal established under international law".[160] The ICTY also "confirmed the indictment

---

undoubtedly became customary international law after 1945, with the 2010 adoption of the Rome Statute's Article 8*bis* definition by all Rome Statute States Parties, see International Criminal Court, Assembly of States Parties 2010, a strong argument exists that the Article 8*bis* definition has become the current manifestation of customary international law.

[153] Reisinger Coracini 2010, p. 756, n 59. The United States was no proponent of the crime of aggression being incorporated into the Rome Statute *at all*. Accordingly, its qualms or purported qualms about the definition should be considered in that context. See Koh and Buchwald 2015 (US views).

[154] See, e.g., Council of Europe, Newsroom 2022 (Parliamentary Assembly of the Council of Europe calling for a tribunal that would "have the power to issue international arrest warrants and not be limited by State immunity or the immunity of heads of State and government and other State officials").

[155] See, e.g., Zelenskyy 2023.

[156] ICJ 2002, *Arrest Warrant*, note 10, paras 51, 61 ("holders of high-ranking office in a State, such as the Head of State, Head of Government and Minister for Foreign Affairs, enjoy immunities from jurisdiction in other States" but may be prosecuted before *certain international courts* such as the ICTY, ICTR, or ICC). In the case of Russia, the positions of the troika are held by President Vladimir Putin, Prime Minister Mishustin, and Foreign Minister Lavrov. See Hamilton 2023, p. 56 ("The optics would be galling if an aggression tribunal proceeded to trial against a comparatively lesser-ranked official while failing to indict Putin for a war that he launched").

[157] ICJ 2002, *Arrest Warrant*, note 10.

[158] Special Court for Sierra Leone (2004) *Prosecutor v. Charles Ghankay Taylor*, SCSL-2003-01-I, Appeals Chamber Decision on Immunity from Jurisdiction ("*Prosecutor v. Taylor*").

[159] International Criminal Court (2019) *Prosecutor v. Al-Bashir,* Judgment in the Jordan Referral re Al-Bashir Appeal, ICC-02/05-01/09 OA2, Ap. Ch., para 162 ("There was no Head of State immunity that would have prevented Jordan from executing the [ICC] warrant for the arrest and surrender [of then-President al-Bashir of Sudan] issued by the Court"). For further discussion, see Kreß 2019.

[160] For details, see Reisinger Coracini and Trahan 2022.

against former President Slobodan Milošević of the Federal Republic of Yugoslavia and transmitted his arrest warrant to all UN Member States at a time when Milošević was still a sitting Head of State".[161] Additionally, the ICC issued a summons against Uhuru Kenyatta, who later became President of Kenya; while the case against him was later withdrawn, it was not withdrawn on grounds of head of state immunity (i.e., he presumptively lacked such immunity before the ICC).[162]

As Professor Reisinger Coracini and I demonstrate elsewhere, an international tribunal is one established under international law, that prosecutes crimes under international law, where the tribunal's establishment represents the will of the international community as a whole.[163] The Appeals Chamber of the Special Court for Sierra Leone convincingly explained the reason for the distinction between national and international courts:

> This result attaches because of the principle that one sovereign state does not adjudicate on the conduct of another state; the principle of state immunity derives from the equality of sovereign states and therefore has no relevance to international criminal tribunals which are not organs of a state but derive their mandate from the international community.[164]

In this respect, international courts are inherently different from national ones.

As mentioned earlier, while the ICJ in the *Yerodia* (Arrest Warrant) case listed the ICTY, ICTR, and ICC as international tribunals to which such personal immunities do not attach,[165] it did not limit itself to those tribunals. For example, the Special Court for Sierra Leone detailed why that tribunal (despite hybrid features) was also an *international* one where such immunities would not apply:

a. The Special Court is not part of the judiciary of Sierra Leone and is not a national court.
b. The Special Court is established by treaty and has the characteristics associated with classical international organisations (including legal personality; the capacity to enter into agreements with other international persons governed by international law; privileges and immunities; and an autonomous will distinct from that of its members).

---

[161] International Criminal Tribunal for the former Yugoslavia (1999) *Prosecutor v. Milošević*, IT-99-37-I, Decision on Review of Indictment and Application for Consequential Orders. The case was terminated upon the death of Milošević. See International Criminal Tribunal for the former Yugoslavia (nd) *Slobodan Milošević, "Kosovo, Croatia & Bosnia"*, IT-02-54, Case Information Sheet. https://www.icty.org/x/cases/slobodan_milosevic/cis/en/cis_milosevic_slobodan_en.pdf. Accessed 19 August 2025 (proceedings terminated on 14 March 2006 after Milošević's death on 11 March 2006).

[162] International Criminal Court (nd-c) *The Prosecutor v. Uhuru Muigai Kenyatta*, ICC-01/09-02/11, Case Information Sheet. https://www.icc-cpi.int/sites/default/files/CaseInformationSheets/KenyattaEng.pdf. Accessed 19 August 2025. The Kenyatta summons does not provide as much precedent as the other situations discussed because Kenya, as a Rome Statute State Party, agreed to the suspension of Head of State immunity in Article 27 of the Rome Statute. See Rome Statute (1998) (as amended), note 18, Article 27.

[163] See Reisinger Coracini and Trahan 2022

[164] *Prosecutor v. Taylor*, note 158, para 51.

[165] ICJ 2002, *Arrest Warrant*, note 10, para 61.

c. The competence and jurisdiction *ratione materiae* and *ratione personae* are broadly similar to that of ICTY and the ICTR and the ICC, including in relation to the provisions confirming the absence of entitlement of any person to a claim of immunity.
d. Accordingly, there is no reason to conclude that the Special Court should be treated as anything other than an international tribunal or court, with all that implies for the question of immunity for a serving Head of State.[166]

The same would be true of a tribunal established upon the recommendation of the UN General Assembly and by agreement between the UN and Ukraine. That is: (a) it would not be part of the judiciary of Ukraine and thus not a national court; (b) it would be established by treaty and have the characteristics associated with classical international organizations (including legal personality, the capacity to enter into agreements with other international persons governed by international law, privileges and immunities, and an autonomous will distinct from that of its members); and (c) it would have the competence and jurisdiction *ratione materiae* and *ratione personae* broadly similar to that of the ICTY, the ICTR, and the ICC, including in relation to the provisions confirming the absence of entitlement of any person to claim immunity.[167] Thus, (d) it would be an international court or tribunal, with all that implies for the question of immunity for a serving Head of State and other members of the troika.[168]

The ruling of the Special Court for Sierra Leone in the *Charles Taylor* case that Taylor's indictment was valid, *even though issued while he was a sitting Head of State of a neighboring country*,[169] would be directly on point. Even though the Special Court possessed hybrid features (for example, benches of judges appointed both internationally and by Sierra Leone),[170] the Appeals Chamber ruled that, having been formed by agreement between the UN and Sierra Leone, its formation made it an international tribunal that could overcome personal immunities.[171] Thus, the Appeals Chamber of the Special Court ruled that even though Taylor was President

166 *Prosecutor v. Taylor*, note 158, para 41.

167 Reisinger Coracini and Trahan 2022.

168 Ibid.

169 *Prosecutor v. Taylor*, note 158, para 53.

170 Agreement on the Establishment of a Special Court, Article 2 (composition of the Special Court and appointment of judges).

171 The Appeals Chamber also focused on Security Council Resolution 1315 that initiated the establishment of the Court. *Prosecutor v. Taylor*, note 158, para 37, citing United Nations Security Council Resolution 1315. It found that the "Security Council acts on behalf of the members of the United Nations". Ibid., para 38. It therefore concluded: "The Agreement between the United Nations and Sierra Leone is thus an agreement between all members of the United Nations and Sierra Leone. This fact makes the Agreement an expression of the will of the international community. The Special Court established in such circumstances is truly international". Ibid. The same reasoning would apply to an aggression-specific tribunal created upon the recommendation of either the UN Security Council (acting, for example, under Chapter VI of the UN Charter, with mandatory abstention of a party to the dispute, Russia, applying) or the UN General Assembly—the subsequent agreement between the UN and Ukraine would represent the will of the international community. See UN Charter, note 20, Article 27(3) ("in decisions under Chapter VI . . . a party to a dispute shall

of Liberia at the time of his indictment, "the official position of the Applicant as an incumbent Head of State at the time when these criminal proceedings were initiated against him [was] not a bar to his prosecution by this court".[172] This ruling would have been directly applicable regarding proceedings against President Putin and other members of the troika vis-à-vis a tribunal created by agreement between the UN and Ukraine after a UN General Assembly resolution.

Our view on the need for an international tribunal was not unanimously accepted. Kevin Jon Heller, for example, argued:

> A Special Tribunal would not find it easier to prosecute Russian officials for aggression than a national court. A Special Tribunal is not necessary to affirm the unacceptability and criminality of aggression. And a Special Tribunal would be no less obligated than a national court to honour the personal immunity of people like Putin and Lavrov.[173]

While his writing in that instance may have been focused on the proposal by Philippe Sands and Gordon Brown[174]—and the present author would agree with that assessment[175]—the same conclusions would certainly not be true if the tribunal were formed by agreement between the UN and Ukraine and recommended or endorsed by the UN General Assembly. Heller, in other writing, appears to concede that a General Assembly endorsement of a tribunal established by agreement between the UN and Ukraine *could* set aside personal immunities if the endorsing resolution were well-supported and cross-regional.[176] He admits that personal immunities, by contrast, *would* apply before a national court.[177]

---

abstain from voting"). Just as the Security Council acts on behalf of the members of the UN, so too does the UN General Assembly, which is composed of the members of the UN.

172 Prosecutor v. Taylor, note 158, para 53.

173 Heller 2022a.

174 See Sect. 5.2.1.

175 See notes 12–13 and accompanying text (concern whether a tribunal established through "pooled jurisdiction" could overcome personal immunities).

176 Heller 2024, p. 16 ("a court should be considered 'international' as long as it 'can make a convincing claim to directly embody the 'collective will'"; suggesting this could be met by a General Assembly resolution endorsing a tribunal where the resolution is supported by a very large and representative majority of states). See also Dannenbaum 2022a ("If it is correct to say that status immunities do not apply before international courts *qua* international courts, a court created by the General Assembly would have the strongest claim to that status"). Heller, however, takes the position that the ICJ's *Arrest Warrant* case and Special Court's *Charles Taylor* case were wrongly decided and that Article 27 of the Rome Statute (irrelevance of official capacity) is invalid, at least in certain circumstances. See, e.g., Heller 2022a (questioning the basis for the ICJ's ruling that personal immunity would not apply before the ICC, at least in certain circumstances); Heller 2024, p. 10 (arguing that the Special Court's *Charles Taylor* case and Article 27 of the Rome Statute do not manifest or establish customary international law); Heller 2024, p. 11 ("if national courts cannot set aside personal immunities (and it is undisputed that they cannot), the international courts they create cannot either"). He thereby implies that Rome Statute Article 27—precluding the application of Head of State immunity—is invalid.

177 Heller 2024, p. 22 ("there is no question that [personal immunity] applies before national [courts]"). See also McDougall 2022 ("foreign domestic courts will be unable to exercise jurisdiction over persons who enjoy personal immunity (including Putin and Lukashenko) during their

Functional immunity (i.e. immunity *ratione materiae*)—which provides "lasting immunity to state officials for official acts they performed in their position"[178]—would not impose an impediment regarding an international tribunal. The issue of functional immunity arises, if at all, at the national level.[179]

5.3.4.4 The Issue of Trials *in Absentia*

An issue that later emerged as significant was whether or not the tribunal should be permitted to conduct trials *in absentia.*[180] Ukraine's Code of Criminal Procedure allows for such trials,[181] and there was a very real concern that high- or mid-level Russian leaders implicated in the crime might not be able to be apprehended.

Others took the position that trials in *absentia* could be seen as violating due process protections,[182] absent narrow circumstances such as where an accused has been present and voluntarily chooses to be absent during trial.[183] As mentioned,

---

term in office"). Some have presented a creative, if completely untested, alternative argument of disregarding immunities on the basis of self-defense. See Corten and Koutroulis 2022, pp. 29–31 (discussing the theory).

[178] Hamilton 2023, p. 44.

[179] On functional immunity, see United Nations General Assembly, International Law Commission 2022, pp. 190–91 (suggesting functional immunity for the crime of aggression does apply before another state's domestic courts). For states taking the view that the ILC erred in leaving the crime of aggression off its list of crimes as to which functional immunity does not apply, see, e.g., Pacheco 2024. As to why the ILC needs to add the crime of aggression back to its list of crimes as to which functional immunity does not apply before another state's domestic courts, see UN General Assembly, International Law Commission 2025b. The ILC's Drafting Committee has now done so. See UN General Assembly, International Law Commission 2025a.

[180] The debate came to the fore particular during deliberations of the "Core Group" of states over the establishment of a tribunal through the Council of Europe. See Chap. 7, Sect. 7.3.4.

[181] See T.M.C. Asser Institute (nd) Trials *in absentia* (trials *in absentia* "have always been allowed under the Criminal Procedure Code of Ukraine . . ."); see Code of Criminal Procedure of Ukraine 2012 (as amended), note 106, Article 262 ("[The] [t]rial court considers the case in the presence of the defendant whose appearance in court is necessarily required. In the absence of the defendant, the case may be considered only on [an] exceptional basis: 1) when the defendant stays outside the limits of Ukraine and evades appearing in court; 2) if the defendant requests that his/her case related to [a] crime which may not be punished with confinement be considered in his/her absence. However, if so, the court may find that [the] defendant's appearance is necessarily required"). The website of Ukraine's Office of the Prosecutor General states that Ukraine has 437 registered crimes of aggression involving 736 suspects. Prosecutor General's Office, Crimes Committed during the Full-Scale Invasion of the RF. https://gp.gov.ua/en. Accessed 17 September 2025. Because Ukraine permits trials *in absentia*, a number of these prosecutions are likely being carried out *in absentia.*

[182] "Some member states, notably Italy, frequently try defendants in their absence, but the practice is not allowed in other EU member states". Brunsden 2008.

[183] See, e.g., T.M.C. Asser Institute (nd) Trials *in absentia* ("There are two general scenarios where [it is seen as legitimate to proceed in the absence of the accused]: (i) where the accused is removed from court for disrupting proceedings and the prosecution or court decide to continue in his absence; and (ii) where the accused does not show up at trial (or ceases to attend midway through) and the prosecution or court decide to continue in his absence . . . . [In the second scenario] a decision to

all recent[184] international criminal and hybrid tribunals absent one (the STL)[185] do not permit or have not permitted trials *in absentia* despite also facing difficulties associated with apprehending accused for trials before those tribunals.[186] Trials *in absentia* also raise problematic optics: what exactly is achieved through a trial where there is no accused?[187] In part due to the STL having held trials *in absentia*, there are lingering questions about what the tribunal accomplished.[188] Article 14(3)(d) of the International Covenant on Civil and Political Rights ("ICCPR")—to which Ukraine is a party[189]—provides that a person facing a criminal charge has the right to be informed of the charges and tried in his or her own presence.[190] While trials *in absentia* are not prohibited by international law, one view is that "they are strongly

---

continue in absence will only be lawful if the prosecution can demonstrate that the accused waived his right to be present") (also discussing "[t]he question of what constitutes a legitimate waiver and what evidence the State must produce to demonstrate that waiver").

184 The Nuremberg Tribunal tried Martin Bormann *in absentia*, although it later turned out that Bormann was already deceased by the time of trial. Schwarz 2016.

185 See STL Statute, note 64, Article 22. "The STL is the only institution which explicitly allows trials in the complete absence of the accused. The ICTY, ICTR, SCSL and the ECCC have allowed partial trials under exceptional circumstances while the ICC Rules of Procedure and Evidence were changed in 2013 which allow for the accused not to be present during part of his trial". Rikhof 2018.

186 A long complex process led to the apprehension and transfer of Slobodan Milošević, Ratko Mladić, and Radovan Karadžić to the ICTY, and Charles Taylor to the Special Court for Sierra Leone. For background on arrests in the former Yugoslavia, see, e.g., Borger 2016. The ICC has a number of outstanding arrest warrants. See Statista Research Department 2024 (as of November 2024, the ICC had 22 outstanding arrest warrants).

187 One report summarizes the concern:

> At the outset it must be remembered that the primary—and overriding—duty of a criminal court is to conduct a fair trial. The defendant is, and must always be, the central figure. The trial is the accused's opportunity to challenge evidence against him and to present his account. It is his opportunity to tell his version of the story. To conduct a trial without the accused is like trying to stage Hamlet without Hamlet. The story of Hamlet cannot be fully told without the Prince himself on stage. It would not be the same play. Without the accused (even with the best supporting cast of judges, prosecutors and witnesses) the trial is not the same trial. For this reason, international law is cautious about *in absentia* proceedings and they have generally been absent from the international arena . . . .

T.M.C. Asser Institute (nd) Trials *in absentia*. But see Massimino 2023 (arguing in favor of trials *in absentia*: first, it would be appropriate considering the heinous nature of the crime; second, it would help fulfill the rights of the victims; third, it would be helpful in the preservation of evidence; and fourth, due process safeguards could be provided).

188 See, e.g., Wählisch 2017.

189 United Nations Treaty Body Database nd.

190 ICCPR, note 81, Article 14(3)(d). Alexander Schwarz writes:

> From the wording of the Covenant, it may be concluded that *in absentia* trials are generally not permissible under the ICCPR. The meaning of article 14(3)(d) of the ICCPR is explained further in General Comment 13 of the Human Rights Committee (HRC), which makes it clear that "[w]hen exceptionally for justified reasons trials *in absentia* are held, strict observance of the rights of the defence is all the more necessary". Even though the HRC leaves the exact meaning of "justified reasons" open, it is clear that, although *in absentia* proceedings

disfavoured", and some might argue that they "compromise a defendant's ability to exercise his or her rights under the ICCPR".[191]

One scholar explains the concern with trials *in absentia*:

> [I]nternational practice, as well as the majority of scholarly opinions, exclude *in absentia* trials, as they are viewed as a tool of authoritarian regimes depriving effective defence. [Justice Antonio] Cassese himself underlined that: "Indeed on many occasions, undemocratic states have used trials *in absentia* to convict and sentence political dissidents living abroad." While he upholds that his home country, Italy, allows such trials, he notes that most other countries in the world—among them the United States and Germany—have ruled them out. Iran and Pakistan use the procedure as common practice in criminal trials, whereas China has declared an unconditional prohibition of trial *in absentia*. Russia banned trials *in absentia* in its reformed Code of Criminal Procedure in 2002. According to Dmitri Kozak, President Putin's Deputy Chief of Staff, the revised code is intended to give Russia "a criminal procedure that corresponds to that of world standards and of civilized countries". The Statute of the International Criminal Court, which may be the most ground-breaking and authoritative agreement within the field of international criminal law, declares the presence of the accused to be an explicit precondition.[192]

Differences of opinion on the question of trials *in absentia* emerged between different stakeholders in the international community, with Ukrainian officials arguing for the expressive value of arrest warrants and *in absentia* proceedings, whereas other states, at least in many rounds of later negotiations, did not share their views on trials *in absentia*.[193]

5.3.4.5 The Relationship with the ICC

Another area that presented complexities concerned the relationship of the tribunal with the ICC. In particular, two considerations emerged: (1) whether an additional tribunal prosecuting a crime that was designed to be prosecuted before the ICC would undermine the work of the ICC, as some claimed; and (2) if there were two tribunals *and* the same person were accused by both *and* the person were in custody, which tribunal would prosecute first.

David Scheffer, in his writing, for example, emphasized that any aggression tribunal would need to work cooperatively with the ICC,[194] which was already active

---

are not *per se* impermissible within the sphere of the ICCPR, they are only possible in exceptional cases.

Schwarz 2016 (citations omitted).

[191] Heller 2024, p. 22.

[192] Wählisch 2017, pp. 309–10.

[193] Interview with a Participant in the Core Group Negotiations, 25 July 2025, discussed in Chap. 7.

[194] See Scheffer 2022b; see also Sluiter 2023 ("In the case of adequate coordination, there can be a good division of labour and mutual reinforcement. But there is also a risk that—despite all good intentions—the new aggression tribunal will be regarded as a competitor of, or an alternative to, the ICC and that the question arises of what the value and relevance of the ICC actually is if another tribunal is also needed").

in the situation, gathering evidence of war crimes and crimes against humanity and having issued several arrest warrants.[195] During the Yale Club meeting, Ukrainian Ambassador Sergiy Kyslytsya emphasized that an aggression tribunal would not compete with, but complement, the ICC.[196]

This situation became complicated when ICC Prosecutor, Karim Khan, expressed his concern about the establishment of an ad hoc aggression tribunal—even though the ICC could not prosecute the crime of aggression in the current situation. He articulated the view that "[w]e should avoid fragmentation, and instead work on consolidation".[197] He called for a "focus on mobilizing . . . what already exists" and raised concern about "self-indulgen[ce] in creating things that we'd like", rather than "putting [what we already have] into action effectively".[198] Such views were not unanimous within the ICC, with then ICC President Piotr Hofmański initially expressing a favorable view of establishing a separate tribunal,[199] although less favorable when speaking on the record.[200] Eventually it seemed that the ICC, which risked being seen as a spoiler, blocking justice that it could not pursue, appeared to decide on a policy of not having a formal policy on the issue.[201]

While a special agreement on cooperation probably would be required between the ICC and a special aggression tribunal to govern various aspects of their relationship,[202] a particular question arose as to the application of *ne bis in idem* (the prohibition on double jeopardy). Specifically, which tribunal would prosecute first in the event that the ICC and special tribunal were to seek to try the same accused who was in custody? Might the second trial risk being precluded due to the prohibition on double jeopardy? Of course, this situation might never arise. But if it did, obviously "the same individual cannot be in the custody of and on trial before . . . two tribunals at the same time".[203]

As to how the timing might play out, Rome Statute Article 20 provides:

> 2. No person shall be tried by another court *for a crime* referred to in Article 5 for which that person has already been convicted or acquitted by the Court.

---

195 See, e.g., International Criminal Court, Press Release 2023.

196 Representatives of Latvia, Liechtenstein, and Ukraine to the UN 2022, pp. 2–3.

197 Quell 2022.

198 Dannenbaum 2022b, p. 863, citing PBS News Hour 2022. See also Hathaway 2023 ("[Khan] tried to throw cold water on the proposal to create a special tribunal to try the crime of aggression . . . . Khan's position may be motivated more by a desire to keep the limelight on himself than by principled objection").

199 Recollection of the author from a meeting with President Hofmański.

200 He reportedly stated: "I think that, from a broader point of view, setting up the aggression tribunal is not a legitimate step for States to take, simply because States decided to put a very complicated trigger mechanism [for ICC jurisdiction over the crime of aggression] in the Kampala amendments". Haxton 2024.

201 Observations of the author.

202 Scheffer 2022b.

203 Ibid.

3. No person who has been tried by another court for conduct also proscribed under Articles 6, 7, 8 or 8 *bis* shall be tried by the Court *with respect to the same conduct* unless the proceedings in the other court:
   (a) Were for the purpose of shielding the person concerned from criminal responsibility for crimes within the jurisdiction of the Court; or
   (b) Otherwise were not conducted independently or impartially in accordance with the norms of due process recognized by international law and were conducted in a manner which, in the circumstances, was inconsistent with an intent to bring the person concerned to justice.[204]

Importantly, paragraph 2 refers to the same "crime" being tried by another court, whereas paragraph 3 refers to "the same conduct" being at issue before two courts. Thus, under paragraph 2, if the ICC were to prosecute first, no issue of double jeopardy would arise, because proceedings before an aggression tribunal would be *for a different crime* than proceedings before the ICC. There would be no risk of double jeopardy attaching. By contrast, paragraph 3 suggests that if an aggression tribunal were to prosecute an individual first for the crime of aggression, but some of *the conduct* at issue also formed the basis of charges before the ICC (such as war crimes charges),[205] the second trial before the ICC could risk being precluded.[206]

While not all scholars shared the assessment that there is such a risk,[207] out of an abundance of caution, the foregoing analysis suggests that, all else being equal, the ICC should prosecute first if a person were to be in custody and charged by both

[204] Rome Statute (1998) (as amended), note 18, Articles 20(2)–(3) (emphasis added). Article 20(1) states: "Except as provided in this Statute, no person shall be tried *before the Court* with respect to conduct which formed the basis of crimes for which the person has been convicted or acquitted *by the Court*". Ibid., Article 20(1) (emphasis added). Paragraph 1 thus "prohibits the ICC from repeatedly trying the person for the same culpable conduct for which the person has already been convicted or acquitted by the ICC". Nuridzhanian and McDougall 2024.

[205] It is not impossible to imagine that an order to invade certain territory (assume it is predominantly civilian occupied) could also result in war crimes being committed against the civilian population. Thus, there is some potential for overlap in the underlying conduct. David Scheffer also envisions that this overlap could arise. See Scheffer 2022b. Gaiane Nuridzhanian and Carrie McDougall, however, maintain that the same conduct would not be at issue. See Nuridzhanian and McDougall 2024 ("Engaging in the planning of other crimes, even if undertaken at the same time and in the same place, is factually distinct conduct. A discussion about instructions to be given to armed forces about their rules of engagement, or the fact that troops will not be prosecuted for violations of international humanitarian law, or about the strategic or operational benefits of the large-scale commission of war crimes (for example, that it might weaken the victim population's morale and ability to resist and cause a victim State to surrender) is simply not the same conduct as planning a State act of aggression").

[206] See Scheffer 2022b (reaching the same conclusion).

[207] See note 205 (Nuridzhanian and McDougall arguing the same conduct would not be at issue). Nuridzhanian and McDougall also argue that no such risk arises because "another court" in paragraph 3 refers only to another domestic court, but not another international or internationalized tribunal—they believe double-jeopardy to be inapplicable between two international tribunals. Nuridzhanian and McDougall 2024. Other scholars, however, do not share their reading of Article 20(3). See Reisinger Coracini and Tallgren 2016, p. 916 ("'by another court' also encompasses international or internationalized courts. Courts in this context are to be understood as international adjudicating bodies, including, e. g., the ad hoc international criminal tribunals, other mixed or

tribunals. Should an aggression tribunal prosecute first, but *in absentia*, assuming none of the considerations in Rome Statute Article 20(3)(a) or (b) are implicated, the same concerns could arise. Namely, pursuant to Article 20(2), if the ICC prosecutes second, charges, if any, based on *the same conduct* that was at issue in the *in absentia* trial could be precluded during a second trial.[208]

5.3.4.6 The Issue of Selectivity

Aside from questions about the particular features of the tribunal was the question of political will and, in particular, the issue of selectivity. One suspects that for some states, the issue of selectivity was a positive—some states no doubt *did want* to prosecute Russian leaders for the crime of aggression and not open the door to prosecution of the crime more broadly. Yet, for many others, a concern arose about having an ad hoc response: why only prosecute aggression when Russian leaders are implicated? And, of course, this raised the issue, mentioned above, of the US- and UK-led invasion of Iraq and why it escaped similar judicial scrutiny.[209] Of course, the context also was different—Iraq did not press for prosecution of the crime, whereas Ukrainian officials have quite vociferously done so. Furthermore, as detailed in Chap. 1, the state of the law was less developed in 2003: the definition of the crime of aggression was still being negotiated; no ICC jurisdiction was yet activated; neither the United States nor Iraq were parties to the Rome Statute (which is still true); neither had ratified the Kampala crime of aggression amendments (which is still true); and the amendments are not retroactive in any event.[210] Thus, many of the legal preconditions were lacking.[211]

As will be discussed in the next chapter, the attraction of selectivity was no doubt at play for some states, such as the United States and the United Kingdom, which proposed (along with Germany) establishing some form of Ukrainian domestic hybrid chamber to prosecute Russian leaders implicated in aggression.[212] These states later came to endorse the Council of Europe led approach that will be discussed in Chap. 7.[213] While it is difficult to document that selectivity was an *attraction* for these states—with the exception of Germany which supports broader jurisdiction

---

hybrid courts and tribunals and potential regional criminal courts"). For a discussion of double jeopardy under the statute that has been agreed on, see Chap. 7, Sect. 7.4.1 (the Tribunal's relationship with the ICC and *ne bis in idem*).

[208] See Rome Statute (1998) (as amended), note 18, Article 20(2).

[209] See Chap. 1, Sect. 1.1; see also Traoré 2022 ("The ongoing Libyan catastrophe has also triggered considerable resentment across Africa. Many Africans see NATO's 2011 intervention, especially the regime change in Libya, as blatantly unlawful"). On the 2025 bombing of Iranian nuclear facilities and US strikes against Venezuelan boats, see note 17.

[210] Activation of jurisdiction over the crime was effective only on 17 July 2018. International Criminal Court, Assembly of States Parties 2017.

[211] See Chap. 1, Sect. 1.1.

[212] See Chap. 6.

[213] See Chap. 7.

before the ICC over the crime of aggression[214]—other G7 states do not support broader ICC jurisdiction over the crime.[215] Thus, for these states, the undeniable optics exist that they *do appear* only to support prosecuting Russian leaders for aggression and not accountability for the crime more broadly. This conclusion is further supported by the crime of aggression's negotiating history. As detailed in Chap. 3, it was the United States that led the effort to truncate the ICC's jurisdiction over the crime in 2010 at the Kampala Review Conference[216] and the United Kingdom and France that led the efforts to further limit, or attempted to further limit, the ICC's jurisdiction in 2017 when the ASP activated jurisdiction.[217]

For many others, both academics and states, the question of selectivity was, and no doubt remains, a concern. Kevin Jon Heller—who did not support establishing an international tribunal[218]—wrote:

> [T]he war in Iraq [did not] lead to high-profile calls for creating a Special Tribunal for the Punishment of the Crime of Aggression Against Iraq . . . . So to create a Special Tribunal now for Russia's invasion of Ukraine would . . . send a message that the "international community" cares about some crimes of aggression more than others.[219]

Kai Ambos similarly wrote:

> [I]t is not easy to provide a[n aggression tribunal] with sufficient legitimacy in the eyes of the world, above all in the eyes of the Global South (which is fundamentally skeptical about

---

[214] On 4 April, Germany, Costa Rica, Sierra Leone, Slovenia, and Vanuatu submitted to the UN Secretary-General the text of a proposed amendment to harmonize the ICC's jurisdiction over all four crimes. Crime of Aggression, amendment proposal 2025.

[215] Statements by Canada, France and the United Kingdom before the Special Working Group on Amendments (2025) (as observed by the author who was present). See also Hamilton 2023 ("Powerful states have been reticent to let international criminal law encroach on decisions about the use of force").

[216] International Crisis Group 2023 ("In negotiations over the activation of the crime at Kampala, the United States worked behind the scenes to ensure that the Rome Statute amendments would not create any criminal exposure for U.S. personnel"); Peskin and Boduszyński 2022 ("In 2010, the U.S., Britain and France, fearful that charges of the crime of aggression might be deployed against them or their allies, undermined a potentially valuable legal tool that could now apply to Russia's invasion of Ukraine"); Heller 2024, p. 13 (a "selectivity problem concerns the identity of the states that would create a Special Tribunal and then oversee its operation. The ICC does not have jurisdiction over acts of aggression committed by non-state parties primarily because of the US's fervent opposition, while other powerful states—most notably the United Kingdom, France, Canada, Australia, and New Zealand—managed to exclude from jurisdiction aggressive acts committed by state parties unless they 'opt-in' by ratifying the aggression amendments. Without the efforts of those states, it is likely that the OTP's current investigation in Ukraine would include aggression as well as war crimes and crimes against humanity".); Corten and Koutroulis 2022, pp. 37–38 ("Certain States that seem now open to the possibility of creating an international tribunal for Ukraine have prevented the Court from having a broad jurisdiction on the crime of aggression. In terms of legitimacy, it goes without saying that such a position should be changed to show that judging acts of aggression is from now on considered imperative, universally and not only in the Ukrainian case").

[217] See Chap. 3, Sects. 3.2.3–3.2.4. Whether their attempt to narrow jurisdiction was successful is an open issue. See Chap. 3, Sect. 3.2.4.

[218] Heller 2022a.

[219] Ibid.

> the Western Ukraine policy)[.] . . . [O]ne wonders . . . why such a tribunal was not set up during the unlawful (US-led) invasion of Iraq.[220]

Such critiques present a broader question about the legitimacy of the selective application of justice. To this author, the answer is twofold. First, one *should not have selective application of justice*—hence, why the author (and many others) advocate fixing the ICC's jurisdiction over the crime of aggression more broadly by harmonizing the ICC's jurisdiction over all four Rome Statute crimes.[221] This would create considerably more jurisdiction before the ICC over the crime, reducing the potential for the selective application of justice and the potential need for ad hoc solutions.

Second, however, there is a more pragmatic response that considers the history of the field of international justice. It cannot be disputed that states have chosen to establish international or hybrid criminal tribunals in some situations and not others. International or hybrid tribunals were established for crimes committed in the former Yugoslavia, Rwanda, Sierra Leone, Lebanon, Bosnia, Kosovo, Cambodia, East Timor, Chad, and the Central African Republic.[222] Yet, no international or hybrid tribunals were established for crimes committed in Syria, Yemen, Myanmar, China, and many other similar situations. Sometimes it was an issue of politics—that the country would not support the establishment of such a tribunal[223] or that the UN Security Council had no will to create one (either a lack of overall will/interest of its

---

[220] Labuda 2024, p. 277, quoting Ambos 2023.

[221] See note 47 (academics and states' representatives endorsing a two-track approach); for the Rome Statute amendment proposal of the Global Institute for the Prevention of Aggression, see Global Institute for the Prevention of Aggression (nd-a) Amendment Proposal. https://crimeofaggression.info/wp-content/uploads/GIPA-model-amendment-proposal_9-September-2023.pdf. Accessed 19 August 2025; see also Global Institute for the Prevention of Aggression (nd-b) GIPA's Reasons for the Proposed Amendment. https://crimeofaggression.info/wp-content/uploads/GIPA-Proposal-Short_25-September-2023.pdf. Accessed 19 August 2025 (GIPA's reasons for the proposed amendment); Trahan 2023b; Chap. 8 (discussing the 2025 proposed amendment text). See also Corten and Koutroulis 2022, p. 35 ("It must be borne in mind that the creation of a 'special' or ad hoc court or tribunal is always problematic in terms of legitimacy . . . . [I]t is always preferable to create competent judicial bodies on an institutional and permanent level and when such bodies exist, to prefer resorting to them instead of creating special tribunals").

[222] They are, respectively: the ICTY, the ICTR, the Special Court for Sierra Leone, the STL, the State Court in Bosnia-Herzegovina (previously a hybrid but now in its purely domestic phase), the Kosovo Specialist Chambers and Specialist Prosecutor's Office (and previous Regulation 64 Panels within Kosovo's court system), the ECCC, the Special Panels for Serious Crimes (in East Timor), the Extraordinary African Chamber within the courts of Senegal (prosecuting crimes committed in Chad), and the Special Criminal Court in the Central African Republic ("CAR").

[223] This, for example, was true of Syria under the regime of former President Bashar al-Assad.

members[224] or due to the veto of a permanent member).[225] Additionally, by 2002, states largely came to focus their energies primarily on one standing institution, the ICC, rather than ad hoc responses.[226] Yet, the ICC only possesses funding to prosecute a handful of cases in each situation and has limitations in terms of its jurisdiction.[227] Even within an ICC situation, because the Prosecutor cannot prosecute all crimes, selectivity comes into play in terms of which crimes and crime scenes are investigated and prosecuted.

The author is not defending selectivity—far from it. Yet, the undeniable reality is that selectivity is often present in the field of international justice. Tom Dannenbaum writes: "international criminal law has always been characterized by some degree of selectivity", but that does not suggest an ad hoc aggression tribunal should be held to a "higher normative standard".[228] Selectivity stems in part from (a) the veto power of the permanent members of the UN Security Council; (b) states having a choice whether or not to become parties to treaties, including the Rome Statute; and (c) the finite nature of resources and that states often have a choice as to whether and how much funding to provide.[229] First, at the Security Council, there is a built-in problem with referrals to the ICC—a permanent member can veto a referral to the ICC that involves its own nationals or crimes committed on its territory, or the nationals of an ally or crimes committed on the territory of an ally. This means that referrals, which also can be blocked for other political reasons, suffer from selectivity. This is not the fault of the ICC, but stems from the veto power given in 1945 to the permanent members of the UN Security Council.[230] The veto also provides a limitation as to which tribunals will be established by the Security Council; if there are perpetrators

[224] For example, establishing an international or hybrid tribunal to prosecute crimes in the DRC has never attracted sufficient political interest within the Security Council, despite massive death tolls and the ICC only being able to take up a handful of cases addressing crimes committed there. See Moszynski 2008 (5.4 million people have died in Democratic Republic of Congo since 1998); International Criminal Court (nd-d) Situation in the Democratic Republic of the Congo, ICC-01/04. https://www.icc-cpi.int/drc. Accessed 19 August 2025 (three convictions; two other cases; renewed investigations opened).

[225] A tribunal for crimes committed within China against the Uyghur population, for example, has never been proposed. For crimes against the Uyghurs, see Global Accountability Network 2022b.

[226] Two exceptions are the Special Criminal Court in CAR and the Kosovo Specialist Chambers and Specialist Prosecutor's Office. The Special Criminal Court in CAR is operating in tandem with the ICC to complement its work. For background on the court, see Labuda 2018. The Kosovo Specialist Chambers is prosecuting cases that predate the commencement of the ICC's jurisdiction. See KSC at a Glance (nd). https://www.scp-ks.org/sites/default/files/public/content/documents/20250311-KSC-AT-GLANCE-EN.pdf. Accessed 19 August 2025 (jurisdiction over crimes committed between 1 January 1998 and 31 December 2000).

[227] International Criminal Court (nd-e) The States Parties to the Rome Statute. https://asp.icc-cpi.int/states-parties. Accessed 19 August 2025; Rome Statute (1998) (as amended), note 18, Articles 12–13 (jurisdiction as to genocide, war crimes and crimes against humanity); Articles 15*bis*–15*ter* (jurisdiction as to the crime of aggression).

[228] Dannenbaum 2022b, p. 868.

[229] This would be less true if a tribunal is funded out of the UN's budget and thus through assessed contributions.

[230] See UN Charter (1945), note 20, Article 27(3).

from a permanent member or its ally, no doubt, no tribunal will be established. Second, selectivity stems from the fact that states have the option whether or not to join the Rome Statute. Until there is universal ratification of the Rome Statute, there will be uneven application of the rule of law and selective application of justice—the ICC will be able to investigate and prosecute in some situations and not in others that are equally meritorious but beyond its jurisdictional reach.[231] Third, selectivity also stems from resource limitations, both in terms of whether states will pay to establish an international or internationalized tribunal, or fund it sufficiently,[232] and funding limitations mean the ICC must be selective in the cases it pursues.

The question then becomes whether one supports a Darfur or Libya referral by the Security Council to the ICC,[233] when other equally meritorious referrals (e.g., regarding crimes committed in Syria)[234] cannot happen? Does one support the selective application of justice through ad hoc tribunals established in some situations but not others? Does one support the justice that the ICC is able to pursue based on where it possesses jurisdiction, recognizing that there may be equally meritorious cases in situations where it does not possess jurisdiction? Does one support the justice the ICC is able to pursue based on the funding states provide to it, when it lacks funding to investigate or prosecute other perhaps equally meritorious cases? To this author, the answer is unequivocally in the affirmative.[235]

On this issue, former ICC President, Judge Chile Eboe-Osuji wrote:

> Let us remember that the same arguments [about selective justice] were heard in 1945 and the following years, about the establishment of the Nuremberg and Tokyo Tribunals. Those were arguments made by sensible people driven by a certain view of purity of principles—in the moment. But they were unconcerned, or not sufficiently concerned, that their arguments might have—in the moment—resulted in impunity, let alone serious injustice for victims of the grave atrocities that had been committed . . . . Now looking back, those precedents of 1945 and 1946—reproached by some then as "flawed"—have been celebrated by most . . . as worthy precedents for the ICC and the earlier ad hoc tribunals for Rwanda and the former Yugoslavia . . . . So, too, it *will* be for [an international tribunal for the crime of aggression against Ukraine]. I strongly support its establishment. Years from now, it would

---

[231] The same is true of other treaties. States choose whether or not to become parties to conventions such as the Torture Convention or Genocide Convention, and whether to accept the ICJ's jurisdiction as to disputes and interpretative questions related to them. See Convention against Torture and Other Cruel, Inhuman, or Degrading Treatment or Punishment (1984) 1465 UNTS 85, Article 30.1 (disputes and interpretative questions may be submitted to the ICJ); Convention on the Prevention and Punishment of the Crime of Genocide (1948), Article IX (same).

[232] The establishment of the Special Court for Sierra Leone and ECCC on the basis of voluntary contributions meant that these institutions were perpetually forced to fundraise. The voluntary contribution model was utilized as a response to the perceived high cost of the ICTY and ICTR. See Skilbeck 2008, p. 10 (high costs). On the history of the establishment of these tribunals and questions of funding, see, e.g., Scheffer 2013.

[233] United Nations Security Council Resolution 1593 (2005) (Darfur); United Nations Security Council Resolution 1971 (2011) (Libya).

[234] The referral—attempted while Bashir al-Assad was still in power—was vetoed by Russia. See United Nations Security Council Resolution 348 (2014) (draft) (vetoed by Russia and China).

[235] See also Dannenbaum 2022b, p. 868 ("the selectivity of the past has not undermined predecessor institutions").

> have correctly earned its place as one of the building blocks in the never-ending construction project of international law.[236]

Others argued that the more international the effort to establish the aggression tribunal, the more it would reduce concerns as to selectivity; conversely, the less legitimate or multilateral the tribunal's establishment, the more prevalent such concerns would be.[237]

Yet, the question of selectivity has undoubtedly influenced the views of at least some states about establishing another ad hoc tribunal. As mentioned, various academics and states who support establishing a special tribunal on the crime of aggression only do so in conjunction with insisting on broader accountability for the crime of aggression through expansion of the ICC's jurisdiction.[238]

5.4 The Views of Ukraine and Other States in Support of an International Tribunal Established Through the United Nations

Unsurprisingly, Ukrainian officials were early endorsers of establishing an international tribunal through the UN. The Ukrainian government backed the idea of a special tribunal as early as March 2022.[239] Subsequently, President Zelenskyy called for the establishment of a special tribunal for the crime of aggression in his statement dated 22 September 2022 at the General Debate of the seventy-seventh

---

[236] Eboe-Osuji 2023; see also Eboe-Osuji 2024. Carrie McDougall writes:

> [W]hile the relative merits of accountability and equality are frequently debated in selectivity literature, we do not have to choose between these values. The reality is that if we refuse to support justice initiatives when they are available unless justice everywhere is possible, we would effectively have to give up on the international criminal justice project. This will not help victims in places like Syria or Yemen. It will simply send a message that serious international crimes can be committed by the powerful with impunity—which will lead to further crimes. The international community can support the proposed tribunal while acknowledging that justice is selective, and that this is unacceptable . . . . [T]he best chance we have of making justice less selective is by demonstrating that international criminal justice mechanisms can apply justice impartially and fairly, and that they are an indispensable part of the international security architecture.

McDougall 2023a. See also Dannenbaum 2022a ("The failure to hold accountable those who have waged such wars is lamentable. However, the revival of the crime of aggression has to begin somewhere. The invasion of Ukraine, as one of the most blatantly aggressive wars in the past 80 years, offers an opportunity to begin that revival").

[237] See Corten and Koutroulis 2022, p. 37.

[238] See note 47 (academics and states' representatives endorsing a two-track approach). Heller also supports broader ICC jurisdiction over the crime of aggression. Heller 2024, p. 24. On the proposal to harmonize the ICC's jurisdiction over all four of its core crimes, see Chap. 8.

[239] Kuleba 2022.

Session of the UN General Assembly.[240] Zelenskyy took this view in particular due to the issue of immunities: "'We understand who gave the orders. These people must not be untouchable. This is very important for us, this is one of the fundamental issues'".[241] Ambassador-at-Large of the Foreign Ministry of Ukraine Anton Korynevych expressed the same view: "there is an urgent need to establish an ad hoc international tribunal"; "[b]ecause of the personal immunities of the Troika leaders, it must be international".[242]

Additional states that were particularly supportive of establishing an international tribunal included Albania, Belgium, Estonia, Guatemala, Latvia, Liechtenstein, Lithuania, Luxembourg, Marshall Islands, North Macedonia, Poland, and Ukraine, which collectively authored an FAQ (Frequently Asked Questions) about establishing an international tribunal.[243] Albania, Belgium, Costa Rica, the Czech Republic, Estonia, Guatemala, Latvia, Liechtenstein, Lithuania, Luxembourg, Marshall Islands, North Macedonia, and Poland additionally issued a Joint Statement in support of establishing an international tribunal.[244] Other supporters included the

---

240 Kreß 2022, p. 23, citing Zelenskyy 2022b.

241 Zelenskyy 2023. See also Zelenskyy 2022a; Pietromarchi 2022 ("Ukrainian President Volodymyr Zelenskyy has urged the United States to support the creation of a special tribunal to try the Russian leadership with the crime of aggression for waging war on Ukraine"); Mueller 2022 (Ukrainian Foreign Minister Dmytro Kuleba calling for an international tribunal); Office of the President of Ukraine Press Release (2023) Special International Tribunal Should Become an Effective Way to Punish Russia for Its Aggression against Ukraine - Andriy Smyrnov. https://www.president.gov.ua/en/news/specialnij-mizhnarodnij-tribunal-maye-stati-diyevim-sposobom-84405. Accessed 19 August 2025.

242 Korynevych et al. 2023, pp. 378–79.

243 Just Security nd-b. See also Joint Statement by Estonia, Latvia and Lithuania 2022; Joint Declaration by the Speakers of the Parliaments of Estonia, Finland, Latvia, Lithuania, Poland and Ukraine on Further Supporting Ukraine and on Russia's Hybrid Activities in Europe (2025). https://www.riigikogu.ee/wpcms/wp-content/uploads/2025/01/Joint-Declaration-03.02.2025.pdf. Accessed 19 August 2025 ("We emphasize the need to establish a Special International Tribunal for the crime of aggression with the broadest cross-regional support and legitimacy".); Ministry of Foreign Affairs of the Republic of Lithuania, The Ministers of Estonia, Latvia and Lithuania Call to Establish a Special Tribunal to Investigate the Crime of Russia's Aggression (2022). https://www.urm.lt/en/news/928/the-ministers-of-estonia-latvia-and-lithuania-call-to-establish-a-special-tribunal-to-investigate-the-crime-of-russias-aggression:35099. Accessed 19 August 2025 (foreign ministers of Estonia, Latvia and Lithuania call to establish a Special Tribunal to investigate the crime of Russia's aggression).

244 Joint Statement on the Accountability for the Crime of Aggression Committed on the Territory of Ukraine, by Albania, Belgium, Costa Rica, Czech Republic, Estonia, Guatemala, Latvia, Liechtenstein, Lithuania, Luxembourg, Marshall Islands, North Macedonia and Poland (2023). https://un.mfa.ee/joint-statement-on-the-accountability-for-the-crime-of-aggression-committed-on-the-territory-of-ukraine/. Accessed 19 August 2025 ("Joint Statement on the Accountability 2023") ("We believe that an international tribunal, before which the immunities granted by international law to the most senior leadership of a state do not apply, is best placed to deliver the above described objectives. We therefore call on the international community to actively engage in discussions on the establishment of such a tribunal, in particular through decisions of the United Nations General Assembly").

European Union, President of the Commission,[245] NATO's Parliamentary Assembly, the Parliamentary Assembly and Committee of Ministers of the Council of Europe, and the European Parliament.[246] A news report suggested that The Netherlands offered to host the international tribunal.[247]

Yet, the concern about selectivity continued to linger, particularly from non-European states. Some were (appropriately) asking why so much emphasis was being placed on pursuing accountability for aggression only in the situation of Ukraine. As to the views of African states, Sâ Benjamin Traoré wrote:

> The split between African states in the voting [on UNGA resolutions related to Ukraine[248]] also reflects the divide in public opinion about the Ukrainian crisis across African countries. While the West has shown unfailing support for Ukraine, Africa and the rest of the world have adopted a more ambivalent position .... There is a vast feeling—especially in public opinions and ordinary citizens—around the duplicity of western states when it comes to respecting international law. The perception is that the western zealotry over Ukraine—and not for other situations of blatant violation of international law—is troubling, shocking and nothing short of hypocrisy and double standards in international politics.[249]

While agreeing with the accusations of hypocrisy and double-standards,[250] Traoré took the view that: "denouncing double-standards legalism [and] western hypocrisy is not antithetical to condemning the unlawful use of force by Russia in Ukraine unequivocally".[251] He argued: "In the face of what is [undoubtedly] a blatant violation of the prohibition of the use of force in international relations, this voting attitude by African counties on Ukraine appears surprising—if not shocking. It seems at odds with Africa's usual zero tolerance for acts of aggression which stems from its anti-colonial and anti-domination history".[252] He therefore urged African states to take a firm stance and unequivocally condemn Russia's illegal use of force.[253]

---

[245] European Commission 2022 (statement by President von der Leyen calling for "a specialised court, backed by the United Nations, to investigate and prosecute Russia's crime of aggression").

[246] See note 44.

[247] Reuters 2022 ("The Netherlands would be willing to house a new, U.N.-backed tribunal to try Russia's invasion of Ukraine, Dutch Foreign Minister Wopke Hoekstra said").

[248] For details of the voting, see Traoré 2022.

[249] See, e.g., ibid.

[250] Ibid. ("When other states take liberties with fundamental principles of international law without facing the same reactions that Russia is facing, it gives the legitimate impression to Africans—and the rest of the world—that compliance with international law is only for some states and not for western states"). See also Van Schaack 2022 (expressing concerns with the perception of bias, double-standards, and selective justice).

[251] Traoré 2022.

[252] Ibid.

[253] Ibid. He writes:

> [T]here are at least two reasons Africa must not lose sight of the importance of expressing their legal views and condemnation of Russia's unlawful use of force in Ukraine .... Firstly, as a matter of principle, Africa abhors aggression. This should be the case regardless of who the aggressor is. Although most African countries were still under colonialism and therefore absent during the adoption of the UN Charter, the prohibition of the use of force in international relations is probably one of the UN principles unreservedly endorsed by

In a similar vein, but taking the logic one step further, Patryk Labuda argued that Russia's invasion of Ukraine was an attempt at imperial conquest and therefore all states, but particularly those that have suffered under imperialism or colonialism, should support Ukraine's quest for accountability for the crime of aggression.[254]

Despite such eloquent arguments, by and large these views have not significantly resonated. Only a few non-European states have actively supported the establishment of an international tribunal[255] and only a few have actively supported the later proposal of establishing a tribunal through the Council of Europe.[256] Many non-European or non-"western" states have chosen to remain silent.[257] Of course, a state's silence—which is susceptible to differing interpretations[258]—does not necessarily reflect a legal position *against* the crime of aggression being prosecuted (or in defense of Russia). As to a freestanding aggression tribunal, it may reflect a stance against selective prosecution or a decision to avoid taking a position on what could appear to be a fight between old Cold War rivals.[259] Alternatively, it may reflect other strategic or economic alliances or interests and not legal considerations at all.[260]

> all of them when assessing international sovereignty. This long standing firm stance against aggression in international relations is deeply grounded in Africa's troubling history. Africa's history is made of aggression for religious, economic, or political reasons . . . . The second principled reason that must guide Africa's positioning vis-à-vis the Ukraine situation is the importance of the principle of territorial integrity to African countries. The question African states must ask themselves is what value territorial integrity has to them and whether they are ready to give up on it. This is highly relevant because Russia's military intervention in Ukraine is a blatant violation of Ukraine's territorial integrity.

Ibid.

[254] See Labuda 2024.

[255] See Just Security nd-b (supporters include Guatemala and Marshall Islands); Joint Statement on the Accountability 2023, note 244 (supporters include Costa Rica, Guatemala, and Marshall Islands).

[256] Non-European States in the Core Group of States supporting the establishment of an aggression-specific tribunal included Australia, Costa Rica, Guatemala, Japan, and the United States, until the 2025 Strasbourg meeting when the United States withdrew.

[257] As will be detailed in Chap. 8, there is much more support within "non-Western" states for harmonizing the ICC's jurisdiction over all four Rome Statute crimes. See Chap. 8. In earlier negotiations before the SWCGA and at the 2010 Review Conference, states from all regions were active and constructive participants. For a detailed account of the Kampala negotiations, see Kreβ and von Holtzendorff 2010; Reisinger Coracini 2010; Trahan 2011. For an account of the negotiations from 1998 to 2010, see Barriga and Kreβ 2012.

[258] Traoré 2022; Azaria 2025.

[259] See Traoré 2022 (suggesting these arguments). The United States was a proponent of an aggression tribunal (first a hybrid one and later one established through the Council of Europe) until the United States withdrew from the negotiations regarding the latter during the Trump administration.

[260] See, e.g., Dannenbaum 2022b, p. 869 ("Russia has significant economic, natural resource and security influence over states across multiple continents"); Traoré 2022 ("voting patterns of most global south countries at the UNGA are shaped by the political interests of the day"; "the rise of China's presence in Africa and the increasing Russian 'return' in many African regions—think of CAR, Mali and, Libya, Guinea, Sudan, for instance—have also influenced the positioning of many African countries").

5.5 Conclusion

In the face of Russia's 2022 full-scale invasion of Ukraine, a significant number of academics and states called for the establishment of an international tribunal to prosecute the crime of aggression, formed by agreement between the United Nations and Ukraine, upon the recommendation of the UN General Assembly. While technical questions arose as to various aspects of the proposal, they did not appear to be insurmountable. One *could* overcome personal immunities of the troika through the establishment of an international tribunal. One *could* choose to avoid holding trials *in absentia*. Furthermore, the method proposed for establishing the tribunal appeared to be quite possible. What became the most significant impediment, however, became the question of political will. Once the G7 came to oppose establishing an international tribunal, as will be described in the next chapter, it was feared that the proposal might not garner a sufficiently persuasive number of votes within the UN General Assembly. Thus, the strongest framework to revive the enforcement of *jus ad bellum* law through the lens of international criminal responsibility was not to be. For a variety of reasons, certain states opted for a different approach and setting a weaker precedent.

References

Africa News (2022) UN Report Shows Rwandan Army Intervened in DRC's Troubled East. https://www.africanews.com/2022/12/23/un-report-shows-rwandan-army-intervened-in-drcs-troubled-east/. Accessed 19 August 2025

Ambos K (2023) A Ukraine Special Tribunal with Legitimacy Problems? Verfassungsblog. https://verfassungsblog.de/a-ukraine-special-tribunal-with-legitimacy-problems/. Accessed 19 August 2025

Andrassy J (1956) Uniting for Peace. American Journal of International Law 50: 563–82

Azaria D (2025) State Silence across International Law: Meaning, Context, and Developments. Oxford University Press, Oxford

Barriga S, Kreß C (2012) The *Travaux Préparatoires* of the Crime of Aggression. Cambridge University Press, Cambridge

BBC News (2023) What Is the South China Sea Dispute? https://www.bbc.com/news/world-asia-pacific-13748349. Accessed 19 August 2025

Bodeen C (2023) China Reaffirms Its Military Threats against Taiwan Weeks before Its Presidential Election. Associated Press. https://apnews.com/article/china-taiwan-elections-military-threats-ea68fa11a0b172c31162c0ff128cabf7. Accessed 19 August 2025

Borger J (2016) The Butcher's Trail: How the Search for Balkan War Criminals Became The World's Most Successful Manhunt. Other Press, New York

Brunsden J (2008) EU Deal Struck on Trials in Absentia. Politico. https://www.politico.eu/article/eu-deal-struck-on-trials-in-absentia/. Accessed 19 August 2025

Collinson S (2025) Trump's Threats to Greenland, Canada and Panama Explain Everything About America First. CNN. https://www.cnn.com/2025/01/08/politics/trump-greenland-canada-panama-analysis/index.html. Accessed 19 August 2025

Corell H (2020) Introductory Note: Agreement Between the United Nations and the Royal Government of Cambodia Concerning the Prosecution Under Cambodian Law of Crimes

Committed During the Period of Democratic Kampuchea. United Nations Audiovisual Library of International Law. https://legal.un.org/avl/ha/abunac/abunac.html. Accessed 12 May 2025

Corell H (2023) A Special Tribunal for Ukraine on the Crime of Aggression—The Role of the U.N. General Assembly. Just Security. https://www.justsecurity.org/85116/a-special-tribunal-for-ukraine-on-the-crime-of-aggression-the-role-of-the-u-n-general-assembly. Accessed 19 August 2025

Corten O, Koutroulis V (2022) In-Depth Analysis: Tribunal for the Crime of Aggression Against Ukraine - a Legal Assessment. European Parliament. https://www.europarl.europa.eu/RegData/etudes/IDAN/2022/702574/EXPO_IDA(2022)702574_EN.pdf. Accessed 15 May 2025

Cotovio V, Goodwin A (2024) Venezuela Builds Forces Near Border with Guyana Despite Agreement to De-Escalate. CNN. https://www.cnn.com/2024/02/09/americas/venezuela-guyana-border-troops-intl-latam/index.html. Accessed 19 August 2025

Council of Europe, Newsroom (2022) PACE Calls for an Ad Hoc International Criminal Tribunal to Hold to Account Perpetrators of the Crime of Aggression against Ukraine. https://www.coe.int/en/web/portal/-/pace-calls-for-an-ad-hoc-international-criminal-tribunal-to-investigate-war-crimes-in-ukraine. Accessed 19 August 2025

Dannenbaum T (2022a) Mechanisms for Criminal Prosecution of Russia's Aggression Against Ukraine. Just Security. https://www.justsecurity.org/80626/mechanisms-for-criminal-prosecution-of-russias-aggression-against-ukraine/. Accessed 4 May 2025

Dannenbaum T (2022b) A Special Tribunal for the Crime of Aggression? Journal of International Criminal Justice 20: 859–73

Datar A (2020) Bar & Bench. https://www.barandbench.com/columns/the-origins-of-justice-must-be-seen-to-be-done

Eboe-Osuji C (2023) Letter to Editor: On So-Called Selectivity and a Tribunal for Aggression Against Ukraine. Just Security. https://www.justsecurity.org/85060/letter-to-editor-on-so-called-selectivity-and-a-tribunal-for-aggression-in-ukraine/. Accessed 19 August 2025

Eboe-Osuji C (2024) End of Immunity: Holding World Leaders Accountable for Aggression, Genocide, War Crimes, and Crimes against Humanity. Prometheus Books, Essex

European Commission (2022) Statement by President von der Leyen on Russian Accountability and the Use of Russian Frozen Assets. https://ec.europa.eu/commission/presscorner/detail/en/statement_22_7307. Accessed 19 August 2025

Global Accountability Network (2022a) Ukraine Task Force, Proposal for a Resolution by the United Nations General Assembly and Accompanying Proposal for a Statute of a Special Tribunal for Ukraine on the Crime of Aggression. https://www.havc.se/res/SelectedMaterial/specialtribunalukraine7sep2022.pdf. Accessed 19 August 2025

Global Accountability Network (2022b) A Multi-Generational Effort to Eliminate the Uyghurs: An Ongoing Genocide. https://www.globalaccountabilitynetwork.org/_files/ugd/a982f0_6b218a6e88324ca385b3b0d044e1770f.pdf. Accessed 19 August 2025

Goldston J (2022) Model Indictment for the Crime of Aggression Committed against Ukraine. Just Security. https://www.justsecurity.org/81411/osji-model-indictment-for-the-crime-of-aggression-committed-against-ukraine/. Accessed 19 August 2025

Green R (2022) Devastation Prompts Calls for Accountability in International Courts. International Bar Association. https://www.ruthsineadgreen.com/2022/03/14/ukraine-devastation-prompts-calls-for-accountability-in-international-courts/. Accessed 19 August 2025

Hamilton R (2023) Ukraine's Push to Prosecute Aggression: Implications for Immunity *Ratione Personae* and the Crime of Aggression. Case Western Reserve Journal of International Law 55: 39–60

Hathaway O (2022a) A Crime in Search of a Court: How to Hold Russia Accountable. Foreign Affairs. https://www.foreignaffairs.com/articles/ukraine/2022-05-19/crime-search-court. Accessed 19 August 2025

Hathaway O (2022b) The Case for Creating an International Tribunal to Prosecute the Crime of Aggression Against Ukraine (Part I). Just Security. https://www.justsecurity.org/83117/the-case-for-creating-an-international-tribunal-to-prosecute-the-crime-of-aggression-against-ukraine/. Accessed 19 August 2025

Hathaway O (2023) Russia's Crime and Punishment: How to Prosecute the Illegal War in Ukraine. Foreign Affairs. https://www.foreignaffairs.com/ukraine/russia-crime-and-punishment-illegal-war-in-ukraine. Accessed 19 August 2025

Hathaway O, Mills M, Zimmerman H (2023) The Legal Authority to Create a Special Tribunal to Try the Crime of Aggression upon the Request of the UN General Assembly. Just Security. https://www.justsecurity.org/86450/the-legal-authority-to-create-a-special-tribunal-to-try-the-crime-of-aggression-upon-the-request-of-the-un-general-assembly/. Accessed 19 August 2025

Hathaway O, Shapiro S (2017) The Internationalists: How a Radical Plan to Outlaw War Remade the World. Simon & Schuster, New York

Haxton E (2024) Interview of the Former President of the ICC, Judge Piotr Hofmański. EJIL:*Talk!* https://www.ejiltalk.org/interview-of-the-former-president-of-the-icc-judge-piotr-hofmanski/. Accessed 19 August 2025

Heller K (2022a) Creating a Special Tribunal for Aggression against Ukraine Is a Bad Idea. Opinio Juris. https://opiniojuris.org/2022/03/07/creating-a-special-tribunal-for-aggression-against-ukraine-is-a-bad-idea/. Accessed 19 August 2025

Heller K (2022b) The Best Option: An Extraordinary Ukrainian Chamber for Aggression. Opinio Juris. https://opiniojuris.org/2022/03/16/the-best-option-an-extraordinary-ukrainian-chamber-for-aggression/. Accessed 19 August 2025

Heller K (2024) Options for Prosecuting Russian Aggression against Ukraine: A Critical Analysis. Journal of Genocide Research 26: 1–24

Independent International Commission of Inquiry on Ukraine (2023) Report of the Independent International Commission of Inquiry on Ukraine to the Human Rights Council. UN Doc. A/HRC/52/6

International Criminal Court (nd-a) Judges Who's Who. https://www.icc-cpi.int/judges/judges-who-s-who. Accessed 19 August 2025

International Criminal Court (nd-b) Assembly of States Parties to the Rome Statute, History of the Special Working Group on the Crime of Aggression. https://asp.icc-cpi.int/crime-of-aggression/History-CoA. Accessed 12 October 2025.

International Criminal Court (nd-c) *The Prosecutor v. Uhuru Muigai Kenyatta*, ICC-01/09-02/11, Case Information Sheet. https://www.icc-cpi.int/sites/default/files/CaseInformationSheets/KenyattaEng.pdf. Accessed 19 August 2025

International Criminal Court (nd-d) Situation in the Democratic Republic of the Congo, ICC-01/04. https://www.icc-cpi.int/drc. Accessed 19 August 2025

International Criminal Court (nd-e) The States Parties to the Rome Statute. https://asp.icc-cpi.int/states-parties. Accessed 19 August 2025

International Criminal Court, Assembly of States Parties (2010) Review Conference, The Crime of Aggression, ICC Doc. RC/Res.6

International Criminal Court, Assembly of States Parties (2017) Activation of the Jurisdiction of the Court Over the Crime of Aggression, Res. ICC-ASP/16/Res. 5

International Criminal Court, Press Release (2023) Situation in Ukraine: ICC Judges Issue Arrest Warrants against Vladimir Vladimirovich Putin and Maria Alekseyevna Lvova-Belova. https://www.icc-cpi.int/news/situation-ukraine-icc-judges-issue-arrest-warrants-against-vladimir-vladimirovich-putin-and. Accessed 19 August 2025

International Crisis Group (2023) A New Court to Prosecute Russia's Illegal War? https://www.crisisgroup.org/global-ukraine/new-court-prosecute-russias-illegal-war. Accessed 19 August 2025

Israeli Defense Forces (2024) The IDF Struck Strategic Weapons Stockpiles in Syria. https://www.idf.il/en/mini-sites/idf-press-releases-israel-at-war/december24-pr/the-idf-struck-strategic-weapons-stockpiles-in-syria/. Accessed 19 August 2025

Jackson R (1945) Chief of Counsel for the United States, Opening Statement at Nuremberg, 21 November 1945 in Trial of the Major War Criminals Before the International Military Tribunal, Nuremberg 14 November 1945–1 October 1948, Vol. II

Johnson L (2022) United Nations Response Options to Russia's Aggression: Opportunities and Rabbit Holes. Just Security. https://www.justsecurity.org/80395/united-nations-response-options-to-russias-aggression-opportunities-and-rabbit-holes/. Accessed 19 August 2025

Just Security (nd-a) Just Security Series: U.N. General Assembly and International Criminal Tribunal for the Crime of Aggression Against Ukraine. https://www.justsecurity.org/tag/un-general-assembly-and-international-criminal-tribunal-for-aggression-against-ukraine/. Accessed 19 August 2025

Just Security (nd-b) Frequently Asked Questions (FAQ): A Special Tribunal for the Crime of Aggression against Ukraine, Endorsed by Albania, Belgium, Estonia, Guatemala, Latvia, Liechtenstein, Lithuania, Luxembourg, Marshall Islands, North Macedonia, Poland and Ukraine. https://www.justsecurity.org/wp-content/uploads/2023/01/FAQ_Special-Tribunal-for-the-Crime-of-Aggression.pdf. Accessed 19 August 2025

Komarov A, Hathaway O (2022) The Best Path for Accountability for the Crime of Aggression Under Ukrainian and International Law: A Treaty Between Ukraine and the UN General Assembly is the Way to Proceed, Just Security. https://www.justsecurity.org/81063/the-best-path-for-accountability-for-the-crime-of-aggression-under-ukrainian-and-international-law/. Accessed 19 August 2025

Kopelman E (1991), Ideology and International Law: The Dissent of the Indian Justice at the Tokyo War Crimes Trial. NYU Journal of International Law and Politics 23: 373–444

Koh H, Buchwald T (2015) The Crime of Aggression: The United States Perspective. The American Journal of International Law 109: 257–95

Korynevych A, Senatorova O, Shepitko M (2023) Prosecution of the Crime of Aggression in International Law and Ukrainian Jurisdiction: Challenges and Prospects. Polish Yearbook of International Law XLIII: 367–79

Kreβ C (2019) Preliminary Observations on the ICC Appeals Chamber's Judgment of 6 May 2019 in the Jordan Referral re Al-Bashir Appeal. TOAEP Occasional Paper Series. https://www.toaep.org/ops-pdf/8-kress. Accessed 19 August 2025

Kreβ C (2022) The Ukraine War and the Prohibition of the Use of Force in International Law. Occasional Paper Series No. 12

Kreβ C, Barriga S (eds) (2016) The Crime of Aggression: A Commentary. Cambridge University Press, Cambridge

Kreβ C, Hobe S, Nuβberger A (2023) The Ukraine War and the Crime of Aggression: How to Fill the Gaps in the International Legal System. Just Security. https://www.justsecurity.org/84783/the-ukraine-war-and-the-crime-of-aggression-how-to-fill-the-gapsin-the-international-legal-system. Accessed 19 August 2025

Kreβ C, von Holtzendorff L (2010) The Kampala Compromise on the Crime of Aggression. Journal of International Criminal Justice 8: 1179–217

Kuleba D (2022) Foreign Minister, Ukraine, A Criminal Tribunal for Aggression in Ukraine. https://www.chathamhouse.org/events/all/research-event/criminal-tribunal-aggression-ukraine. Accessed 19 August 2025

Kuzmin G, Panin I (2017) Russia. In: Kreß C, Barriga S (eds) The Crime of Aggression: A Commentary. Cambridge University Press, Cambridge

Labuda P (2018) The Special Criminal Court in the Central African Republic. ASIL Insights 22

Labuda P (2024) Countering Imperialism in International Law: Examining the Special Tribunal for Aggression against Ukraine through a Post-Colonial Eastern European Lens. Yale Journal of International Law 49: 271–310

Lippman M (1991) Nuremberg: Forty Five Years Later. Connecticut Journal of International Law 7: 1–64

Masol S (2024) Are You a Leader? Ukraine's Supreme Court Clarifies the Definition of the Crime of Aggression. EJIL:*Talk!* https://www.ejiltalk.org/are-you-a-leader-ukraines-supreme-court-clarifies-the-definition-of-the-crime-of-aggression. Accessed 19 August 2025

Massimino I (2023) The Crime of Aggression and Trials *in Absentia*: The Only Short-Term Response to Finding Putin and Other Russian Leaders Accountable. Indiana Law Review 58. https://indianalawreview.com/2023/08/29/the-crime-of-aggression-and-trials-in-absentia-the-only-short-term-response-to-finding-putin-and-other-russian-leaders-accountable/. Accessed 19 August 2025

Massimino I (2024) The ICC and *in-Absentia* Proceedings: Finding a Response to the Difficulties of Executing Arrest Warrants. ESIL Reflections 13. https://esil-sedi.eu/wp-content/uploads/2024/05/Massimino-Vol.13-Issue-9.pdf. Accessed 5 May 2025

McDougall C (2022) Why Creating a Special Tribunal for Aggression against Ukraine is the Best Available Option: A Reply to Kevin Jon Heller and Other Critics. Opinio Juris. https://opiniojuris.org/2022/03/15/why-creating-a-special-tribunal-for-aggression-against-ukraine-is-the-best-available-option-a-reply-to-kevin-jon-heller-and-other-critics/. Accessed 19 August 2025

McDougall C (2023a) The Imperative of Prosecuting Crimes of Aggression Committed Against Ukraine. Journal of Conflict and Security Law 28: 203–30

McDougall C (2023b) Why Ukraine Needs an International – not Internationalised –Tribunal to Prosecute the Crimes of Aggression Committed Against It. Polish Review of International and European Law 12: 1–91

McDougall C (2024) Expanding the ICC's Jurisdiction Over the Crime of Aggression. Journal of International Criminal Justice 22: 543–64

Moszynski P (2008) 5.4 million People Have Died in Democratic Republic of Congo Since 1998 Because of Conflict, Report Says. BMJ 336: 235

Mueller J (2022) Ukrainian Diplomat Calls for Russia to Face Tribunal Ahead of 2023 Peace Summit. The Hill. https://thehill.com/policy/international/3788804-ukrainian-diplomat-calls-for-russia-to-face-tribunal-ahead-of-2023-peace-summit/#:~:text=Ukrainian%20Foreign%20Minister%20Dmytro%20Kuleba%20is%20calling%20for,to%20a%20new%20interview%20with%20The%20Associated%20Press. Accessed 19 August 2025

NATO Parliamentary Assembly (2022) Declaration Standing with Ukraine, 111 SESP 22 E rev.1 fin. https://www.nato-pa.int/download-file?filename=/sites/default/files/2022-05/111%20SESP%2022%20E%20rev.1%20fin%20-%20DECLARATION%20ON%20UKRAINE.pdf

Nuridzhanian G, McDougall C (2024) On Double Jeopardy, the ICC, and the Special Tribunal for the Crime of Aggression. Just Security. https://www.justsecurity.org/91314/on-double-jeopardy-the-icc-and-the-special-tribunal-for-the-crime-of-aggression/#:~:text=Article%20(1)%20of%20the,or%20acquitted%20by%20the%20ICC. Accessed 19 August 2025

Nevitt M (2025) Using Labels, Not Law to Justify Lethal Force: Inside the Venezuelan Boat Strike. Just Security. https://www.justsecurity.org/119985/labels-ustify-lethal-force-venezuelan-boat-strike/. Accessed 21 November 2025

Pacheco J (2024) Where Do States Stand on Official Immunity under International Law. Just Security. https://www.justsecurity.org/94830/where-do-states-stand-on-official-immunity-under-international-law. Accessed 19 August 2025

PBS News Hour (2022) International Criminal Court Prosecutor on the Pursuit of Justice for Russian War Crimes: Full Transcript. https://www.pbs.org/newshour/show/international-criminal-courts-top-prosecutor-discusses-justice-for-russian-war-crimes. Accessed 19 August 2025

Peskin V, Boduszyński M (2022) Putin's Crime of Aggression in Ukraine and the International Criminal Court. LA Times. https://www.latimes.com/opinion/story/2022-03-05/vladimir-putin-crime-aggression-ukraine-international-criminal-court. Accessed 19 August 2025

Pietromarchi V (2022) Ukraine Wants a Special Tribunal to Prosecute Putin. Can It Work? Al Jazeera. https://www.aljazeera.com/news/2022/12/7/ukraine-wants-a-special-tribunal-to-prosecute-putin-can-it-work. Accessed 19 August 2025

Quell M (2022) ICC Prosecutor Opposes EU Plan for Special Ukraine Tribunal. AP News. https://apnews.com/article/russia-ukraine-war-crimes-netherlands-the-hague-ursula-von-der-leyen-9e83e1107064ef6e9c375576b998373a. Accessed 19 August 2025

Reisinger Coracini A, Tallgren I (2016) Article 20. In: Triffterer O, Ambos K (eds) (2016) Rome Statute of the International Criminal Court: A Commentary, 3rd edn. Beck/Hart, Oxford

Reisinger Coracini A, Trahan J (2022) The Case for Creating a Special Tribunal to Prosecute the Crime of Aggression Committed Against Ukraine (Part VI): On the Non-Applicability of Personal Immunities. Just Security. https://www.justsecurity.org/84017/the-case-for-creating-a-special-tribunal-to-prosecute-the-crime-of-aggression-committed-against-ukraine-part-vi-on-the-non-applicability-of-personal-immunities/. Accessed 19 August 2025

Reisinger Coracini A (2010) The International Criminal Court's Exercise of Jurisdiction Over the Crime of Aggression – at Last ... in Reach ... Over Some. Göttingen Journal of International Law 2: 745–89

Reisinger Coracini A (2022) The Case for Creating an International Tribunal to Prosecute the Crime of Aggression against Ukraine (Part II). https://www.justsecurity.org/83201/tribunal-crime-of-aggression-part-two/. Accessed 19 August 2025

Reisinger Coracini A (2025) Email from Astrid Reisinger Coracini 5 September 2025

Representatives of Latvia, Liechtenstein, and Ukraine to the UN (2022) Letter dated Aug. 12, 2022 from the Reps. of Latvia, Liechtenstein and Ukraine to the United Nations addressed to the Secretary-General, UN Doc. A/ES-11/7-S/2022/616

Reuters (2022) Netherlands Willing to House Special Court for Russia Invasion of Ukraine, Minister Says. https://www.reuters.com/world/europe/netherlands-willing-house-special-court-russia-invasion-ukraine-minister-says-2022-12-12/. Accessed 19 August 2025

Rikhof J (2018) Analysis: The Special Tribunal for Lebanon: A Unique Situation. Global Justice Journal Queen's Law. https://globaljustice.queenslaw.ca/news/analysis-the-special-tribunal-for-lebanon-a-unique-institution. Accessed 19 August 2025

Rosen B, Bridgeman T, Gerami N (2025) The Day After US Strikes on Iran's Nuclear Program: Law & Policy. Just Security. https://www.justsecurity.org/115234/policy-legal-iran-nuclear-strikes/. Accessed 18 July 2025

Sands P (2017) East-West Street: On the Origins of "Genocide" and "Crimes against Humanity". Alfred A. Knopf, New York

Sands P (2022) Putin's Use of Military Force Is a Crime of Aggression. Financial Times. https://www.ft.com/content/cbbdd146-4e36-42fb-95e1-50128506652c. Accessed 19 August 2025

Scheffer D (2013) All The Missing Souls: A Personal History of the War Crimes Tribunals. Princeton University Press, Princeton

Scheffer D (2022a) The Case for Creating an International Tribunal to Prosecute the Crime of Aggression Against Ukraine (Part IV). Just Security. https://www.justsecurity.org/83290/tribunal-crime-of-aggression-part-four-2/. Accessed 19 August 2025

Scheffer D (2022b) Forging A Cooperative Relationship Between International Criminal Court and A Special Tribunal for Aggression Against Ukraine. Just Security. https://www.justsecurity.org/83757/forging-a-cooperative-relationship-between-intl-crim-court-and-a-special-tribunal-for-russian-aggression-against-ukraine/. Accessed 19 August 2025

Schwarz A (2016) The Legacy of the *Kenyatta* case: Trials *in Absentia* at the International Criminal Court and Their Compatibility with Human Rights. African Human Rights Law Journal 16: 99–116

Skilbeck R (2008) Funding Justice: The Price of War Crimes Trials. Human Rights Brief 15: 6–10

Sluiter G (2023) The Criminal Justice Response to the War in Ukraine One Year Later - the Arrest Warrant against Putin from the ICC and the Discussion of a Special "Aggression Tribunal" - Rethinking SLIC. Rethinking SLIC Blog. https://rethinkingslic.org/blog/criminal-law/169-the-criminal-justice-response-to-the-war-in-ukraine-one-year-later-the-arrest-warrant-against-putin-from-the-icc-and-the-discussion-of-a-special-aggression-tribunal. Accessed 19 August 2025

Special Court for Sierra Leone, Outreach and Special Affairs Section (2011) *Wetin Na Di Sp shal Kot?* The Special Court Made Simple, 2nd edn. https://www.rscsl.org/Documents/The%20Special%20Court%20Made%20Simple.pdf. Accessed 19 August 2025

Stahn C, van den Herik L (ed) (2010) Future Perspectives on International Criminal Justice. T.M.C. Asser Press, The Hague

Statista Research Department (2024) Outstanding Arrest Warrants by the International Criminal Court (ICC) as of November 2024, by Place of Crime. https://www.statista.com/statistics/1555855/icc-outstanding-arrest-warrants/#:~:text=As%20of%20November%202024%2C%20there%20were%2022%20outstanding,Putin%2C%20and%20Prime%20Minister%20of%20Israel%20Benjamin%20Netanyahu. Accessed 19 August 2025

The Elders (2022) The Elders Call for a Criminal Tribunal to Investigate Alleged Crime of Aggression in Ukraine. https://theelders.org/news/elders-call-criminal-tribunal-investigate-alleged-crime aggression-ukraine. Accessed 19 August 2025

Trahan J (2011) Negotiating the Amendment on the Crime of Aggression: Proceedings at the Kampala Review Conference on the International Criminal Court. International Criminal Law Review 11: 49–104

Trahan J (2022a) UN General Assembly Should Recommend Creation of Crime of Aggression Tribunal for Ukraine: Nuremberg is Not the Model. Just Security. https://www.justsecurity.org/80545/u-n-general-assembly-should-recommend-creation-of-crime-of-aggression-tribunal-for-ukraine-nuremberg-is-not-the-model/. Accessed 19 August 2025

Trahan J (2022b) The Case for Creating an International Tribunal to Prosecute the Crime of Aggression against Ukraine (Part III). Just Security. https://www.justsecurity.org/83238/tribunal-crime-of-aggression-part-three/. Accessed 19 August 2025

Trahan J (2023a) Legal Issues Surrounding Veto Use and Aggression. Case Western Reserve Journal of International Law 55: 93–146

Trahan J (2023b) Amending the Kampala Amendments: A Proposal to Harmonize the ICC's Jurisdiction, Opinio Juris. https://opiniojuris.org/2023/10/02/amending-the-kampala-amendments-a-proposal-to-harmonize-the-iccs-jurisdiction/. Accessed 19 August 2025

Traoré S B (2022) Making Sense of Africa's Massive Abstentions During the Adoption of the UNGA Resolution on the Aggression Against Ukraine. AfricLAW. https://africlaw.com/2022/04/21/making-sense-of-africas-massive-abstentions-during-the-adoption-of-the-unga-resolution-on-the-aggression-against-ukraine/. Accessed 19 August 2025

United Nations General Assembly (1999) Report of the Group of Experts for Cambodia Established Pursuant to General Assembly Resolution 52/135 (1999). http://hrlibrary.umn.edu/cambodia-1999.html Accessed 19 August 2025

United Nations General Assembly (2011) Third Report on Immunity of State Officials from Foreign Criminal Jurisdiction by Roman Anatolevich Kolodkin, Special Rapporteur on the Immunity of State of Officials from Foreign Criminal Jurisdiction, UN Doc. A/CN.4/646

United Nations General Assembly, International Law Commission (2022) Draft Article on the Immunity of State Officials from Foreign Criminal Jurisdiction, in Report of the International Law Commission, Seventy-Third Session, General Assembly, Ordinary Records, 77th Sess., Supp No. 10, UN Doc. A/7710

United Nations General Assembly, International Law Commission (2025a) Immunity of State Officials from Foreign Criminal Jurisdiction, A/CN.4/L.1017. https://documents.un.org/doc/undoc/ltd/g25/076/63/pdf/g2507663.pdf. Accessed 28 September 2025

United Nations General Assembly, International Law Commission (2025b) Second Report on Immunity of State Officials from Foreign Criminal Jurisdiction by Claudio Grossman Guiloff, Special Rapporteur, UN Doc. A/CN.4/780. https://documents.un.org/doc/undoc/gen/g25/012/32/pdf/g2501232. Accessed 19 August 2025

United Nations Security Council (2000) Report of the Secretary-General on the Establishment of a Special Court for Sierra Leone, UN Doc. S/2000/915

United Nations Treaty Body Database (nd) Ratification Status for ICCPR, https://tbinternet.ohchr.org/_layouts/15/TreatyBodyExternal/Treaty.aspx?Treaty=CCPR

UNTS (nd). https://treaties.un.org/pages/showDetails.aspx?objid=08000002801572a2

Van Schaack B, Ambassador-at-Large for Global Criminal Justice, U.S. Dept. of State (2022) The SOAS Annual Justice Lecture: Building Justice. https://state.gov/building-justicecriminal-accountability-and-the-road-to-peace-questions-on-justice-in-libya-and-beyond. Accessed 19 August 2025

Wählisch M (2017) Legitimacy Defects and Legal Flaws of the Special Tribunal for Lebanon: Dilemmas of the "Peace through Justice" Theorem. In: Hayashi N, Bailliet C (eds) (2017) The Legitimacy of International Criminal Tribunals. Cambridge University Press, Cambridge

Zelenskyy V (2022a) President of Ukraine Volodymyr Zelenskyy (2022) We Must Create a Special Tribunal on the Crime of Aggression Against Ukraine - Address by President Volodymyr Zelenskyy to the Participants of the Public Debate "War and Law" in Paris. https://www.president.gov.ua/en/news/mayemo-stvoriti-specialnij-tribunal-shodo-zlochinu-agresiyi-78285. Accessed 5 May 2025

Zelenskyy V (2022b) Speech by the President of Ukraine at the General Debate of the 77th Session of the UN General Assembly (2022). https://www.legal-tools.org/doc/wh08nu/. Accessed 19 August 2025

Zelenskyy V (2023) President of Ukraine Volodymyr Zelenskyy (2023) Official website, President: Ukraine Stands against Hybrid Formats of Tribunal for Russian Crime of Aggression. https://www.president.gov.ua/en/news/ukrayina-vistupaye-proti-gibridnih-formativ-tribunalu-shodo-82669. Accessed 19 August 2025

Other Documents

Agreement between the United Nations and the Government of Sierra Leone on the Establishment of a Special Court for Sierra Leone (2002) 2178 UNTS 137

Agreement for the Prosecution and Punishment of the Major War Criminals of the European Axis, Charter of the International Military Tribunal (1945) 59 Stat. 1544, 82 UNTS 279

Cambodia (2004) Law on the Establishment of the Extraordinary Chambers, with Inclusion of Amendments as Promulgated on 27 October 2004. NS/RKM/1004/006. https://www.eccc.gov.kh/sites/default/files/legal-documents/KR_Law_as_amended_27_Oct_2004_Eng.pdf. Accessed 19 August 2025

Chatham House (2022) A Criminal Tribunal for Aggression in Ukraine. https://www.chathamhouse.org/events/all/research-event/criminal-tribunal-aggression-ukraine. Accessed 5 May 2025

Charter of the United Nations (1945) 33 UNTS 933

Code of Criminal Procedure of Ukraine 2012 (as amended). https://cjad.nottingham.ac.uk/documents/implementations/pdf/Ukraine-Criminal_Procedure_Code_amend_2020.pdf. Accessed 19 August 2025

Combined Statement and Declaration Calling for the Creation of a Special Tribunal for the Punishment of the Crime of Aggression against Ukraine (2002) Gordon & Sarah Brown. https://gordonandsarahbrown.com/wp-content/uploads/2022/03/Combined-Statement-and-Declaration.pdf. Accessed 19 August 2025

Convention against Torture and Other Cruel, Inhuman, or Degrading Treatment or Punishment (1984) 1465 UNTS 85

Convention on the Prevention and Punishment of the Crime of Genocide (1948) 78 UNTS 277

Council of Europe (2022) Consequences of the Aggression of Russian Federation against Ukraine – Accountability for International Crimes, Committee of Ministers, 1442nd Meeting, CM/Del/Dec(2022)1442/2.3

Council of Europe Parliamentary Assembly (2022) The Russian's Federation's Aggression against Ukraine: Ensuring Accountability for Serious Violations of International Humanitarian Law and Other International Crimes, Resolution 2436

Crime of Aggression, Amendment Proposal (2025). https://treaties.un.org/doc/Publication/CN/2025/CN.162.2025-Eng.pdf. Accessed 19 August 2025

Criminal Code of the Russian Federation No. 63-Fz of 13 June 1996, as Amended (1996)

Criminal Code of Ukraine, No 2341-III from 5 April 2001, Edition from 7 September 2024 (2024). https://zakon.rada.gov.ua/laws/show/en/2341-14#Text. Accessed 19 August 2025

Definition of "Aggressor" at the League of Nations Conference for the Reduction and Limitation of Armaments on the 6th February 1933 (nd). http://www.letton.ch/lvx_33sdn.htm. Accessed 19 August 2025

Draft Agreement between the United Nations and the Royal Government of Cambodia Concerning the Prosecution under Cambodian Law of Crimes Committed During the Period of Democratic Kampuchea (2003)

European Parliament (2022) Resolution of 19 May 2022 on the Fight Against Impunity for War Crimes in Ukraine, P9_TA(2022)0218

Global Institute for the Prevention of Aggression (nd-a) Amendment Proposal. https://crimeofaggression.info/wp-content/uploads/GIPA-model-amendment-proposal_9-September-2023.pdf. Accessed 19 August 2025

Global Institute for the Prevention of Aggression (nd-b) GIPA's Reasons for the Proposed Amendment. https://crimeofaggression.info/wp-content/uploads/GIPA-Proposal-Short_25-September-2023.pdf. Accessed 19 August 2025

Global Institute for the Prevention of Aggression (2022) Statement by Members of the Council of Advisors on Russia's Invasion of Ukraine. https://crimeofaggression.info/wp-content/uploads/GIPA-Statement_24-March-2022-7.pdf. Accessed 19 August 2025

International Court of Justice (nd) *Application of the Convention on the Prevention and Punishment of the Crime of Genocide (The Gambia v. Myanmar)*

International Court of Justice (2002) *Arrest Warrant of 11 April 2000 (Democratic Republic of Congo v. Belgium)*, Judgment, 2002 ICJ Rep. 3

International Court of Justice (1986) *Case Concerning Military and Paramilitary Activities in and Against Nicaragua (Nicaragua v. United States)*, Merits, 1986 ICJ Rep. 14

International Court of Justice (1954) *Effect of Awards of Compensation Made by the UN Administrative Tribunal*, Advisory Opinion, 1954 ICJ Rep. 47

International Court of Justice (2012) *Jurisdictional Immunities of the State (Germany v. Italy)*, Judgment, 2012 ICJ Rep. 99

International Covenant on Civil and Political Rights (1966) 999 UNTS 171

International Criminal Court (2019) *Prosecutor v. Al-Bashir,* Judgment in the Jordan Referral re Al-Bashir Appeal, ICC-02/05-01/09 OA2, ACh

International Criminal Tribunal for the former Yugoslavia (nd) *Slobodan Milošević, "Kosovo, Croatia & Bosnia,"* IT-02-54, Case Information Sheet. https://www.icty.org/x/cases/slobodan_milosevic/cis/en/cis_milosevic_slobodan_en.pdf. Accessed 19 August 2025

International Criminal Tribunal for the former Yugoslavia (1999) *Prosecutor v. Milošević*, IT-99-37-I, Decision on Review of Indictment and Application for Consequential Orders

International, Impartial and Independent Mechanism for Syria (nd). https://www.ungeneva.org/en/about/organizations/IIIM-Syria. Accessed 19 August 2025

International Military Tribunal for the Far East (1946) Special Proclamation by the Supreme Commander for the Allied Powers at Tokyo

International Military Tribunal 1946) Judgment of 1 October 1946 in The Trial of German Major War Criminals. Proceedings of the International Military Tribunal Sitting at Nuremberg, Germany, Part 22 (22 August 1946 to 1 October 1946)

Interview with a Participant in the Core Group Negotiations, 25 July 2025

Joint Declaration by the Speakers of the Parliaments of Estonia, Finland, Latvia, Lithuania, Poland and Ukraine on Further Supporting Ukraine and on Russia's Hybrid Activities in Europe (2025). https://www.riigikogu.ee/wpcms/wp-content/uploads/2025/01/Joint-Declaration-03.02.2025.pdf. Accessed 19 August 2025

Joint Statement on the Accountability for the Crime of Aggression Committed on the Territory of Ukraine, by Albania, Belgium, Costa Rica, Czech Republic, Estonia, Guatemala, Latvia, Liechtenstein, Lithuania, Luxembourg, Marshall Islands, North-Macedonia and Poland (2023). https://un.mfa.ee/joint-statement-on-the-accountability-for-the-crime-of-aggression-committed-on-the-territory-of-ukraine/. Accessed 19 August 2025

KSC at a Glance (nd) https://www.scp-ks.org/sites/default/files/public/content/documents/20250311-KSC-AT-GLANCE-EN.pdf. Accessed 19 August 2025

Lomé Peace Agreement between the Government of Sierra Leone and the Revolutionary United Front of Sierra Leone (1999)

Ministry of Foreign Affairs of the Republic of Lithuania, The Ministers of Estonia, Latvia and Lithuania Call to Establish a Special Tribunal to Investigate the Crime of Russia's Aggression (2022). https://www.urm.lt/en/news/928/the-ministers-of-estonia-latvia-and-lithuania-call-to-establish-a-special-tribunal-to-investigate-the-crime-of-russias-aggression:35099. Accessed 19 August 2025

Office of the President of Ukraine Press Release (2023) Special International Tribunal Should Become an Effective Way to Punish Russia for Its Aggression against Ukraine - Andriy Smyrnov. https://www.president.gov.ua/en/news/specialnij-mizhnarodnij-tribunal-maye-stati-diyevim-sposobom-84405. Accessed 19 August 2025

OSCE Parliamentary Assembly (2022) Resolution on the Russian's Federation War of Aggression against Ukraine and Its People, and Its Threat to Security across the OSCE Region

Prosecutor General's Office, Crimes Committed during the Full-Scale Invasion of the RF. https://gp.gov.ua/en. Accessed 17 September 2025

Protocol Additional to the Geneva Conventions of 12 August 1949, and Relating to the Protection of Victims of International Armed Conflicts (1977)

Public International Law and Policy Group (nd) Draft Law for a Ukrainian High War Crimes Court. https://static1.squarespace.com/static/5900b58e1b631bffa367167e/t/62d6c27baae10b6ca51cadb7/1658241661209/DRAFT+Ukraine+High+War+Crimes+Court.pdf. Accessed 19 August 2025

Rome Statute of the International Criminal Court (1998) 2187 UNTS 3 (as amended)

Rules of Procedure and Evidence of the International Criminal Tribunal for the former Yugoslavia, as amended (1994)

Special Court for Sierra Leone (2004a) *Prosecutor v. Charles Ghankay Taylor*, SCSL-2003-01-I, Appeals Chamber Decision on Immunity from Jurisdiction

Special Court for Sierra Leone (2004b) *Prosecutor v. Morris Kallon and Brima Buzzy Kamara*, SCSL-2004-15 AR72(E) and SCSL-2004-16-AR72(E), Decision on Challenge to Jurisdiction: Lomé Accord Amnesty (Appeals Chamber)

Statements by Canada, France and the United Kingdom before the Special Working Group on Amendments (2025)

Statute of the International Criminal Tribunal for Rwanda (1994) SC Res. 955

Statute of the International Criminal Tribunal for the former Yugoslavia (1993) SC Res. 827

Statute of the Special Court for Sierra Leone (2002)

Statute of the Special Tribunal for Lebanon (2007) attached to United Nations Security Council Resolution 1757 (2007)

T.M.C. Asser Institute (nd) Trials *in absentia*

United Nations General Assembly Resolution 351 (IV) (1949)

United Nations General Assembly Resolution 52/135 (1998)

United Nations General Assembly Resolution 57/228B (2003)

United Nations General Assembly Resolution 71/248 (2016)

United Nations General Assembly Resolution ES-11/1 (2022)

United Nations General Assembly Resolution ES-11/2 (2022)
United Nations General Assembly Resolution ES-11/4 (2022)
United Nations General Assembly Resolution ES-11/L.10 (2025)
United Nations Security Council Resolution 827 (1993)
United Nations Security Council Resolution 955 (1994)
United Nations Security Council Resolution 1593 (2005)
United Nations Security Council Resolution 1757 (2007)
United Nations Security Council Resolution 1971 (2011)
United Nations Security Council Resolution 348 (2014) (draft) (vetoed by Russia and China)
United Nations Security Council Resolution 155 (2022) (draft) (vetoed by the Russian Federation)
United Nations Security Council Resolution 2623 (2022)

Chapter 6
An Opposing Plan: Calls for Establishing a Ukrainian Hybrid Chamber to Prosecute Aggression

Contents

Abstract In response to the proposals for the creation of an international criminal tribunal for the situation of Ukraine to be established through the United Nations, the United States, the United Kingdom, and Germany tabled a counterproposal of utilizing a tribunal with some level of hybrid features or support that would be part of Ukraine's domestic legal system. Their proposal raised various difficulties: (1) it would have been unconstitutional under Ukraine's Constitution; (2) it would have protected high-level leaders from prosecution through the application of personal immunities; and (3) it most likely would have failed as to the appearance of impartiality. Also, proceedings before a national judicial institution would neither convey the gravity of the situation—violation of the core norm against the use of force contained in the UN Charter by a permanent member of the UN Security Council no less—nor the international character of the crime of aggression as a threat to the international order. As a result, the establishment and judgments of such a Ukrainian domestic chamber would have created fairly weak precedent and little if any deterrence. During much of 2023, the competing international tribunal proposal and hybrid Ukrainian chamber proposal resulted in a deadlock in the negotiations to establish a tribunal for the situation.

Keywords Hybrid tribunal · Ukrainian chamber · Proposal by Germany · Proposal by the United Kingdom · Proposal by the United States · Constitutionality ·

J. Trahan, *The Crime of Aggression and Russia's Invasion of Ukraine*,
https://doi.org/10.1007/978-94-6265-763-2_6

Immunity · Impartiality · Appearance of impartiality · Legitimacy · Views of Ukraine · Core Group negotiations · Stalemate in negotiations

6.1 Introduction

This chapter explores the competing proposal tabled by Germany, the United Kingdom, and the United States, which they described as a "hybrid tribunal", but which was basically a plan to use a Ukrainian chamber with international features or support. For many reasons, this proposal appeared to be far weaker than the proposal for an international tribunal established through the United Nations. It faced potential constitutional impediments within the Ukrainian system and would result in personal immunity for top Russian leaders. Nor was it seen to carry nearly the same precedential weight as an international tribunal, because having Ukrainian judges adjudicating cases of Russian aggression—potentially *in absentia* as is permitted under Ukrainian law—would lack the appearance of impartiality, even if actual impartiality could be achieved. The G7 states came to endorse this Ukrainian hybrid model; meanwhile Ukraine opposed it. Thereafter, months of negotiations ensued within a Core Group of States[1] working to establish consensus on how to move forward with a crime of aggression tribunal for the situation. Yet, during the first year of negotiations within the Core Group, deadlock resulted between those states that supported the establishment of an international tribunal and those that supported utilizing a domestic Ukrainian one. Clearly, a third way would need to be found in order for a crime of aggression tribunal to be established in the situation of Ukraine.

6.2 The Competing "Hybrid" Tribunal Proposals

In light of vocal support for establishing an international tribunal for the crime of aggression in the situation of Ukraine, detailed in the last chapter, by the spring of 2023 several states developed a competing proposal. These states referred to their proposals as supporting establishment of a "hybrid tribunal". Yet, that labeling was somewhat confusing. A hybrid tribunal can be established through the UN by bilateral agreement between the UN and the country in question such that it qualifies as an international tribunal. An example is the Special Court for Sierra Leone.[2] Alternatively, a hybrid tribunal can also be established within the judicial system of a single state, such as the Extraordinary Chambers in the Courts of Cambodia

---

[1] The full name is "the Core Group on the Establishment of a Special Tribunal for the Crime of Aggression against Ukraine".

[2] See Agreement between the United Nations and the Government of Sierra Leone on the Establishment of a Special Court for Sierra Leone (2002) 2178 UNTS 137. On why the Special Court for Sierra Leone was an international tribunal and what makes a tribunal an international one, see Chap. 5, Sect. 5.3.4.3.

("ECCC"), having hybrid features (i.e., features from the national system as well as international features).[3] The proposals—which lacked specificity and were not entirely consistent with each other—were either for the latter model (a hybrid tribunal that is part of Ukraine's domestic legal system), or were really not hybrid tribunal proposals as all. They centered around crime of aggression prosecutions occurring before a domestic Ukrainian chamber with some unspecified level of international support or features.[4]

6.2.1 The Proposals by Germany, the United Kingdom, and the United States

Germany was the first to develop an alternative tribunal proposal. In a speech by Germany's then Federal Foreign Minister Annalena Baerbock on 16 January 2023, Baerbock expressed support for a hybrid Ukrainian chamber. While presenting a bold vision of the importance of international law, the UN Charter, and the need to prosecute the crime of aggression, as to a tribunal, Baerbock proposed the following:

> Our idea, with a number of partners, is . . . that there is a way to strengthen the International Criminal Court rather than weakening it, in the form of a court that derives its jurisdiction from Ukrainian criminal law. What would be important for me and, I believe, for many others would be for this court to be supplemented by an international component. Of course there cannot be a special procedure for one aggressor – what we establish must be supported by as many as possible of the world's states. It is therefore important to us to have an international component, for example with a location outside Ukraine, with financial support from partners and with international prosecutors and judges, to reinforce the impartiality and the legitimacy of this court.[5]

On 20 January 2023, the United Kingdom made a similar pronouncement. The UK's Foreign, Commonwealth and Development Office issued a statement that: "The UK would be willing to explore a 'hybrid' tribunal (a specialised court integrated into Ukraine's national justice system with international elements)".[6] The statement added that "[a]ny new tribunal would also need sufficient international support and must not undermine the existing accountability mechanisms".[7]

---

[3] See Cambodia, Law on the Establishment of the Extraordinary Chambers, with Inclusion of Amendments as promulgated on 27 October 2004 (2004) NS/RKM/1004/006. https://www.legal-tools.org/doc/9b12f0/pdf/. Accessed 7 August 2025. The Kosovo Specialist Chambers and Specialist Prosecutor's Office were also created within the court system of Kosovo, although the tribunal sits in The Hague. See Karnavas 2017 ("[T]he KSC is a specialized chamber within the Kosovo Judiciary".).

[4] A wide variety of tribunals are encompassed within the label "hybrid tribunal". For background on hybrid tribunals, see, e.g., Ainley and Kersten 2025; Naughton 2018; Trahan 2018, pp. 890–96 (discussing different models). There exists no precise line delimiting when a national tribunal becomes a "hybrid" one. See also note 11 on hybrid tribunals.

[5] Baerbock 2023. See also Ghaedi and Romaniec 2023.

[6] UK Press Release 2023.

[7] Ibid.

Finally, then US Ambassador for Global Criminal Justice Beth Van Schaack, in a speech on 27 March 2023 that was quite strong in terms of the need for accountability, articulated the following approach as to a tribunal:

> The United States supports the development of an internationalized tribunal dedicated to prosecuting the crime of aggression against Ukraine. Although a number of models have been under consideration, and these have been analyzed closely, we believe an internationalized court that is rooted in Ukraine's judicial system, but that also includes international elements, will provide the clearest path to establishing a new Tribunal and maximizing our chances of achieving meaningful accountability. We envision such a court having significant international elements – in the form of substantive law, personnel, information sources, and structure.[8]

Van Schaack added that an internationalized national court "builds upon the example of other successful hybrid justice mechanisms" and will "facilitate broader cross-regional international support".[9]

Thus, all three states[10] suggested utilizing a Ukrainian court with certain hybrid (i.e., internationalized) features. By calling for the tribunal to be located outside Ukraine with international prosecutors and judges, Germany appeared to articulate the most "internationalized" form for the tribunal. The UK's statement was so fragmentary that it was difficult to ascertain what precisely they were endorsing. Meanwhile, the United States was clearly proposing a court within Ukraine's judicial system, with some international elements (such as substantive law, personnel, information sources, and structure).[11]

---

[8] Van Schaack 2023.

[9] Ibid.

[10] Denmark also supported such a model, at least by May 2023. See text accompanying note 83. Eventually the full G7 came to support the proposal. See note 85.

[11] "It is sometimes not easy to decide whether a particular court fits the typology of a hybrid court...". Naughton 2018, p. 6. Elena Naughton of the International Center for Transitional Justice suggests that hybrid tribunals usually share the following features: (a) jurisdiction over international crimes; (b) at least some application of international procedural and substantive law; (c) composition consisting of both national and international judges, prosecutors, and staff; and (d) usually some international funding. Ibid. The hybrid tribunals established to date are: the Special Court for Sierra Leone, the ECCC, the Extraordinary African Chambers within the Courts of Senegal (which prosecuted crimes committed in Chad), the Kosovo Specialist Chambers and Specialist Prosecutor's Office (and prior to that, Regulation 64 Panels within Kosovo's court system), the State Court in Bosnia-Herzegovina, the Special Panels for Serious Crimes (in East Timor), the Special Tribunal for Lebanon, and the Special Criminal Court in the Central African Republic.

6.3 The Weaknesses of the Hybrid Proposals

In calling for the utilization of a chamber within Ukraine's judicial system with some international features,[12] the proposal suffered from a number of defects. First, implementing a special hybrid tribunal within the Ukrainian court system would be unconstitutional under Ukraine's Constitution. Second, high-level leaders would be immune from prosecution before such a tribunal (even if the tribunal possessed international features). Third, utilizing a Ukrainian chamber (presumably with at least a majority of Ukrainian judges serving on it)[13] to adjudicate cases related to Russian aggression would lack the appearance of impartiality, if not actual impartiality. This could prove extremely problematic in terms of legitimacy and the appearance of legitimacy. In turn, this begged the question of why it would attract the cross-regional endorsements and support that Germany and the United States suggested. It would also not reflect the gravitas of what was at stake—a flagrant breach of the UN Charter. Fourth, the tribunal would not further the goals usually associated with establishing a hybrid tribunal. Finally, and quite significantly, Ukraine opposed the hybrid approach, and a hybrid chamber could hardly be created without Ukraine's backing. The proposals appeared to present a truly weak alternative to establishing an international criminal tribunal through the United Nations endorsed by the UN General Assembly.[14] Furthermore, as will be examined below, one suspects that supporting a weak tribunal model may have been precisely what the proponents of the hybrid Ukrainian chamber had in mind. Each of these topics is explored *seriatim* below.

6.3.1 The Constitutional Problem

An initial concerning feature was that Ukraine's Constitution prohibits the formation of "special" or "extraordinary" chambers while the country is in a state of martial law or a state of emergency. Specifically, Article 125 of the Ukrainian Constitution states that the "[e]stablishment of extraordinary and special courts is not permitted".[15] Article 157 further states that "[t]he Constitution of Ukraine shall not be amended in conditions of martial law or a state of emergency".[16]

Alexander Komarov and Oona Hathaway explain the source of the prohibition:

---

[12] See Korynevych et al. 2023, pp. 274–75 ("The . . . concept is an internationalised (hybrid) court, i.e. *as part of the Ukrainian judicial system*, with varying degrees of internationalization . . .".) (emphasis added).

[13] Germany, for example, suggested adding international judges. See Baerbock 2023.

[14] Hamilton 2023b; Trahan 2023b.

[15] Ukraine, Constitution of Ukraine, adopted at the Fifth Session of the Verkhovna Rada of Ukraine on 28 June 1996, as amended (1996). https://www.refworld.org/legal/legislation/natlegbod/1996/en/42875. Accessed 11 October 2024.

[16] Ibid.

> Th[e prohibition] is directly rooted in Ukraine's status as a post-Soviet state. At the time the Constitution was adopted in 1996, the memory of special and extraordinary tribunals which took place during the Soviet era was still fresh. "Extraordinary and special courts" essentially were forms of extrajudicial simplified "justice" serving totalitarian goals, such as [tribunals] during The Great Purge and special courts in the Gulag system, as well as various military tribunals created in the former Soviet Union. "Special courts" are understood as separate domestic judicial institutions with their own system for consideration of certain categories of cases (usually criminal). "Extraordinary courts" are considered to be domestic courts that are formed to consider a specific (usually criminal) case on the basis of a special act of the relevant public authority.[17]

The constitutional requirements meant that the establishment of a hybrid chamber within Ukraine's court system could only have been pursued once martial law or the state of emergency ends and the Constitution is amended.[18] Such a plan could have resulted in years of delay, since, as of late 2025, it is quite unclear when the conflict will end. Rebecca Hamilton posed the question:

> Could a sufficiently motivated Ukrainian government find a way to creatively lawyer around this hurdle? Maybe. But . . . [e]ven if some creative lawyering approach somehow succeeded and on a workable timeframe, it could undermine the commitment to the rule of law that undergirds the legitimacy of any such project.[19]

Suggesting an approach that was constitutionally defective under Ukraine's Constitution was not a strong start.

6.3.2 The Immunity Problem

An additional difficulty with conducting crime of aggression trials through a chamber established as part of Ukraine's court system—even one with international elements or support—pertains to the issue of immunity. The issue of personal immunity was discussed previously at length[20] and therefore will be revisited only briefly.

As previously explained, in proceedings before a domestic court, personal immunity would exempt the highest-level Russian (as well as other)[21] leaders from prosecution. Specifically, the "troika"—the Head of State, the Head of Government, and the Minister of Foreign Affairs—possess personal immunity before another state's domestic courts while in office.[22] As detailed in Chap. 5, while such immunities do not

---

[17] Komarov and Hathaway 2022a.

[18] Ibid.; see also Komarov and Hathaway 2022b. The Special Tribunal that has been agreed upon by the Council of Europe and Ukraine, which will be discussed in Chap. 7, by contrast, would not be established *within* Ukraine's court system.

[19] Hamilton 2023b.

[20] See Chap. 5, Sect. 5.3.4.3.

[21] For the role of Belarus, see Chap. 4, Sect. 4.2.3. For the role of North Korea, see Chap. 4, Sect. 4.2.4.

[22] For discussion of the *Yerodia* (Arrest Warrant) decision of the International Court of Justice ("ICJ"), see Chap. 5, Sect. 5.3.4.3. See also International Court of Justice (2002) *Arrest Warrant of*

apply before an international tribunal, they are not overcome in proceedings before the domestic courts of another state.[23] Thus, pursuant to the ICJ's *Yerodia*/Arrest Warrant ruling,[24] a domestic chamber (even with international elements) would not be an international tribunal that would be able to overcome such immunities.[25]

Furthermore, as discussed in earlier chapters, the definition of the crime of aggression in the Rome Statute of the International Criminal Court ("ICC") encompasses only those at the leadership level.[26] Thus, prosecuting the troika was seen as imperative. It was difficult to imagine Ukraine agreeing to a plan that would give immunity to Russian President Putin, and thus impunity while in office.[27] Anton Korynevych, who serves as Ambassador-at-Large in the Ministry of Foreign Affairs of Ukraine, and his colleagues thus wrote: "many countries are concerned that the hybrid (internationalised) model, which will essentially be a Ukrainian domestic court, will delay or even eliminate the prospect of bringing Russian and Belarusian Troika members to justice, as they will enjoy personal immunity before the domestic hybrid court".[28]

The inability to prosecute high-level leaders would, in turn, have potential implications regarding the legitimacy of the tribunal. Lithuanian Vice-Minister at the Lithuanian Ministry of Foreign Affairs, Gabija Grigaite-Daugirde, explained:

---

11 April 2000 (Democratic Republic of Congo v. Belgium), Judgment, 2002 ICJ Rep. 3, paras 51, 61.

[23] See Chap. 5, Sect. 5.3.4.3.

[24] Further development of the law in future is of course possible.

[25] See Coracini and Trahan 2022. Even Kevin Jon Heller agreed with this point: "A hybrid tribunal established as part of the Ukrainian judicial system . . . would not be sufficiently international to set aside Putin and Lavrov's personal immunity". Heller 2023. He offered two ideas to "internationalize" a hybrid tribunal created within Ukraine's judicial system: "(1) a General Assembly resolution asking the U.N. to create a hybrid tribunal with Ukraine; and (2) an agreement between the U.N. and Ukraine to create that tribunal". Ibid. Yet the US, UK, and German proposals contained neither of these ideas nor were they pursued thereafter. For discussion of why the Sierra Leone Special Court, which was not formed within Sierra Leone's court system, by contrast, was sufficiently international to overcome immunities, see Chap. 5, Sect. 5.3.4.3.

[26] See Rome Statute of the International Criminal Court (1998) 2187 UNTS 90 (as amended), Article 8*bis*(1) ("Rome Statute (1998) (as amended)"). For discussion of the leadership clause, see Chap. 3, Sect. 3.3.2; Chap. 4, Sect. 4.4.5. The definition of the crime in the Ukrainian Criminal Code does not contain a leadership clause, although something akin to it has been read into the definition. See Korynevych et al. 2023, p. 378 (the Grand Chamber of the Ukrainian Supreme Court has read something akin to the leadership clause into the Ukrainian law); Criminal Code of Ukraine, No 2341-III from 5 April 2001 (2024) https://zakon.rada.gov.ua/laws/show/en/2341-14#Text. Accessed 28 September 2025, Article 437.

[27] See President of Ukraine 2023. As will be discussed in Chap. 7, the Special Tribunal that has been agreed upon by the Council of Europe and Ukraine does (unfortunately) recognize the personal immunity of the troika while they are in office, by suspending proceedings against them. See Chap. 7, Sect. 7.4.2.2. This result eventually emerged as a necessary condition for obtaining the G7's support for the tribunal. Ibid.

[28] Korynevych et al. 2023, p. 375, citing Smyrnov 2024. See also Labuda 2024, p. 300 ("There is little doubt that a hybrid tribunal based on Ukraine's criminal jurisdiction would not be able to prosecute Russia's leadership".).

> Understanding that – according to international law as it stands today – personal immunities for political and military leaders of an aggressor state should be applied, serious doubts arise as to whether domestic jurisdictions would be able to meet expectations for the legitimacy of the results of criminal investigations, because even arrest warrants for the crime of aggression committed by Russian political and military leadership could not be issued.[29]

For this reason, establishing a specialized hybrid Ukrainian chamber was quickly denounced, particularly by the Government of Ukraine.[30] The concern was that it made little sense to prosecute a leadership crime and immunize the top-level leaders, allowing them to pin responsibility on those in levels below in the hierarchy. Such a result could even *embolden* top-level leaders, by entrenching impunity—allowing them to escape individual criminal responsibility, in this instance, for a full-scale invasion of a neighboring state. Rebecca Hamilton argued that "the optics would be galling if an aggression tribunal proceeded to trial against a comparatively lesser-ranked official while failing to indict Putin for a war that he launched".[31]

Functional immunities (covering acts performed in an official capacity) could also prove problematic in proceedings before a national court if the initial (but likely erroneous)[32] approach taken by the International Law Commission ("ILC")[33] were to be followed. The application of functional immunities would pose even more difficulties because, unlike personal immunities, they do not expire when a person's term in office ends. If functional immunities were applicable, they would serve as a permanent bar to proceedings before another state's national courts.[34]

---

[29] Grigaite-Daugirde 2023, p. 304.

[30] President of Ukraine 2023 ("We understand who gave the orders. These people must not be untouchable. This is very important for us, this is one of the fundamental issues".); Kuleba 2022 (calling for "holding the Russian Federation *and its leadership accountable* for the crime of aggression against Ukraine") (emphasis added). See also Sect. 6.3.5 (Zelenskyy rejecting "hybrid formats").

[31] Hamilton 2023a, p. 56.

[32] For why the initial approach was incorrect and such functional immunities do not attach, see Pacheco 2024; United Nations General Assembly, International Law Commission 2025b; Dannenbaum 2022, p. 862 ("The better view is that aggression is no different from other international crimes involving state violations – foreign courts have competence and functional immunities do not apply".).

[33] See United Nations General Assembly, International Law Commission 2022, pp. 190–91 (leaving the crime of aggression off the list of crimes to which functional immunity does not apply before another state's domestic courts). The ILC's Drafting Committee has now rectified this error. See United Nations General Assembly, International Law Commission 2025a.

[34] Van Alebeek 2008, p. 114 (functional immunity "is not dependent on an official's term of office"); United Nations General Assembly, International Law Commission 2022, draft Article 4.1 (personal immunity terminates when a person's term in office ends).

6.3.3 The Legitimacy Problem

Perhaps most significantly, a Ukrainian chamber, consisting of Ukrainian judges (even if a few international judges were to join them), would lack the appearance of legitimacy. This would prove true even if the Ukrainian jurists were the most distinguished jurists and wrote superlatively well-reasoned opinions. As Grigaite-Daugirde wrote: "In cases when victim states try to prosecute the leaders of an aggressor state, it would be difficult for them to escape 'the taint of victor's justice', and such prosecutions could hardly be perceived as ensuring maximum legitimacy and impartiality".[35] Carrie McDougall described the situation as "victim's revenge", noting that "[e]ven if a Ukrainian prosecution for aggression received the sort of extensive international support that is on offer, Ukrainian authorities are unlikely to be perceived as acting in a wholly impartial manner".[36] Similarly, Patryk Labuda wrote that "the weightiest argument against a hybrid tribunal may be the potential perception of Ukraine acting as a prosecutor and judge in its own case".[37] Because the crime of aggression has not been enforced at the international level since the prosecutions before the International Military Tribunal at Nuremberg and the International Military Tribunal for the Far East (Tokyo), it was vital to get it right. The tribunal would need to possess both legitimacy and the appearance of legitimacy.[38]

While Chap. 5 discussed the reasons to establish an international tribunal (thus, the arguments will not be repeated), suffice it to say that what Germany, the United Kingdom, and the United States were proposing appeared to be a truly weak response to the large-scale invasion of a neighboring state by a permanent member of the UN Security Council. As previously discussed,[39] the crime of aggression enforces the core norm contained in the UN Charter, Article 2(4), prohibiting aggressive use of force.[40] "The Article 2(4) prohibition on the use of force is the cornerstone of th[e] effort [articulated in the UN Charter, to 'save succeeding generations from the scourge of war'] and of the post-World War II international legal system in general".[41] The ICJ in the *Armed Activities* case "called the prohibition against the use of force 'a

---

[35] Grigaite-Daugirde 2023, p. 304. "Victor's justice" is perhaps not the right phrase, because Ukraine has not been victorious in expelling Russian forces from its territory; yet the phrasing is nonetheless evocative.

[36] McDougall 2023, p. 217. See also Dannenbaum 2022, p. 862 ("prosecutions in a victim state's courts risk the taint of apparent partiality, which would compromise the[] ability to vindicate the aggression ban").

[37] Labuda 2024, p. 305.

[38] See Grigaite-Daugirde 2023, p. 306 ("Bearing in mind that the investigation into the crime of aggression committed by the political and military leadership of Russia, a permanent member of the UN Security Council, against Ukraine will be an historical investigation on par with the Nuremberg trial, any legality, legitimacy, impartiality or quality deficit should be avoided from the very beginning . . .".).

[39] See Chap. 5, Sect. 5.3.1 (Why Establish an International Tribunal).

[40] Charter of the United Nations (1945) 33 UNTS 933, Article 2(4) ("UN Charter (1945)").

[41] O'Connell 2024, p. 333.

cornerstone of the United Nations Charter'",[42] and acclaimed legal scholar Louis Henkin called Article 2(4) "the principal norm of international law in our time".[43]

For the tribunal to have authoritative weight and establish significant precedent that could potentially deter other states from committing aggression, or Russia from committing additional aggression, it could not be formed as part of the Ukrainian domestic legal system. Such an approach would fail to provide the kind of powerful statement that would be imperative if leaders in the future were to be deterred. As Claus Kreβ explains:

> The establishment of an internationalized Ukrainian tribunal would fail to send out this message: [t]he institutional design would not clearly convey the international character of the crime of aggression and would emphasize Ukraine's national interest as the immediate victim rather than that of the international community as a whole.[44]

Moreover, the problem of legitimacy of using a hybrid Ukrainian chamber would be compounded exponentially if Ukraine were to conduct aggression trials *in absentia* as it is permitted to do,[45] and has done,[46] under Ukrainian law.

6.3.4 The Absence of the Traditional Benefits Associated with Hybrid Tribunals

While perhaps not the most significant concern, it is worth noting that the establishment of a hybrid chamber within Ukrainian legal system to prosecute the crime of aggression would not advance most of the goals typically associated with hybrid tribunals. Some of the traditional arguments in favor of hybrid tribunals include: (1) capacity building; (2) local ownership; (3) cost savings; and (4) being situated in the country where the crimes occurred, which can make the court's work more readily visible to victim and perpetrator populations.[47] Yet, when a tribunal is seeking to adjudicate inter-state aggression, these benefits would not necessarily follow.[48]

For example, one benefit of hybrid tribunals is that they allow national judges and staff to work alongside experienced internationals at all levels, which may help

---

[42] Kreβ 2022, p. 1, citing International Court of Justice (2005) *Armed Activities on the Territory of Congo (Democratic Republic of Congo v. Uganda)*, Judgment, 2005 ICJ Rep. 168, para 148.

[43] Henkin 1971, p. 544.

[44] Nuremberg Academy (2023) Nuremberg Academy Lectures-Claus Kreβ. YouTube. https://www.youtube.com/watch?v=mkQNFiclqmQ. Accessed 7 August 2025.

[45] See Code of Criminal Procedure of Ukraine 2012 (2020). https://cjad.nottingham.ac.uk/documents/implementations/pdf/Ukraine-Criminal_Procedure_Code_amend_2020.pdf. Accessed 7 August 2025, Article 262.

[46] McDougall 2023, p. 216 (former Ukrainian President Viktor Yanukovych was tried *in absentia* by Ukraine for complicity in waging a war of aggression), citing Sayapin 2018.

[47] See, e.g., Trahan 2018, pp. 885–88 (interviewees discussed the benefits of hybrid tribunals in terms of efficiency, successful outreach facilitated by being located in situation countries, and capacity building).

[48] Labuda 2024, pp. 274, 303–04.

with capacity building when the domestic judges and staff resume work in their home institutions.[49] While that would also be the case in the current context, it was *precisely the involvement of local judges that would also be seen as problematic*. As discussed above, Ukrainian judges—particularly when adjudicating cases involving the conduct of leaders of a neighboring state that has invaded their country—would likely lack the appearance of impartial arbiters. In this context, difficulties would arise from local ownership.[50]

Various hybrid tribunals have also been located in their situation countries[51] rather than in a country at a distance, as the initial ad hoc tribunals were.[52] Being located in closer proximity to victim and perpetrator populations can bring justice "closer to home".[53] Yet, as mentioned, such an approach also can prove problematic. Moreover, in the current situation, Germany did not propose locating the tribunal in Ukraine, and recruitment and operational challenges would have surfaced if the tribunal were established in an active war zone.

---

[49] See, e.g., Trahan 2018, pp. 887–88 (interviews with Robert Petit, Hassan Jallow, and Serge Brammertz discussing capacity building). National prosecutors and judges may not previously have handled cases related to genocide, crimes against humanity, war crimes, or the crime of aggression.

[50] Serge Brammertz, for example, discussed the difficulty of "local ownership" in the context of Lebanon:

> [O]ne problem created by proximity to the crime scene, is that the closer you are getting to the area where their crimes have been committed, the higher the likelihood that people you would hire would be at least perceived as being biased towards one or the other side in the conflict, which in an extreme situation would indeed be an argument to go for an ad hoc [international] solution where you have a kind of ad hoc tribunal which is located elsewhere and where the entire team is composed by professionals who have no link at all to the region.

Ibid., p. 901 (interview with Serge Brammertz). International tribunals can also contribute to capacity building. For example, the International Criminal Tribunal for the former Yugoslavia ("ICTY") is acknowledged to have done so by helping with the establishment of the hybrid State Court in Bosnia-Herzegovina. See, e.g., United Nations International Criminal Tribunal for the former Yugoslavia (nd) Capacity Building, http://www.icty.org/en/outreach/capacity-building. Accessed 13 March 2018.

[51] For example, the Special Court for Sierra Leone sat in Freetown, Sierra Leone, and the ECCC sat in Phnom Penh, Cambodia. Two hybrid tribunals, however, have been located in The Hague—the Special Tribunal for Lebanon and the Kosovo Specialist Chambers and Specialist Prosecutor's Office. For background, see Statute of the Special Tribunal for Lebanon (2007) attached to United Nations Security Council Resolution 1757 (2007); Background (nd) Kosovo Specialist Chambers & Specialist Prosecutor's Office. https://www.scp-ks.org/en/background. Accessed 15 October 2025.

[52] The ICTY sat in The Hague, Netherlands (not in any of the countries of the former Yugoslavia) and the International Criminal Tribunal for Rwanda ("ICTR") sat in Arusha, Tanzania (not in Rwanda). Given that all the existing international and hybrid tribunals (other than the ICC) are "ad hoc", calling only the ICTY and ICTR "ad hoc" is somewhat misleading. See Trahan 2018, p. 844, n 17 (interview with William Schabas: "Actually the better way to describe all these institutions is to say they are ad hoc. They are created for a particular situation, particular circumstances".). Notwithstanding, it is the ICTY and ICTR that are referred to as the "ad hoc" tribunals.

[53] See, e.g., Trahan 2018, p. 888 (interview with Serge Brammertz discussing "local ownership").

Hybrid tribunals can also result in cost savings.[54] Indeed, the Special Court for Sierra Leone—a hybrid tribunal, although international in its creation, with many international features[55]—had a significantly reduced budget compared to the budgets of the ICTY and the ICTR.[56] However, a hybrid tribunal is not *inherently* less expensive.[57] It all depends on what is expected of the tribunal. An international tribunal could be narrowly focused in its design and mandate, having a relatively small budget. Conversely, a domestic chamber with hybrid features could be broadly focused in its design and mandate, necessitating a larger budget. The cost would depend on such factors as: (1) what time period the prosecutions would be expected to cover; (2) how many individuals would be investigated and/or prosecuted; and (3) the complexity of the cases involved. The cost would not depend on the presence or absence of hybrid features.[58]

Thus, it was far from clear that the benefits typically associated with hybrid tribunals would be achieved through the establishment of a hybrid Ukrainian chamber. Or, to the extent some benefits could be achieved, these might easily be outweighed by the difficulties associated with utilizing a Ukrainian chamber. Patryk Labuda thus concluded: "[T]he traditional arguments in favor of hybrid tribunals, such as capacity building and local ownership, are less relevant for inter-state aggression, where the symbolic and expressive dimension of international criminal tribunals

---

[54] See, e.g., Trahan 2018, pp. 885–86 (interviews with Brenda Hollis and David Crane discussing efficiency).

[55] See note 2 (Special Court for Sierra Leone).

[56] See Cassese 2006 (on cost). For background on the establishment of these tribunals, see Scheffer (2013).

[57] See, e.g., Trahan 2018, pp. 897–901 (interviewees discussing that the Special Court for Sierra Leone was not as cost effective as originally envisioned).

[58] Tom Dannenbaum explains that:

> Cost mitigation [of an international tribunal] could include an "accordion structure", allowing for the reduction of staffing and other (potentially) variable costs during periods of low activity and the expansion of capacity when conditions require. And adjustable space sharing arrangement may also be appropriate. Such measures would accommodate a long interval between issuance of an arrest warrants [*sic*] and the beginning of trials.

Dannenbaum 2022, p. 965.

outweighs any longer-term 'shadow effects' on the domestic rule of law".[59] For this and other reasons, "[f]ew scholars have argued in favor of a hybrid tribunal".[60]

6.3.5 *Ukrainian Opposition to the Hybrid Approach*

A final, but extremely significant additional impediment associated with the hybrid Ukrainian chamber was that *Ukraine did not wish to pursue it.*[61] While the Ukrainian Government initially seemed open to both models, by May 2023, President Zelenskyy announced that his government would "work without any hybrid formats . . . . We have seen the Minsk agreements since 2014—they were a kind of hybrid peace . . . . Therefore, Ukraine does not want to agree to any hybrid peace, [a] hybrid tribunal as a continuation of this".[62]

Zelenskyy seemed deeply suspicious of the proposal to utilize a hybrid Ukrainian chamber. He stated: "Only one institution is capable of responding to the original crime—the crime of aggression, a tribunal . . .[, n]ot something hybrid that can formally close the topic . . .[,] not some compromise that will allow politicians to say that the case is allegedly done . . .[,] but a true, full-fledged tribunal. True and

---

[59] Labuda also writes:

> As Antonio Cassese argued in regard to the Special Court for Sierra Leone, it "was designed to improve on the tribunals for the former Yugoslavia and Rwanda, which were perceived to be marred by four essential flaws": their costliness, lengthiness, "remoteness from the territory where crimes had been committed," and "unfocused character," resulting in the prosecution of low-ranking targets. However, these traditional benefits of hybridity do not apply in the Russia Ukraine context.

Labuda 2024, p. 303, citing Cassese 2006. Cassese's assessment of the ad hoc tribunals may have occurred before lower-level warrants were withdrawn and other lower-level cases were transferred back to the situation countries; both tribunals predominantly prosecuted high- or at least relatively high-level perpetrators. For background on the ICTY, see, e.g., Trahan and Vukusic 2020, in Stahn et al. 2020; Trahan 2019, in Sterio and Scharf 2019.

[60] Labuda 2024, n 155. For one scholar arguing for a hybrid approach, see Heller 2024, pp. 12–15 (A hybrid tribunal would have "significant practical advantages over a Special Tribunal, because it would build on Ukraine's functioning judicial system, avoiding the need to create a new tribunal *ex nihilo* . . . . Equally important, though, a [hybrid] would minimize perceptions of inter-conflict selectivity, despite being limited to Russia's invasion of Ukraine".). Heller ignores that building on Ukraine's functioning judicial system was *precisely the source of the problem* in terms of the lack of appearance of impartiality, constitutional impediments, and the application of personal immunities. For discussion of the problem of selectivity, see Chap. 5, Sect. 5.3.4.6. For rare added support for the hybrid approach, see Scharf et al. 2023. For a rebuttal, see, e.g., Trahan 2023a.

[61] Patryk Labuda wrote: "Since hybrids cannot, by definition, be imposed upon a sovereign state, the 'hybrid court for Ukraine' amounts to a contradiction in terms, with some analysis echoing westsplaining by ignoring Ukrainian agency and imposing arrangements on an Eastern European state against its will". Labuda 2024, p. 304 (footnotes omitted).

[62] Ibid., p. 299, citing European Pravda 2023; President of Ukraine 2023.

full justice".[63] Andrii Smyrnov, then Deputy Head of the Office of the President of Ukraine, expressed similar views. He "rejected the idea of a hybrid tribunal as unconstitutional . . . . He also suggested that anchoring such a tribunal in Ukraine's justice system would create an impression that the crime of aggression is merely a bilateral dispute between Ukraine and Russia".[64] A hybrid Ukrainian chamber, quite simply, could not be established without the Ukrainian Government being on board.

6.3.6 *The Motivations of the Proponents*

The weaknesses of the model proposed by Germany, the United Kingdom, and the United States begs the question of why powerful states would advocate such a weak approach to accountability. Given the serious tensions that have existed between the three countries and Russia over the invasion of Ukraine, as well as more broadly, these countries could hardly be attempting to "protect" President Putin from judicial scrutiny. Thus, the inevitable conclusion is that these states were willing to "go easy" on Putin in order to avoid the precedent of establishing an international criminal tribunal that could prosecute a head of state for the crime of aggression. The three countries appeared to be acting out of self-interest: the fear that the legality of their leaders' uses of force might be questioned in the future. They were undoubtedly concerned about the precedent they could set.

At the same time, having vociferously condemned Russia's invasion and advocated for accountability, including for the crime of aggression,[65] Germany, the United Kingdom, and the United States could hardly back out of the endeavor altogether. They could, however, water down the proposal and weaken the justice to be delivered. Their call for utilization of a hybrid Ukrainian chamber appeared to be just such a light-handed approach to justice. While it would establish some precedent in terms of prosecuting the crime of aggression, it would not set a particularly powerful precedent and might even set a fairly illegitimate one. Moreover, trials within a Ukrainian court were guaranteed not to set any precedent for trying the highest-level leaders (the troika).

It certainly seemed that these states had no interest in living up to the promise made by US Chief Prosecutor at Nuremberg, Robert H. Jackson, also invoked in Chap. 3. In his Opening Statement, Jackson declared:

> The ultimate step in avoiding periodic wars, which are inevitable in a system of international lawlessness, is to make statesmen responsible to law. And let me make clear that while this

[63] Ibid., p. 299, citing Clancy 2023. The Minsk Agreements refer to a series of international agreements attempting to end the war in the Donbas between the Ukrainian Armed Forces and Russian separatist groups. See, e.g., Hodunova 2025.

[64] International Crisis Group 2023, citing Shashkova 2023.

[65] Baerbock 2023 (the "Charter has not stopped Russia's President from waging a brutal war of aggression against Ukraine"; "[a]ccountability is what matters"); Van Schaack 2023 ("There is no question that Russia's aggression against Ukraine is a manifest violation of the UN Charter"; "justice and accountability [are] imperatives").

> is first applied against German aggressors, the law includes, and if it is to serve a useful purpose *it must condemn, aggression by other nations, including those which sit here now in judgment.*[66]

Quite ironically, two of the states that sat in judgment at Nuremberg (the United States and the United Kingdom) appeared to be weakening the precedent that would be set for trying nationals of the successor state (Russia) to a large part of another Nuremberg ally (the USSR) for the crime of aggression. Moreover, it seemed that the motivation was to ensure that US and UK leaders would not have to face similar scrutiny should they commit such a crime in the future. Germany, by contrast, was in a different position, because it *has supported broader accountability* with respect to prosecuting the crime of aggression, by leading, as will be discussed in Chap. 8, the efforts to create more jurisdiction over the crime of aggression before the ICC.[67]

Powerful states were in a potential Catch-22. Any precedent set in the situation of Ukraine could become precedent in future situations. More powerful states are the ones that periodically do make recourse to the use of force as they have more powerful and effective militaries, and they do not always do so in conformity with the constraints of international law.[68] As Philippe Sands wrote: "The momentum soon confronted the realpolitik: Britain, France, Germany and the US were—to put it mildly[—]initially trepidatious. It was perhaps not so much a matter of principle, more self-preservation: if a tribunal were to be created today in relation to Russia, then why not tomorrow in relation to us?".[69] Patryk Labuda similarly wrote: "many scholars question the United [States'] bona fides in making what appear to be self-interested arguments. In particular, critics point out that a hybrid tribunal would have less 'precedential value' than a General Assembly-backed international tribunal, thereby decreasing the likelihood that future tribunals will be created in cases of aggression by Western states".[70]

Rebecca Hamilton expressed an interesting alternative view when she queried whether the United States actually would be better off with aggression prosecutions conducted before an internationalized national court. She wrote:

---

[66] International Military Tribunal 1947, p. 154 (emphasis added).

[67] See Chap. 8.

[68] For discussion of the 2003 incursion into Iraq by the United States and United Kingdom, see Chap. 1, Sect. 1.1. See also Dannenbaum 2022, p. 871 ("The devastating UK- and US-led invasion of Iraq was characterized at the time as a 'crime of aggression' by British Foreign Office lawyer Elizabeth Wilmshurst"), citing Wilmshurst 2005. One might also add US and Israeli strikes in 2025 against Iranian nuclear facilitates to the list of uses of force lacking a cogent legal basis. See Rosen et al. 2025. See also Chap. 5, note 28 (other recent problematic uses of force).

[69] Sands 2023. France joined in endorsing the hybrid Ukrainian chamber approach, which, as mentioned, eventually all G7 states endorsed. See note 85.

[70] Labuda 2024, p. 301, citing Clancy 2023 ("According to a source familiar with the core group discussions, . . . it's the G7, led by the US, Britain and France, who are pushing back against establishing a tribunal through a General Assembly resolution. Their motivation, the source says, is a purely political attempt to avoid setting a precedent for the international prosecution for the crime of aggression".); Hamilton 2023b ("[T]he United States may seek to thwart the emergence of an international tribunal that could potentially be repurposed or expanded to pursue future cases of aggression perpetrated by other states (the United States included)".).

> The United States may seek to thwart the emergence of an international tribunal that could potentially be repurposed or expanded to pursue future cases of aggression perpetrated by other states (the United States included). But if those inside the U.S. government believe that by instead supporting an "internationalized national court" in Ukraine they are somehow limiting the replicability or generalizability of the effort, they are mistaken.
>
> The precedent being established here is that *any* state that is a victim of aggression – or, in a future scenario, merely *perceives itself* to be a victim of aggression – can, with the support of allied states, create an internationalized national court to prosecute its (actual or perceived) aggressor. Unlike a truly international tribunal, an "internationalized national court" is endlessly replicable; it requires one aggrieved state and some minimum number of supporting states.[71]

6.4 The Resulting Stalemate in the Core Group Negotiations

By the spring of 2023, a Core Group of States was formed for the purpose of identifying consensus on an approach for establishing a tribunal to prosecute the crime of aggression in the situation of Ukraine.[72] The possibility of reform of the Rome Statute to increase the ICC's jurisdiction over the crime of aggression in such a way that it would encompass the conduct of Russian nationals (along with the conduct of nationals of other non-States Parties) remained a theoretical possibility.[73] Yet, no one was betting on this outcome or its occurrence in time to benefit Ukraine.[74] Also, as will be detailed in Chap. 8, of the G7 group of states, only Germany has been supportive of the ICC having more jurisdiction over the crime of aggression.[75] Other

---

[71] Hamilton 2023b.

[72] Kyiv Independent News Desk 2023. The group expanded to approximately 40 states. See Korynevych et al. 2023, p. 374 (the Core Group has approximately 40 states).

[73] On what the proposed amendment would cover, see Chap. 8. If negotiations by the ICC's Assembly of States Parties ("ASP") to amend the Rome Statute and harmonize the ICC's jurisdiction over all four Rome Statute crimes were successful *and* were a new amendment to that effect to enter into force for Ukraine while the war or annexation is ongoing, the ICC would possess jurisdiction not only over war crimes, genocide, and crimes against humanity committed on the territory of Ukraine, but also jurisdiction over the crime of aggression. Now that negotiations to harmonize jurisdiction have been put off until 2029—a topic covered in Chap. 8—the possibility of the ICC possessing jurisdiction over the crime in the situation of Ukraine seems more remote.

[74] See International Criminal Court (2025) Special Session, The Review of the Amendments on the Crime of Aggression. ICC-ASP/S-1/Res.1. https://asp.icc-cpi.int/sites/default/files/asp_docs/ICC-ASP-S-1-Res.1-ENG.pdf. Accessed 16 October 2025 (delaying negotiations until an intersessional meeting in 2027 and a Special Session of the ASP in 2029). Any amendment could not apply retroactively. See Rome Statute (1998) (as amended), note 26, Article 24 (non-retroactivity).

[75] During the lead-up to a Special Session of the ICC's ASP held in July 2025, Germany led the Group of Friends, consisting of states that supported such an increase in the ICC's jurisdiction over the crime of aggression. An amendment proposal to harmonize jurisdiction over all four Rome Statute crimes was tabled by Germany, along with Costa Rica, Sierra Leone, Slovenia, and Vanuatu. See Costa Rica, Germany, Sierra Leone, Slovenia, and Vanuatu (2025) Proposal of Amendment. https://treaties.un.org/doc/Publication/CN/2025/CN.162.2025-Eng.pdf. Accessed 7 August 2025.

G7 states appear wary of the ICC having more jurisdiction over the crime.[76] As will be discussed in Chap. 8, the G7 (other than Germany), through their support for accountability regarding the crime of aggression in the situation of Ukraine but not more broadly, create the distinct optics of only endorsing the selective application of justice when it comes to the crime of aggression.[77]

As mentioned in Chap. 5, most (but by no means all) of the states in the Core Group were European.[78] While aggression poses a truly global risk, it is understandable that European countries were particularly interested in establishing an aggression tribunal in the situation. For states located in the proximity of Russia, the threat of Russian aggression was seen as an existential threat to their national security. European countries were also feeling the impact of receiving significant numbers of Ukrainian refugees[79] and sharing, with the United States, the cost of providing military support to Ukraine.[80]

The Core Group commenced meeting in various European cities every other month, with approximately forty states attending, along with representatives of the European Union and Council of Europe.[81] From the first meeting in January 2023 through May 2023, momentum grew for a tribunal to be established through the United Nations, recommended by the UN General Assembly.[82] Then, at a May 2023 meeting in Tallinn, Estonia, the United Kingdom and Denmark proposed an "internationalized national tribunal" and those became the competing models until January 2024.[83] Thus, a stalemate developed between those states that preferred the establishment of an international tribunal established through the United Nations and those that preferred a hybrid Ukrainian chamber,[84] with all G7 states eventually endorsing the latter model.[85] In light of the stalemate, pressure mounted for states to find a third

---

[76] As will be detailed in Chap. 8, various of the G7 states, joined by a few other states, did their best to derail the negotiations on the topic that took place 7–9 July 2025 at the United Nations during a Special Session of the ICC's ASP. See Trahan 2025. Canada, the United Kingdom, France, Japan, and New Zealand tabled a resolution that would have delayed the negotiations to harmonize jurisdiction until 2/3rds of States Parties had ratified the Kampala crime of aggression amendments, which could have taken decades. See International Criminal Court, Assembly of States Parties 2025, Annex II, para 9.

[77] See Chap. 8, Sect. 8.5 (State Opposition to Harmonizing Jurisdiction).

[78] The non-European states in the Core Group included Australia, Costa Rica, Guatemala, Japan and the United States, until the 2025 Strasbourg meeting when the United States withdrew.

[79] Statista nd.

[80] Wolf and Davis 2024.

[81] See note 72 (approximately 40 states in the Core Group).

[82] Interview with a Participant in the Core Group Negotiations, 25 July 2025.

[83] Ibid.

[84] Ibid.

[85] At the G7 Foreign Ministers' meeting in Japan in April 2023, the Foreign Ministers of the G7 stated: "We support exploring the creation of an internationalized tribunal based in Ukraine's judicial system to prosecute the crime of aggression against Ukraine". See United Kingdom, Foreign, Commonwealth and Development Office 2023 (agreed to by the foreign ministers of Canada, France, Germany, Italy, Japan, the United Kingdom, and the United States, as well as the High Representative of the European Union).

way to establish the tribunal or risk no tribunal being established. The efforts to reach agreement on this third way—which emerged in the form of agreement on a tribunal to be established by agreement between the Council of Europe and Ukraine—are detailed in the following chapter.

6.5 Conclusion

By spring 2023, Germany, the United Kingdom, and the United States developed an alternative proposal of establishing a specialized chamber within Ukraine's court system, with hybrid features, rather than an international tribunal. The proposal represented a far weaker response than the proposed international criminal tribunal established through the United Nations. The Ukrainian chamber would arguably be unconstitutional under Ukraine's Constitution, would result in personal immunities shielding top-level Russian (or other)[86] leaders, and likely would suffer in terms of the appearance of legitimacy, with Ukrainian judges adjudicating cases involving Russian aggression. As a result, it would create weak precedent, failing to reflect the gravitas of the situation—that a large-scale offense against the international order was at stake. The countries proposing this hybrid model were no doubt in a Catch-22. Any precedent set whereby Russian (or other) leaders faced scrutiny for the crime of aggression against Ukraine could also become precedent for exposing their leaders to future judicial scrutiny. Ultimately, with states in the Core Group split as to which model to support, neither the proposal for the international tribunal nor the one for a hybrid Ukrainian chamber attracted sufficient support to proceed.

References

Ainley K, Kersten M (eds) (2025) Hybrid Justice: Innovation and Impact in the Prosecution of Atrocity Crimes. Oxford University Press, Oxford

Baerbock A (2023) Strengthening International Law in Times of Crisis – Speech by Federal Foreign Minister Annalena Baerbock in The Hague, Federal Foreign Office (2023) https://www.auswaertiges-amt.de/en/newsroom/news/strengthening-internationallaw-in-times-of-crisis/2573492?view. Accessed 18 July 2025

Cassese A (2006) Report on the Special Court for Sierra Leone. https://www.rscsl.org/Documents/Cassese%20Report.pdf. Accessed 7 August 2025

Clancy D (2023) The Divide Hardens on What a Special Court for the Crime of Aggression by Russia Should Look Like. PassBlue

Coracini A, Trahan J (2022), The Case for Creating a Special Tribunal to Prosecute the Crime of Aggression Committed Against Ukraine (Part VI): On the Non-Applicability of Personal Immunities. Just Security. https://www.justsecurity.org/84017/the-case-for-creating-a-special-tribunal-to-prosecute-the-crime-of-aggression-committed-against-ukraine-part-vi-on-the-non-applicability-of-personal-immunities/. Accessed 7 August 2025

[86] For the roles of Belarus and North Korea, see Chap. 4, Sects. 4.2.3–4.2.4.

Dannenbaum T (2022) A Special Tribunal for the Crime of Aggression? Journal of International Criminal Justice 20: 859–73

European Pravda (2023) Zelenskyy Calls on U.N. General Assembly to Approve Resolution in Support of Special Tribunal Creation. Ukrainska Pravda. https://www.pravda.com.ua/eng/news/2023/03/3/7391931/. Accessed 7 August 2025

Ghaedi M, Romaniec R (2023) Germany's Baerbock Calls for Special Ukraine Tribunal at ICC. Deutsche Welle. https://www.dw.com/en/germanys-baerbock-calls-for-special-ukrainetribunal-at-icc/a-64408862. Accessed 18 July 2025

Grigaite-Daugirde G (2023) Crime of Aggression against Ukraine: Legality and Legitimacy of Domestic Prosecutions in Third States. Polish Yearbook of International Law XLIII: 299–309

Hamilton R (2023a) Ukraine's Push to Prosecute Aggression: Implications for Immunity *Ratione Personae* and the Crime of Aggression. Case Western Reserve Journal of International Law 55: 39–60

Hamilton R (2023b) An Assessment of the United States' New Position on an Aggression Tribunal for Ukraine. Just Security. https://www.justsecurity.org/85765/an-assessment-of-the-united-states-new-position-on-an-aggression-tribunal-for-ukraine. Accessed 7 August 2025

Heller K (2023) The Jordan Appeal Supports a Hybrid Tribunal Denying Personal Immunity. Opinio Juris. https://opiniojuris.org/2023/02/06/the-jordan-appeal-judgment-supports-a-hybrid-tribunal-denyingpersonal-immunity. Accessed 18 July 2025

Heller K (2024), Options for Prosecuting Russian Aggression against Ukraine: A Critical Analysis. Journal of Genocide Research, 26: 1–24

Henkin L (1971) The Reports of the Death of Article 2(4) Are Greatly Exaggerated. American Journal of International Law 65: 544–48

Hodunova K (2025) What Were the Minsk Agreements and Why Did They Fail to Bring Peace in Ukraine? The Kyiv Independent. https://kyivindependent.com/what-were-the-minsk-agreements-and-why-did-they-fail-to-bring-peace-in-ukraine/. Accessed 1 August 2025

International Criminal Court, Assembly of States Parties (2025) Report of the Working Group on Amendments Regarding Its Work on the Review of the Kampala Amendments Concerning the Exercise of Jurisdiction with Regard to the Crime of Aggression. ICC-ASP/S-1/2. https://asp.icc-cpi.int/sites/default/files/asp_docs/ICC-ASP-S-1-2-ENG.pdf. Accessed 18 July 2025

International Crisis Group (2023) A New Court to Prosecute Russia's Illegal War? https://www.crisisgroup.org/global-ukraine/new-court-prosecute-russias-illegal-war. Accessed 4 May 2025

International Military Tribunal (1947) Trial of Major German War Criminals by the International Military Tribunal Sitting at Nuremberg Germany, Vol. II. Hein & Co., Buffalo

Karnavas M (2017) Kosovo Specialist Chamber–Part I: Its Statute and Rules of Procedure and Evidence in a Nutshell. International Criminal Law Blog. http://michaelgkarnavas.net/blog/2017/05/24/kosovo-specialist-chambers-part-1/. Accessed 7 August 2025

Komarov A, Hathaway O (2022a) Ukraine's Constitutional Constraints: How to Achieve Accountability for the Crime of Aggression. Just Security. https://www.justsecurity.org/80958/ukraines-constitutional-constraints-how-to-achieve-accountability-for-the-crime-of-aggression/. Accessed 19 July 2025

Komarov A, Hathaway O (2022b) The Best Path For Accountability for the Crime of Aggression Under Ukrainian and International Law. Just Security. https://www.justsecurity.org/80958/ukraines-constitutional-constraints-how-to-achieve-accountability-for-the-crime-of-aggression/. Accessed 7 August 2025

Korynevych A, Senatorova O, Shepitko M (2023) Prosecution of the Crime of Aggression in International Law and Ukrainian Jurisdiction: Challenges and Prospects. Polish Yearbook of International Law XLIII: 367–79

Kreβ C (2022) The Ukraine War and the Prohibition of the Use of Force in International Law. Occasional Paper Series No. 12

Kuleba D (2022) Statement by Minister of Foreign Affairs of Ukraine Dmytro Kuleba on the Initiative to Create a Tribunal for Bringing the Leadership of the Russian Federation to Justice for the Crime of Aggression Against Ukraine, Ukrainian Government (2022) Press Center Permanent

Mission of Ukraine to the United Nations. https://ukraineun.org/en/press-center/535-/. Accessed 7 August 2025

Kyiv Independent News Desk (2023) President's Office (2023) 36 Countries in Core Group on Special Tribunal for Russian Crime of Aggression. https://kyivindependent.com/presidents-office-36-countries-in-core-group-on-special-tribunal-for-russian-crime-of-aggression. Accessed 7 August 2025

Labuda P (2024) Countering Imperialism in International Law: Examining the Special Tribunal for Aggression against Ukraine through a Post-Colonial Eastern European Lens. Yale Journal of International Law, 49: 271–310

McDougall C (2021) The Crime of Aggression under the Rome Statute of the International Criminal Court, 2nd edn. Cambridge University Press, Cambridge

McDougall C (2023) The Imperative of Prosecuting Crimes of Aggression Committed against Ukraine. Journal of Conflict and Security Law 28: 203–30

Naughton E (2018) Committing to Justice for Serious Human Rights Violations: Lessons from Hybrid Tribunals. International Center for Transitional Justice. https://www.ictj.org/publication/committing-justice-serious-human-rights-violations-lessons-hybrid-tribunals. Accessed 18 July 25

O'Connell M (2024) What Remains of Law against War. Georgetown Law Journal 113: 319–85

Pacheco J (2024) Where Do States Stand on Official Immunity under International Law, Just Security. https://www.justsecurity.org/94830/where-do-states-stand-on-official-immunity-under-international-law. Accessed 7 August 2025

President of Ukraine (2023) Ukraine Stands Against Hybrid Formats of Tribunal for Russian Crime of Aggression. https://www.president.gov.ua/en/news/ukrayina-vistupaye-proti-gibridnih-formativ-tribunalu-shodo-82669. Accessed 7 August 2025

Rosen B, Bridgeman T, Gerami N (2025) The Day After US Strikes on Iran's Nuclear Program: Law & Policy. Just Security. https://www.justsecurity.org/115234/policy-legal-iran-nuclear-strikes/. Accessed 18 July 2025

Sayapin S (2018) A Curious Aggression Trial in Ukraine: Some Reflections on the Alexandrov and Yerofeyev Case. Journal of International Criminal Justice 16: 1093–104

Scharf M, Williams P, Dutton Y, Sterio M (2023) The United States' Proposal on Prosecuting Russians for the Crime of Aggression Against Ukraine Is a Step in the Right Direction. Just Security. https://www.justsecurity.org/85886/the-united-states-proposal-onprosecuting-russians-for-the-crime-of-aggression-against-ukraine-is-a-step-in-the-right-direction. Accessed 7 August 2025

Sands P (2023) There Can Be No Impunity for the Crime of Aggression against Ukraine. Financial Times

Scheffer D (2013) All The Missing Souls: A Personal History of the War Crimes Tribunals. Princeton University Press, Princeton

Shashkova M (2023) Putin and His Doppelgängers Must Be Tried at a War Crimes Tribunal - Deputy Head of Zelensky's Office. Kyiv Post. https://www.kyivpost.com/post/14386. Accessed 7 August 2025

Smyrnov A (2024) It is Only a Full-Fledged Tribunal That Will Allow Lifting the Immunity of the President, Prime Minister and Foreign Minister of Russia – Andriy Smyrnov, President of Ukraine (2024) https://tinyurl.com/3nmhdpk5. Accessed 30 August 2024

Stahn C, Agius C, Brammertz S, Hocking J, Rohan C (eds) (2020) Legacies of the International Criminal Tribunal for the Former Yugoslavia: A Multidisciplinary Account. Oxford University Press, Oxford

Statista (nd) Estimated Number of Refugees from Ukraine Recorded in Europe and Asia since February 2022 as of July 2024, by Selected Country. https://www.statista.com/statistics/1312584/ukrainian-refugees-by-country. Accessed 7 August 2025

Trahan J (2018) Views of the Future of the Field of International Justice: A Scenarios Project Based on Expert Consultations. American University International Law Review 33: 837–941

Trahan J (2019) Examining the Benchmarks by which to Evaluate the ICTY's Legacy. In: Sterio M, Scharf M (eds) (2019) The Legacy of Ad Hoc Tribunals in International Criminal Law: Assessing the ICTY's and ICTR's Most Significant Legal Accomplishments. Cambridge University Press, Cambridge

Trahan J (2023a) Why a "Hybrid" Ukrainian Tribunal on the Crime of Aggression Is Not the Answer. Just Security. https://www.justsecurity.org/85019/why-hybrid-ukrainian-tribunal-on-crime-of-aggression-is-not-the-answer. Accessed 7 August 2025

Trahan J (2023b) Don't Be Fooled by U.S. Smoke and Mirrors on the Crime of Aggression. Just Security. https://www.justsecurity.org/85986/dont-be-fooled-by-u-s-smoke-and-mirrors-on-the-crime-of-aggression. Accessed 7 August 2025

Trahan J (2025) Crime of Aggression Negotiations Blocked by France, the United Kingdom, and Canada. Opinio Juris. https://opiniojuris.org/2025/07/31/crime-of-aggression-negotiations-blocked-by-france-the-united-kingdom-and-canada/. Accessed 30 July 2025

Trahan J, Vukusic I (2020) The Legacy of the ICTY: The Three-Tiered Approach to Justice in Bosnia-Herzegovina and Benchmarks for Measuring Success. In: Stahn C, Agius C, Brammertz S, Hocking J, Rohan C (eds) Legacies of the International Criminal Tribunal for the Former Yugoslavia: A Multidisciplinary Account. Oxford University Press, Oxford

UK Press Release (2023) UK Joins Core Group Dedicated to Achieving Accountability for Russia's Aggression against Ukraine. https://www.gov.uk/government/news/ukraine-uk-joins-core-group-dedicated-to-achieving-accountability-for-russias-aggression-against-ukraine. Accessed 18 July 2025

United Kingdom, Foreign, Commonwealth and Development Office (2023) G7 Japan 2023 Foreign Ministers' Communiqué. https://www.gov.uk/government/publications/g7-japan-2023-foreign-ministers-communique/g7-japan-2023-foreign-ministers-communique-18-april-2023-karuizawa-nagano. Accessed 7 August 2025

United Nations General Assembly, International Law Commission (2022) Draft Article on the Immunity of State Officials from Foreign Criminal Jurisdiction, in Report of the International Law Commission, Seventy-Third Session, General Assembly, Ordinary Records, 77th Sess., Supp No. 10, UN Doc. A/7710

United Nations General Assembly, International Law Commission (2025a) Immunity of State Officials from Foreign Criminal Jurisdiction, UN Doc. A/CN.4/L.1017. https://documents.un.org/doc/undoc/ltd/g25/076/63/pdf/g2507663.pdf. Accessed 28 September 2025

United Nations General Assembly, International Law Commission (2025b) Second Report on Immunity of State Officials from Foreign Criminal Jurisdiction by Claudio Grossman Guiloff, Special Rapporteur, UN Doc. A/CN.4/780. https://documents.un.org/doc/undoc/gen/g25/012/32/pdf/g2501232.pdf. Accessed 13 May 2025

Van Alebeek R (2008) The Immunity of States and Their Officials in International Criminal Law and International Human Rights Law. Oxford University Press, Oxford

Van Schaack B (2023) Ambassador Van Schaack's Remarks on the U.S. Proposal to Prosecute Russian Crimes of Aggression (2023) U.S. Department of State. https://2021-2025.state.gov/ambassador-van-schaacks-remarks/. Accessed 18 July 2025

Wilmshurst E (2005) Wilmshurst Resignation Letter. BBC News

Wolf C, Davis E (2024) Countries That Have Committed the Most Aid to Ukraine. U.S. News. https://www.usnews.com/news/best-countries/articles/these-countries-have-committed-the-most-aid-to-ukraine. Accessed 7 August 2025

Other Documents

Agreement between the United Nations and the Government of Sierra Leone on the Establishment of a Special Court for Sierra Leone (2002) 2178 UNTS 137

Background (nd) Kosovo Specialist Chambers & Specialist Prosecutor's Office, https://www.scp-ks.org/en/background. Accessed 15 October 2025

Cambodia, Law on the Establishment of the Extraordinary Chambers, with Inclusion of Amendments as promulgated on 27 October 2004 (2004) NS/RKM/1004/006. https://www.legal-tools.org/doc/9b12f0/pdf/. Accessed 7 August 2025

Charter of the United Nations (1945) 33 UNTS 933

Code of Criminal Procedure of Ukraine 2012 (2020). https://cjad.nottingham.ac.uk/documents/implementations/pdf/Ukraine-Criminal_Procedure_Code_amend_2020.pdf. Accessed 7 August 2025

Costa Rica, Germany, Sierra Leone, Slovenia, and Vanuatu (2025) Proposal of Amendment. https://treaties.un.org/doc/Publication/CN/2025/CN.162.2025-Eng.pdf. Accessed 18 July 2025

Criminal Code of Ukraine, No 2341-III from 5 April 2001 (2024). https://zakon.rada.gov.ua/laws/show/en/2341-14#Text. Accessed 28 September 2025, art 437

International Criminal Court (2025) Special Session, The Review of the Amendments on the Crime of Aggression. ICC-ASP/S-1/Res.1. https://asp.icc-cpi.int/sites/default/files/asp_docs/ICC-ASP-S-1-Res.1-ENG.pdf. Accessed 16 October 2025

International Court of Justice (2002) *Arrest Warrant of 11 April 2000 (Democratic Republic of Congo v. Belgium)*, Judgment, 2002 ICJ Rep. 3

International Court of Justice (2005) *Armed Activities on the Territory of Congo (Democratic Republic of Congo v. Uganda)*, Judgment, 2005 ICJ Rep. 168

Interview with a Participant in the Core Group Negotiations, 25 July 2025

Nuremberg Academy (2023) Nuremberg Academy Lectures-Claus Kreβ. YouTube. https://www.youtube.com/watch?v=mkQNFiclqmQ. Accessed 7 August 2025

Rome Statute of the International Criminal Court (1998) 2187 UNTS 90 (as amended)

Statute of the Special Tribunal for Lebanon (2007) attached to United Nations Security Council Resolution 1757 (2007)

Ukraine, Constitution of Ukraine, adopted at the Fifth Session of the Verkhovna Rada of Ukraine on 28 June 1996, as amended (1996). https://www.refworld.org/legal/legislation/natlegbod/1996/en/42875. Accessed 11 October 2024

United Nations International Criminal Tribunal for the Former Yugoslavia (nd) Capacity Building. http://www.icty.org/en/outreach/capacity-building. Accessed 13 March 2018

Chapter 7
Agreement on a Third Way: Establishing a Tribunal Through the Council of Europe

Contents

Abstract This chapter describes the final negotiations that led to agreement on an aggression tribunal to be established by the Council of Europe and Ukraine. It also details the content of that agreement, focusing specifically on the key contentious issues that arose during the negotiations and how they were resolved. These included: the definition of the crime; head of state immunity; how cases are initiated; and trials *in absentia*. The chapter also provides an overview of the remainder of the Tribunal's statute and discusses the role of the Management Committee tasked with assisting with the administration and management of the Tribunal. The chapter additionally examines how states would join in endorsing and funding the Tribunal through an Enlarged Partial Agreement. Procedural steps need to occur and funding must be procured before the Tribunal can commence operations. Due to compromises made in the final agreement, whether the Tribunal can bring some measure of justice to the people of Ukraine remains to be seen. Much depends on the support the Tribunal receives from states, the functioning of the Tribunal, and whether any accused will be apprehended. Yet even if the Tribunal only holds trials *in absentia* and issues

J. Trahan, *The Crime of Aggression and Russia's Invasion of Ukraine*,
https://doi.org/10.1007/978-94-6265-763-2_7

indictments for accused who remain at large, this would still bring recognition to the crime committed and harms inflicted on the victims. While it is a weaker tribunal than could have been established, the Tribunal is absolutely necessary. Its existence would ensure that leaders implicated in the invasion of Ukraine—the largest and deadliest military operation in Europe since World War II—do not escape consequences and set at least some precedent for the prosecution of the crime of aggression.

Keywords Core Group negotiations · Council of Europe · Definition of the crime of aggression · Personal immunities · Independent prosecutor · Transfer of proceedings · Trials *in absentia* · Final agreement · Funding the Tribunal · Tribunal Statute · Tribunal Agreement · Enlarged Partial Agreement · Prospects for the Tribunal · Legitimacy of the Tribunal · Challenges ahead

7.1 Introduction

This chapter discusses the proposal that eventually emerged and was accepted by both groups of states in the Core Group.[1] They agreed that the Special Tribunal for the Crime of Aggression against Ukraine ("Special Tribunal" or "Tribunal") would be formed by agreement between Ukraine and the Council of Europe, with states from other regions able to join in endorsing the Tribunal. Such broader backing could increase the Tribunal's base of support beyond being solely a regionally backed tribunal, making it more international. As of late 2025, hurdles remain. Specifically, states in the Council of Europe (and beyond) must decide whether to become parties to a certain Enlarged Partial Agreement;[2] and/or enter into cooperation agreements with the Tribunal. They must also ensure that the Tribunal has sufficient funding to operate. Key issues as to the Tribunal's operations have been resolved, including the question of immunities, the issue of trials *in absentia*, and whether there will be a fully independent prosecutor or cases will be referred or transferred from Ukraine. The Tribunal will utilize a definition of the crime that is similar, but not identical, to the internationally accepted definition of the crime of aggression found in Article 8*bis* of the Rome Statute of the International Criminal Court ("ICC").[3] The compromises reached on some of the issues—particularly suspending proceedings against top Russian (and other) leaders—present the question of when too many compromises

[1] The Core Group's full name is "the Core Group on the Establishment of a Special Tribunal for the Crime of Aggression against Ukraine".

[2] Council of Europe (2025) Draft Resolution Establishing the Enlarged Partial Agreement on the Management Committee of the Special Tribunal for the Crime of Aggression against Ukraine, dated 18 June 2025. https://www.riigiteataja.ee/aktilisa/2170/2202/6002/760XV_Ukraina_ingl_k_L1.pdf. Accessed 28 September 2025 ("Enlarged Partial Agreement"). The Council of Europe's role in the establishment of the Special Tribunal was possible as Russia had been expelled from the Council of Europe. See Council of Europe, Committee of Ministers 2022.

[3] Rome Statute of the International Criminal Court (1998) 2187 UNTS 90, as amended ("Rome Statute (1998) (as amended)"), Article 8*bis*.

suggest that one should decline to pursue the establishment of a tribunal. The author does not suggest that this point was reached, since failing to pursue accountability for the crime of aggression in the situation would also prove a profound mistake. The chapter closes by addressing some of the challenges ahead if or when the Tribunal becomes operational. Above all, the Tribunal must prove itself to be a fair and credible one in its operations so that the potential to ensure at least some measure of justice and deterrence is not squandered.

7.2 Negotiations Within the Core Group for a Tribunal Established Through the Council of Europe

After the stalemate that developed during 2023 as to the form an aggression tribunal could take, described in Chap. 6,[4] states in the Core Group set off in earnest to find a third way to proceed. Some ideas included the establishment of a tribunal by agreement between the UN and Ukraine, pursuant to a Security Council resolution under Chapter VI of the UN Charter.[5] Under Chapter VI, mandatory abstention of a party to the dispute (Russia) would apply, meaning Russia should not be able to veto the resolution.[6] Yet that idea never attracted significant support.[7] A report prepared at the request of the Asser Institute reflects another model that was floated and

[4] See Chap. 6, Sect. 6.4.

[5] This was the method by which the Special Court for Sierra Leone was established. Namely, as discussed in Chap. 5, Sect. 5.3.4.1, the UN Security Council under a Chapter VI resolution requested that the UN Secretary-General negotiate an agreement between the UN and Sierra Leone, see SC Res. 1315 (2000), para 1. The tribunal was subsequently established by agreement between the UN and Sierra Leone. See Agreement between the United Nations and the Government of Sierra Leone on the Establishment of a Special Court for Sierra Leone (2002) 2178 UNTS 137.

[6] UN Charter Article 27(3) states that "in decisions under Chapter VI, and under paragraph 3 of Article 52, a party to a dispute *shall* abstain from voting". See Charter of the United Nations (1945) 33 UNTS 933 ("UN Charter") (emphasis added). It does not say "may"; it says "shall". For the argument that the UN Security Council could have recommended the establishment of a special aggression tribunal for the situation of Ukraine under a Chapter VI resolution, see, e.g., Trahan 2024, pp. 49–51.

[7] Even if Russia abstained on the vote—and it is unclear whether that could have been achieved since mandatory abstention is inconsistently applied—it seemed unlikely that the other permanent members of the Security Council would have supported the approach.

discarded.[8] While the search for a common approach continued, a team of prosecutors within the European Union Agency for Criminal Justice Cooperation ("EuroJust")—named the International Centre for the Prosecution of the Crime of Aggression against Ukraine ("ICPA")[9]—was set up in The Hague, Netherlands, and began compiling evidence of the commission of the crime.[10]

Because most states in the Core Group were European,[11] an obvious contender for a middle-ground approach between establishing an international tribunal through the UN and utilizing a Ukrainian chamber with hybrid features was to establish a regionally backed tribunal. Indeed, by January 2024, attention shifted to the involvement of the Council of Europe,[12] which had already endorsed the creation of an ad hoc tribunal in the situation in January 2023.[13] (At that time, the Council of Europe endorsed the establishment of an international tribunal with no personal immunities applying;[14] yet, as explained in Chap. 6, the G7 refused to support that approach.)[15]

Once the idea of a Council of Europe/Ukraine tribunal became the focus of the Core Group negotiations, the Committee of Ministers of the Council of Europe on 30 April 2024, gave the mandate to the Secretary-General of the Council of Europe to

---

[8] The report describes the following proposal:

> When the discussions in the Core Group reached an impasse in September 2023, the European External Action Service and the services of the European Commission (DG Justice and Legal Service) floated the idea of [another] model. According to their approach, . . . the Tribunal should be set up by a multilateral agreement between the Core Group-participating states and receive international legal personality . . . . This . . . option allowed the Core Group process to move forward, but many delegations felt that negotiating a multilateral treaty between 40 states would be too cumbersome.

Chlevickaitė et al. 2025, p. 22.

[9] Ukraine, Lithuania, Latvia, Estonia, Poland, Romania and the United States appointed prosecutors to the ICPA. See European Union Agency for Criminal Justice Cooperation nd; see also European Union Agency for Criminal Justice Cooperation 2023.

[10] The name is misleading as the ICPA has no capacity to conduct prosecutions. It was primarily intended to support national investigations. Ibid.

[11] As mentioned in earlier chapters, the Core Group consisted of approximately forty states as well as representatives of the European Union and the Council of Europe; approximately five states were non-European (Australia, Costa Rica, Guatemala, Japan and the United States, until the 2025 Strasbourg meeting when the United States withdrew).

[12] Interview with a Participant in the Core Group Negotiations, 25 July 2025 ("25 July 2025 Interview").

[13] Parliamentary Assembly (2023) Resolution 2482, Legal and Human Rights Aspects of the Russian Federation's Aggression against Ukraine ("Parliamentary Assembly, Resolution 2482").

[14] The Parliamentary Assembly of the Council of Europe adopted a resolution calling for the creation of a special tribunal with a statute that would "clearly state that personal immunities would not apply to incumbent State officials, in line with the practice of other international criminal tribunals . . .". Ibid., para 7.3.

[15] See Chap. 6, Sect. 6.4. France and Germany, of course, are members of the Council of Europe, but came not to endorse the approach articulated by the Parliamentary Assembly in its 2023 resolution. See Parliamentary Assembly, Resolution 2482, note 13.

prepare necessary documents.[16] At that point, states were still "brainstorming as to what the Tribunal would look like".[17] In May 2024, Liechtenstein hosted a seminar with Ukraine and the Council of Europe on potential features of such a tribunal and after that "momentum picked up".[18] On 7 June 2024, the Parliamentary Assembly of the Council of Europe formally called for an "agreement between the Council of Europe and the Government of Ukraine on the establishment of a special tribunal for the crime of aggression . . . against Ukraine".[19] The Parliamentary Assembly noted that "the proposal of establishing such a tribunal by an agreement between the Council of Europe and Ukraine is the best *feasible* option".[20] They did not claim it was the best option.

7.3 Key Issues During the Negotiations

Throughout 2024 and until March 2025, the Core Group continued to meet for the purpose of agreeing on various key issues. They included: the definition of the crime of aggression to be utilized; whether personal immunities would apply and exempt top Russian leaders (the "troika") from prosecution; whether the tribunal would have an independent prosecutor or receive cases referred or transferred from Ukraine; and whether the tribunal would be able to conduct trials *in absentia*.[21] Each of these topics is discussed in turn below.

7.3.1 The Definition of the Crime of Aggression to Be Utilized

A key issue during the negotiations centered on what definition of the crime of aggression to utilize. As discussed in earlier chapters, during the trials before the International Military Tribunal at Nuremberg and the International Military Tribunal for the Far East (Tokyo) it was "war" that was contained within the definition of the crime.[22] However, as discussed in Chap. 2, intervening UN General Assembly and Security Council resolutions, particularly when addressing state responsibility,

---

[16] Council of Europe, Committee of Ministers 2024.

[17] 25 July 2025 Interview, note 12.

[18] Ibid.

[19] Parliamentary Assembly (2024) Resolution 15998, Legal and Human Rights Aspects of the Russian Federation's Aggression against Ukraine.

[20] Ibid. (emphasis added).

[21] 25 July 2025 Interview, note 12 (identifying these as the key issues during the negotiations).

[22] See Charter of the International Military Tribunal (1945) 85 UNTS 251 ("London Charter 1945"), Article 6(a) (defining "crimes against peace" as the "waging of a war of aggression, or a war in violation of international treaties, agreements or assurances, or participation in a common plan or conspiracy for the accomplishment of any of the foregoing"); International Military Tribunal for the Far East (1946) Special Proclamation by the Supreme Commander to the Allied Powers at Tokyo,

focused on an "act of aggression".[23] "Act of aggression" is a lower threshold than war and aligns more with the UN Charter's prohibition of "the use of force",[24] which is also a threshold lower than war.[25] As discussed in Chap. 3, when it came time to define the crime for purposes of the ICC's Rome Statute, States Parties chose a middle ground by encompassing an "act of aggression" in the definition of the crime, but requiring that the act of aggression rise to the level of a "manifest" violation of the UN Charter to constitute the crime of aggression.[26] They thereby raised the threshold so that not every act of aggression or use of force would be included.

During the Core Group negotiations, the debate resurfaced, with the vast majority of states advocating use of the Rome Statute's definition of the crime,[27] which had been accepted by consensus by all Rome Statute States Parties[28] and is recognized as customary international law.[29] These states argued that it was important not to undermine the Rome Statute.[30]

However, France and the United States[31] argued for the Nuremberg and Tokyo Tribunal approach of only covering a war of aggression.[32] Both states advocated for a narrow approach with regard to accountability.[33] The United States argued that only the Nuremberg definition represents customary international law, an argument no other state supported.[34] France additionally argued that only the UN Security Council holds the authority to determine what constitutes an act of aggression,[35] an argument that had been raised and rejected during negotiations leading up to the 2010

---

as amended ("Tokyo Charter 1946"), Article 5(a) (similar). See also Chap. 2, Sect. 2.4 (discussing the London Charter and Nuremberg trial).

[23] See, e.g., UN General Assembly Resolution 3314 (XXIX) (1974) (enumerating various acts of aggression). "From 1973 to 1990, the Security Council adopted thirty-four resolutions in which it made express reference to the concept of 'act of aggression', primarily against apartheid South Africa and 'the illegal regime in Southern Rhodesia' for acts of aggression against neighbouring states; and two against Israel . . .". Strapatsas 2017, p. 178. See also Chap. 2, Sect. 2.6.

[24] UN Charter, note 6, Article 2(4).

[25] For example, US military strikes into Iran in 2025 were an illegal use of force under Article 2(4) of the UN Charter, but did not erupt into full-scale war with Iran. See, e.g., Rosen et al. 2025.

[26] Rome Statute (1998) (as amended), note 3, Article 8*bis*; Chap. 3, Sect. 3.2.2.

[27] 25 July 2025 Interview, note 12. Astrid Reisinger Coracini was the only academic to address the Core Group; she briefed them on the definition of the crime of aggression.

[28] International Criminal Court, Assembly of States Parties 2010.

[29] See Chap. 5, Sect. 5.3.4.2 (see particularly Coracini note 152 in Chap. 5; but see McDougall disagreeing on the content of the customary international law definition of the crime).

[30] 25 July 2025 Interview, note 12.

[31] Ibid.

[32] London Charter 1945, note 22; Tokyo Charter 1946, note 22.

[33] 25 July 2025 Interview, note 12.

[34] Ibid. For why the Article 8*bis* definition represents customary international law, see Chap. 5, Sect. 5.3.4.2.

[35] 25 July 2025 Interview, note 12. The French later seemed to give up on their own theory in the context of the Core Group negotiations. See note 169. But that did not stop France from raising it in the lead-up to the July 2025 Special Session of the ICC's Assembly of States Parties. See Chap. 8, Sect. 8.5.

Kampala Review Conference, since the UN Security Council does not pronounce on issues of individual criminal responsibility.[36]

The debate did not much matter in terms of its application before the Special Tribunal. Russian leaders arguably had committed both an "act of aggression" (or multiple acts of aggression) and launched a war of aggression.[37] Yet, the approach *did* matter greatly in terms of the development of international law and upholding previous advances in the law.[38] One concern was to avoid creating fragmentation that would potentially weaken the approach taken in the Rome Statute by utilizing a different definition. Furthermore, to retreat to the 1945 standard utilized at Nuremberg and Tokyo would not only embrace an outdated approach but could run the risk of inappropriately suggesting that it is only when aggression rises to the level of war that individual criminal responsibility attaches.

While no single part of the agreement on the Tribunal was resolved in isolation—i.e., it was a "package deal"—ultimately, as one of the last issues to be resolved, Liechtenstein, France, and the United States[39] negotiated a formulation of the crime of aggression that is close to the Rome Statute's Article *8bis* formulation. However, as will be discussed further below,[40] troubling language contained in the definition could suggest that only a "war" will rise to the level of the crime of aggression, at least for purposes of the Special Tribunal.

---

[36] During the negotiations within the Special Working Group on the Crime of Aggression ("SWGCA"), some of the permanent members of the UN Security Council repeatedly raised the argument that under Article 39 of the UN Charter, only the Security Council can determine the existence of an act of aggression. See UN Charter, note 6, Article 39. Therefore, they argued that the Security Council should serve as "gatekeeper", whereby absent it determining the existence of an act of aggression, no referral to the ICC should be possible. In fact, Security Council referrals to the ICC including the crime of aggression are possible (see Rome Statute (1998) (as amended), note 3, art 15*ter*), but the Security Council's role is not exclusive. Most other states rejected the approach of having the Security Council serve as sole gatekeeper and felt that reflecting the Security Council's ability to refer situations involving aggression, and having the first chance to do so, would suffice. Thus, crime of aggression investigations and prosecutions can also initiate through State Party referral or the ICC Prosecutor acting *proprio motu*, although they cannot proceed without the Security Council first having been given six months to make a determination and authorization from the ICC's Pre-Trial Division. See ibid., Article 15*bis*(6)–(8). For the negotiating history of the SWGCA, see Barriga and Kreß 2012; for negotiations during the 2010 Kampala Review Conference, see Trahan 2011.

[37] For why leaders of the Russian Federation are implicated, see Chap. 4, Sect. 4.4.2 (legal analysis of Russia having committed an "act of aggression").

[38] See Chap. 5, Sect. 5.3.4.2 (why use the Rome Statute definition).

[39] 25 July 2025 Interview, note 12 (it was those three states that reached the agreement on the definition). Other states in the Core Group went along with that agreement.

[40] See Sect. 7.4.2.1.

7.3.2 *Whether Personal Immunities Would Exempt Top Leaders from Prosecution*

Probably the most contentious issue during the negotiations[41] involved the issue of whether personal immunities would exempt top leaders (the "troika"—the Head of State, Head of Government, and Minister of Foreign Affairs) from prosecution.[42] As discussed in Chap. 6, Ukraine had previously rejected the idea of establishing a Ukrainian chamber with some degree of international support or features largely because trials before it would have involved personal immunity for the troika.[43]

Two issues were actually at play: first, whether prosecutions before a tribunal established primarily through regional arrangements *could* avoid the application of personal immunity. Second, regardless of what might be possible, it was necessary to find an approach on which the Core Group could agree.

As detailed in Chap. 5, personal immunities do not prevent prosecution of the troika before an international tribunal, but they do prevent such prosecutions before a domestic tribunal.[44] Yet the case law leaves open the question of how the law would apply to a tribunal established by an international agreement (an agreement between Ukraine and the Council of Europe) that represents primarily the will of Council of Europe member states (i.e., regional will),[45] rather than the will of the full international community.

One answer could be to ensure that the Tribunal represents *more than* the will of the Council of Europe, by making it possible for countries from other regions to be able to join in endorsing the Tribunal,[46] as 19 countries beyond the four Allies did in endorsing the Nuremberg Tribunal's Charter.[47] Indeed, as discussed further below, it will be possible for states both within the Council of Europe and beyond to join in supporting the Special Tribunal.[48] But, in order for the Special Tribunal judges to be able to rule on whether the Tribunal possesses sufficient international support (ideally cross-regional and representative) to constitute the "will of the international community" such that it would be an international tribunal to which personal immunities would not attach, the Tribunal Statute would need to at least be silent on the

---

[41] 25 July 2025 Interview, note 12.

[42] See International Court of Justice (2002) *Arrest Warrant of 11 April 2000 (Democratic Republic of Congo v. Belgium)*, Judgment, 2002 ICJ Rep. 3, discussed in Chap. 5, Sect. 5.3.4.3.

[43] See Chap. 6, Sect. 6.3.2.

[44] See Chap. 5, Sect. 5.3.4.3.

[45] See, e.g., Nuridzhanian 2025, p. 15 ("it is less clear whether the Special Tribunal, established based on an agreement between one state and a regional organisation, can be considered as representing 'the will of international community' for the purpose of non-applicability of state official immunity".); Chlevickaitė et al. 2025, p. 40 ("the tribunal would neither be a domestic mechanism *stricto sensu*, nor would it be purely international").

[46] This is possible under the Enlarged Partial Agreement. See Enlarged Partial Agreement, note 2.

[47] Nineteen states additionally adhered to, or acceded to, the London Charter. See UNTS nd. The states joining were from various regions, including Australia, Ethiopia, Haiti, Honduras, India, New Zealand, Panama, Paraguay, Uruguay. Ibid.

[48] See Sect. 7.4.3.

issue.[49] The outcome would then depend on how many states, including those from other regions, could be enticed to support the Tribunal.

A group of states referred to as the "Core Core Group" (consisting of Liechtenstein, Latvia, Lithuania, Estonia, Poland, Luxembourg, Switzerland, Belgium, and Romania) insisted that personal immunities not apply.[50] The intermediate position would have been to leave the Tribunal Statute silent on the issue, leaving the answer to judicial interpretation. More powerful states—the G7, joined by Denmark and Norway—however, insisted that personal immunities *must apply* during the troika's terms in office.[51] As discussed in Chap. 6, the G7 were likely not aiming to "protect" President Putin from prosecution, but acting out of self-interest, avoiding setting precedent that potentially could be applied against their leaders.[52] While President Zelenskyy had been outspoken on this issue, insisting that personal immunities must not apply,[53] Ukraine's representative in the negotiations, Ambassador Anton Korynevych, who chaired the Core Group, was more cautious, undoubtedly wary of antagonizing the G7.[54]

As detailed below,[55] it was the G7 approach that largely prevailed, with proceedings against the troika suspended during their terms in office. This likely was quite a bitter pill for Ukraine to swallow. It would be difficult to explain to the Ukrainian public why top Russian leaders—especially President Putin—would have proceedings against them suspended.[56]

7.3.3 Whether the Tribunal Would Have a Fully Independent Prosecutor or Receive Cases Referred or Transferred from Ukraine

The issue also arose whether the Tribunal would have a fully independent prosecutor who would decide which cases to pursue, or whether referrals or transfers of investigations would come from the Ukrainian authorities. This question, in turn, was linked to the immunities question. With referrals or transfers, Ukraine arguably could only refer or transfer cases it had the power to investigate or prosecute, and thus personal immunities would apply.

---

49 For discussion of what makes a tribunal international, see note 194; see also Chap. 5, Sect. 5.3.4.3.
50 25 July 2025 Interview, note 12.
51 Ibid.
52 See Chap. 6, Sect. 6.3.6.
53 See Chap. 6, Sect. 6.3.5.
54 25 July 2025 Interview, note 12.
55 See Sect. 7.4.2.2.
56 On the Tribunal's need to conduct outreach, see Sect. 7.5.

All states except France and the EU representative initially argued for a fully independent prosecutor.[57] The vast majority of states opposed transfers of proceedings or indictments.[58] A fully independent prosecutor would likely be viewed as more internationally acceptable and more legitimate—assuming the selection of a highly-qualified individual. Receiving cases initiated by Ukraine could make the Tribunal appear less independent, with concerns that this could impact the Tribunal's appearance of legitimacy.

France, in opposing an independent prosecutor and preferring transfer of proceedings, was arguably hoping to ensure that there would be no head of state prosecutions.[59] Had there been only transfer of proceedings, the Statute would not have had to say anything on the immunities question; Ukraine could not have transferred proceedings against a sitting head of state. Thus, once the issue of head of state immunity had been resolved (as discussed above), the issue could have been dropped.[60] However, at the February 2025 meeting in Brussels, Ukraine started arguing for referrals.[61] On this, as will be detailed below,[62] that position prevailed[63]—at least to some extent. The result, under the author's reading of the Statute, is that both routes will be open. That is, while proceedings, information, or evidence may be referred by the Ukrainian Prosecutor General to the Tribunal Prosecutor, it may be possible to read the Statute to allow the Tribunal Prosecutor to act independently.

7.3.4 Whether the Tribunal Would Be Able to Conduct Trials in Absentia

A final significant issue, also discussed in Chap. 5,[64] was whether the Tribunal would be able to conduct trials *in absentia*. Only Ukraine argued for such trials,[65] no doubt concerned that it would be extremely difficulty to apprehend high-level Russian (or other) leaders and have them transferred to the Tribunal. Also, the approach was consistent with Ukrainian law,[66] so it would not appear unusual to the Ukrainian

---

[57] 25 July 2025 Interview, note 12.

[58] Ibid.

[59] Ibid.

[60] Ibid.

[61] Email with a Participant in the Core Group Negotiations, 19 September 2025.

[62] See Sect. 7.4.2.3.

[63] 25 July 2025 Interview, note 12.

[64] See Chap. 5, Sect. 5.3.4.4.

[65] 25 July 2025 Interview, note 12.

[66] Code of Criminal Procedure of Ukraine (2020). https://cjad.nottingham.ac.uk/documents/implementations/pdf/Ukraine-Criminal_Procedure_Code_amend_2020.pdf. Accessed 28 September 2025, Article 262.

public,[67] whereas it would seem unfamiliar to those hailing from many other judicial systems.[68]

All states other than Ukraine opposed trials *in absentia.*[69] As detailed in Chap. 5, due process concerns exist with such trials, as well as concerns that trials absent an accused could appear less than fully legitimate,[70] thereby potentially affecting the Tribunal's appearance of legitimacy. As will be detailed below, while Ukraine prevailed and the Tribunal will be able to conduct trials *in absentia*, procedural protections have been built into the Statute as to the conduct of such trials.[71]

7.3.5 Weighing All the Compromises

All of these compromises, along with the fact that the Tribunal would not be an international one established through the United Nations, presented a profound conundrum to states during the Core Group negotiations. Should states continue to pursue the establishment of a tribunal riddled with compromises? Furthermore, the Tribunal also would only be able to prosecute the crime of aggression in the situation of Ukraine, and thereby only pursue selective justice.[72]

A similar question—when compromises are too numerous to accept—emerged during the negotiations to establish the Extraordinary Chambers in the Courts of Cambodia ("ECCC").[73] The concern arose that the Government of Cambodia might manipulate the work of the tribunal. Having co-investigative judges and co-prosecutors (one UN appointed and one Cambodia appointed), as well the tribunal's location in Phnom Penh and the fact that it was part of the Cambodian legal system,[74]

---

[67] See Chlevickaitė et al. 2025, p. 18 ("The vast majority of domestic war crime trials in Ukraine are conducted *in absentia*. This is known widely, and, with all valid concerns, the society is used to it").

[68] For discussion of concerns with conducting trials *in absentia*, see Chap. 5, Sect. 5.3.4.4.

[69] 25 July 2025 Interview, note 12.

[70] See Chap. 5, Sect. 5.3.4.4.

[71] See Sect. 7.4.2.4.

[72] The issue of selectivity is discussed in Chap. 5, Sect. 5.3.4.6.

[73] For background on the negotiations, see Scheffer 2013.

[74] See Agreement between the United Nations and the Royal Government of Cambodia Concerning the Prosecution under Cambodian law of Crimes Committed During the Period of Democratic Kampuchea (2003) https://www.eccc.gov.kh/en/documents/legal/agreement-between-united nations-and-royal-government-cambodia-concerning-prosecution. Accessed 28 September 2025. As to the structure of the ECCC, Open Society Justice Initiative explains how it worked:

> Its hybrid structure places Cambodians and internationals in positions as judges on trial, pre-trial, and supreme court judicial chambers; as co prosecutors; as co-investigating judges; and as defense counsel. In each judicial chamber, Cambodian judges outnumber international judges. However, a supermajority voting requirement for each judicial chamber is intended to ensure that at least one international judge concurs on most decisions, including any decision to stop the investigation or prosecution of an accused person. This provision is intended as a

meant that the ECCC was ripe for Cambodian Government interference. Due to historic Cambodian control over its judiciary, this problem was foreseen years before the ECCC was established.[75] In fact, negotiations to establish the ECCC broke down out of concern about such manipulation and that Cambodia was not negotiating in good faith.[76] The contrary view—that negotiations should continue and the tribunal should be established—was motivated by the fact that the ECCC was likely the only justice that would be possible for the estimated 1.5–2 million murders by the Khmer Rouge.[77] Thus, proponents took the view that potentially flawed justice was better than none at all. The tribunal ultimately proceeded, and in fact it *was* manipulated (especially into prematurely closing cases 003 and 004).[78] Notwithstanding, it was able to deliver extremely significant verdicts in cases 001 and 002.[79] What lesson could one take from this experience? The perfect is the enemy of the good.[80] Sometimes a perfect solution cannot be achieved. The ECCC's work represented a truly

---

> method to break judicial deadlocks and ensure that domestic political interference does not protect certain accused persons from prosecution.

Open Society Justice Initiative 2019, p. 2.

[75] For background on the negotiations to establish the ECCC, see Scheffer 2013, pp. 384–402.

[76] Ibid., pp. 401–02.

[77] Open Society Justice Initiative 2019, p. 6 (using the estimate of 1.5–2 million).

[78] For details on what cases 003 and 004 would have alleged, see ibid., pp. 7–14.

[79] "Case 001 [involved] the prosecution of Kaing Guek Eav, alias Duch, the warden of the notorious Tuol Sleng Prison in Phnom Penh" in which an estimated 14,000–17,000 individuals perished. Ibid., p. 3; Visit Cambodia nd. "Case 002, based on a 400-page indictment, originally included charges against four persons alleged to have been senior leaders of the Khmer Rouge . . .". Open Society Justice Initiative 2019, p. 3. It was severed into two cases: the first trial, Case 002/01 concerned forced population transfers by the Khmer Rouge; the second trial, Case 002/02, charged genocide, war crimes and crimes against humanity. Ibid., pp. 3–4. "The factual base [of Case 002/02] . . . included five cooperatives and worksites, four security centers, internal purges in the North and East Zones, the treatment of ethnic Vietnamese and Cham Muslim minority populations, and the regulation of marriage, including rape within the context of forced marriage". Ibid., p. 4.

[80] The saying is attributed to Voltaire. See Voltaire 1780, p. 250 ("*Le mieux est l'ennemi du bien*").

significant accomplishment, even if it did not achieve all that it could have absent the interference.[81]

As to the Special Tribunal, its Statute certainly contains less than ideal features. It is far less than ideal that the Tribunal will not be an international one established through the UN, and will only deliver selective justice[82]—only examining the crime of aggression in the situation of Ukraine (which, admittedly, also would have been the case had it been established through the UN). On the other hand, to have no justice in the situation for the crime of aggression—the largest and deadliest military operation in Europe since World War II[83]—would have proven a profound setback for the rule of law and the endeavor to prosecute the crime of aggression.[84] Ultimately, it is probably too early to determine whether the Tribunal—assuming it receives sufficient ratifications or acceptances of the Enlarged Partial Agreement[85] and sufficient funding to commence operations—will be seen as fully legitimate. As will be detailed below, as of late 2025 various steps are required before the Tribunal can become operational.[86]

---

[81] Evaluating the design of the ECCC, David Scheffer writes:

> There is no question that the ideal court for the investigation and prosecution of the senior Khmer Rouge leaders and other masterminds of the atrocity crimes during the Pol Pot era—namely, one with state-of-the art constitutional construction mandating international participation and compliance with the entire body of international standards of due process—was not achieved. But the negotiating history reveals how much was accomplished against considerable odds and despite many reversals of fortune.

Scheffer 2008, p. 254.
As to the significance of the verdict in Case 002, Open Society Justice Initiative writes:

> The judgment against Nuon Chea and Khieu Samphan is an undeniable accomplishment for the ECCC . . . . [T]he . . . judgment covers an astonishing range of crimes and crime sites throughout Cambodia. Nuon Chea and Khieu Samphan [were] the most senior leaders of the Khmer Rouge [then] still alive. Although they generally refused to testify at the trial, the evidence presented, . . . [went] a long way toward explaining the nature of the Khmer Rouge's criminality. This spread havoc over the entire country and affected nearly every Cambodian alive at the time, killing 1.5 to 2 million. While it is easy to lament that Cambodians waited too long to see justice and that many who suffered died before it occurred, it is heartening to know that some justice did come before all of the senior leaders of the Khmer Rouge atrocities passed away. Future generations will benefit from this accomplishment and an enhanced understanding of Cambodian history.

Open Society Justice Initiative 2019, p. 6.

[82] For discussion of the problem of selectivity, see Chap. 5, Sect. 5.3.4.6.

[83] McFaul and Person 2024, p. 34 ("On February 24, 2022, Russian president Vladimir Putin launched a full-scale invasion of Ukraine, expanding dramatically the war against Ukraine he began in 2014 and starting the largest war in Europe since World War II").

[84] See, e.g., Nuridzhanian 2025, p. 27 ("While some commentators question the legitimacy of the Special Tribunal, I belong to those who consider its creation indispensable for ensuring accountability for the crime of aggression".) (footnote omitted).

[85] See Sect. 7.4.3 (discussing the Enlarged Partial Agreement).

[86] See Sect. 7.5 (key challenges).

7.4 The Final Agreement on the Tribunal Statute

During 19–21 March 2025, the Core Group held its final meeting in Strasbourg, France, and concluded its work after fourteen rounds of negotiations.[87] It had reached agreement on three legal instruments required to establish the Tribunal:[88]

- an Agreement between the Council of Europe and the Government of Ukraine on the Establishment of the Special Tribunal for the Crime of Aggression against Ukraine (the "Tribunal Agreement");[89].
- a Statute of the Special Tribunal for the Crime of Aggression against Ukraine (the "Tribunal Statute");[90] and
- a draft Enlarged Partial Agreement on the Management Committee of the Special Tribunal for the Crime of Aggression against Ukraine (the "Enlarged Partial Agreement").[91]

Approval at the political level was given at a Ministerial Meeting of the Core Group in Lviv, Ukraine, on 9 May 2025.[92] Ukraine formally requested the establishment of the Tribunal by a letter sent to the Secretary General of the Council of Europe on 13 May 2025.[93] On 24 June 2025, the Council of Europe's Committee of Ministers decided to: "authorise the Secretary General to sign the Agreement, to which the Statute of the Tribunal [was] annexed; authorise the establishment of an Enlarged Partial Agreement on the Management Committee of the Special Tribunal; and resume consideration of the establishment of the Enlarged Partial Agreement once a sufficient number of states have pledged to ensure [the Tribunal's] sustainability, including in budgetary terms".[94] The President of Ukraine and the Secretary General of the Council of Europe signed the Tribunal Agreement, with annexed Tribunal Statute, in Strasbourg, France on 25 June 2025.[95] Ukraine's Parliament ratified the Agreement, with annexed Tribunal Statute, in early July 2025.[96]

---

[87] Chlevickaitė et al. 2025, p. 28.

[88] Council of Europe nd. "[Thirty-eight] states (including Ukraine), the Council of Europe, the European Commission and the European External Action Service signed off [on the] three draft documents". Forde 2025.

[89] Agreement between the Council of Europe and the Government of Ukraine on the Establishment of the Special Tribunal for the Crime of Aggression against Ukraine (2025). https://rm.coe.int/agreement-and-statut-english/1680b66127

[90] Statute of the Special Tribunal for the Crime of Aggression against Ukraine (2025). https://search.coe.int/cm?i=0900001680b678ca. Accessed 28 September 2025 ("Tribunal Statute"). According to a participant in the Core Group negotiations, five or six countries did not vote in favor of the Tribunal Statute. 25 July 2025 Interview, note 12. Compare Forde, note 88.

[91] See Enlarged Partial Agreement, note 2.

[92] Council of Europe nd.

[93] Pecorella 2025.

[94] Council of Europe nd. On the question of funding, see Sect. 7.4.3.

[95] Council of Europe nd.

[96] Ukrainska Pravda 2025.

7.4.1 *Some of the Tribunal's Key Features*

The Tribunal Statute contains fifty-four articles.[97] Some of the Tribunal's key features are described below. The resolution of the most contentious issues is detailed in the following section.

Who May Be Prosecuted

The Tribunal Statute provides for the establishment of an ad hoc criminal tribunal to prosecute persons "who bear the greatest responsibility for the crime of aggression against Ukraine".[98] Jurisdiction is based on the "territorial jurisdiction of Ukraine".[99] While not expressly stated, the Statute allows the Tribunal to prosecute not only Russian, but also Belarusian or other nationals. An FAQ ("Frequently Asked Questions") prepared by the Council of Europe explains: "As the Special Tribunal will deal with establishing accountability for the crime of aggression committed against Ukraine, Belarusian or North Korean individuals could potentially be prosecuted if evidence shows they played a significant role in the crime of aggression against Ukraine".[100] The requirement that only those who bear the "greatest responsibility" for the crime of aggression may be prosecuted[101] was probably unnecessary, as the crime is a "leadership crime"—only leaders with the ability to control or direct the political or military action of a state will be encompassed by the definition of the crime.[102]

---

97 See Tribunal Statute, note 90.

98 Tribunal Agreement, note 89, Article 1.1; Tribunal Statute, note 90, Article 1. See Magliveras 2025 ("It is not clear from the Agreement whether the term 'persons' covers only natural persons (individuals) or legal persons (organisations) as well. This is not a rhetorical question: the notion of 'criminal organisation' was enshrined in Articles 9 et seq. of the Charter of the International Military Tribunal and it featured prominently in the Nuremberg Trials . . .".). Because organizations have not been prosecuted before the international and hybrid tribunals operating over the last few decades, had the Statute intended to allow for such prosecutions, it should have made that clear; thus, legal persons are no doubt excluded.

99 Tribunal Statute, note 90, Article 1. Gaiane Nuridzhanian explains:

> According to customary international law rules on national jurisdiction, a state can criminalise any acts committed in its own territory, and undertake any actions within its own territory necessary to enforce its criminal laws. The territorial jurisdiction of the state extends also to crimes initiated abroad but completed on that state's territory. Ukraine may therefore assert its territorial jurisdiction with respect to crimes initiated abroad but completed on its territory.

Nuridzhanian 2025, p. 11 (internal citations omitted).

100 Council of Europe nd.

101 Tribunal Statute, note 90, Article 1.

102 Ibid., Article 2(1) (the crime applies to "a person in a position effectively to exercise control over or to direct the political or military action of a State"); Article 4(1) (individual criminal responsibility attaches to a "person in a position effectively to exercise control over or to direct the political or military action of a State"). Another view is that the reference to those who bear the "greatest responsibility" might be giving a signal that only a limited number of those who are truly the most

The Temporal Start Date

The Statute contains no express temporal start date for jurisdiction.[103] This could suggest that there is leeway to investigate and prosecute persons implicated in the illegal annexation of Crimea, not solely the 2022 invasion.[104] However, as will be discussed below,[105] the Tribunal Statute's definition of the crime could be read to suggest that only a "war" of aggression is encompassed. Under that reading, leaders responsible for the illegal annexation of Crimea might not be able to be prosecuted if the annexation were viewed in isolation; however, if viewed as the start of the war, then such charges could be included.[106]

Modes of Responsibility

In addition to the requirement that a perpetrator must satisfy the leadership clause and be a person who bears "the greatest responsibility" for the crime of aggression, the definition of the crime requires the perpetrator to have been involved in the "planning, preparation, initiation or execution" of the crime.[107] Those words operate in conjunction with the modes of responsibility (defined in Article 4(1)), covering those who "planned, instigated, ordered or committed, or attempted to commit"[108] the crime of aggression. The latter expands the field of responsibility, for example, to those who ordered the planning of the crime, or planned the initiation of the crime, but a role in the "planning, preparation, initiation, or execution" of the crime is always required, as it is part of the definition of the crime. This is similar to the Rome Statute, where the language of Article *8bis* requires that the perpetrator be involved in the "planning, preparation, initiation or execution" of the crime of aggression, but the modes of responsibility in Rome Statute, Article 25 (individual criminal responsibility) and article 28 (command responsibility) additionally apply.[109]

The Tribunal Statute is silent on the application of command responsibility; thus, it appears to be excluded. Although the doctrine probably would have had limited applicability, given that only leaders fall within the definition, this author would have expressly included command responsibility. Even those who are considered leaders

---

culpable should be tried; it also could be a signal to Ukraine to refer only such proceedings. Coracini 2025; on initiating cases, see Sect. 7.4.2.3.

[103] "[T]he Statute does not explicitly indicate the temporal and spatial scope of the Special Tribunal's jurisdiction". Nuridzhanian 2025, p. 4.

[104] See Heller 2025 (taking this view: "Art[icle] 1 does not contain any temporal limitation. That absence is critical, because it means the [Tribunal] will be able to prosecute not only the Russian political and military leaders responsible for the 2022 invasion, but also those responsible for, *inter alia*, the unlawful invasion and annexation of Crimea in 2014").

[105] See Sect. 7.4.2.1.

[106] The Nuremberg Tribunal did not convict for "acts" of aggression against Austria and Czechoslovakia, but only convicted for events involving "war"—from the invasion of Poland onward. See Clark 2007.

[107] Tribunal Statute, note 90, Article 2(1).

[108] Ibid., Article 4(1).

[109] For added discussion of the interaction of these provisions, see Chap. 4, Sect. 4.4.4.

can have superiors above them in the hierarchy of command structures. Thus, the doctrine could have (or have had) some applicability.

The Tribunal Statute also excludes responsibility based on "aiding and abetting" and does not expressly list co-perpetration or acting pursuant to a common purpose. The exclusion of aiding and abetting as a mode of responsibility could limit or eliminate potential charges against North Korean or Belarusian leaders (discussed in Chap. 4). For example, North Korea arguably has not committed its own independent act of aggression but aided and abetted that of Russia.[110] While Belarus committed its own independent act of aggression (allowing the initial launch of Russian forces from its territory)[111] so that its leaders could be charged on that basis, Belarus' leaders arguably also aided and abetted other acts by Russia, which could not be charged.[112]

Even though no form of co-perpetration is expressly included in the modes of responsibility, there may be some potential for theories of group perpetration to be read into the word "committed", as was done before the ICTY and ICTR.[113] It would have been preferable for the Statute to have included command responsibility, as well as aiding and abetting, and co-perpetration (expressly) as forms of individual criminal responsibility.

The Seat of the Tribunal

Although states planned for the Tribunal to sit in The Hague, Netherlands,[114] as of late 2025, the Netherlands had not yet formally agreed to host it, although it is expected to do so. The Tribunal Agreement states that the Tribunal "shall have its

[110] See Chap. 4, Sect. 4.4.2 (analyzing "act of aggression" and the conduct of North Korea). Alternatively, one might be able to argue that the leadership of North Korea played a role in the "execution" of the crime, so perhaps could be charged on that basis.

[111] Belarus' act of aggression was clearly part of the launch of the war, so that even if the Tribunal Statute is read in Article 2(4) to require "war", its actions would be encompassed. See Sect. 7.4.2.1 (discussing whether "war" is required by the Tribunal's definition of the crime).

[112] See Chap. 4, Sect. 4.4.2 (analyzing "act of aggression" and the conduct of Belarus).

[113] The ad hoc tribunals prosecuted under a theory known as "joint criminal enterprise" ("JCE"), which was not listed under either tribunal's statute. The theory was read into the word "committed", since it was a form of group commission. See, e.g., International Criminal Tribunal for the former Yugoslavia (2003) *Prosecutor v. Krnojelac*, Case No. T-97-25-A, Appellate Judgment, para 29 ("Article 7(1) of the [ICTY] Statute does not make explicit reference to 'joint criminal enterprise.' However, the Appeals Chamber recalls that, after considering the question in the *Tadić* Appeals Judgment, it concluded that participation in a joint criminal enterprise as a form of liability, or the theory of common purpose as the Chamber referred to it, was implicitly established in the Statute . . ."); see also International Criminal Tribunal for the former Yugoslavia (1999) *Prosecutor v. Tadić*, Case No. IT-94-1-A, Appellate Judgment. An Asser Institute report alternatively suggests possible expansion of the modes of individual criminal responsibility through the application of Ukrainian law. See Chlevickaitė et al. 2025, p 30, citing Tribunal Statute, note 90, Article 3(c) (including, as applicable law, although hierarchically a lower source of authority than the Tribunal Statute, "provisions of the substantive criminal law of Ukraine relating to the prosecution and punishment of the crime of aggression").

[114] A draft Tribunal Agreement dated 21 March 2025 stated that the Tribunal shall sit in The Hague (Article 2.1), with the ability to sit elsewhere (Article 2.2). See Agreement between the Council of Europe and the Government of Ukraine on the Establishment of the Special Tribunal for the Crime of Aggression against Ukraine (draft dated 21 March 2025) (on file with the author).

seat in one of the States that has joined the Enlarged Partial Agreement [discussed below], subject to the conclusion of a host State agreement".[115] Apparently, The Netherlands has expressed willingness to host the Tribunal on the condition that a sufficient number of states enter into cooperation agreements with the Tribunal.[116]

The Prosecutor, Deputy Prosecutor, and Judges

The Tribunal will be led by Chambers, the Office of the Prosecutor, and the Registry.[117] The Office of the Prosecutor will be led by a Prosecutor and at least one Deputy Prosecutor.[118] A roster of fifteen judges are to be elected,[119] who "can be activated depending on the needs of the Tribunal".[120] The Tribunal's President, who will be the Presiding Judge of the Appeals Chamber,[121] will appoint the judges to serve as Pre-Trial Judge (consisting of one judge), the Trial Chamber (consisting of three judges), and the Appeals Chamber (consisting of five judges).[122] The judges, who will serve for nine year staggered terms,[123] shall attempt to achieve unanimity in their decision-making, but, failing that, decisions shall be made by a majority.[124] The Prosecutor and Deputy Prosecutor(s) shall serve for seven year terms[125] and the Registrar for a four year term.[126]

---

[115] Tribunal Agreement, note 89, Article 2.

[116] 25 July 2025 Interview, note 12 (no precise number of cooperation agreements was mentioned). See Chlevickaitė et al. 2025, p. 28 ("According to Article 9(4) of the Draft [Enlarged Partial Agreement], the host state agreement between the Netherlands and the Tribunal would only enter into force upon the conclusion of a minimum number of such cooperation agreements with a minimum number of commitments relating to cooperation in the areas of (a) witness protection and relocation; (b) execution of sentences; and (c) release, including interim release"). The Netherlands is not mentioned in the final version of the Enlarged Partial Agreement.

[117] Tribunal Statute, note 90, Article 6.

[118] Ibid., Article 9.

[119] Ibid., Article 8(2). For qualifications and election of the judges, see ibid., Article 8. For the argument that it was a "missed opportunity" for the Statute not to require "Ukrainian judges to serve on trial and appellate . . . panels", see Heller 2025 (noting that "although Ukrainian judges can be elected to the [Tribunal], there will never be more than one at any given time"). Fully international panels make the Tribunal look more international and avoid the problematic optics that Ukrainian judges could be seen to lack sufficient impartiality, but simultaneously give Ukraine less ownership in the process.

[120] Chlevickaitė et al. 2025, p. 31.

[121] Tribunal Statute, note 90, Article 7(5).

[122] Ibid., Article 7(1). For the functioning of the Pre-Trial judge, the Trial Chamber, and the Appeals Chamber, see ibid., Articles 25, 26, 41–43.

[123] The judges need not be appointed simultaneously. See ibid., Article 8(2).

[124] Ibid., Article 35(3).

[125] Ibid., Article 10(4). For qualifications and election of the Prosecutor, see ibid., Article 10.

[126] Ibid., Article 12(2). The Secretary-General of the Council of Europe would appoint the Registrar. Ibid.

The Registrar and Victim Representation

The Registrar is charged with the "administration and servicing" of the Special Tribunal.[127] He or she[128] is to establish a Victim and Witness Unit, a Detention Unit, and a Defense Unit.[129]

A minimal provision addresses the representation of victims during proceedings. It states:

> Where groups of victims are identified by the Special Tribunal as specially affected by conduct which formed the basis of the crime as specified in the indictment, the Special Tribunal shall allow them to be collectively represented by legal counsel while ensuring the observance of the rights of the accused, a fair and impartial trial and an efficient conduct of the proceedings.[130]

The Statute thus allows for collective representation, but there is no right of victims to participate in the proceedings.[131] This was likely done due to the enormous number of potential victims. Given the large-scale and divergent types of harms inflicted upon the people and state of Ukraine (and beyond),[132] potentially many victim groups could warrant collective representation. It will be important for the Tribunal to include such victim groups, who would need to be "identified by the Special Tribunal as specially affected". The Rules of Procedure and Evidence will need to specify the details as to victim representation.[133]

Due Process/Fair Trial Protections

As to due process, the Statute contains provisions that address the right to a fair trial, the presumption of innocence, rights during investigation, and the rights of the

---

[127] Ibid., Article 11(1).

[128] On gender and geographic representation, see ibid., Article 8(1) (judges), Article 13(2) (staff).

[129] Ibid., Article 11(3)(a)–(c). For protection of witnesses, see ibid., Article 21.

[130] Ibid., Article 22.

[131] See Chlevickaitė et al. 2025, p. 32 (describing a three step process: (a) identification of a group of victims as specially affected "by conduct which formed the basis of the crime as specified in the indictment", (b) which allows for the group to be collectively represented by legal counsel, although (c) the Tribunal can still reject participation of a victim group if it endangers the rights of the accused, a fair and impartial trial and the efficient conduct of proceedings); ibid., p. 42 (criticism of the victim participation provisions in the Statute as falling short of full victim participation).

[132] For discussion of the types of harm inflicted upon Ukraine due to the invasion, see Chap. 4, Sect. 4.3. See also Heller 2025 ("it is . . . not obvious which individuals in Ukraine should be considered "specially affected" by Russia's aggression. I presume the drafters were thinking of individuals killed and injured by Russia during the invasion. But will the category of 'specially affected victims' be limited to civilians—or will it include soldiers? There is no evident reason for a more restrictive interpretation, given that Ukrainian soldiers have been killed or injured only because Russia chose to criminally invade their country".); Chlevickaitė et al. 2025, p. 14 ("Aggression can affect not only the society of an invaded, occupied or bombarded nation, but also the people of an aggressor state [e.g., Russia or Belarus]").

[133] Coracini 2025; see Tribunal Statute, note 90, Article 15 (the judges shall draft Rules of Procedure and Evidence).

accused.[134] The FAQ prepared by the Council of Europe states: "The Special Tribunal will follow internationally and regionally recognised standards of due process and the rule of law—for instance, those of the European Convention on Human Rights—ensuring fair trials, defence rights and judicial independence".[135] Strict adherence to due process/fair trial protections will be important.

The Tribunal's Relationship with the ICC and *Ne bis in Idem*

As to the Tribunal's relationship with the ICC, the Statute states that: "The Special Tribunal shall cooperate with the International Criminal Court on all matters of mutual concern", and provides for the Tribunal to enter into a cooperation agreement with the ICC.[136] The Statute also states that when a person is detained by the ICC, "the Special Tribunal shall give priority to the proceedings before the International Criminal Court".[137]

The latter provision (giving priority in prosecuting to the ICC), could have been seen as prudent, given double-jeopardy (*ne bis in idem*) might preclude a second trial by the ICC if the Special Tribunal were to prosecute first, should an accused be in custody and wanted by both tribunals.[138]

The opposite risk does not appear to arise: if the ICC conducts the first trial of an accused, the Tribunal Statute suggests the Special Tribunal could still conduct a second trial. Article 17(1) of the Tribunal Statute addresses the prohibition of double-jeopardy as it relates to two trials before the Special Tribunal. It "bars the Special Tribunal from trying a person 'with respect to the same conduct which formed the basis of crimes for which the person has *already been convicted or acquitted*

[134] See Tribunal Statute, note 90, Article 16 (right to a fair trial), Article 18 (presumption of innocence), Article 19 (rights during an investigation), Article 20 (rights of the accused). Gaiane Nuridzhanian enumerates the due process guarantees contained in the Statute:

> the presumption of innocence, the right to remain silent, the right to be informed of charges, the right to legal assistance, the right to interpretation and translation, the right to adequate time and facilities for the preparation of the defence, the right to question witnesses, the right, subject to exceptions . . . to be present at the trial and the right not to be tried twice. In addition, the Statute contains rules on sentencing and penalties and the procedure for their enforcement. It provides a right to appeal, to request revision of a conviction or sentence and to retrial of a case tried in the absence of the accused. The Statute also guarantees freedom from arbitrary detention and the right to obtain compensation in case of unlawful arrest or detention.

Nuridzhanian 2025, p. 19 (citing various articles).

[135] Council of Europe nd.

[136] Tribunal Statute, note 90, Article 46(1).

[137] Ibid., Article 46(2).

[138] The Rome Statute provides: "No person who has been tried by another court for conduct also proscribed under articles 6, 7, 8 or 8 *bis* shall be tried by the Court with respect to the *same conduct* unless the proceedings in the other court [were to shield the person or not conducted according to due process etc.]. Rome Statute (1998) (as amended), note 3, Article 20 (3) (emphasis added). As to how this might play out, for example, war crimes charges before the ICC could rest on evidence of an order that also was at issue in a crime of aggression case. Thus, there is some possibility of overlap in underlying conduct. For added discussion, see Chap. 5, Sect. 5.3.4.5.

by the Special Tribunal' itself'".[139] Article 17(2) addresses the prohibition as it relates to the Special Tribunal and a trial before a national court. It "bars the Special Tribunal from trying a person for conduct constituting the crime of aggression if the person has already been tried for the same conduct by a *national court* [with certain exceptions]".[140] There is no comparable prohibition "as between the Special Tribunal and other international criminal courts"[141] such as the ICC.

Yet, even if not addressed by the Special Tribunal Statute, a question exists if a second trial before the Special Tribunal that concerns *conduct* that was at issue in a first trial before the ICC might not violate general principles of international law (the general rule as to *ne bis in idem*).[142] In that case, a second trial before the Special Tribunal might still be precluded.[143] The two tribunals obviously will not prosecute the same charges—at least for now, absent a Rome Statute amendment to the ICC's jurisdiction; thus, the clearer violation (trials based on the same charges) would not arise.

Cooperation

In addition to cooperation with the ICC, the Special Tribunal may request information or documents from the UN and other international organizations or bodies and may enter into cooperation arrangements or agreements with such organizations or bodies.[144] The Ukrainian authorities are obliged to cooperate fully with the Special Tribunal.[145] Member States and Associate Member States[146] (who will be discussed

---

[139] Nuridzhanian 2025, p. 23 (emphasis added), quoting Tribunal Statute, note 90, Article 17(1).

[140] Nuridzhanian 2025, p. 23 (emphasis added).

[141] Ibid.

[142] See Tribunal Agreement, note 89, Rec 15 ("Attaching the greatest importance to due process and fair trial standards, including the principles of *nullum crimen sine lege* and *ne bis in idem*, in accordance with international and European human rights standards . . ."); Tribunal Statute, note 90, Article 3 (after the Tribunal Statute and Rules of Procedure and Evidence, the Special Tribunal, shall apply "applicable treaties, customary international law and *general principles of law*") (emphasis added).

[143] Robin Geiß and Jelena Bäumler explain:

> [T]he ECtHR has expressed that the guarantee of *ne bis in idem* prevents a defendant not only from being punished twice for the same facts, but also from being prosecuted or tried twice. To this effect, it has interpreted that the notion of the 'same offence' corresponds to 'those facts which constitute a set of concrete factual circumstances involving the same defendant and inextricably linked together in time and space, the existence of which must be demonstrated in order to secure a conviction or institute criminal proceedings'.

Geiß and Bäumler nd, para 39, citing European Court of Human Rights (2009) *Zolotukhin and Human Rights Training Institute of the Paris Bar Association (Intervening) v. Russia*, Merits and Just Satisfaction, App. No. 14939/03, ECHR 2009-I 291, IHRL 3277, para 84. "Even though 'there is no general rule of international law that imposes an international obligation to comply with *ne bis in idem*', . . . it has been widely and internationally recognized as a judicial guarantee through different international instruments". Ibid., para 50, quoting Vervaele 2014, p. 171.

[144] Tribunal Statute, note 90, Article 47.

[145] Ibid., Article 48(1); see also Tribunal Agreement, note 89, Article 7(1)–(2).

[146] Tribunal Statute, note 90, Article 49(3); see also Tribunal Agreement, note 89, Article 7(3).

below)[147] are also asked to cooperate with the Tribunal, pursuant to the terms of the cooperation agreements they enter with it.[148] According to an Asser Institute report, "the Core Group also worked on a 'template cooperation agreement' . . . [whereby] each [Enlarged Partial Agreement] state could choose from the template text a set of cooperation obligations . . .".[149]

Additional Provisions

The Tribunal Statute includes a host of additional articles. They include the following: (i) the working language of the Tribunal shall be English;[150] (ii) the Tribunal's judges shall draft and adopt its Rules of Procedure and Evidence;[151] (iii) an accused may enter a guilty plea;[152] (iv) the judges have a time limit by which to render their judgments;[153] (v) a person who is convicted can be sentenced to serve time up to life imprisonment,[154] as well as the payment of fines and confiscation of assets or

---

[147] See Sect. 7.4.3.

[148] Enlarged Partial Agreement, note 2, Article 9(2) ("[e]ach member or associate member shall seek to co-operate [with the Tribunal] within the limits of its national legislation . . ."); Tribunal Statute, note 90, Article 48(3)–(4) (the Tribunal may request assistance from member and associate members and enter into cooperation agreements with them).

[149] Chlevickaitė et al. 2025, p. 28.

[150] Tribunal Statute, note 90, Article 14(1). "[T]he Tribunal shall determine in its Rules of Procedure and Evidence in what circumstances and under which conditions other languages may be used (in particular, Russian and Ukrainian), taking into account the official languages of the [Council of Europe] (which are English and French)". Chlevickaitė et al. 2025, p. 31.

[151] Tribunal Statute, note 90, Article 15.

[152] Ibid., Article 29.

[153] Ibid., Article 35(6) ("[t]he written decision under this article shall be delivered within ten months from the date the closing statements end, unless special circumstances justify a delivery within fifteen months").

[154] An Asser Institute report suggests a potential issue as to the length of sentences:

> [The Trial Chamber's ability to impose imprisonment for up to 30 years as well as well as life imprisonment], goes beyond the level of penalties under Article 437 of the [Ukrainian Criminal Code], as it stood in 2014 or in 2022. This difference in penalties between domestic law and the Statute may raise the question of compliance with the principle of *nullum crimen, nulla poena sine lege* under Article 7 of the [European Convention on Human Rights], which expressly prohibits under paragraph 1, second sentence, to impose a "heavier penalty than the one that was applicable at the time when the criminal offence was committed".

Chlevickaitė et al. 2025, pp. 34–35, citing European Convention on Human Rights (1953) ETS No. 005, Article 7 ("European Convention on Human Rights").

Article 36(1) of the Tribunal Statute provides that "[t]he Trial Chamber may impose the following penalties for the crime of aggression: (a) imprisonment for a specified number of years, which may not exceed a maximum of thirty years; or (b) a term of life imprisonment when justified by the extreme gravity of the crime and the individual circumstances of the convicted person". Tribunal Statute, note 90, Article 36(1). The Ukrainian Criminal Code expanded its penalties for the crime of aggression in October 2024. See Law of Ukraine (2025) On Amendments to the Criminal and Criminal Procedure Codes of Ukraine in Connection with the Ratification of the Rome Statute of the International Criminal Court and Amendments thereto, Bulletin of the Verkhovna Rada (VVR), No. 10. https://zakon.rada.gov.ua/laws/show/4012-20#n33 [read in translation]. Accessed 17 September

property;[155] (vi) the Tribunal has jurisdiction over offences against the administration of justice;[156] and (vii) a provision addresses the protection of national security information.[157]

Closure of the Tribunal

When the President of the Tribunal confirms that "all investigations, pre-trial proceedings, trials and appeals commenced before the Special Tribunal have been completed and all possible appeal rights in such proceedings have lapsed", excluding those associated with the troika (whose proceedings were suspended),[158] and that certain steps have been taken as to any fugitives who remain at large, the President shall recommend to the Management Committee, discussed below, to dissolve the Tribunal.[159] Thereafter, a Residual Mechanism would be established to assume remaining prosecutorial and judicial functions.[160]

7.4.2 *Resolution of the Most Contentious Issues*

While many details in the Tribunal Statute could warrant further examination, the section below focusses on the resolution of the most contentious issues that arose during the negotiations.

7.4.2.1 The Definition of the Crime

As described above,[161] as to the definition of the crime of aggression, the two competing approaches were (a) using the definition found in Rome Statute Article *8bis*, or (b) encompassing only a "war" of aggression as was done at Nuremberg and

---

2025. See also Heller 2025 (questioning how the judges would determine when a defendant deserves less than a life sentence given that the Nuremberg Judgment states that aggression is the "supreme" international crime (thus, an extremely grave crime necessarily is involved) and only leaders may be prosecuted before the Special Tribunal).

[155] Tribunal Statute, note 90, Article 36 (the assets or property would need to be "derived directly or indirectly from the crime of aggression . . ."). The Statute provides that "funds collected through fines or confiscation measures" would be ordered "to be transferred" to the reparation mechanism being established". Ibid., Article 37.

[156] Ibid., Article 32.

[157] Ibid., Article 33.

[158] On suspension of proceedings against the troika, see Sect. 7.4.2.2.

[159] Tribunal Statute, note 90, Article 54(1)(a).

[160] Ibid., Article 54(2).

[161] See Sect. 7.3.1.

Tokyo[162] (and under Ukrainian law).[163] The outcome was that the Tribunal Statute largely tracks the Rome Statute Article 8*bis* definition, except in a few respects, one of them being potentially quite significant.

Article 2 of the Tribunal Statute states:

> (1) For the purpose of this Statute, "crime of aggression" means the planning, preparation, initiation or execution, by a person in a position effectively to exercise control over or to direct the political or military action of a State, of an act of aggression which, by its character, gravity and scale, constitutes a manifest violation of the Charter of the United Nations.
> (2) For the purpose of paragraph 1 "act of aggression" means the use of armed force by a State against the sovereignty, territorial integrity or political independence of another State, or in any other manner inconsistent with the Charter of the United Nations.
> (3) For the purpose of determining whether an act of aggression, by its character, gravity and scale, constitutes a manifest violation of the Charter of the United Nations, the Special Tribunal shall take into account UNGA resolution 3314 (XXIX) of 14 December 1974 and all relevant UNGA resolutions with respect to Ukraine, including those recited in the Preamble of the bilateral Agreement between the Council of Europe and Ukraine.
> (4) For the purpose of this Statute, in the context of the aggression against Ukraine, an act of aggression which is determined by its character, gravity and scale to constitute a manifest violation of the Charter of the United Nations, shall also be deemed to constitute a war of aggression.[164]

Paragraph (1) replicates verbatim Article 8*bis*(1) of the Rome Statute. Paragraph (2) replicates verbatim the first sentence of Article 8*bis*(2) of the Rome Statute.

Paragraph (3) introduces a new feature—that the Tribunal shall "take into account" various UN General Assembly resolutions, some of which have condemned Russian aggression. As mentioned above, the French argued that only the UN Security Council may determine whether an act of aggression has been committed,[165] but Russia had vetoed such a determination in the present situation.[166] Thus, relying on a Security Council determination would not have been possible.[167] The General Assembly, however, has made such a determination,[168] and therefore that body is referenced.[169] One wonders how that would mesh with the requirement of proof beyond a reasonable doubt and whether the accused could rebut the factual basis, or

---

[162] See London Charter 1945, note 22; Tokyo Charter 1946, note 22.

[163] Criminal Code of Ukraine, No 2341-III from 5 April 2001 (2024) https://zakon.rada.gov.ua/laws/show/en/2341-14. Accessed 28 September 2025, Article 437. See also Grzebyk 2023 (analysis of criminal codes of Eastern European states).

[164] Tribunal Statute, note 90, Article 2.

[165] 25 July 2025 Interview, note 12.

[166] UN Security Council Resolution 155 (2022) (vetoed by the Russian Federation).

[167] 25 July 2025 Interview, note 12.

[168] See, e.g., United Nations General Assembly Resolution ES-11/1 (2022) ("deplores in the strongest terms the aggression by the Russian Federation against Ukraine in violation of Article 2 (4) of the Charter"); United Nations General Assembly Resolution 79/184 (2024) ("condemning ... the war of aggression against Ukraine by the Russian Federation in violation of Article 2 (4) of the Charter ...").

[169] 25 July 2025 Interview, note 12. That the French agreed to a Tribunal that takes into account determinations by the UN General Assembly suggests that they gave up on their own theory that

whether the resolutions are intended to be conclusive. The Tribunal Statute contains no language that "[a] determination of an act of aggression by an organ outside the Court shall be without prejudice to the Court's own findings under this Statute", as is contained in Rome Statute Articles 15*bis*(9) and 15*ter*(4).[170] These are important safeguards to ensure that an accused has the ability to rebut fully the evidence presented and that a determination by an outside body is not conclusive as to the facts. Presumably that would be the case here, although it is less than fully clear. Paragraph (3) also references UN General Assembly Resolution 3314 rather than listing the acts of aggression contained in it (as Rome Statute Article 8*bis* does), which is a slight difference, in that the resolution contains other provisions that could be drawn upon. The inclusion of the reference to UN General Assembly resolution 3314 was important, as it is a good indicator of all the acts of aggression intended to be encompassed within the definition, and reliance on it helps align the Special Tribunal's definition with the Article 8*bis* definition.

Paragraph (4) is where the real "smoke and mirrors" come in: it suggests that an act of aggression that meets the "manifest" criteria *is* a war of aggression. This could imply that it is only a "war" of aggression that would meet the "manifest threshold" requirement as to an act of aggression. That position would be contrary to the Rome Statute definition, which leaves open the possibility that an act of aggression, as listed in Article 8*bis*(2),[171] could meet the "manifest" threshold without full-scale war.

Specifically, the Rome Statutes definition makes clear that the following acts of aggression (originally from UN General Assembly Resolution 3314 and expressly listed in Article 8*bis*) can amount to the crime of aggression—as long as they rise to the level of a "manifest" violation of the UN Charter:

(a) The invasion or attack by the armed forces of a State of the territory of another State, or any military occupation, however temporary, resulting from such invasion or attack, or any annexation by the use of force of the territory of another State or part thereof;
(b) Bombardment by the armed forces of a State against the territory of another State or the use of any weapons by a State against the territory of another State;
(c) The blockade of the ports or coasts of a State by the armed forces of another State;
(d) An attack by the armed forces of a State on the land, sea or air forces, or marine and air fleets of another State;
(e) The use of armed forces of one State which are within the territory of another State with the agreement of the receiving State, in contravention of the conditions provided for in the agreement or any extension of their presence in such territory beyond the termination of the agreement;
(f) The action of a State in allowing its territory, which it has placed at the disposal of another State, to be used by that other State for perpetrating an act of aggression against a third State;
(g) The sending by or on behalf of a State of armed bands, groups, irregulars or mercenaries, which carry out acts of armed force against another State of such gravity as to amount to the acts listed above, or its substantial involvement therein.[172]

---

only the Security Council may make a determination whether an act of aggression has occurred. See note 35 and accompanying text (French argument).

170 Rome Statute (1998) (as amended), note 3, Articles 15*bis*(9), 15*ter*(4).

171 See ibid., Article 8*bis*(2).

172 Ibid.

Thus, for example, under Rome Statute Article *8bis*(2)(a), "any annexation" is encompassed as an act of aggression and there is no requirement that "war" be involved. A "bloodless" annexation could amount to the crime of aggression, if it is of sufficient "character, gravity and scale" to be a "manifest" Charter violation (e.g., it could be a clear violation that is large in scale). Yet, the same is not necessarily true under the Special Tribunal Statute, where the above listed acts are not enumerated (although they are referenced), and Paragraph (4) seems to impose a separate requirement that such an act constitute "war" before being encompassed within the definition. Thus, it appears that the G7, who only wanted to criminalize "war", have basically re-written the Rome Statute's text to serve their ends,[173] although it might be possible to read the convoluted language of Paragraph 4 differently.[174]

In any event, Article 5 of the Statute states: "Nothing in this Statute shall be interpreted as limiting or prejudicing in any way existing or developing rules of international law for purposes other than this Statute".[175] Additionally, Paragraph (4) states that the definition is "[f]or the purpose of this Statute" and "in the context of aggression against Ukraine". Thus, whatever the Tribunal Statute contains in Paragraph (4) will not impact how Rome Statute Article 8*bis* is read and should not impact the development of international law.[176]

Another reasons for the language of Paragraph (4) could have been to foreclose any argument that a different standard than provided for under Ukrainian (and Russian and Belarusian)[177] law was being applied. This could help foreclose the argument

---

[173] See Pecorella 2025 ("the ICC Statute provides individual criminal responsibility for those political or military leaders of an aggressor state when they commit *an act* of aggression. In this respect, the definition provided by the Statute of the Special Tribunal may well constitute a regression to the Nuremberg time, when Article 6a of the IMT Charter only criminalized aggressive wars".); see London Charter 1945, note 22, Article 6(a).

[174] Kevin Jon Heller argues: "if anything, the curious language *expands* what we mean by a war of aggression, because Art[icle] 2(4) deems *any* manifest violation of the UN Charter a war of aggression, which would seem to go well beyond both Nuremberg jurisprudence and Res[olution] 3314". Heller 2025. That reading is plausible, although potentially not what the drafters intended.

[175] Tribunal Statute, note 90, Article 5.

[176] But see Pecorella 2025 ("I find unconvincing that a multilateral agreement . . . regulating one of the most fundamental aspects of the system established by the UN Charter, to which it makes express reference, can have no effects on the development of international law rules governing the crime of aggression").

[177] Criminal Code of the Russian Federation No. 63-Fz, as amended (1996), Article 353; Criminal Code of the Republic of Belarus (1999), Article 122.

that the principle of *nullum crimen sine lege* (no crime without law)[178] was being violated.[179]

As mentioned, one consequence of Paragraph (4) is that it may be difficult for the Tribunal to prosecute leaders involved in the illegal annexation of Crimea (or illegal attempted annexations in the Donbas)[180]—if viewed in isolation. For example, the annexation of Crimea only involved limited fighting;[181] thus, on its own, it would appear difficult to characterize as war (if that is required by Paragraph (4)).[182] However, if the entire course of conduct, from the illegal annexation of Crimea in 2014, to the subsequent insurgency in the Donbas, up to and including the 2022 invasion were characterized as part of the war, then it could be encompassed.[183] Alternatively, one might view the annexation of Crimea in 2014 and the insurgency in the Donbas starting in 2014 as "preparation" or, at the very least, the "initiation" of the invasion that became full-scale in 2022.[184] That one of the General Assembly resolutions included in the recitals in the Tribunal Agreement condemned the annexation of Crimea is perhaps some indication that the Core Group intended the annexation of Crimea to be included.[185]

---

[178] Gaiane Nuridzhanian explains:

> The principle of legality, or *nullum crime sine lege*, is a general principle of law enshrined in, among other instruments, Art[icle] 7 [of the European Convention on Human Rights]. The principle prohibits holding a person criminally responsible for an act which did not constitute a criminal offence under national or international law at the time when the act was committed. Recital 15 to the [Tribunal] Agreement emphases the importance of "due process and fair trial standards, including the principles of *nullum crimen sine lege* . . . in accordance with international and European human rights standards".

Nuridzhanian 2025, p. 7, n. 26, quoting Tribunal Agreement, note 89, Rec 15; see also European Convention on Human Rights, note 154, Article 7.

[179] See Nuridzhanian 2025, pp. 7–8 ("the adoption of a narrower understanding of an act of state element for the purpose of the definition of the crime of aggression is required by the principle of legality"[;] "for this reason, Article 2 (4) of the Statute brings the element of 'a war of aggression' into the definition of the crime of aggression"). But see note 154 (suggesting a potential *nulla poena sine lege* problem as to sentencing).

[180] See Chap. 4, Sect. 4.2.1 (The Earlier Illegal Annexation of Crimea and Russian Proxy Forces in the Donbas).

[181] Ibid.

[182] See note 174 (Heller reading the language differently). Under Heller's reading, one would only need to ascertain that a "manifest" UN Charter violation occurred, with the definition equating a manifest violation to war.

[183] The Judgment of the International Military Tribunal for the Far East (Tokyo) was criticized for finding all aspects of the war in the Pacific to be part of one pre-planned conspiracy by Japanese leaders, when, in fact, the war contained different phases in response to events as they unfolded. See Kopelman 1991, pp. 419–20.

[184] Trahan 2025. According to Gleb Bogush: the invasion and illegal annexation of Crimea played a crucial role in the 2022 invasion of southern Ukraine. Crimea served as a staging ground for the southern offensive, facilitating the rapid occupation of key areas and cities. For example, the eastern thrust from Crimea proved decisive in the encirclement and fall of Mariupol. Emails with Gleb Bogush 7 April 2025, 3 July 2025.

[185] Gaiane Nuridzhanian argues:

7.4.2.2 The Application of Personal Immunities

As mentioned above, states also held starkly divergent views on whether personal immunity should apply and prevent prosecution of the troika during their terms in office.[186] On this issue, the G7 approach—in favor of immunity—largely prevailed.

In its early provisions, the Tribunal Statute appears to take a strong stance on the irrelevance of official capacity. Article 4(2), which is similar to Rome Statute Article 27(1),[187] states:

> For the purpose of this Statute, the official position of any accused person at the time of the alleged commission of a crime, whether as Head of State or Government, a member of a government or parliament, an elected representative or a government official, shall not relieve such person of criminal responsibility nor mitigate punishment.[188]

Unfortunately, later in the Statute, Article 23(5) specifies that indictments against the "troika" may not be confirmed and proceedings regarding them are to be suspended during their terms in office. It states:

> Where the indictment concerns a Head of State, Head of Government or Minister of Foreign Affairs, the Pre-Trial Judge shall not confirm the indictment and shall order the proceedings be suspended until that person no longer holds that office or an appropriate waiver has been presented to the Special Tribunal. During the suspension, the Pre-Trial Judge shall not otherwise act upon the indictment.[189]

The latter article makes clear that the troika could be indicted (that is, an indictment could be prepared and potentially even made public), but it could not be confirmed during the troika's terms in office, absent a waiver of immunities.[190] No

---

> Among the resolutions directly mentioned in the preamble of the Agreement are those denouncing the unlawful use of force against the territorial integrity of Ukraine and condemning Russia's occupation and annexation of Crimea, part of Ukraine's territory, since 2014. The indirect reference to these resolutions in Article 2 of the Statute combined with the lack of express limitation on the temporal jurisdiction leaves the Special Tribunal with the discretion to determine the temporal scope of the cases before it and extend its temporal jurisdiction to any crime of aggression against Ukraine committed prior to the full-scale invasion of 2022.

Nuridzhanian 2025, pp. 10–11 (internal citations omitted).

Common Article 2 to the Geneva Conventions additionally supports the conclusion that the annexation of Crimea, even viewed in isolation, amounts to war. See, e.g., Convention (I) for the Amelioration of the Condition of the Wounded and Sick in Armed Forces in the Field 1949, Article 2 ("The Convention [which almost exclusively applies to international armed conflict] shall also apply to all cases of partial or total *occupation* of the territory of a High Contracting Party, *even if the said occupation meets with no armed resistance*".) (emphasis added). Thus, occupation alone can create a state of international armed conflict. See Grzebyk 2025 (making this argument).

186 See Sect. 7.3.2.

187 See Rome Statute (1998) (as amended), note 3, Article 27(1).

188 Tribunal Statute, note 90, Article 4(2).

189 Ibid., Article 23(5).

190 Such a waiver by the individual's state of nationality would be difficult to imagine absent a change of government.

arrest warrants could be issued for their arrests.[191] The Council of Europe's FAQ explains that "investigations and the gathering of evidence can be conducted [and] indictments can be prepared,"[192] and the "Special Tribunal Prosecutor will be able to publish a formal document setting out the charges and material facts in each case".[193] At that point, however, the Special Tribunal would need to suspend its work against the troika.

Because the Statute is not silent on the issue of personal immunities, the argument as to whether the tribunal is "international enough" to avoid the application of personal immunities[194] is moot. That is, regardless of the number of countries that endorse the Tribunal by joining the Enlarged Partial Agreement (discussed below),[195] financially supporting it, or entering into cooperation agreements with it, the argument that the Tribunal should be treated as an international tribunal for purposes of personal immunity is foreclosed by the express language of the Statute.[196]

The slight good news is that the topic is handled procedurally and not as a matter of international law. Chapter 1 (Jurisdiction and Applicable Law) contains a strong statement on the irrelevance of official capacity.[197] It is in a much later section on procedure that the suspension of proceedings is addressed,[198] with the suspension done as a procedural step.[199] Because it was somewhat unclear how immunities would have applied (or not) had they not been expressly addressed, the result is something of a middle-ground. Arguably such a middle-ground is appropriate for a regionally supported tribunal, which itself represents a middle-ground approach between an international tribunal supported by the international community and a

[191] Nuridzhanian 2025, p. 16.

[192] Council of Europe nd.

[193] Ibid.

[194] See Sect. 7.3.2. See also Nuridzhanian 2024 ("There are three cumulative criteria for a criminal tribunal to be deemed international. First, the process of [the] tribunal's establishment must involve more than one State. . . . Second, an international tribunal must be established based on international law . . . . Third, the tribunal must not be formally incorporated into any domestic legal system"). Compare Coracini and Trahan 2022 ("To qualify as a[n] international criminal court or tribunal, a court must fulfill two conditions: (1) it must be established under international law, and (2) it must sufficiently reflect the will of the international community as a whole to enforce crimes under customary international law"; also noting that the Rome Statute set aside personal immunities, with that provision entering into force, along with the remainder of the Rome Statute, with the ratification of sixty states); see also International Criminal Court (2019) *Prosecutor v. Omar Hassan Ahmad Al-Bashir,* Judgment in the Jordan Referral re Al-Bashir Appeal, No. ICC-02/05-01/09 OA2, para 115 ("international courts act on behalf of the international community as a whole"); Nuridzhanian 2024 (agreeing that "to overcome the personal immunities, the tribunal must be acting on behalf of the 'international community as a whole'").

[195] See Sect. 7.4.3.

[196] See Chlevickaitė et al. 2025, p. 38 ("it does not have to be decided whether the Tribunal could speak in the name of the international community to overcome 'troika' immunity or not, since the rules in the Statute decide that question in a procedural way").

[197] Tribunal Statute, note 90, Article 4(2).

[198] Ibid., Article 23(5).

[199] 25 July 2025 Interview, note 12.

Ukrainian chamber.[200] The Tribunal at least has the power to issue an indictment against heads of state while they are in office.[201]

Additionally, the G7 states originally also took a problematic stand on the issue of functional immunities, arguing for their application.[202] As discussed in Chap. 5, functional immunity applies to official acts performed while a person holds office and do not expire when the term of office ends.[203] To have recognized functional immunities before the Special Tribunal could have paralyzed its proceedings and arguably would have been incorrect as a matter of international law. The Drafting Committee of the International Law Commission ("ILC") has affirmed that functional immunities (*ratione materiae*) do not apply before the domestic courts of another state[204] and they do not apply at the international level for crimes under international law.[205] Thus, the Tribunal Statute appropriately states: "Functional immunity shall not apply before the Special Tribunal".[206]

7.4.2.3 Initiating Cases

As mentioned above,[207] during the Core Group negotiations, states also took divergent views on the question of how cases would be initiated—whether through a fully independent prosecutor or by referral or transfer of proceedings from Ukraine.

The Tribunal Statute, in Article 23(1), provides that "criminal proceedings, information or evidence related to a crime within the jurisdiction of the Special Tribunal" will be "refer[red]" by the Prosecutor General of Ukraine to the Prosecutor of the Special Tribunal.[208] The Statute thus "would allow Ukraine to refer the dossiers of domestic investigations related to the crime of aggression to the Prosecutor of the Special Tribunal who could then draw on evidence accumulated within the framework of the International Centre for the Prosecution of the Crime of Aggression (ICPA) to pursue prosecutions".[209] The Tribunal Prosecutor would not be obligated to act on the information provided, as Article 23(2) states that "[i]f the Prosecutor

---

[200] Ibid.

[201] Ibid.

[202] Ibid.

[203] See Chap. 5, Sect. 5.3.4.3; Hamilton 2023, p. 44; Nuridzhanian 2025, p. 13 ("Functional immunity, or immunity *ratione materiae*, refers to the immunity of serving or former state officials from foreign criminal jurisdiction in respect of acts committed in their official capacity").

[204] United Nations General Assembly, International Law Commission (2025). See also Hamilton 2023, p. 44 ("There is broad agreement that functional immunity is not a bar to the prosecution of serious international crimes, even in foreign domestic courts"). As of late 2025, the full ILC has not yet formally endorsed the view.

[205] Goldston and Khalfaoui 2023.

[206] Tribunal Statute, note 90, Article 23(4).

[207] See Sect. 7.3.3.

[208] Tribunal Statute, note 90, Article 23(1).

[209] Forde 2025.

decides not to proceed with an investigation, he or she shall draw up a reasoned archiving order and notify Ukraine thereof".[210]

These provisions do not appear to rule out the ability of the Tribunal Prosecutor to also act on information that he or she gathers independently. Tribunal Statute Article 24(3) enumerates a long list of powers that the Prosecutor has, and none of them is conditioned on approval of the Ukrainian authorities.[211] Thus, it is possible to read the Tribunal Statute to allow for both referral of proceedings, information, and evidence from the Ukrainian Prosecutor General, and independent action by the Tribunal Prosecutor.[212] Admittedly, this reading may not be what the drafters intended, and others read the Prosecutor's powers to be limited to Ukraine's referrals.[213] In either event, the Prosecutor's independence is preserved, because he or she would have the leeway to decide not to proceed with criminal proceedings referred by Ukraine's Prosecutor General.[214] It may also be useful that the Statute not only provides for referral of "proceedings", but also "information" and "evidence". This gives the Tribunal Prosecutor the ability to open an investigation in a case where proceedings have not been opened (and perhaps could not, for immunity reasons, be opened) in Ukraine, as long as information or evidence has been referred.[215]

The Tribunal Statute also mentions "referral" from Ukraine, not "transfer".[216] According to one participant in the Core Group negotiations, it was felt that this would not differ much from a self-referral under the Rome Statute, whereby a State Party may refer a situation to the ICC Prosecutor, including one involving its own nationals and/or crimes committed on its territory.[217]

---

[210] Tribunal Statute, note 90, Article 23(2).

[211] Ibid., Article 24(3).

[212] But see 25 July 2025 Interview, note 12 (noting that France might argue otherwise).

[213] See, e.g., Heller 2025 ("This seemingly innocuous provision [Article 23(1)] actually means that the [Special Tribunal's] docket will be completely controlled by Ukraine: unless *a particular Russian suspect* is referred by Ukraine's Prosecutor General, the [Tribunal] Prosecutor will be powerless to investigate or prosecute. In other words, under the [Tribunal] Statute, the Prosecutor has no *proprio motu* power whatsoever".) (emphasis added). Heller's reading is incorrect; nothing requires a particular suspect to be referred. The Statute expressly allows for referral of evidence or information, without proceedings being initiated against a particular accused.

[214] Tribunal Statute, note 90, Article 23(2).

[215] Coracini 2025. Given that referral of "information" or "evidence" can trigger the Tribunal Prosecutor's work, whether the Tribunal Statute is read to give the Tribunal Prosecutor fully independent powers may not matter much, since the provisions of "information" or "evidence" is a fairly low threshold to satisfy.

[216] Tribunal Statute, note 90, Article 23(1).

[217] 25 July 2025 Interview, note 12. For referral to the ICC of a situation by a State Party, see Rome Statute (1998) (as amended), note 3, Article 14.

7.4.2.4 The Ability to Conduct Trials *in Absentia*

Finally, as to the issue of whether the Tribunal should be able to hold trials *in absentia,*[218] Ukraine prevailed in its desire that the Tribunal be able to do so. Article 28(1) of the Statute states:

> Where, upon confirmation of the indictment under Article 25, paragraph 2, of this Statute, the accused does not appear before the Special Tribunal, the Special Tribunal may conduct proceedings in his or her absence:
>
> (a) when he or she has waived his or her right to be present in an unequivocal manner; or
> (b) if all reasonable steps have been taken to secure his or her appearance before the Special Tribunal and to inform the person of the charges and the consequences of his or her non-appearance before the Special Tribunal, and the interests of justice so require.[219]

The Statute goes on to provide for various procedural safeguards.[220] The FAQ prepared by the Council of Europe explains that:

> Trials *in absentia* will have to be accompanied with procedural safeguards such as the right to legal representation of the interests and rights of the accused. Persons tried *in absentia* will have the right to request a retrial if they subsequently appear before the Special Tribunal in person, unless they waive that right or accept the initial judgment.[221]

---

[218] See Sect. 7.3.4.

[219] Tribunal Statute, note 90, Article 28(1).

[220] The Statute provides that:

> (2) When hearings are conducted in the absence of the accused, the Special Tribunal shall ensure that:
> (a) the accused has been duly notified or served with, or otherwise been given notice through publication in the media or communication to his or her State of residence or nationality of:
> (i) the indictment;
> (ii) the date, time and place of the hearing; and
> (iii) the consequences of his or her non-appearance before the Special Tribunal; and
> (b) the accused has designated a defence counsel of his or her own choosing, to be remunerated either by the accused or, if the accused is proved to be indigent, by the Special Tribunal; whenever the accused refuses or fails to appoint a defence counsel, such counsel is to be assigned by the Defence Unit with a view to ensuring full representation of the interests and rights of the accused.
> (3) In case of a conviction in the absence of the accused, the convicted person shall have the right to a retrial in his or her presence before the Special Tribunal or a successor mechanism, unless he or she
> (a) has waived in writing his or her right to a retrial; or
> (b) accepts the judgment.
>
> Ibid., Article 28(2)–(3).

[221] Council of Europe nd. It is possible that convictions *in absentia* could help with the freezing of assets of those convicted, with the Special Tribunal transferring them to the Register of Damages/Claims Commission process. 25 July 2025 Interview, note 12. For the Register of Damages, see Committee of Ministers, Council

Given the divergent views on whether the Special Tribunal for Lebanon ("STL"), a tribunal that held trials *in absentia*, was worth the effort and cost,[222] the jury is still out as to the optics of holding trials *in absentia* at the international/hybrid tribunal level, and, as discussed further below, what they would mean for the legitimacy of the Special Tribunal.[223] The author generally disfavors such trials. In the present context, however, they would permit trials against high-level leaders (excluding the troika) to be conducted before the Special Tribunal. Without the *in absentia* option, there could be the anomalous situation of Ukraine proceeding with trials (*in absentia* or in the presence of the accused) against lower-level perpetrators, but no trials proceeding against higher-level perpetrators before the Special Tribunal, unless they are apprehended.[224]

Thus, the negotiators ultimately produced a largely well-crafted Statute. This author may not concur with some of the drafting decisions of the Core Group—e.g., suspending proceedings against the troika, the changes from the Rome Statute's definition of the crime, the possible tying of the Prosecutor's hands to what is referred by Ukraine, the decision to permit trials *in absentia,* as well as the omission of "aiding and abetting" as a form of responsibility[225]—but that is the nature of negotiations. Had there been no concessions, there also would have been no Tribunal.[226]

---

of Europe (2023) Resolution CM/Res (2023) Establishing the Enlarged Partial Agreement on the Register of Damage Caused by the Aggression of the Russian Federation against Ukraine. https://rd4u.coe.int/documents/358068/372244/CM_Res%282023%293+-+Statute.pdf/2cebbb65-c86d-61c6-06c2-dca378ecd900?t=1708702115594. Accessed 8 August 2025 ("Committee of Ministers 2023"). For the Claims Commission, see note 262.

[222] See, e.g., Wählisch 2017; Chlevickaitė et al. 2025, p. 39 ("The [STL] only managed, 14 years and almost a billion US Dollars later, to complete one substantive *in absentia* trial before it shut down in December 2023".) (citing sources); Heller 2025 ("The STL should serve as a cautionary tale for the [Special Tribunal], with nothing to show for its 14 years of efforts other than the conviction of three suspects *in absentia* [one conviction affirmed on appeal] who will probably never be captured".); Lobel and Milaninia 2025 ("The STL's *in absentia* model was widely perceived to have lacked sufficient legitimacy and impact, undermining public confidence in the STL's authority and contributing to perceptions of limited deterrent or expressive value").

[223] The author agrees with Gaiane Nuridzhanian when she writes: "While in theory Article 28 of the Statute envisages necessary procedural safeguards, it is their application in practice that will determine the fairness of the *in absentia* trials before the Special Tribunal". Nuridzhanian 2025, p. 22. See International Federation for Human Rights et al. 2025 ("The possibility of holding trials *in absentia* . . . marks a regressive development from previously established international criminal tribunals"; "trials *in absentia* may affect perceptions of objectivity and impartiality of trials where an accused person is not present to defend themselves").

[224] Coracini 2025.

[225] The author, as of yet, has not found an explanation why aiding and abetting was omitted from the forms of individual criminal responsibility. Perhaps it was dropped to reinforce the requirement that only those who bear the "greatest responsibility" be tried. Tribunal Statute, note 90, Article 1. Aiding and abetting could be seen as an ancillary form of responsibility.

[226] The G7 no doubt had the upper hand in the negotiations as some of those states are also the key weapons suppliers to Ukraine. The Insider 2022.

7.4.3 The Role of the Management Committee and the Enlarged Partial Agreement

A final topic relevant to the operation of the Special Tribunal pertains to the role of the Management Committee. The idea of a Management Committee derives from the practice of the Special Court for Sierra Leone, which also had such a Committee.[227] The Management Committee would undertake some of the functions that the Assembly of States Parties does for the ICC.[228] The work of the Special Tribunal's Management Committee is governed by the Enlarged Partial Agreement, which also provides the mechanism whereby states both within and beyond the Council of Europe would join in endorsing the Tribunal and financing its operations. States that become parties to the Enlarged Partial Agreement would be entitled to nominate up to two representatives to the Management Committee, thereby gaining a voice in the Tribunal's administration.[229]

The Management Committee is tasked with assisting in the administrative and managerial aspects of the Tribunal's operations.[230] It would make nominations and elect the roster of judges,[231] as well as the Prosecutor and Deputy Prosecutor(s).[232] The Tribunal's President would also provide yearly updates to the Management

---

[227] See Mochochoko and Tortora 2004 (discussing the Management Committee of the Special Court for Sierra Leone).

[228] For background on the ASP, see Trahan 2020.

[229] Enlarged Partial Agreement, note 2, Article 4(1).

[230] Ibid., Article 1(2).

[231] Tribunal Statute, note 90, Article 8(4). The FAQ specifies:

> Members and Associate Members of the Management Committee will be able to propose candidates for the roster of judges. Nominated candidates will not need to be a national of a state that is Member or Associate Member of the Management Committee. The roster will include 15 judges. An independent advisory panel will recommend the most suitable candidates for the roster of judges to the Management Committee. The Management Committee will elect the judges to the roster by secret ballot, by an absolute majority and for a nine-year period.

Council of Europe nd.

[232] Tribunal Statute, note 90, Article 10(4). The FAQ provides:

> Candidates for the role of Prosecutor will be proposed by states that are Members or Associate Members of the Management Committee. Nominations for the post of Prosecutor should preferably be made with the support of multiple states. The nominated candidate would not need to be a national of a state that is Member or Associate Member of the Management Committee. The advisory panel will recommend the most suitable candidates to the Management Committee. The Prosecutor will be elected by secret ballot by an absolute majority of the Management Committee.
>
> The term will be seven years, without the possibility of re-election. The Deputy Prosecutor(s) will be elected in the same way as the Prosecutor, from a list of candidates provided by the Prosecutor for a term of seven years and without the possibility of re-election.

Council of Europe nd.

Committee on the work of the Tribunal,[233] and, as mentioned, would recommend to the Management Committee when the Tribunal should cease operations.[234]

The Management Committee will also set the Tribunal's budget and allocate the amount of contributions to be made by states.[235] As to the cost of the Tribunal, the Council of Europe's FAQ states that: "While exact costs are still being worked out, the cost is likely to be similar to that of other international or internationalised criminal tribunals".[236] The Enlarged Partial Agreement provides that the "Management Committee shall determine the amount of the annual contribution of its members and the recommended voluntary contributions of its associate members".[237]

Under the Enlarged Partial Agreement, certain states may automatically become Members or Associate Members.[238] Other states may become Members or Associate Members with the permission of the Management Committee.[239] Members would contribute financially to the Tribunal, whereas Associate Members would have the option to contribute.[240] Thus, states can decide whether they wish to support the Tribunal by joining the Enlarged Partial Agreement and whether they wish to contribute financially to its operations. States that do not contribute do not have the same rights as states that do.[241] A certain level of funding is required before the Tribunal may commence operations.[242]

It will be extremely important to ensure that enough states become Members and Associate Members to the Enlarged Partial Agreement, both to demonstrate commitment to the Tribunal's work and to ensure that it has sufficient funding to operate.

---

233 Tribunal Statute, note 90, Article 52(1).

234 Ibid., Article 54(1).

235 Enlarged Partial Agreement, note 2, Article 8(1)–(2).

236 Council of Europe nd.

237 Enlarged Partial Agreement, note 2, Article 8.1.

238 Ibid., Article 3.1 ("Any member or observer State of the Council of Europe and the European Union, any other State that has voted in favour of the United Nations General Assembly Resolution A/RES/ES-11/6 of 23 February 2023, or any State and international organisation that has participated in the Core Group on the Establishment of a Special Tribunal for the Crime of Aggression against Ukraine may become a member or associate member of the Management Committee by notification addressed to the Secretary General").

239 Ibid., Article 3.2.

240 Ibid., Article 8.2.

241 25 July 2025 Interview, note 12. Associate Members participating in meetings of the Management Committee do not have the right to vote, except during a year in which the Associate Member makes a voluntary contribution reaching a certain level. Enlarged Partial Agreement, note 2, Article 5(4)–5(5).

242 See Tribunal Agreement, note 89, Article 6(2).

7.5 Key Challenges

As of late 2025, various technical steps remain before the Tribunal can become operational. They include, first, the ratification or acceptance of the Enlarged Partial Agreement by Member States of the Council of Europe as well as other states that wish to do so. Second, enough Member States and Associate Member States need to be willing to finance the Tribunal, whether through assessed contributions by Member States or voluntary contributions by Associate Member States. Only once there is sufficient funding for the Tribunal's first year of operations and pledges for the second and third years of operations, can the first phase of operations commence.[243] Third, enough countries need to be willing to enter into cooperation agreements[244] with the Tribunal for The Netherlands to be willing to host it; otherwise, another host country will need to be found.[245] Fourth, a Host State Agreement must be concluded with the host state. Fifth, cooperation agreements with states as well as the ICC and/ or other organizations will be needed. These steps require both political will and monetary commitments.[246] A wildcard might be whether the establishment of the Tribunal could be derailed by a peace agreement between Russia and Ukraine—i.e., whether Russia demands that the Tribunal be scrapped as a condition for such an agreement and there is acquiescence to that demand.[247]

Once the preconditions are met (if they are), the Management Committee would need to elect a highly-qualified roster of judges and a highly qualified Prosecutor and Deputy Prosecutor(s), and the Tribunal would need to hire highly qualified staff. The Tribunal would then face the task of operating both efficiently and fairly.

Additionally, the Tribunal also must *be seen* to operate efficiently and fairly,[248] which would be facilitated by its having an effective Press or Outreach Office to explain the Tribunal's work.[249] Neither the Tribunal's founding documents nor the

---

[243] Ibid.

[244] States (other than Ukraine which is required to cooperate) have the option whether to enter into cooperation agreements with the Tribunal. The Tribunal Agreement provides that Member and Associate Member States "will" cooperate with the Tribunal "within the framework of cooperation agreement or other arrangements and within the limits of their national legislation and their international obligations"—suggesting that such states *should* be entering cooperation agreements. See Tribunal Agreement, note 89, Article 7(3). It may also be possible for the Tribunal Prosecutor to request Ukraine to seek cooperation from states with which Ukraine has cooperation agreements. Coracini 2025.

[245] 25 July 2025 Interview, note 12.

[246] "Agreement on the technical process of developing a Special Tribunal for the Crime of Aggression may not translate into concrete political support to establish it". Forde 2025.

[247] While the Tribunal Statute precludes an amnesty grant impacting on its proceedings, see Tribunal Statute, note 90, Article 4(3), that addresses a different topic.

[248] It was Justice Pal, writing in dissent to the Judgment of the Tokyo Tribunal, who wrote that justice "should be conducted in such a way as not only to assure that justice is done but also to create the impression that it is being done". International Military Tribunal for the Far East (1953) Dissentient Judgment, p. 7, as quoted in Kopelman 1991, p. 403.

[249] See also Chlevickaitė et al. 2025, p. 18 (mentioning the need for public outreach around the Tribunal).

Council of Europe's FAQ contains any mention of such an office. The work of the Press or Outreach Office would include making clear what the Tribunal will be tasked with accomplishing and what it will not be able to accomplish. It is crucial for the public and others to hold realistic expectations to avoid disappointment.[250] The Council of Europe issuing "explainers", such as its FAQ, probably would not suffice. It will not be easy to explain, particularly to the Ukrainian public, why the troika was essentially granted immunity (suspended proceedings) during their terms in office.[251] Nor will it be easy to explain, particularly to the broader public in other regions, how selective justice[252] advances justice overall. The latter could prove particularly challenging if some of the states that support the Special Tribunal (particularly the G7 states, aside from Germany)[253] keep resisting giving the ICC more jurisdiction over the crime of aggression in other situations, a topic explored in the next chapter.

7.6 Conclusion

The Tribunal represents an innovation, as it would be the first free-standing ad hoc tribunal designed to prosecute the crime of aggression. As such, assuming it is established, it will have an immensely important task.[254] It remains to be seen whether the Tribunal can live up to the expectations of accomplishing justice vis-à-vis the crime of aggression in the situation of Ukraine, which may influence views on the prosecution of the crime of aggression more broadly. The number of countries that join in supporting the Tribunal—whether by joining the Enlarged Partial Agreement, financing the Tribunal, and/or entering into cooperation agreements with it—could in turn impact the Tribunal's legitimacy.[255] The more broadly supported the Tribunal is, the more legitimate its establishment is likely to be considered. Yet, that is only

250 On the importance of reasonable expectations, see Trahan 2019 (evaluating the accomplishments of the ICTY and discussing the benchmarks for measuring the success of a tribunal).

251 "Recent sociological polls indicate that 76% of Ukrainians believe that justice cannot be reached without the accountability of those who designed th[e] attack on Ukraine and perpetrated ensuing conflict-related crimes". Chlevickaitė et al. 2025, p. 11, n. 58, citing Rating Group 2024.

252 For discussion of the problem of selectivity, see Chap. 5, Sect. 5.3.4.6.

253 Germany is in a different position because it has supported broader accountability when it comes to prosecuting the crime of aggression, by leading, as will be discussed in Chap. 8, the efforts to create more jurisdiction over the crime of aggression before the ICC. See Chap. 8, Sect. 8.4.1 (Germany's role).

254 "The tribunal would be only the third in human history—after the Nuremberg and Tokyo tribunals—to prosecute aggression. This is therefore a watershed moment in which the entirety of humanity (or at least the most representative form of it) must be persuaded and enabled to participate". Chlevickaitė et al. 2025, p. 40.

255 See, e.g., ibid., p. 37 ("[T]he legitimacy of the tribunal could further be increased by political means. An obvious avenue is . . . to seek broad cross-regional support for the future [Enlarged Partial Agreement]. In addition, Ukraine and its allies may consider seeking a positive reference to the tribunal in a future resolution of the UN [General Assembly] . . .".).

the beginning. The Tribunal will need to conduct its proceedings with impeccable fairness, since trying high-level leaders, should they be apprehended, is potentially the most difficult task a tribunal can face.[256]

The question of the Tribunal's legitimacy will loom large. It is not solely Russian aggression that deserves to be prosecuted; as long as the G7 states (excluding Germany) continue to be hesitant to accept broader jurisdiction over the crime, accusations of selectivity will haunt the work of the Special Tribunal. This is a problem not of the Tribunal's making. No matter how well it performs, these criticisms necessarily will persist. Moreover, due to the way in which the issue of personal immunities was addressed, the Tribunal will also face the glaring optics of prosecuting high-level leaders (should they be apprehended), *except* the highest-level troika. The holding of trials *in absentia* also may not be seen to achieve a great deal; the jury is out on whether proceedings *in absentia* are seen to advance justice.[257] The more individuals can be tried in person, the more the Tribunal will be seen to achieve, assuming the trials are well-conducted and charges well-supported by the evidence. If the Tribunal's sole accomplishments turn out to be trials *in absentia* and the issuance of indictments against the troika that cannot be confirmed, its achievements may not prove very convincing, at least in terms of delivering justice.[258] The more states enter into cooperation agreements with the Tribunal, the greater the likelihood that arrest warrants will be executed and perpetrators apprehended and tried in person. The use of sealed warrants would increase the chances of apprehensions.

Even without in person trials, the Tribunal will likely advance the historical record, detailing the roles of the leadership-level in the invasion of Ukraine (and possibly the illegal annexation of Crimea),[259] as well as exposing—with proper victim participation[260]—the multitude of harms and crimes inflicted on the people and state of Ukraine. This alone could bring some solace and recognition to the victims, particularly if coupled with monetary recovery through the existing Register of Damages[261] and Claims Commission that is being established.[262]

---

[256] See, e.g., Wald 2009.

[257] See, e.g., Nuridzhanian 2025, p. 20 ("The absence of the accused during the trial can undermine the fairness of proceedings, but, on the other, trials *in absentia* serve to prevent impunity in cases where the accused chooses to evade justice").

[258] See Forde 2025 ("If a Special Tribunal only focusses on a small group of elite prosecutions, at a tremendous cost and with no guarantee of ever apprehending let alone convicting these suspects, what does this do for individual justice in Ukraine and the broader system of international criminal justice?"; yet concluding: "[t]o sustain a rules-based order and the integrity of international law, the international community *must* pursue meaningful accountability for the crime of aggression").

[259] See notes 180–185 and accompanying text (whether the annexation of Crimea is encompassed).

[260] See notes 130–133 and accompanying text (discussing group victim representation).

[261] See Committee of Ministers 2023, note 221. The Register of Damages allows "Ukrainian citizens and residents [to] submit claims for damage or destruction of residential immovable property as well as claims for the death of an immediate family member". Forde 2025.

[262] See Didkovska 2025. "The Claims Commission will serve as the second integral element of Ukraine's international compensation mechanism, alongside the Register of Damage for Ukraine, established by the Council of Europe". Ibid. (emphasis omitted).

While the Tribunal Statute presents a new form of tribunal[263]—a regionally supported ad hoc tribunal designed to prosecute the crime of aggression—it will be the history books that pronounce on whether the international community comes to see its work, assuming it is established, as legitimate. On balance, the Tribunal Statute contains many compromises; yet, if the alternative is *no justice* for high-level perpetrators of the crime of aggression, the author considers the Special Tribunal to be essential.[264] It may not create the most legitimate and weightiest of precedent—as a fully international tribunal established through the UN could have—but the absence of accountability in the current context also would have proven a profound setback for the rule of law and prosecution of the crime of aggression. The G7 States have not made the commitment to the rule of law that one would have wished for—as they, except for Germany, have only endorsed selective justice for the crime of aggression, and all of them have ensured that the troika cannot be prosecuted by the Special Tribunal while in office. Yet, they have at least made a commitment to the rule of law and the prosecution of the crime of aggression. Now they must ensure that the Tribunal is sufficiently supported and funded to enable it to perform its work.

References

Barriga S, Kreß C (2012) The *Travaux Préparatoires* of the Crime of Aggression. Cambridge University Press, Cambridge

Chlevickaitė G, Busol K, Hoffmeister F, Owiso O (2025) The Special Tribunal for the Crime of Aggression Against Ukraine. Legal Assessment and Policy Recommendations Asser Institute. https://www.asser.nl/media/798017/asser-special-tribunal-report-25062025.pdf. Accessed 18 August 2025

Clark R (2007) Nuremberg and the Crime Against Peace. Washington University Global Studies Law Review 6: 527–50

Coracini A (2025) Presentation of Astrid Reisinger Coracini 23 September 2025

Coracini A, Trahan J (2022) The Case for Creating a Special Tribunal to Prosecute the Crime of Aggression Committed Against Ukraine (Part VI): On the Non-Applicability of Personal Immunities, Just Security. https://www.justsecurity.org/84017/the-case-for-creating-a-special-tribunal-to-prosecute-the-crime-of-aggression-committed-against-ukraine-part-vi-on-the-non-applicability-of-personal-immunities/. Accessed 26 September 2025

Council of Europe (nd) Frequently Asked Questions – Special Tribunal for the Crime of Aggression against Ukraine. https://www.coe.int/en/web/portal/frequently-asked-questions. Accessed 23 July 2025

Council of Europe, Committee of Ministers (2022) Consequences of the Aggression of the Russian Federation against Ukraine. CM/Del/Dec(2022)1428ter/2.3. https://search.coe.int/cm?i=0900001680a5d7d9. Accessed 27 October 2025

[263] "This marks the first time in history that a dedicated tribunal is being established to investigate and prosecute the crime of aggression". Chlevickaitė et al. 2025, p. 4.

[264] See, e.g., Forde 2025 ("failure to secure meaningful accountability for Russia's egregious crimes in Ukraine will embolden the perpetrator, inspire other authoritarian states and will inevitably make us all less safe"); Chlevickaitė et al. 2025, p. 38 ("the statute enjoys a high level of legitimacy, supported by at least 40 states and the oldest human rights institution in Europe . . .").

Council of Europe, Committee of Ministers (2024) Meeting of the Ministers' Deputies on 30 April 2024, News. https://www.coe.int/en/web/cm/news/-/asset_publisher/hwwluK1RCEJo/content/883 meeting-of-the-ministers-deputies-on-30-april-2024. Accessed 28 September 2025

Didkovska M (2025) Kyiv Initiates Talks on Claims Commission Treaty for Ukraine. The Gaze. https://thegaze.media/news/kyiv-initiates-talks-on-claims-commission-treaty-for-ukraine. Accessed 12 August 2025

European Union Agency for Criminal Justice Cooperation (nd) International Centre for the Prosecution of the Crime of Aggression against Ukraine. https://www.eurojust.europa.eu/international-centre-for-the-prosecution-of-the-crime-of-aggression-against-ukraine. Accessed 28 September 2025

European Union Agency for Criminal Justice Cooperation (2023) Press Release, European Union Agency for Criminal Justice Cooperation (2023) History in the Making-the International Centre for the Prosecution of the Crime of Aggression Against Ukraine Starts Operations at EuroJust. https://www.eurojust.europa.eu/news/history-makinginternational-centre-prosecution-crime-aggression-against-ukraine-starts-operations-at-eurojust. Accessed 28 September 2025

Forde A (2025) The Road Not (Yet) Taken: A Special Tribunal for the Crime of Aggression against Ukraine. Opinio Juris. https://opiniojuris.org/2025/04/16/the-road-not-yet-taken-a-special-tribunal-for-the-crime-of-aggression-against-ukraine/. Accessed 19 August 2025

Geiß R, Bäumler J (nd) Max Planck Encyclopedias of International Law. Oxford Public International Law. *Ne bis in idem*. https://doi.org/10.1093/law:epil/9780199231690/law-9780199231690-e66. Accessed 26 September 2025

Goldston J, Khalfaoui A (2023) In Evaluating Immunities Before a Special Tribunal for Aggression Against Ukraine, the Type of Tribunal Matters. Just Security. https://www.justsecurity.org/84959/in-evaluating-immunities-before-a-special-tribunal-for-aggression-against-ukraine-the-type-of-tribunal-matters/. Accessed 12 August 2025

Grzebyk P (2023) Crime of Aggression Against Ukraine: The Role of Regional Customary Law. Journal of International Criminal Justice, 21: 435–59

Grzebyk P (2025) Personal Scope of Responsibility for the Crime of Aggression: The Case of Russian Aggression Against Ukraine. In: Šturma P, Lipovský M (eds) Special Judicial Mechanism for the Crime of Aggression Committed against Ukraine. Brill | Nijhoff, Leiden

Hamilton R (2023) Ukraine's Push to Prosecute Aggression: Implications for Immunity *Ratione Personae* and the Crime of Aggression. Case Western Reserve Journal of International Law 55: 39–60

Heller K (2025) The New STCoA: The Good, the Bad, the Curious, and the Terrible. Opinio Juris. https://opiniojuris.org/2025/07/11/the-new-stcoa-the-good-the-bad-the-curious-and-the-terrible/. Accessed 19 August 2025

International Criminal Court, Assembly of States Parties (2010) Review Conference, The Crime of Aggression, ICC Doc. RC/Res.6

International Federation for Human Rights, Amnesty International, the International Commission of Jurists (2025) Ukraine: Establishment of the Special Tribunal for the Crime of Aggression Must Ensure Victims-Centered Justice. https://www.amnesty.org/en/latest/news/2025/05/ukraine-establishment-of-the-special-tribunal-for-the-crime-of-aggression-must-ensure-victims-centered-justice/. Accessed 19 August 2025

Kopelman E (1991) Ideology and International Law: The Dissent of the Indian Justice at the Tokyo War Crimes Trial. NYU Journal of International Law & Politics 23: 373

Lobel H, Milaninia N (2025) Building a Special Tribunal for the Crime of Aggression Against Ukraine. EJIL: *Talk!* https://www.ejiltalk.org/building-a-special-tribunal-for-the-crime-of-aggression-against-ukraine/. Accessed 19 August 2025

Magliveras K (2025) The Council of Europe's Special Tribunal for the Crime of Aggression Against Ukraine: A New Type of Internationalized Criminal Justice? https://internationallaw.blog/2025/07/07/the-council-of-europes-special-tribunal-for-the-crime-of-aggression-against-ukraine-a-new-type-of-internationalized-criminal-justice/. Accessed 19 August 2025

McFaul M, Person R (2024) Why Putin Invaded Ukraine. In: Brands H (ed) War in Ukraine: Conflict, Strategy, and the Return of a Fractured World. Johns Hopkins University Press, Baltimore

Mochochoko P, Tortora G (2004) The Management Committee for the Special Court for Sierra Leone. In: Romano C, Nollkaemper A, Kleffner J (eds) (2004) Internationalized Criminal Courts: Sierra Leone, East Timor, Kosovo, and Cambodia. Oxford University Press, Oxford

Nuridzhanian G (2024) International Enough? A Council of Europe Special Tribunal for the Crime of Aggression. Just Security. https://www.justsecurity.org/96320/council-of-europe-ukraine-tribunal/. Accessed 19 August 2025

Nuridzhanian G (2025) The Newly Established Special Tribunal for the Crime of Aggression Against Ukraine: Jurisdiction, Immunities and Due Process. https://doi.org/10.2139/ssrn.5359650. Accessed 26 September 2025

Open Society Justice Initiative (2019) Recent Developments at the Extraordinary Chambers in the Courts of Cambodia. https://www.justiceinitiative.org/uploads/979d6668-cde4-4ae2-9018-b758dc5a7d6c/briefing-eccc-recent-developments-20180118.pdf. Accessed 24 July 2025

Pecorella G (2025) The Crime of Aggression: A Preliminary Look at Ukraine's Special Tribunal. International Law Blog. https://internationallaw.blog/2025/07/01/the-crime-of-aggression-a-preliminary-look-at-ukraines-special-tribunal/. Accessed 19 August 2025

Rating Group (2024) Justice in the Context of Russian Armed Aggression. https://ratinggroup.ua/en/research/ukraine/justicecontext-russian-armed-aggression.html. Accessed 28 September 2025

Rosen B, Bridgeman T, Gerami N (2025) The Day After US Strikes on Iran's Nuclear Program: Law & Policy. Just Security. https://www.justsecurity.org/115234/policy-legal-iran-nuclear-strikes/. Accessed 18 July 2025

Scheffer D (2008) The Extraordinary Chambers in the Courts of Cambodia. In: Bassiouni M C (ed) International Criminal Law, Volume 3: International Enforcement. Brill | Nijhoff, Leiden

Scheffer D (2013) All The Missing Souls: A Personal History of the War Crimes Tribunals. Princeton University Press, Princeton

Strapatsas N (2017) The Practice of the Security Council Regarding the Concept of Aggression. In Kreβ C, Barriga S (eds) (2017) The Crime of Aggression: A Commentary. Cambridge University Press, Cambridge

The Insider (2022) The 30 Countries Supplying Ukraine with Weapons: A Detailed List. https://theins.ru/en/news/251226. Accessed 21 August 2025

Trahan J (2011) Negotiating the Amendment on the Crime of Aggression: Proceedings at the Kampala Review Conference on the International Criminal Court. International Criminal Law Review 11: 49–104

Trahan J (2019) Examining the Benchmarks by Which to Evaluate the ICTY's Legacy. In: Sterio M, Scharf M (eds) The Legacy of Ad Hoc Tribunals in International Criminal Law: Assessing the ICTY's and ICTR's Most Significant Legal Accomplishments. Cambridge University Press, Cambridge

Trahan J (2020) The Assembly of States Parties. In: Oosterveld V, deGuzman M (eds) The Elgar Companion to the International Criminal Court. Edward Elgar Publishing, Cheltenham, UK

Trahan J (2024) The Role of the UN Security Council and General Assembly In Responding to the Invasion of Ukraine. Polish Review of International and European Law 12: 23–64

Trahan J (2025) Emails with Gleb Bogush, 7 April 2025, 3 July 2025

Ukrainska Pravda (2025) Ukrainian Parliament Ratifies Agreement on Establishment of Special Tribunal for Russian Aggression. https://www.pravda.com.ua/eng/news/2025/07/15/7521820/. Accessed 6 August 2025

UNTS (nd) https://treaties.un.org/pages/showDetails.aspx?objid=08000002801572a2. Accessed 28 September 2025

Vervaele J (2014) European Criminal Justice in the Post-Lisbon Area of Freedom, Security and Justice. *Editoriale Scientifica*, Naples

Visit Cambodia (nd) S21 Prison, Tuol Sleng nd. https://visitcambodia.info/tour/s21-prison-tuol-sleng/. Accessed 21 August 2025

Voltaire (1780) *Questions sur l'Encyclopédie, par des Amateurs*. Vol. 2. Unnamed Publisher, Geneva
Wald P (2009) Tyrants on Trial: Keeping Order in the Courtroom. Open Society Justice Initiative. https://www.justiceinitiative.org/uploads/7f44003a-5c7a-452e-a44a-0ccd86202ae4/tyrants_20090911.pdf. Accessed 10 August 2025
Wählisch M (2017) Legitimacy Defects and Legal Flaws of the Special Tribunal for Lebanon: Dilemmas of the "Peace through Justice" Theorem. In: Hayashi N, Bailliet C (eds) The Legitimacy of International Criminal Tribunals. Cambridge University Press, Cambridge

Other Documents

Agreement between the Council of Europe and the Government of Ukraine on the Establishment of the Special Tribunal for the Crime of Aggression against Ukraine (2025). https://rm.coe.int/agreement-and-statut-english/1680b66127. Accessed 28 September 2025
Agreement between the Council of Europe and the Government of Ukraine on the Establishment of the Special Tribunal for the Crime of Aggression against Ukraine (draft dated 21 March 2025) (on file with the author)
Agreement between the United Nations and the Royal Government of Cambodia Concerning the Prosecution under Cambodian law of Crimes Committed During the Period of Democratic Kampuchea (2003). https://www.eccc.gov.kh/en/documents/legal/agreement-between-united nations-and-royal-government-cambodia-concerning-prosecution. Accessed 28 September 2025
Agreement between the United Nations and the Government of Sierra Leone on the Establishment of a Special Court for Sierra Leone (2002) 2178 UNTS 137
Charter of the International Military Tribunal (1945) 85 UNTS 251
Charter of the United Nations (1945) 33 UNTS 933
Code of Criminal Procedure of Ukraine (2020). https://cjad.nottingham.ac.uk/documents/implementations/pdf/Ukraine-Criminal_Procedure_Code_amend_2020.pdf. Accessed 28 September 2025
Committee of Ministers, Council of Europe (2023) Resolution CM/Res (2023) Establishing the Enlarged Partial Agreement on the Register of Damage Caused by the Aggression of the Russian Federation against Ukraine. https://rd4u.coe.int/documents/358068/372244/CM_Res%282023%293+-+Statute.pdf/2cebbb65-c86d-61c6-06c2-dca378ecd900?t=1708702115594. Accessed 8 August 2025
Convention (I) for the Amelioration of the Condition of the Wounded and Sick in Armed Forces in the Field (1949)
Council of Europe (2025) Draft Resolution Establishing the Enlarged Partial Agreement on the Management Committee of the Special Tribunal for the Crime of Aggression against Ukraine, dated June 18, 2025. https://www.riigiteataja.ee/aktilisa/2170/2202/6002/760XV_Ukraina_ingl_k_L1.pdf. Accessed 28 September 2025
Criminal Code of the Republic of Belarus (1999)
Criminal Code of the Russian Federation No. 63-Fz, as amended (1996)
Criminal Code of Ukraine, No 2341-III from 5 April 2001 (2024). https://zakon.rada.gov.ua/laws/show/en/2341-14#Text. Accessed 28 September 2025
European Convention on Human Rights (1953) ETS No. 005
European Court of Human Rights (2009) *Zolotukhin and Human Rights Training Institute of the Paris Bar Association (Intervening) v. Russia*, Merits and Just Satisfaction, App. No. 14939/03, ECHR 2009-I 291, IHRL 3277
International Center for the Prosecution of the Crime of Aggression Against Ukraine (ICPA) (nd). https://www.eurojust.europa.eu/intemational-centre-for-theprosecution-of-the-crime-of-aggression-against-ukraine. Accessed 28 September 2025

International Court of Justice (2002) *Arrest Warrant of 11 April 2000 (Democratic Republic of Congo v. Belgium)*, Judgment, 2002 ICJ Rep. 3
International Criminal Court (2019) *Prosecutor v. Omar Hassan Ahmad Al-Bashir*, Judgment in the Jordan Referral re Al-Bashir Appeal, No. ICC-02/05-01/09 OA2
International Criminal Tribunal for the former Yugoslavia (2003) *Prosecutor v. Krnojelac*, Case No. T-97-25-A, Appellate Judgment
International Criminal Tribunal for the former Yugoslavia (1999) *Prosecutor v. Tadić*, Case No. IT-94-1-A, Appellate Judgment
International Military Tribunal for the Far East (1953) Dissentient Judgment
International Military Tribunal for the Far East (1946) Special Proclamation by the Supreme Commander to the Allied Powers at Tokyo, as amended
Interview with a Participant in the Core Group Negotiations, 25 July 2025
Interview with a Participant in the Core Group Negotiations, 19 September 2025
Law on the Establishment of the Extraordinary Chambers, with Inclusion of Amendments (2004) NS/RKM/1004/006. https://cjad.nottingham.ac.uk/documents/implementations/pdf/Cambodia-Extraordinary_Chambers_2004.pdf Accessed 12 May 2025. Accessed 28 September 2025
Law of Ukraine (2025) On Amendments to the Criminal and Criminal Procedure Codes of Ukraine in Connection with the Ratification of the Rome Statute of the International Criminal Court and Amendments thereto, Bulletin of the Verkhovna Rada (VVR), No. 10. https://zakon.rada.gov.ua/laws/show/4012-20#n33 [read in translation]. Accessed 17 September 2025
Parliamentary Assembly (2023) Resolution 2482, Legal and Human Rights Aspects of the Russian Federation's Aggression against Ukraine
Parliamentary Assembly (2024) Resolution 15998, Legal and Human Rights Aspects of the Russian Federation's Aggression against Ukraine
Rome Statute of the International Criminal Court (1998) 2187 UNTS 90, as amended
Statute of the Special Tribunal for the Crime of Aggression against Ukraine (2025). https://search.coe.int/cm?i=0900001680b678ca. Accessed 28 September 2025
United Nations General Assembly, International Law Commission (2025) Immunity of State Officials from Foreign Criminal Jurisdiction, A/CN.4/L.1017. https://documents.un.org/doc/undoc/ltd/g25/076/63/pdf/g2507663.pdf. Accessed 28 September 2025
United Nations General Assembly Resolution 3314 (XXIX) (1974)
United Nations General Assembly Resolution ES-11/1 (2022)
United Nations General Assembly Resolution 79/184 (2024)
United Nations Security Council Resolution 1315 (2000)
United Nations Security Council Resolution 155 (2022)

Chapter 8
Advancing Peace and Justice More Broadly: The Need to Harmonize the International Criminal Court's Jurisdiction over All Four of Its Crimes

Contents

Abstract This book has focused on accountability for the crime of aggression in the situation of Ukraine. Yet, that accountability should not be pursued in only one situation, as the selective enforcement of justice is inherently problematic and, at most, a second-best solution. For this reason, some of those working on the establishment of a special tribunal for the crime of aggression in the situation of Ukraine have also insisted on broader accountability regarding the crime. The most obvious route is to amend the Rome Statute of the International Criminal Court ("ICC"), which at present creates fairly limited jurisdiction over the crime of aggression. To address this problem, States Parties to the Rome Statute have submitted a proposal to harmonize the ICC's jurisdiction over all four of the ICC's core crimes, which would create considerably more jurisdiction over the crime of aggression before the ICC than at present. Yet powerful states, to date, have successfully blocked this reform agenda, delaying negotiations until 2029. This chapter details the amendment proposal and how a limited group of influential states were able to derail adoption of a harmonization amendment at the 7–9 July 2025 Special Session of the ICC's Assembly of States Parties. It also discusses why harmonization of jurisdiction is imperative in order to attempt to enforce and potentially deter the crime of aggression more broadly and not only in the situation of Ukraine.

J. Trahan, *The Crime of Aggression and Russia's Invasion of Ukraine*,
https://doi.org/10.1007/978-94-6265-763-2_8

Keywords Gap in ICC jurisdiction · Harmonization of jurisdiction · Rome Statute amendment proposal · Working Group on Amendments · Special Session of the Assembly of States Parties

8.1 Introduction

This chapter acknowledges that creating a tribunal to adjudicate the crime of aggression in the situation of Ukraine would not resolve the gap in ICC jurisdiction that exists vis-à-vis the crime. This must be resolved if aggression is to be meaningfully prosecuted and state actors deterred (to the extent possible) from committing the crime in the future. The chapter considers why States Parties to the Rome Statute[1] of the International Criminal Court ("ICC") should amend the Statute (specifically, the Kampala crime of aggression amendments)[2] to harmonize the ICC's jurisdiction over all four of its core crimes. Such an amendment would create considerably more jurisdiction before the ICC over the crime of aggression than presently exists. The chapter makes the case that there is no coherent reason for the ICC to have only the sliver of jurisdiction that it possesses over the crime, a situation that only entrenches double-standards, exceptionalism, and impunity. Harmonizing the ICC's jurisdiction would also provide a broader answer to states that question the focus on the crime of aggression only in the situation of Ukraine. It would make clear that this is not a crime that should be enforced only in one situation, but should be prosecuted more systematically in order to make a meaningful contribution to global stability and world peace. Unfortunately, in the Special Session of the ICC's Assembly of States Parties ("ASP") held in July 2025, a limited group of powerful states was able to block the negotiations that could have resulted in the ICC having more jurisdiction over the crime, deferring the topic to future negotiations to be held in 2029.[3]

8.2 The Gap in the ICC's Jurisdiction over the Crime of Aggression

Chapter 3 explained the existing gap in the ICC's jurisdiction that has resulted in the ICC's lack of jurisdiction over the crime in the situation of Ukraine.[4] That chapter additionally described the negotiations that led to the agreement by States Parties as to the definition of the crime of aggression,[5] now contained in Article 8*bis* of the

[1] Rome Statute of the International Criminal Court (1998) 2187 UNTS 90 (as amended) ("Rome Statute (1998) (as amended)").

[2] International Criminal Court, Assembly of States Parties 2010.

[3] For the ASP resolution deferring negotiations until 2029, see International Criminal Court 2025b.

[4] See Chap. 3, Sect. 3.2.5.

[5] See Chap. 3, Sect. 3.2.2 (definition).

ICC's Rome Statute,[6] as well as agreement[7] on the conditions for the ICC's exercise of jurisdiction over the crime.[8] A brief recap will detail how the ICC's jurisdiction over the crime currently operates.

The ICC's general default jurisdictional rule that is applicable to the crimes of genocide, war crimes, and crimes against humanity is found in Articles 12 and 13 of the Rome Statute. It provides for ICC jurisdiction over: (a) crimes committed on the territory of a States Party;[9] (b) crimes committed by the nationals of a State Party;[10] and (c) crimes committed in a situation referred to the ICC by the UN Security Council.[11] As to the crime of aggression, (c) is also true—i.e., the Security Council may make referrals regarding the crime.[12] However, as to (a) and (b) (which apply to situations initiated by State Party referral or the Prosecutor acting *proprio motu*), a different jurisdictional regime exists vis-à-vis the crime of aggression.

Although the ICC does possess jurisdiction over the crime of aggression when its work is initiated by State Party referral or the Prosecutor acting *proprio motu*, as to (a) crimes committed on the territory of a State Party and (b) crimes committed by the nationals of a State Party, two carve-outs to that jurisdiction exist. Under Rome Statute Article 15*bis*(4), a State Party may "opt out" of the ICC's jurisdiction over the crime of aggression,[13] and under Article 15*bis*(5), the nationals of, and crimes committed on the territories of, non-States Parties are completely excluded from the ICC's jurisdiction over the crime.[14] These two provisions were negotiated in 2010 at the Review Conference held in Kampala, Uganda.[15] The second carve-out is the reason there is no jurisdiction over the crime of aggression committed in the territory of Ukraine, as Russia, as well as Belarus and North Korea,[16] are

---

[6] See Rome Statute (1998) (as amended), note 1, Article 8*bis*.

[7] See Chap. 3, Sects. 3.2.3–3.2.4 (jurisdiction).

[8] See Rome Statute (1998) (as amended), note 1, Articles 15*bis*, 15*ter*.

[9] Ibid., Article 12(2)(a) (including crimes committed on board a vessel or aircraft where the state of registration is a State Party). A non-State Party may also lodge an ad hoc declaration accepting jurisdiction. See ibid., Article 12(3).

[10] Ibid., Article 12(2)(b).

[11] Ibid., Article 13(b).

[12] See ibid., Article 15*ter*.

[13] Article 15*bis*(4) states:

> The Court may, in accordance with article 12, exercise jurisdiction over a crime of aggression, arising from an act of aggression committed by a State Party, unless that State Party has previously declared that it does not accept such jurisdiction by lodging a declaration with the Registrar. The withdrawal of such a declaration may be effected at any time and shall be considered by the State Party within three years.

Ibid., Article 15*bis*(4).

[14] Article 15*bis*(5) states: "In respect of a State that is not a party to this Statute, the Court shall not exercise its jurisdiction over the crime of aggression when committed by that State's nationals or on its territory". Ibid., Article 15*bis*(5).

[15] See International Criminal Court, Assembly of States Parties 2010.

[16] For the roles of Russia, Belarus, and North Korea, see Chap. 4, Sect. 4.2.

all non-States Parties.[17] That answer does not change despite Ukraine having first accepted the ICC's jurisdiction on an ad hoc basis[18] and later ratified the Rome Statute, including the Kampala crime of aggression amendments.[19] Under the present jurisdictional regime, the only method by which the ICC could possess jurisdiction over the crime of aggression in the situation of Ukraine would be through a referral by the UN Security Council.[20] Such a referral is an obvious non-starter since Russia, as a permanent member of the UN Security Council, would be able to veto it.[21] Because the crime of aggression is committed in both the "aggressor" and "victim" state, under normal jurisdictional rules, the fact that the crime is impacting in Ukraine (part of it is occurring there) would normally suffice to create jurisdiction given Ukraine's consent to the ICC's exercise of jurisdiction.[22] That, however, is not true if the nationals of non-States Parties and crimes committed on the territories of non-States Parties are exempt from the ICC's jurisdiction as to the crime, as is currently the case.

After the 2010 Review Conference, jurisdiction was arguably further limited in 2017, when the ICC's ASP decided to activate the ICC's jurisdiction over the crime.[23] The United Kingdom and France (joined by a handful of aligned states)[24] insisted on a narrow interpretation of the 2010 Kampala crime of aggression amendments. Under their interpretation, *both* the aggressor state *and* the victim state need to be Rome Statute States Parties that have ratified the crime of aggression amendments

---

[17] For Rome Statute States Parties, see United Nations Treaty Collection nd-a.

[18] For Ukraine's Article 12(3) declarations, see International Criminal Court nd-a.

[19] Ukraine became a State Party to the Rome Statute on 1 January 2025. See International Criminal Court 2025a.

[20] Rome Statute (1998) (as amended), note 1, Article 15*ter* (Security Council referrals).

[21] Charter of the United Nations (1945) 33 UNTS 933 ("UN Charter (1945)"), Article 27(3) (veto power). For a general theory that legal limits to the veto inherently exist due to other obligations of international law, reference is made to Trahan J (2020) Existing Legal Limits to Security Council Veto Power in the Face of Atrocity Crimes. Cambridge University Press, Cambridge.

[22] As noted in Chap. 7, Gaiane Nuridzhanian explains:

> According to customary international law rules on national jurisdiction, a state can criminalise any acts committed in its own territory, and undertake any actions within its own territory necessary to enforce its criminal laws. The territorial jurisdiction of the state extends also to crimes initiated abroad but completed on that state's territory. Ukraine may therefore assert its territorial jurisdiction with respect to crimes initiated abroad but completed on its territory.

Nuridzhanian 2025, p. 11 (internal citations omitted). See also Grzebyk 2025 ("every state has a right to prosecute crimes committed on its territory (territorial jurisdiction)"; "[i]f the state has a right to execute jurisdiction in particular circumstances, it has also the sovereign right to authorize an international court to execute its jurisdiction on behalf of this state").

[23] Jurisdiction did not immediately activate after the Kampala Review Conference, but was subject to a delay. One year needed to pass after thirty States Parties had ratified or accepted the Kampala crime of aggression amendments, and one more decision by the ASP was needed after 1 January 2017. See Rome Statute (1998) (as amended), note 1, Articles 15*bis*(2)–(3);15*ter*(2)–(3).

[24] See Kreβ 2018, p. 9 (citing Canada, Colombia, Japan, and Norway joining the French/UK reading, and Liechtenstein, Argentina, Botswana, Samoa, Slovenia, and Switzerland opposing it).

and the aggressor state must not have opted out of jurisdiction.[25] No such agreement had been negotiated in 2010.[26] Yet, during negotiations in 2017, the United Kingdom and France prevailed in having their interpretation reflected in paragraph (2) of the ASP's resolution that activated the ICC's jurisdiction over the crime.[27]

However, after the decision to adopt the resolution, approximately ten States Parties took the floor to state that that was *not the agreement* as to jurisdiction.[28] These states insisted that it would suffice for *either* the aggressor *or* the victim state to be a State Party that had ratified the Kampala crime of aggression amendments as long as the aggressor State Party had not opted out of jurisdiction (the "broad interpretation").[29] Furthermore, these states succeeded in preserving that argument, at least to some extent, by adding language to the resolution that provides a reminder that the ICC's judges will be the final arbiters of jurisdiction.[30] The debate over this interpretative question remains unresolved.[31] However, that question is *not* at

---

[25] Ibid., p. 8.

[26] That the UK/French reading does not make sense is illustrated by the fact that under their reading, a State Party would have to ratify the Kampala crime of aggression amendments to be able to opt out of them. But why would a State Party do that if it could just decide not to ratify? The UK/French reading renders Article 15*bis*(4) a useless provision. Moreover, the rules on treaty interpretation disfavor an interpretation that would render treaty language a nullity. See International Law Commission (1966) Draft Articles on the Law of Treaties with Commentaries, Yearbook of the ILC, Vol. II, Commentary to Article 31, p. 219, para 6 ("Properly limited and applied, the [principle of effectiveness] requires that a provision be interpreted so as to give it the fullest effect and not to render it meaningless or ineffective"); Oxford Reference 2014 ("An approach to treaty interpretation [requires] that a treaty must be interpreted so as to give meaning and effect to all its terms rather than rendering them redundant or meaningless"); Ratner 2014, p. 25 (similar); International Court of Justice (1949) *Corfu Channel (United Kingdom v. Albania)*, Judgment of 9 April 1949, ICJ Rep. 1949, p. 24 (similar).

The alternative reading, that all States Parties are "in" the jurisdiction, which is why an "opt out" was created, makes far more sense. Under this reading, all that would be needed would be for one of the aggressor State Party or the victim State Party to have ratified the Kampala crime of aggression amendments and for the aggressor not to have opted out of jurisdiction. See Permanent Mission of Liechtenstein to the United Nations (2013) Handbook: Ratification and Implementation of the Kampala Amendments to the Rome Statute of the ICC, p. 9 ("Permanent Mission of Liechtenstein to the United Nations 2013") ("the amendments must have been ratified by and entered into force for at least one of the States Parties involved – be it the presumed aggressor or the victim State").

[27] International Criminal Court, Assembly of States Parties 2017, para 2.

[28] Trahan 2018b, p. 218.

[29] See, e.g., Permanent Mission of Liechtenstein to the United Nations 2013, note 26, p. 9.

[30] International Criminal Court, Assembly of State Parties 2017, para 3 ("Reaffirm[ing] paragraph 1 of article 40 and paragraph 1 of article 119 of the Rome Statute in relation to the judicial independence of the judges of the Court"). See also Rome Statute (1998) (as amended), note 1, Article 119(1) ("Any dispute concerning the judicial functions of the Court shall be settled by the decision of the Court").

[31] See Trahan 2018b (arguing that the modification of jurisdiction was invalid); McDougall 2024 (arguing that the Activating Resolution did not amount to a "subsequent agreement" under the Vienna Convention on the Law of Treaties and that if the resolution is only a "supplementary means of interpretation", it would be of lesser weight when interpreting the Kampala amendments); McDougall 2021 (setting forth the arguments in detail). Compare Kreß 2018, p. 12 ("This language is no more than a statement of the obvious fact that the ASP cannot replace the Court as the judicial

issue regarding the situation of Ukraine, because it is the non-State Party carve-out, mentioned above, that is the impediment to the ICC's exercise of jurisdiction over the crime of aggression in the situation of Ukraine.

If the UK/French reading of the Activating Resolution is correct, then the ICC's jurisdiction over the crime of aggression is *truly minimal.* It would only exist if *both* the aggressor state *and* the victim state are Rome Statute States Parties that have ratified the Kampala crime of aggression amendments and the aggressor state has not opted out of jurisdiction. As of late 2025, there are forty-nine States Parties that have ratified the crime of aggression amendments.[32] Thus, only when one of the forty-nine States Parties invades or commits another act of aggression against another of the forty-nine States Parties would jurisdiction over the crime exist before the ICC, as long as the aggressor State Party has not opted out of jurisdiction.[33]

If the "broad interpretation" is correct, only *one* of the States Parties involved, either the aggressor *or* the victim state, would have to have ratified the Kampala crime of aggression amendments, as long as the aggressor state has not opted out of jurisdiction.[34] That creates slightly more ICC jurisdiction over the crime. Yet, under both readings, crimes committed by the nationals of, and on the territories of, non-States Parties are completely excluded from jurisdiction. Furthermore, the possibility of a referral by the UN Security Council of a situation in which the crime of aggression appears to have been committed[35] seems remote.

The fact that, since the ICC's jurisdiction over the crime commenced in 2018,[36] the ICC has been unable to pursue a single crime of aggression investigation or prosecution[37] is ample evidence that the jurisdictional regime is too narrow—under either interpretive approach and given the non-State Party carve-out.

---

body charged with applying the law in complete independence"). For the Vienna Convention on the Law of Treaties, see Vienna Convention on the Law of Treaties (1969) 1155 UNTS 331, 8 ILM 679 ("Vienna Convention on the Law of Treaties").

[32] United Nations Treaty Collection nd-b.

[33] Only two states have exercised such opt out declarations, Guatemala and Kenya. See International Criminal Court nd-b. Because these two States have not ratified the amendments, their decision to opt-out can be interpreted as state practice validating the broad interpretation of jurisdiction.

[34] For more on the "broad" and "narrow" interpretations, see also McDougall 2024, pp. 546–47.

[35] See Rome Statute (1998) (as amended), note 1, Article 15*ter* (Security Council referrals).

[36] International Criminal Court, Assembly of State Parties 2017 (activating jurisdiction effective 17 July 2018).

[37] This is not because there is no aggression occurring. For one discussion of annexation and related threats, see, e.g., Niyo 2025 (considering the full-scale Russian invasion of Ukraine, Israel's continued military activities in the occupied Palestinian territories, Morocco's assertive claims over Western Sahara, and Rwanda's alleged involvement in the eastern Democratic Republic of the Congo (DRC) through a proxy, the March 23 Movement (M23)).

8.3 Why Harmonize Jurisdiction over Rome Statute Crimes

The glaring lack of jurisdiction over the crime of aggression in the situation of Ukraine has highlighted these restrictions contained in the ICC's jurisdictional regime. This in turn has prompted States Parties to try to ameliorate the situation by proposing an amendment to the Rome Statute that would harmonize the ICC's jurisdiction over all four Rome Statute crimes[38] (a "harmonization amendment").[39] As discussed in previous chapters, this route was not pursued as a solution in the situation of Ukraine, as it was predicted that the amendment might not be accomplished in time to encompass the situation and would not apply retroactively.[40]

Numerous reasons exist to support increasing the ICC's jurisdiction over the crime of aggression. First, if aggression is the "supreme" crime, as it was held to be in the Judgment of the International Military Tribunal at Nuremberg,[41] there is no reason it should be subject to such a truncated jurisdictional regime before the ICC.[42] The crime is arguably denominated "supreme" not because it is inherently more important or more serious than the other crimes prosecuted before the Nuremberg Tribunal (war crimes and crimes against humanity),[43] but because it can set off a chain of causation that leads to the commission of all the other crimes, most or all of which would

[38] The ICC possesses jurisdiction over genocide, crimes against humanity, war crimes, and the crime of aggression. See Rome Statute (1998) (as amended), note 1, Article 5.1.

[39] See Costa Rica, Germany, Sierra Leone, Slovenia, and Vanuatu (2025) Proposal of Amendment. https://treaties.un.org/doc/Publication/CN/2025/CN.162.2025-Eng.pdf. Accessed 7 August 2025 ("Amendment Proposal 2025").

[40] The prediction on timing was correct. The proposal for a harmonization amendment that States Parties could have adopted in July 2025 was thwarted, with negotiations delayed until 2029. See Sect. 8.7 (discussing the July 2025 negotiations); see also Rome Statute (1998) (as amended), note 1, Article 24 (prohibition on retroactivity). Annexation is a continuing crime; thus, if the amendment is adopted in 2029 and enters into force in Ukraine, there is some possibility of the ICC exercising jurisdiction, if some form of annexation is occurring at the time.

[41] International Military Tribunal (1946) Judgment of 1 October 1946, in The Trial of German Major War Criminals. Proceedings of the International Military Tribunal Sitting at Nuremberg, Germany, Part 22 (22 August 1946 to 1 October 1946), p. 421 ("IMT Judgment").

[42] Kreß 2025, p. 2 ("there was no principled reason why the crime of aggression should continue to be sidelined in the ICC Statute").

[43] Charter of the International Military Tribunal (1945) 85 UNTS 251, Article 6(b) (war crimes); Article 6(c) (crimes against humanity) ("London Charter 1945"). Genocide, ironically, was not one of the crimes prosecuted at Nuremberg, although the word is referenced in the Indictment. See Nuremberg Trial Proceedings Vol. 1 (nd) Indictment: Count Three, https://avalon.law.yale.edu/imt/count3.asp. Accessed 10 September 2025 ("They conducted deliberate and systematic genocide, [namely], the extermination of racial and national groups, against the civilian populations of certain occupied territories in order to destroy particular races and classes of people and national, racial, or religious groups, particularly Jews, Poles and Gypsies and others".); see also Bass 2000, p. 148 ("One of the great ironies of Nuremberg's legacy is that the tribunal is remembered as a product of Allied horror at the Holocaust, when in fact America and Britain, the two liberal countries that played major roles in deciding what Nuremberg would be, actually focused far more on the criminality of Nazi aggression than on the Holocaust") (footnote omitted); Bass 2000, p. 193 (Churchill conversation

not have occurred absent the aggression. The famous quote from the Nuremberg Judgment is that: "To initiate a war of aggression . . . is not only an international crime; it is the supreme international crime differing only from other war crimes in that it contains within itself the accumulated evil of the whole".[44] As Robert H. Jackson, Chief Prosecutor for the United States at Nuremberg, explained: "the other atrocities were all preparatory to [the war] or done in execution of it".[45]

Second, there is no cogent reason for the non-State Party exclusion from jurisdiction. This simply puts non-State Party nationals and crimes committed on their territories in a position that is above the law, which is anathema to the goals of the Rome Statute as articulated in its preamble.[46] The outcome was driven by the bargaining positions of powerful states during the negotiations,[47] but rests on no sound legal arguments.[48] Non-State Party nationals are bound under the Rome Statute not to commit the crimes of genocide, war crimes, and crimes against humanity on the territory of a State Party (or a state that has accepted the ICC's jurisdiction on an ad hoc basis) or face criminal exposure should they do so.[49] Why should they not be similarly bound as to the crime of aggression?

Third, as mentioned, the inability of the ICC to exercise jurisdiction over the crime of aggression in even a single situation since 17 July 2018—the date when its ability

---

with Anthony Eden: the Holocaust was "probably the greatest and most horrible single crime ever committed in the whole history of the world"), citing Gilbert 1981, p. 341.

44 IMT Judgment, note 41, p. 421.

45 Bass 2000, p. 177, quoting Jackson 1945, p. 299.

46 The preamble:

> **Affirm[s]** that the most serious crimes of concern to the international community as a whole must not go unpunished and that their effective prosecution must be ensured . . . ,
>
> **Determine[s]** to put an end to impunity for the perpetrators of these crimes and thus to contribute to the prevention of such crimes . . . , [and]
>
> **Reaffirm[s]** the Purposes and Principles of the Charter of the United Nations, and in particular that all States shall refrain from the threat or use of force against the territorial integrity or political independence of any State, or in any other manner inconsistent with the Purposes of the United Nations[.]

Rome Statute (1998) (as amended), note 1, Recs 4–5, 7. See also Donat Cattin 2023, p. 93, n 13 (the limitations to the Court's jurisdiction on the crime of aggression "are running counter to the object and purpose of the [Rome] Statute, which is to put an end to impunity of the perpetrators of the [four] core crimes that shock humankind").

47 The United States was a strong proponent of the non-State Party exemption during the negotiations in Kampala. According to Carrie McDougall, "the US was the prime mover, but the exclusion of non-States Parties was a unanimous position of the [permanent members] and some of their closest allies". Trahan 2024.

48 Kreβ 2025, p. 2 ("the existing state of legal affairs therefore constituted a double standard reflecting the interests of certain military powers").

49 See Rome Statute (1998) (as amended), note 1, Article 12(2). The Trump Administration declines to acknowledge this provision. See Trump 2025 (as amended to include additional designees) ("The ICC has no jurisdiction over the United States or Israel, as neither country is party to the Rome Statute or a member of the ICC").

to exercise jurisdiction over the crime commenced[50]—speaks volumes about the fact that jurisdiction is too minimal to be of practical utility.

Fourth, when jurisdiction is so limited, States Parties that have ratified the Kampala crime of aggression amendments in the hope of protecting their states and nationals from the crime of aggression fail to receive adequate protection.[51] In many or even most situations, the ICC will lack jurisdiction over the crime even if the State Party seeking protection has ratified the amendments.[52] Smaller and mid-sized states that lack powerful armies and seek the protection of the law are thus unable to achieve the full protection that the jurisdiction of the Rome Statute could otherwise provide.[53]

Fifth, because the ICC cannot exercise jurisdiction over the crime of aggression in so many situations, the ICC is unable to be in a position to deter leaders from committing the crime of aggression.[54] This is quite serious considering that the crime enforces the core norm contained in Article 2(4) of the UN Charter against the use of force.[55] For example, China is a non-State Party; thus, its nationals and aggression committed on (e.g., launched from) its territory are completely outside the ICC's jurisdictional regime. The same is true vis-à-vis the nationals of any non-State Party. Even aggression by a State Party is not necessarily encompassed by the

---

[50] See International Criminal Court, Assembly of State Parties 2017.

[51] The UN Charter's use of force provisions are designed to protect all states. See UN Charter (1945), note 21, Article 2(4) (prohibition of the use of force); supplemented by ch. VII (Security Council force authorizations); Article 51 (right to self-defense). Yet, whether violations trigger a response depends on the politics of voting in the UN Security Council. See note 170 (critique of vetoes). On the limitations on General Assembly powers, see notes 60–64 and accompanying text.

[52] How much protection they would receive is impacted by whether the "narrow" or "broad" interpretation of jurisdiction is correct. See Sect. 8.2. Yet, under either interpretation, as explained, States Parties are not protected from aggression committed by the nationals of a non-State Party or crimes committed on the territory of a non-State Party—even if the victim State Party has ratified the Kampala crime of aggression amendments. Ibid.

[53] Gevorgyan 2025 ("Small or structurally vulnerable states, such as Timor-Leste, the Democratic Republic of the Congo, Vanuatu, Nigeria, Ukraine, Ghana, Armenia and Senegal, supported [harmonization of jurisdiction over all four Rome Statute crimes]. For these states, strengthening the ICC's jurisdiction over aggression is not abstract legal idealism but a concrete strategy for survival in a system that offers little deterrence against unlawful force". "These states seek an international order where legal norms constrain the use of force precisely because they are the ones most exposed when those norms break down").

[54] Grzebyk 2025 ("Only prevention of aggression allows for avoiding deaths on both sides of the conflict – the aggressor's and its victim's"); Gevorgyan 2025 (the current "gap in enforcement . . . carries serious consequences, especially for states vulnerable to unlawful uses of force, and has contributed to the persistence of unchecked aggression around the world").

[55] See UN Charter (1945), note 21, Article 2(4) ("All Members shall refrain in their international relations from the threat or use of force against the territorial integrity or political independent of any state, or in any other manner inconsistent with the Purposes of the United Nations"); see also Rome Statute, note 1, Article 8*bis*(2) ("For the purpose of paragraph 1, 'act of aggression' means the use of armed force by a State against the sovereignty, territorial integrity or political independence of another State, or in any other manner inconsistent with the Charter of the United Nations . . . ."). There are only slight differences between these provisions: (a) UN Charter Article 2(4) also prohibits the "threat" of the use of force, which is not contained in Rome Statute Article 8*bis*, and (b) Rome Statute Article 8*bis* mentions "sovereignty" whereas UN Charter Article 2(4) does not.

ICC's jurisdiction.[56] While it is difficult to demonstrate that international criminal tribunals create deterrence, some studies suggest they have the potential to do so.[57] Yet if there is no jurisdiction and thus not even the *possibility* of ICC investigation or prosecution, then any potential to create deterrence is squandered.

Sixth, if an aggressor state is also a permanent member of the UN Security Council (or a close ally of a permanent member), aggression by the permanent member (or its close ally) almost certainly will not be condemned by that body nor be the subject of other actions by the Council (such as the imposition of sanctions, a no-fly zone, or other coercive or non-coercive measures).[58] Thus, there is likely to be neither individual criminal responsibility nor ramifications imposed by the Security Council.[59] While the General Assembly may address issues when the Security Council fails to act—particularly in a situation where a Uniting for Peace resolution is adopted[60]—there are powers that only the Security Council possesses.[61] Although the General Assembly can condemn aggression, as it has done in the situation of Ukraine,[62] it cannot *impose* or *mandate* any of the forceful, non-forceful, or interim measures that the Security Council can mandate.[63] In almost all situations, the General Assembly can at most *recommend* measures to be taken in the face of a breach of international peace and security.[64]

Seventh, if the ICC's jurisdiction over the crime of aggression is not reformed, then states will need to make do with ad hoc solutions, as is being pursued with the

---

[56] See Sect. 8.2 (explaining jurisdictional limitations).

[57] On whether deterrence is effective at the international level, see, e.g., McAllister 2020; Miller 2023. Deterrence was one of the goals behind the establishment of the Nuremberg Tribunal. Henry Stimson, a crucial US proponent of holding trials at Nuremberg, wrote: "We should always have in mind the necessity of punishing effectively enough to bring home to the German people the wrongdoing done in their name, and thus prevent similar conduct in the future . . .". Bass 2000, p. 157, quoting McCloy-Stimson conversation, 28 August 1944, in Smith 1981, p. 23.

[58] For the Security Council's ability to impose provisional measures, non-forceful measures, and forceful measures, see UN Charter (1945), note 21, Articles 40–42.

[59] Some measures can be taken on a bilateral basis or through a regional arrangement. See, e.g., European Council, Council of the European Union nd.

[60] A Uniting for Peace resolution triggers the UN General Assembly meeting in an Emergency Special Session when the UN Security Council is deadlocked. For the first Uniting for Peace resolution, see United Nations General Assembly Resolution 377A (V) (1950); for the Uniting for Peace resolution passed in the situation of Ukraine, see United Nations Security Council Resolution 2623 (2022).

[61] See Andrassy 1956, p. 572 ("The [Uniting for Peace] Resolution grants the Assembly no greater powers than those it has under Article 10 and 11, paragraph 2"); Carswell 2013, p. 476 ("[T]he resolution serves to reveal the latent potential of the Assembly already residing within the UN Charter, and constructs a procedural framework for its exercise").

[62] United Nations General Assembly Resolution ES-11/1 (2022).

[63] UN Charter (1945), note 21, Articles 40–42.

[64] Compare ibid., ch. IV (UN General Assembly powers) with chs. V–VII (UN Security Council powers). The General Assembly, though, has been able to create an investigative mechanism—the International, Impartial Independent Mechanism ("IIIM") to assist in the investigation and prosecution of serious crimes under international law committed in Syria since March 2011. See United Nations General Assembly Resolution 71/248 (2016).

effort to establish the Special Tribunal for the Crime of Aggression against Ukraine (the "Special Tribunal").[65] Yet, the ICC was created to move beyond the ad hoc approach to the creation of international criminal tribunals that was pursued during the 1990s.[66] It was hoped that a permanent institution would obviate the need for ad hoc solutions.[67] Returning to an ad hoc approach when the ICC cannot exercise jurisdiction over the crime (a) risks undermining the role of the ICC, (b) is highly inefficient, (c) will result in justice only selectively enforced, and (d) where there is no will for selective enforcement, will result in impunity.

Eighth, harmonizing jurisdiction would be an expression of support for the ICC and for strengthening its role. It was always envisioned that the ICC would be able to investigate and prosecute the crime of aggression, starting with the 1998 Rome negotiations when the crime was included in the Rome Statute as one of the four core crimes over which the ICC would have jurisdiction.[68] States Parties considered it to be a core crime from the beginning. States should define the conditions for the exercise of jurisdiction in a way that acknowledges the crime's role and importance in the international criminal justice system that states intended to create at the Rome Conference.

Ninth, harmonization would cure the fragmented, two-tiered approach to jurisdiction that currently exists under the Rome Statute.[69] States Parties that have ratified the Kampala crime of aggression amendments would be asked to ratify the new harmonization amendment. Once those States Parties do so, only one jurisdictional regime would be in place for all four Rome Statute crimes.[70]

---

[65] See Chap. 7 for discussion of the Special Tribunal.

[66] The International Criminal Tribunal for the former Yugoslavia and the International Criminal Tribunal for Rwanda were established during this time period. See United Nations Security Council Resolution 827 (1993); United Nations Security Council Resolution 955 (1994).

[67] With the creation of the ICC, there was initial optimism that the court would be able to address all high-level cases of genocide, war crimes, and crimes against humanity. More than twenty-five years after the 1998 Rome negotiations, it has been recognized that the ICC cannot address all such cases. Thus, there will still be a need for ad hoc tribunals, such as the hybrid Special Criminal Court in the Central African Republic, as well as cases brought in domestic courts under universal jurisdiction or other jurisdictional theories. For background on the Special Criminal Court, see, e.g., Labuda 2018; on the need for multiple levels of accountability, see Trahan 2018a (interviews with tribunal prosecutors on the need for the ICC, hybrid tribunals, and domestic prosecutions).

[68] Rome Statute (1998) (as amended), note 1, Article 5.1. For states that supported the inclusion of the crime of aggression during the 1998 Rome negotiations, see Chap. 3, Sect. 3.2.1.

[69] See Sect. 8.2 (explaining the different jurisdictional regimes as to genocide, war crimes, and the crime against humanity on the one hand, and the crime of aggression on the other).

[70] Once an amended version of Article 15*bis* is adopted, it was not envisioned that States Parties would still have the option to ratify or accept the unamended (i.e., original) version of Article 15*bis*. Trahan 2025e. Minor differences in jurisdiction would still exist. See text accompanying note 114 (six month delay; Pre-Trial Division authorization).

These are some of the reasons the ICC's limited jurisdictional regime over the crime of aggression must be addressed if the ICC is to play a meaningful role in prosecuting the crime and perhaps deterring its commission.

8.4 The Proposal to Harmonize Jurisdiction

Given the desire by a number of states to harmonize the ICC's jurisdiction over all four Rome Statute crimes, a fairly straightforward amendment proposal was tabled by States Parties in the spring of 2025 that would eliminate the ICC's exceptional jurisdictional regime regarding the crime of aggression.[71] The proposed amendment to Rome Statute Article 15*bis* would subject the crime of aggression to the Rome Statute's general jurisdictional regime, contained in Rome Statute Article 12, in situations where a State Party has made a referral or the Prosecutor acts *proprio motu*. The UN Security Council's ability to refer situations involving the crime, addressed in a different article of the Rome Statute, would remain unaffected by the amendment.[72]

8.4.1 The Text of the Amendment Proposal

Civil society organizations ("CSOs") initially promulgated the idea that an amendment was needed to harmonize the ICC's jurisdiction over all four core crimes. Parliamentarians for Global Action ("PGA") first proposed such an amendment in 2022[73] with the Global Institute for the Prevention of Aggression ("GIPA") following.[74] GIPA then issued a proposed amendment text in September 2023.[75] CSOs and States Parties also focused on the need for a harmonization amendment at side-events held during ASP sessions in 2023 and 2024.[76]

---

[71] See Amendment Proposal 2025, note 39.

[72] See Rome Statute (1998) (as amended), note 1, Article 15*ter* (Security Council referrals). Article 15*ter* is not part of the amendment proposal. See Amendment Proposal 2025.

[73] Parliamentarians for Global Action 2022 (calling "for the removal of the procedural conditions of Article 15 *bis* that exempt nationals of States Non Parties to the Statute").

[74] See Global Institute for the Prevention of Aggression 2022. For the Executive Council, Steering Committee, and Council of Advisers of GIPA, see Global Institute for the Prevention of Aggression nd-a. The author serves as Convenor of GIPA.

[75] Global Institute for the Prevention of Aggression nd-b (proposing an amendment text and discussing entry into force). By early 2025, GIPA consolidated its support for the entry into force procedure in Article 121(5). For discussion of entry into force, see Sect. 8.4.2.

[76] See Global Institute for the Prevention of Aggression 2024 News (side-event entitled "Reviewing the ICC's Jurisdiction over the Crime of Aggression: Addressing a Double Standard in International Law" sponsored by Costa Rica, The Gambia, Liechtenstein, Germany, Sierra Leone, Slovenia, Vanuatu, European Center for Constitutional and Human Rights ("ECCHR") and GIPA); Global Institute for the Prevention of Aggression 2023 News (on 8 December 2023, the Permanent Missions of Costa Rica, Estonia, Germany, Liechtenstein and Vanuatu to

In January 2023, Germany committed to reform of the ICC's jurisdiction over the crime of aggression and took on the leadership of a Group of Friends (states committed to that purpose), which eventually consisted of 38 States Parties.[77] In November 2024, the Permanent Representatives of Costa Rica, Germany, Sierra Leone, Slovenia, and Vanuatu sent an informal "discussion paper" to all States Parties.[78] By resolution dated 6 December 2024, the ASP invited the Chair of the ASP's Working Group on Amendments "to convene regular meetings of the Working Group starting early in 2025 to facilitate discussions on the Kampala amendments on the crime of aggression in preparation [for a] Special Session of the Assembly [to be held] from 7 to 9 July 2025 . . .".[79] On 27 January 2025, the current and former Presidents of the ICC's ASP also published a joint statement calling for harmonization of jurisdiction.[80]

During the spring and early summer of 2025, the Working Group on Amendments (a standing body that considers Rome Statute amendment proposals)[81] devoted monthly meetings to the topic, under the able chairmanship of Colombian Ambassador Juan José Quintana.[82] A drafting session held from 27–28 March 2025 hosted by Switzerland for the Group of Friends in Glion, Switzerland, furthered the drafting process. Additionally, a series of regional meetings held in Brasilia, São Paolo, Accra, Seoul, and Berlin, helped galvanize State Party support for the amendment.[83] On 4

---

the UN, and GIPA, sponsored the panel "The ICC and the Crime of Aggression: Harmonizing Jurisdiction and Promoting Universality"); Assembly of State Parties Side Event on the Review of the Kampala Amendments on the Crime of Aggression: Perspective of African States Parties, co-hosted by Ghana, Malawi, Sierra Leone, Switzerland and Africa Legal Aid ("AFLA") (2024). https://www.africalegalaid.com/blog/asp-side-event-on-thenbspreview-of-the-kampala-amendments-on-the-crime-of-aggression-perspective-of-african-states-parties. Accessed 12 September 2025.

77 Baerbock 2023 (Germany's commitment); Kreβ 2025, p. 2 ("consultations were undertaken within a 'Group of Friends', convened by Germany"); Trahan 2025e (38 States Parties in the Group of Friends).

78 See Permanent Missions of Costa Rica, Sierra Leone, Vanuatu, Germany and Slovenia to the United Nations 2024.

79 ICC-ASP/23/Res.1 (2024) Strengthening the International Criminal Court and the Assembly of States Parties, para 163. The Kampala resolution whereby the crime of aggression amendments were adopted called for a review to occur seven years after the start of the ICC's exercise of jurisdiction over the crime. See International Criminal Court, Assembly of States Parties 2010, para 3. Given that the ICC's jurisdiction commenced in 2018 (see International Criminal Court, Assembly of State Parties 2017), the review needed to be in 2025.

80 Just Security 2025 (signed by Päivi Kaukoranta, Silvia Fernández de Gurmendi, O-Gon Kwon, Sidiki Kaba, Tiina Intelmann, Christian Wenaweser, Bruno Stagno Ugarte, and Prince Zeid Ra'ad Al Hussein).

81 For some of its earlier work, see, e.g., Trahan 2012 (describing Rome Statute amendment proposals before the Working Group on Amendments at that time).

82 The Working Group on Amendments held six formal meetings: 30 January, 7 March, 1 April, 6 May, 9 June and 1 July 2025. International Criminal Court, Assembly of States Parties 2025.

83 The Brasilia (25 March), São Paolo (27 March), Seoul (10 April), and Berlin (6 June) meetings were sponsored by Germany. The Accra meeting (20–21 May) was organized by the civil society organization AFLA. A briefing session for States Parties was also held at the African Union Mission

April 2025, after the Glion meeting, Costa Rica, Germany, Sierra Leone, Slovenia, and Vanuatu formally tabled an amendment proposal which they sent to the UN Secretary-General for circulation.[84]

The text of the amendment proposal provided:

Amendments to Article 15 *bis* of the Rome Statute

Article 15bis (4) and (5) are replaced by the following text inserted after Article 15bis (3):

4. The Court may, in accordance with Article 12, exercise jurisdiction over a crime of aggression if one or more of the following States have ratified or accepted the aggression amendments, or have accepted the exercise of the jurisdiction of the Court over the crime of aggression in accordance with paragraph 5:
   (a) The State on the territory of which the conduct in question occurred or, if the crime was committed on board a vessel or aircraft, the State of registration of that vessel or aircraft;
   (b) The State of which the person accused of the crime is a national.
5. If the acceptance of a State that has not ratified or accepted the aggression amendments, or that is not a Party to this Statute, is required under paragraph 4, that State may, by declaration lodged with the Registrar, accept the exercise of jurisdiction by the Court over the crime of aggression in accordance with Article 12, paragraph 3.[85]

The amendment, which was virtually identical to the text proposed by GIPA,[86] would replace the text that created the exceptional jurisdiction regime (Article 15*bis*(4) and (5)) and restore the crime of aggression to the ICC's general jurisdictional regime in Article 12.[87] Paragraph (4) of the amendment would restore the provisions of Rome Statute Article 12(2) and Paragraph (5) of the amendment would restore the provisions of Rome Statute Article 12(3). Thus, pursuant to amended Paragraph (4), the ICC would possess jurisdiction over the crime of aggression: (a) when committed by the nationals of a State Party or (b) when committed on the territory of a State Party[88]—*without carve-outs* vis-à-vis non-State Party nationals or crimes committed on their territories or the possibility for States Parties to file opt out declarations. And, as provided in amended Paragraph (5), Article 12(3) ad hoc declarations would be restored vis-à-vis the crime of aggression.[89] Such declarations allow a state to accept

to the United Nations on 13 June 2025, sponsored by Switzerland and Sierra Leone. See note 124 and accompanying text (AU meeting).

[84] Amendment Proposal 2025, note 39.

[85] Ibid.

[86] See Global Institute for the Prevention of Aggression nd-b.

[87] Kreβ 2025, p. 2 (harmonization "consisted of replacing the 'debilitating conditions', as currently contained in Article 15*bis*(4) and (5) ICC Statute, by those governing other crimes under international law under the Court's jurisdiction, as laid out in Articles 12(2) and (3) of the ICC Statute"). As mentioned, very minor differences in jurisdiction would remain. See text accompanying note 114.

[88] Jurisdiction would include crimes committed on board a vessel or aircraft where the state of registration is a State Party.

[89] Minor language changes were made to fit the original Rome Statute language into the new amendment text.

the ICC's jurisdiction on an ad hoc basis without becoming a party to the Rome Statute, an option that presently exists with regard to the Rome Statute's other three core crimes.[90]

Under the amendment text, States Parties would also resolve the interpretative question discussed above (the broad versus narrow interpretations) in favor of the broad interpretation. *Either* the aggressor *or* the victim State Party would need to ratify the new harmonization amendment for the ICC to have jurisdiction over the crime, because jurisdiction would exist over crimes committed on the territories of States Parties or by their nationals.[91] Under general jurisdictional rules, only part of a crime needs to be committed on the territory of a state for jurisdiction to exist.[92]

As mentioned earlier, the Security Council's ability to make referrals regarding the crime would remain untouched, as the amendment proposal would only address situations involving a State Party referral or the Prosecutor acting *proprio motu*.[93]

8.4.2 Entry into Force

One issue left unresolved by the amendment proposal was which amendment procedure in the Rome Statute should be utilized for the amendment to enter into force. First, "adoption" of (i.e., agreement to) the amendment would be required, either by vote of 2/3 of States Parties or by consensus.[94] That much was uncontroversial. Then, there were at least[95] two possible choices. Either the entry into force provisions in Rome Statute Article 121(4) or those found in Article 121(5) would be utilized. Under Article 121(4), 7/8 of States Parties would need to ratify or accept the amendment, which would enter into force for all States Parties one year after the deposit of the last instrument of ratification or acceptance.[96] Alternatively, under Article 121(5), the amendment would enter into force for each State Party one year after it deposits its instrument of ratification or acceptance.[97]

---

[90] See Rome Statute (1998) (as amended), note 1, Article 12(3).

[91] Grzebyk 2025 ("If the amendment is adopted, the Court would be able to prosecute the crime of aggression if at least one state involved (as a state aggressor or as a state victim of aggression) were a party to the amendments on crime of aggression").

[92] See note 22 (discussing territorial jurisdiction).

[93] See note 72 (Article 15*ter* not part of the amendment proposal).

[94] Rome Statute (1998) (as amended), note 1, Article 121(3).

[95] Because the Rome Statute does not expressly address the amendment of an amendment, it might also be possible to develop another solution that is *sui generis*. For creative ideas, see, e.g., Abken and Rob 2023.

[96] Rome Statute (1998) (as amended), note 1, Article 121(4).

[97] Ibid., Article 121(5). The second sentence of Article 121(5) addresses the exercise of jurisdiction and therefore is inapplicable to the issue of entry into force. It states: "In respect of a State Party which has not accepted the amendment, the Court shall not exercise its jurisdiction regarding a crime covered by the amendment when committed by that State Party's nationals or on its territory". See ibid. This limitation on the exercise of jurisdiction does not apply to the crime of aggression. Unlike

The Rome Statute's text superficially suggests that Article 121(4) should be utilized. Article 121(5) states that it governs "amendment to articles 5, 6, 7 and 8", with Article 121(4) governing all other amendments.[98] An amendment to Article 15*bis* would not be an amendment to Articles 5, 6, 7 or 8.

Yet, a strong argument also exists for utilizing the amendment procedures in Article 121(5). Because the Kampala crime of aggression amendments were accomplished under the entry into force provisions of Article 121(5), the harmonization amendment arguably should follow the same method. The harmonization amendment would be a continuation (or completion) of the Kampala process, suggesting one should remain with the same procedures. In fact, the Kampala crime of aggression amendments themselves represented a *sui generis* solution, since some of the amendments arguably should have used the procedures in Article 121(4) and others should have used those in Article 121(5).[99] Yet, at the 2010 Review Conference, States Parties did not want to employ two different amendment procedures; therefore, they decided to treat all the crime of aggression amendments as one "basket"—using Article 121(5).[100] Thus, in 2010, States Parties in Kampala had already established the precedent of flexible state practice in applying the entry into force provisions to the aggression amendments.[101] That there is no Rome Statute provision addressing the amendment of prior amendments also suggests the need for flexibility when interpreting the amendment provisions.

An additional, but very real, consideration was that waiting for 7/8 of States Parties to ratify or accept a harmonization amendment before entry into force could take decades or might never be accomplished[102]—rendering the whole endeavor of

---

any other Rome Statute amendment, Rome Statute Article 5(2) gave States Parties a mandate to define the conditions for the ICC's exercise of jurisdiction over the crime of aggression. See ibid., Article 5(2). Thus, States Parties were, and are, not limited by the language contained in the second sentence.

98 Rome Statute (1998) (as amended), note 1, Article 121(5).

99 The Kampala amendments included an amendment to Article 5(2). See International Criminal Court, Assembly of States Parties 2010 (amending Article 5). The literal language of the Rome Statute would mandate *that* part of the Kampala amendments be accomplished pursuant to the entry into force provisions of Article 121(5). The remainder of the amendments were *not* amendments to Articles 5, 6, 7 or 8, such that a literal reading of the Rome Statute would require that the entry into force provisions of Article 121(4) be followed. See ibid. (also amending arts 9, 20, and 25, and adding arts 8*bis*, 15*bis* and 15*ter*).

100 See ibid., para 1 ("Decid[ing] to adopt, in accordance with article 5, paragraph 2, of the Rome Statute of the International Criminal Court . . . the amendments to the Statute contained in annex I of the present resolution, which are subject to ratification or acceptance *and shall enter into force in accordance with article 121, paragraph 5*") (emphasis added).

101 Vienna Convention on the Law of Treaties, note 31, Article 31(3)(b) (treaty interpretation shall take into account, together with the context, "any subsequent practice in the application of the treaty which establishes the agreement of the parties regarding its interpretation").

102 At the rate that States Parties have ratified the Kampala crime of aggression amendments (49 ratifications over the past 15 years), ratification by 2/3 of States Parties (83 or 84 states) would take approximately 26 years in total (or 11 more years)—assuming the rate of ratification remains constant, which it probably would not. The States Parties more interested in ratifying likely have already done so, suggesting it could become more difficult to obtain the remaining ratifications.

no practical utility. The high threshold of ratification or acceptance by 7/8 of States Parties provides a strong practical argument against using the amendment procedures of Article 121(4). Furthermore, as a legal matter, one might have concerns that for the last 1/8, the harmonization amendment would enter into force without their consent. Meanwhile, under Article 121(5), all States Parties would have a choice regarding whether to adopt the new harmonization amendment. If they choose to do so, it would enter into force for each State Party one year after it deposits its instrument of ratification or acceptance, gradually increasing the ICC's jurisdiction over the crime.[103]

8.5 State Opposition to Harmonizing Jurisdiction

By spring 2025, during meetings of the ASP's Working Group on Amendments, it had become clear which States Parties did not wish to see any such amendment to the Rome Statute.[104] These states clearly preferred the limited and basically unusable current jurisdictional regime. The United Kingdom and France (as well as Brazil), for example, raised technical questions during the Working Group meetings, while Canada was purely obstructionist, trying to block consideration of the amendment proposal.[105]

The United Kingdom fixated on the fact that the harmonization amendment would restore a state's ability to lodge an Article 12(3) declaration.[106] The United Kingdom questioned why or whether ad hoc declarations should be allowed for a State Party (one that had not ratified the harmonization amendment) as well as a non-State Party, and at what point the ability of states to use Article 12(3) declarations would become available.[107] The easy answer to the UK's questions would be: whatever States Parties negotiate.[108] Yet, the restoration of Article 12(3) declarations was

---

103 Such a gradual increase in jurisdiction is also occurring with the Kampala crime of aggression amendments, only the jurisdictional increases are limited. See Sect. 8.2 ("broad" and "narrow" interpretations; non-State Party carve-out).

104 The author attended these meetings as Convenor of GIPA and thus bases her account on first-hand observations.

105 Ibid.

106 See Rome Statute (1998) (as amended), note 1, Article 12(3).

107 Oral exchange between the author and a UK representative at the AU Mission to the UN, 13 June 2025.

108 Article 12(3) declarations could be made available to either non-States Parties or both States Parties and non-States Parties, although it would be odd to give the ability to use them (a benefit) only to non-States Parties, disadvantaging States Parties—which appeared to be what the United Kingdom was advocating. Similarly, States Parties could also specify when the ability to exercise Article 12(3) declarations would commence. Absent specifying, it presumably would be on entry into force of the amendment. (Under Article 121(5) that would occur one year after the first State Party's ratification or acceptance of the harmonization amendment; under Article 121(4), it would occur one year after 7/8 of States Parties have ratified or accepted the harmonization amendment). The inability to use Article 12(3) declarations regarding the crime of aggression occurred with the

hardly the key feature of the amendment proposal. Thus, it was unclear whether the United Kingdom was actually concerned about these details or was trying to create issues, so that there would be insufficient time to resolve outstanding questions during the three days allotted for the 7–9 July 2025 Special Session of the ASP.

France also raised a variety of technical arguments, including one also raised during the Core Group negotiations[109] (and in Kampala). France argued that under Article 39 of the UN Charter, only the UN Security Council may determine whether a state has committed an act of aggression.[110] Yet, the Security Council does not make determinations of individual criminal responsibility; its role under Article 39 pertains to the conduct of states. Furthermore, even then, its role is not exclusive.[111] Moreover, as explained in Chap. 7, in the negotiations leading up to the 2010 Kampala Review Conference, States Parties had rejected the argument that, due to the Charter's language, Security Council referral should be the only path by which an aggression investigation or prosecution could be initiated before the ICC.[112] States Parties, by consensus adoption of the Kampala crime of aggression amendments, decided that there could also be referrals by State Parties and the Prosecutor could act *proprio motu.*[113] In the event those paths are pursued, pursuant to Rome Statute Article 15*bis*(6)–(8), States Parties did add a delay of six months to allow for the Security Council to make a determination as to an act of aggression, but, in the event that it does not do so, the Kampala amendments provide that the ICC Prosecutor may proceed after receiving authorization from the ICC's Pre-Trial Division.[114] This arrangement

---

adoption of the Kampala aggression amendments (although it only had application in 2018 when jurisdiction commenced), so one might alternatively restore such declarations at the adoption of the harmonization amendment.

[109] See Chap. 7, Sect. 7.3.1.

[110] China also made this argument during the Special Session. See note 147. UN Charter Article 39 states: "The Security Council shall determine the existence of any threat to the peace, breach of the peace, or act of aggression and shall make recommendations, or decide what measures shall be taken in accordance with Articles 41 and 42, to maintain or restore international peace and security". UN Charter (1945), note 21, Article 39. France's argument worked particularly poorly in the context of the Core Group negotiations, since the Special Tribunal statute contains no role for the UN Security Council and expressly references resolutions by the UN General Assembly. See Statute of the Special Tribunal for the Crime of Aggression against Ukraine (2025). https://search.coe.int/cm?i=0900001680b678ca. Accessed 12 September 2025, preamble.

[111] UN Charter Article 24(1) states that the Security Council has "primary responsibility" for the maintenance of international peace and security, but leaves an opening for a role by the UN General Assembly. See UN Charter (1945), note 21, Article 24(1). See also International Court of Justice (1962) *Certain Expenses of the United Nations*, Advisory Opinion, 1962 ICJ Rep. 151, p 163 ("The Charter makes it abundantly clear . . . that the General Assembly is also to be concerned with international peace and security"); International Court of Justice (2004) *Legal Consequences of the Construction of a Wall in the Occupied Palestinian Territory*, Advisory Opinion, 2004 ICJ Rep. 136, para 26 (reaffirming the Security Council's primary, but not exclusive, responsibility for the maintenance of international peace and security).

[112] See Chap. 7, Sect. 7.3.1 (in particular note 36); see also Chap. 3, Sect. 3.2.3.

[113] International Criminal Court, Assembly of States Parties 2010.

[114] See Rome Statute (1998) (as amended), note 1, Article 15*bis* (6)–(8).

was adopted by consensus of all States Parties at the Kampala Review Conference.[115] In short, the French argument—which was also made by permanent members of the Security Council during negotiations of the Special Working Group on the Crime of Aggression ("SWGCA"), particularly those held in Princeton, New Jersey, over the years 2003–2009[116]—had already been advanced and resolved years ago.

Brazil also raised a variety of technical questions that suggested a genuine interest in the outcome of the amendment, but may also have been intended to block progress.[117]

Meanwhile, Canada took the most obstructionist stance during meetings of the Working Group on Amendments, insisting that it was premature to consider any amendment text.[118] Canada argued that States Parties instead should use the scheduled 7–9 July Special Session for a "stocktaking" exercise.[119] "Stocktaking" had occurred at the 2010 Kampala Review Conference.[120] While the topics considered were important, their discussion took valuable time away from the crime of aggression negotiations in 2010 and may have been intended to "run the clock". Canada seemed to want this again, proposing that the "stocktaking" take up the entire 7–9 July Special Session, focusing on issues such as the experiences of States Parties in ratifying the Kampala crime of aggression amendments, but not reaching consideration of any substantive amendment.[121]

[115] International Criminal Court, Assembly of States Parties 2010.

[116] For reports of the SWGCA, see International Criminal Court, Assembly of States Parties 2012. The author was present during the Princeton meetings of the SWGCA and recollects some of the permanent members making this argument.

[117] The Chair of the Working Group, Ambassador Quintana, asked States Parties to submit questions on the amendment proposal to him in writing, which resulted in a document listing questions, with responding answers provided in a separate document. The questions and views of states are summarized in International Criminal Court, Assembly of States Parties 2025, pp. 3–6. Brazil was one of the States Parties that opposed the amendment during the Special Session. See text accompanying note 146 (15 states opposed).

[118] Notes of the author who attended meetings of the Working Group on Amendments.

[119] Ibid.

[120] The topics addressed were: the impact of the Rome Statute system on victims and affected communities; peace and justice; complementarity; and cooperation. Trahan 2011, p. 50, n 3.

[121] Notes of the author, who attended meetings of the Working Group on Amendments.

8.6 State and Civil Society Support for Harmonizing Jurisdiction

A large majority of States Parties that attended the Working Group meetings, on the other hand, appeared genuinely supportive of the harmonization amendment.[122] These States Parties were working to provide answers to questions raised,[123] resisting the effort to waste the upcoming Special Session on "stocktaking", and focusing on building support for the amendment proposal. On 13 June 2025, GIPA, along with the Permanent Missions of Sierra Leone and Switzerland to the UN and the Federal Department of Foreign Affairs of Switzerland, co-organized an informational seminar for legal advisers of States Parties held at the African Union's Mission to the UN, which approximately 75 States Parties attended; the overwhelming majority supported the harmonization amendment.[124]

Civil society played an active role both within the Working Group on Amendments and otherwise.[125] This marked a sharp contrast to the unhelpful role the dominant CSOs had played in Kampala and during the SWGCA negotiations.[126] During those years, only a handful of independently affiliated individuals (primarily academics) were encouraging states to support what became the Kampala crime of aggression amendments, including former Nuremberg Prosecutor Benjamin Ferencz, his son Don Ferencz, Astrid Reisinger Coracini, Claus Kreß, Robbie Manson, Jutta Bertram-Nothnagel, Enid Adler, Carrie McDougall, Roger Clark, Noah Weisbord, myself, and David Donat Cattin on behalf of PGA.[127]

By December 2024, the European Center for Constitutional and Human Rights ("ECCHR") had drafted a position in support of the harmonization amendment[128] and

---

[122] Ibid. It must be acknowledged that a fair number of States Parties attending also remained silent during the meetings. Ibid.

[123] See note 117 (questions raised).

[124] See Global Institute for the Prevention of Aggression 2025a. Trahan 2025d (support).

[125] Bardelle 2025 ("civil society played a central role – advocating for reform, amplifying the voices of victims and survivors of aggression, and providing technical expertise").

[126] See Weisbord in Kreβ and Barriga 2017. Human Rights Watch had never supported the process of defining the crime or the conditions for the ICC's exercise of jurisdiction over it, despite the crime being one of the four core crimes contained in the Rome Statute. The Coalition for the International Criminal Court ("CICC") (constrained by the views of CSOs on its Steering Committee) was unable to play any leadership role. Meanwhile, Amnesty International and the Open Society Foundations released a press release and letter respectively opposing the Kampala amendments. See ibid., p. 1322 ("Amnesty International [in 2010 in Kampala] took a perfectionist stance without acknowledging the repercussions of their position: that it would collapse the negotiations"; "by rejecting the Kampala compromise on perfectionist grounds and then criticising the delegates for the consensus outcome, Amnesty International came across as self-righteous and disconnected"); Neier 2010 (President of the Open Society Foundations: "The current amendment proposal risks politicizing and overburdening the ICC, and undermining the integrity of the Rome Statute").

[127] Some of the academics at various points also represented states: Carrie McDougall (Australia, although not during the Special Session); Astrid Reisinger Coracini (Austria); Claus Kreβ (Germany); and Roger Clark (Samoa).

[128] European Center for Constitutional and Human Rights 2024.

had a sign-on statement eventually joined by more than 80 CSOs.[129] The GIPA also played an active role in proposing text solutions, engaging at Working Group meetings, having its members speak at regional conferences,[130] and organizing events to promote the amendment and answer questions.[131] The African Legal Aid ("AFLA") similarly played an active role in organizing events aimed particularly at engaging with, and giving a voice to, African States Parties.[132] By the spring of 2025, the CICC also took on a constructive role, particularly in arranging for civil society representatives to speak about the experiences of victims of the crime of aggression during meetings of the Working Group on Amendments.[133] The Open Society Justice Initiative was supportive[134] and Human Rights Watch publicly promoted the amendment.[135]

This positive engagement by civil society was reflected in the final memorandum by the Chair of the Working Group on Amendments, which acknowledged:

> Civil society organizations played an active and constructive role in all WGA sessions, strongly endorsing the harmonization proposal and calling for decisive action to close accountability gaps related to the crime of aggression. These organizations emphasized that harmonization is essential for upholding the principle of equal justice, ensuring that victims of aggression have access to meaningful accountability, and preserving the ICC's normative consistency and global standing. They unequivocally stated that harmonization was not merely a technical or legal exercise, but a human rights and justice imperative. In their view, victims of aggression, like those of genocide or war crimes, deserve access to justice and

---

[129] Joint Civil Society 2024 (updated version with 88 signatures).

[130] See note 83 (regional conferences). For details, see Global Institute for the Prevention of Aggression various-dates.

[131] See note 124 and accompanying text (AU meeting); GIPA also co-hosted a meeting sponsored by the Permanent Missions of Germany, Liechtenstein, Switzerland and Vanuatu, held on 8 July 2025 at the German Mission to the UN. Global Institute for the Prevention of Aggression 2025c.

[132] See note 76 (AFLA side-event); note 83 (AFLA conference).

[133] Kreβ 2025, p. 3 ("The Coalition for the International Criminal Court also voiced its support for the reform, and their speakers did so with a clarity and dedication for which there has been no precedent since the negotiations began on the ICC Statute three decades earlier"). The CICC also helped arrange a panel on 7 July entitled "The Devastating Impact on Victims of Aggression and the Case for Harmonization from a Civil Society Perspective". It was co-organized by ECCHR, GIPA, PGA and TRIAL International, and co-sponsored by the Permanent Mission of Switzerland to the UN. See Global Institute for the Prevention of Aggression 2025b. See also Coalition for the ICC 2025.

[134] Trahan 2025c.

[135] Human Rights Watch's briefing note to States Parties contained the following:

> Human Rights Watch calls on states parties to eliminate double standards in the treatment of the crime of aggression under the Rome Statute, and propose amendments that would ensure that, as with other crimes in article 5, the ICC can exercise jurisdiction over the crime of aggression pursuant to a state referral or the prosecutor acting *proprio motu*, when committed by state party nationals or on the territory of states parties.

Human Rights Watch 2024, Sect. III.B.

accountability mechanisms that do not depend on whether their State has accepted a specific jurisdictional clause.[136]

One of the distractions in late spring 2025, however, was the quandary facing the ASP President over whether to proceed with the 7–9 July meeting at the United Nations (as had been scheduled) or to relocate the meeting to The Hague.[137] The concern about meeting in New York stemmed from the imposition of sanctions against ICC judges and prosecutors under an Executive Order by US President Donald J. Trump.[138] It was feared that the US stance (and ability to withhold visas) could prevent civil society members and some state delegations from attending the Special Session, or, worse still, result in threats to individual diplomats and/or their countries.[139] These were very real worries.

However, all the preparatory work for the Special Session had taken place in New York, primarily the meetings of the Working Group on Amendments; thus, it was New York delegates who were "up to speed" on the topic. Therefore, a number of States Parties that supported the harmonization amendment pushed for the negotiations to remain in New York.[140] After much back-and-forth, the decision was made to hold the negotiations in New York as planned. Yet, the two months of indecision about the venue wasted valuable time and proved a distraction during the lead up to the negotiations.

8.7 The Special Session Negotiations and Outcome

The Special Session was off to a mixed start. The final memorandum by the Chair of the Working Group on Amendments included as annexes both the amendment proposal discussed above, submitted by Costa Rica, Germany, Sierra Leone, Slovenia, and Vanuatu,[141] and the text of a proposed resolution submitted by Canada, the United Kingdom, France, Japan, and New Zealand. The latter resolution called

[136] See International Criminal Court, Assembly of States Parties 2025, p. 3.

[137] See Anderson 2025 (discussing "states suggesting a change of venue from New York to The Hague amid uncertainties over the current US visa regime, raising questions over the United Nations['] usual provision of diplomatic privileges to ICC meetings"); Grzebyk 2025 (discussing "attempts to postpone [the Special Session] and move [it] to the Hague for various reasons, [including] potential problems of delegates with the entry to the USA").

[138] See Trump 2025. Three CSOs were placed on the sanctions list after the Special Session. See Rubio 2025.

[139] Threats to states by the United States did occur. See note 149 (threats).

[140] Trahan 2025e.

[141] Amendment Proposal 2025, note 39. On 5 June 2025, Liechtenstein also submitted a draft resolution intended to accompany the amendment. International Criminal Court, Assembly of States Parties 2025. The final iteration is attached as Annex I to International Criminal Court, Assembly of States Parties 2025.

for delaying the negotiations until 2/3 of States Parties had ratified the Kampala crime of aggression amendments,[142] which could have taken decades.[143]

Yet, in Plenary Statements delivered by States Parties at the Special Session, it was clear that the vast majority of States Parties were supportive of the harmonization amendment. Over 50 states spoke in favor of harmonization, with several more if support prior to the Special Session is counted.[144] Thus, "a significant number of States Parties and civil society actors voiced strong support for harmonizing the crime's jurisdictional framework with that of the Court's other core crimes".[145]

Meanwhile, the States Parties opposed to the amendment had grown to fifteen: Argentina, Australia, Brazil, Burkina Faso, Canada, France, Guatemala, Japan, Kenya, Republic of Korea, Mali, New Zealand, Norway, Uganda, and the United Kingdom.[146] Opposition was additionally expressed by two powerful non-States Parties (who would have no vote in the matter but could still exert pressure on other states): China[147] and the United States.[148] Indeed, the United States, which had

---

[142] See International Criminal Court, Assembly of States Parties 2025, Annex II.

[143] See note 102 (calculating rate of ratifications).

[144] Chart prepared by Astrid Reisinger Coracini on file with the author. See also Bardelle 2025 ("Germany delivered a joint statement on behalf of 34 members of the Group of Friends, calling for harmonization. In addition to many European countries, the endorsing states included Chile, Sierra Leone, the State of Palestine, Timor-Leste, Vanuatu, and Zambia. Several other delegations voiced their support in individual statements, including a number of African and Latin American States Parties, such as the Democratic Republic of the Congo (DRC), Ghana, Senegal, Nigeria, as well as Uruguay, Mexico, and Peru. A positive sign was Ukraine's clear endorsement of the reform . . ."); Kreß 2025, p. 3 ("In New York, an impressive cross-regional majority of States Parties present, including, in particular, an overwhelming majority of delegations from Europe (including, notably, Ukraine), a large majority of the delegations from Africa, and a majority of delegations from Latin America rallied behind the reform proposal"); Gevorgyan 2025 ("the division [of states supporting and states opposed to the harmonization amendment] did not follow a simple North–South or ideological line. Rather, it reflected what structural realism would predict: states with greater global influence and military capabilities were more likely to resist legal limits on the use of force, while structurally weaker states supported reforms to strengthen legal protections").

[145] Gevorgyan 2025. On CSO support, see Sect. 8.6.

[146] Notes of the author on file with the author; Trahan 2025b. See Bardelle 2025 ("a smaller but vocal group of states expressed hesitancy, scepticism or outright rejection of the proposed harmonization. France, Canada, the United Kingdom, Japan, New Zealand, Brazil, Australia, Mali, and Uganda were among them"); Kreß 2025, p. 3 ("Canada, France, Japan, New Zealand and the United Kingdom, all of whom, except for New Zealand, had been part of the Special Tribunal initiative, voiced their firm opposition. While only Argentina, Australia and Uganda unambiguously aligned with them, they received further backing from the USA").

[147] Bardelle 2025 ("China argu[ed] [at the Special Session] that only the Security Council has the authority to determine acts of aggression"). This argument had already been resolved decades prior. States Parties had already rejected the misleading conflation of the specific powers of the Security Council under the UN Charter and the criminal justice mandate of the ICC under the Rome Statute. See notes 109–116 and accompanying text.

[148] Gevorgyan 2025 ("States like China and the United States, though not parties to the Rome Statute but present as observer states, opposed the reform").

already threatened states prior to the negotiations, took the floor during the Special Session to deliver another threat.[149]

No consensus emerged despite three days of intensive negotiations to try to find a middle ground between States Parties that supported the harmonization amendment and those that opposed it (or supported delaying negotiations potentially for decades).[150] A significant number of states, led by Liechtenstein, had in the interval developed a balanced compromise proposal. It would have achieved harmonization after a delay (the requirement that 30 States Parties ratify the harmonization amendment) and then the possibility of the ASP blocking entry into force by a vote of 2/3 of States Parties; yet, the states opposed to harmonization would not agree.[151]

Some States Parties had already expressed the desire for consensus adoption in their Opening Statements at the Special Session.[152] Given the number of States Parties present at the Special Session (fewer than one hundred and thus well-short of the full 125 States Parties),[153] it became clear that there was not the required

[149] Bardelle 2025 ("the United States attempted to deter any expansion of the Court's jurisdiction through issuing a threatening statement to all States Parties ahead of the session, reiterating this position on the second day through a high-level representative of the State Department"); Anderson 2025 ("pressure is being put on delegates from a non-member state, the United States, with a sharply worded diplomatic note, seen by Justice Info, which expresses 'grave concerns' over efforts to 'expand the Court's jurisdiction over the crime of aggression, including over non-States Parties'. The *demarche* goes on to threaten to use 'all appropriate and effective diplomatic, political, and legal instruments to block the ICC's assertion of such jurisdiction'"); Gevorgyan 2025 ("The United States, having imposed sanctions on [ICC officials], actively, and seemingly successfully, sought to deter any expansion of the Court's jurisdiction. On the second day of the session, a senior legal adviser to the US State Department delivered a statement threatening to use 'all diplomatic, political, and legal instruments to block ICC overreach'").

[150] International Criminal Court, Assembly of States Parties 2025, Annex II (proposal to delay negotiations until 2/3 of States Parties ratify or accept the Kampala crime of aggression amendments).

[151] Claus Kreβ explains that the States Parties opposed to harmonization

> rejected a finely balanced compromise proposal formulated by Liechtenstein that foresaw a deferral of the reform's entry into force until the deposit of the 30th ratification and, in addition, contained a provision allowing entry into force to be blocked in the event of a decision against proceeding being adopted by a majority of two-thirds of States Parties . . . . Apart from Liechtenstein and the five co-sponsors of the reform proposal, the delegations from Andorra, Armenia, Austria, Belgium, Bolivia, Bosnia-Herzegovina, Bulgaria, Cap[e] Verde, Chile, Cyprus, the Czech Republic, Democratic Republic of Congo, Denmark Ecuador, East Timor, Estonia, Finland, Gabon, The Gambia, Ghana, Greece, Iceland, Ireland, Ivory Coast, Latvia, Liberia, Lithuania, Luxembourg, Malawi, Malta, Mexico, The Netherlands, Nigeria, the State of Palestine, Peru, Poland, Portugal, Romania, Senegal, Slovakia, Slovenia, Spain, South Africa, Sweden, Switzerland, Ukraine and Uruguay stood out by their determination.

Kreβ 2025, p. 3.

[152] Notes of the author on file with the author. See, e.g., Kreβ 2025, p. 3 ("Brazil and South Korea, while touching upon the substance with great circumspection, emphasized the lack of consensus regarding the reform proposal and voiced a clear procedural preference for moving forward only by consensus").

[153] Bardelle 2025 (noting "more than 20 States Parties absent"). Hungary deposited an instrument of withdrawal from the Rome Statute. If that takes effect one year after the instrument's deposit,

2/3 of States Parties needed to adopt the amendment by vote.[154] Therefore it would need to be adopted by consensus. Consensus essentially meant that the States Parties opposed to the amendment had something akin to veto power—that is, any one of them could have blocked consensus.

Given the opponents' ability to block adoption of the harmonization amendment, all that could be agreed on was a resolution committing to a continuation of the process: continuing negotiations in a subgroup of the Working Group on Amendments; a two-day intersessional meeting on the topic in New York in 2027; and a five-day Special Session on the topic in New York in 2029.[155] On a positive note, the final resolution did express the commitment by States Parties "to the aim of strengthening the jurisdiction of the Court over the crime of aggression".[156] The resolution, however, also acknowledged "a deep structural divide among States Parties" on the substantive issues.[157] Any agreement on creating meaningful jurisdiction before the ICC over the crime of aggression will have to wait at least four more years, and likely longer, while the amendment, if any, enters into force.[158]

Summing up the state of affairs, Palestine's Ambassador Majed Bamya eloquently explained:

> It would appear that when we talk of the crime of aggression, we are looking at a hurdles race, where instead of running we continue to walk and where obstacles continue mounting

---

the ICC would have 124 States Parties. See Human Rights Watch 2025. In September 2025, Niger, Mali, and Burkina Faso also announced an intent to withdraw. Reuters 2025.

[154] Bardelle 2025 ("reaching the two-thirds majority required for adoption under Article 121(3) of the Rome Statute would have been difficult"). Not all States Parties registered to attend the Special Session appeared to be in the room simultaneously; fewer than a hundred delegations were present at any one time. With at least fifteen negative votes assured, the margins were too close and time too short to achieve the 83 or 84 positive votes required to adopt the amendment by 2/3 of States Parties. Observations of the author who attended the Special Session. Additionally, some of the States Parties accredited to the Special Session were in arrears concerning payments into the Court's budget for a period that exceeded two years; thus, they had lost the right to vote and they had not requested a waiver to the plenary to exercise it. This revealed a lack of adequate preparation of the Special Session by the competent organs and units of the ASP.

[155] See International Criminal Court 2025b.

[156] Ibid. See Bardelle 2025 ("The adopted resolution offers a modest victory: States Parties committed to revisiting the issue in four years and reaffirmed the majority's intention to strengthen the Court's jurisdiction over the crime of aggression").

[157] Maria Gevorgyan of the Center for Truth & Justice ("CFTJ") explains:

> The resolution acknowledged this divide explicitly:
>
> > Recognizing that many States Parties take the view that there is a gap in jurisdiction over the crime of aggression and advocate for harmonization . . . . Also recognizing that other States Parties take the view that the current provisions reflect a balance agreed at Kampala and confirmed in 2017. . . .
>
> While diplomatically worded, this language captures the political stalemate that continues to hinder reform.
>
> Gevorgyan 2025.

[158] Extremely different timing would be involved depending on which entry into force procedure is used—whether Rome Statute Article 121(4) or Article 121(5). See Sect. 8.4.2.

> and the victims of the crime of aggression are asked to wait in the meantime. The resolution before us does not reflect the urgent need for action or the historical responsibility that falls upon us . . . . However, we have to highlight the constructive approach that prevailed over our discussions. And this is a merit we recognize to all those who were involved in these discussions, whatever their initial positions were. We also have to highlight the important signal that we are all sending by being united at this critical and important juncture. We also highlight our joint commitment reflected in the draft resolution to strengthen the jurisdiction of the court over the crime of aggression and our ability to adopt a way to move forward together on this important matter. We have an obligation of result when it comes to the issue of the crime of aggression.[159]

8.8 Conclusion

It is perhaps unsurprising that certain powerful states (and some of their allies) do not wish to be constrained by the rule of law when it comes to the use of force and therefore disfavor ICC jurisdiction over the crime of aggression that could encompass the actions of their nationals or crimes committed on their territories. A more charitable view would be that they, or some of them, are not inexorably opposed to broader ICC jurisdiction over the crime, but choose to tread cautiously. Some of the same states, ironically (or perhaps predictably), have strongly supported prosecution of the crime of aggression in the situation of Ukraine—but only in that one situation, where the leaders to be investigated and/or prosecuted likely will be Russian, Belarusian, and, perhaps, North Korean.[160] Some of the very same states that created the Nuremberg precedent to end impunity for crimes against peace appear to have embraced a very retrogressive position as to the ICC's jurisdiction over the crime of aggression, a position that stands in stark contrast to their past achievement.

Perhaps that is all the precedent that Nuremberg truly set, as it too represented selective justice—only prosecution by the Allies of the nationals of defeated Axis powers.[161] Yet, that is not what the US Prosecutor at Nuremberg believed the trials stood for.[162] Eighty years after the Nuremberg trial, has the international community come no further than the selective application of justice for the crime of aggression?

---

159 Kreß 2025, pp. 3–4, quoting Ambassador Bamya.

160 See Council of Europe nd ("As the Special Tribunal will deal with establishing accountability for the crime of aggression committed against Ukraine, Belarusian or North Korean individuals could potentially be prosecuted if evidence shows they played a significant role in the crime of aggression against Ukraine"). For the author's concerns whether North Korean nationals could be prosecuted before the Special Tribunal, see Chap. 7, Sect. 7.4.1 (discussing the exclusion from the Tribunal's Statute of "aiding and abetting" as a mode of responsibility).

161 The IMT at Nuremberg prosecuted only Germany nationals, while the International Military Tribunal for the Far East (Tokyo) prosecuted only Japanese nationals. For background on the Nuremberg Tribunal, see, e.g., Bass 2000, ch. 5; for one examination of the Tokyo Tribunal, see, e.g., Kopelman 1991.

162 As previously mentioned, in his Opening Statement, Robert H. Jackson famously declared: "And let me make clear that while this law is first applied against German aggressors, the law includes, and if it is to serve a useful purpose it must condemn aggression by any other nations, including those which sit here now in judgment". Jackson 1947, pp. 98–102.

One would hope we have moved beyond the approach taken in 1945. The obligations against committing aggression are now contained in the UN Charter,[163] commitments all UN Member States are obligated to uphold. Furthermore, the crime of aggression does not provide for individual criminal responsibility regarding *every* use of force violation under the UN Charter; it only applies where a state has committed a "manifest" violation of the Charter.[164] In this way, the crime is more conservative than the obligations contained in the UN Charter.

One would hope that states opposed to broader ICC jurisdiction over the crime of aggression do not envision their state being in a position where they perceive a need to manifestly violate the UN Charter. While some powerful states may not have appropriate regard for the rule of law, at least under certain administrations,[165] most others opposing the amendment are likely wary of broader jurisdiction because it could mean their state and/or leaders would have to explain their state's conduct in situations where legality or illegality is less clear. Admittedly, there are "grey" areas (areas where the law is uncertain) in the area of *jus ad bellum*/the prohibition of the use of force.[166] Yet, this provides no reason to avoid ICC jurisdiction over the crime, because the crime excludes responsibility in areas where genuine legal uncertainty exists. As explained in Chap. 3, through the requirement that an act of aggression must rise to the level of a "manifest" violation of the UN Charter measured by the "character, gravity and scale" of that act, debatable situations are excluded from the definition of the crime.[167] The crime is thus able to adapt over time. As areas of legal uncertainty are resolved, more would be encompassed within the definition. As new areas of the law emerge—for example, in response to emerging technologies[168]—if the law is uncertain, such situations would not be encompassed within the definition until the law is clearer. The definition of the crime is thus relatively conservative in requiring this level of legal clarity and certainty.

Another explanation for the reticence of powerful states might relate to the forum where the issue would arise.[169] One suspects that certain states (the permanent members of the UN Security Council and their close allies) would prefer discussing

---

[163] See UN Charter (1945), note 21, Article 2(4).

[164] See Rome Statute (1998) (as amended), note 1, Article 8*bis*(1) (manifest threshold); for additional discussion of the manifest threshold, see Chap. 3, Sect. 3.2.2.

[165] See Alvarez 2025 (criticizing breaches of international law by the United States, particularly during the second Trump Administration).

[166] See Chap. 3, Sect. 3.2.4 (especially note 77) (acknowledging, for example, divergent views among states on the parameters of self-defense and the issue of so-called "humanitarian intervention").

[167] This requirement of a "manifest" threshold "appropriately limit[s] the Court's jurisdiction to the most serious acts of aggression under customary international law, thus excluding cases of insufficient gravity and falling within a grey area". Report of the Special Working Group on the Crime of Aggression (2008) ICC-ASP/6/20/Add.1, Annex II, para 68; see also Kreß 2009, p. 1138; McDougall 2021, p. 158.

[168] See, e.g., Trahan 2025a.

[169] See Gevorgyan 2025 ("In a system where states act in accordance with their relative power, the resistance of some powerful states to reform is not incidental, but structural").

violations of the UN Charter's use of force provisions only in a forum they control. The UN Security Council provides powerful states with such a forum, with the permanent members uniquely able to shape the Security Council's work through the use of their veto power.[170] In most situations, the permanent members (and their close allies) will not face ramifications (condemnation or other action) before that body for the illegal use of force even where conduct clearly violates the UN Charter.[171] These same states, however, hold no such automatic sway over the ICC. States Parties, such as the United Kingdom and France, are in a position to engage constructively with the ICC and able to nominate their nationals to serve as judges and prosecutor.[172] Other permanent members (the United States and Russia) have chosen to try to influence and harm the ICC through the imposition of sanctions (as well as threats) by the United States[173] and retaliatory arrest warrants and *in absentia* convictions by Russia.[174] These measures are a blatant attempt to exert leverage over, and stymie the work of, an institution over which they hold no veto power.

Standing in stark contrast, particularly to the stances of the United States and Russia, are states that stand on the side of the rule of law and a stronger ICC. While generalizations are inevitably imprecise, one might think of these states as small and mid-sized states that lack powerful armies. Many of these states support prosecution of the crime of aggression before the ICC (and the ICC having adequate jurisdiction to conduct investigations and prosecutions) because they do not wish their state or nationals to become victims of the crime of aggression.[175] The policies of these states may also be shaped by a commitment to the rule of law and the UN Charter system, particularly its provisions on the use of force. Thankfully, more recent wars have not involved anything resembling the cataclysmic death tolls of World War II. Yet, the death tolls from inter-state wars over the last half century are nonetheless staggering.[176] Moreover, judging by voting within the UN General Assembly, the vast

---

[170] On abusive vetoes (ones that shield the perpetration of genocide, war crimes and/or crimes against humanity), see Trahan 2020, 2022a, b. On abusive vetoes that shield the perpetration of aggression, see Trahan 2023.

[171] This was true, for example, when Russia vetoed the resolution that would have condemned its invasion of Ukraine and imposed other measures. See United Nations Security Council Resolution 155 (2022) 155 (vetoed by the Russian Federation). Chapter VI resolutions would be possible, but only if states start applying the UN Charter's mandatory abstention requirement. See UN Charter, note 21, Article 27(3) ("in decisions under Chapter VI . . . a party to a dispute shall abstain from voting").

[172] See Rome Statute 1998 (as amended), note 1, Article 42(4) (election of the prosecutor and deputy prosecutor by States Parties); Article 36 (nomination and election of judges by States Parties).

[173] See Trump 2025 (sanctions); note 149 (threats).

[174] Russia has issued arrest warrants against ICC judges and the ICC Prosecutor. See Radio Free Europe/Radio Liberty 2024. More recently, these became *in absentia* convictions.

[175] Notes of the Special Session on file with the author. See Gevorgyan 2025 ("The failure to adopt meaningful reform ultimately preserves a system that offers the least protection to those most at risk. In this sense, the Special Session did not just stall legal progress, it failed the states that depend on international law for their very existence").

[176] According to one estimate, there were approximately twenty-five interstate wars between 1946 and 2007, resulting in nearly three million battle deaths in total, with the overwhelming

majority of UN Member States do believe that it is wrong and illegal to invade another country,[177] and a fair number have also supported the proposition that individual criminal responsibility must follow.[178]

As to why the rule of law matters, particularly when it comes to the prohibition against the illegal use of force and the importance of prosecuting the crime of aggression, Germany's then Federal Foreign Minister Annalena Baerbock eloquently explained as follows:

> I believe that . . . I don't have to do much to persuade you about my first point, namely the question as to why international law is so indispensable, for our peace and for an international order that is based on rules and not on the law of the strong . . . . After all, it's clear that in a world order based only on power, those who are the strongest and who use their power most ruthlessly will prevail. This means that no smaller country would be able to sleep soundly at night. And it goes without saying that this is the case not only here in Europe, but anywhere in the world where a state must live in fear that a bigger or stronger neighbour might attack it while the world simply looks on. However, international law stipulates that all states are sovereign and equal. It protects the weak against the tyranny of the strong, whether in the north, south, east or west of our common world.[179]

States supporting broader ICC jurisdiction for the crime of aggression endorse this vision. Namely, there must be rule of law that protects states from every region of the globe against the illegal use of force against them. Moreover, individual criminal responsibility must follow where the rule of law fails and states and their nationals become victims of the crime.

The real divergence in views thus comes down to whether selective application of justice is acceptable (or even preferred). States that support the Special Tribunal but do not support expanding the ICC's jurisdiction over the crime of aggression appear to take this view. The opposite view is that selectivity is anathema to a genuine commitment to the rule of law and the crime of aggression must be prosecuted more broadly. For the states supporting the latter view, the Nuremberg trials established powerful precedent, but their selective application of justice must not be emulated; we must progress beyond the precedent set in 1945. Both groups of states are right

---

majority concentrated in the Korean War (1950–1953, 930,084 deaths), the Iran–Iraq War (1980–88, 1,250,000 deaths), and the Indo–Pakistani conflicts (notably 1971, 13,723 deaths). See Sarkees and Wayman 2010. One should also add the carnage from the French and US wars against Vietnam. Goscha nd (First Indochina war fatality estimates of 300,000–500,000); Ziad et al. 2008 (Vietnam fatality estimate over 3 million).

177 See United Nations General Assembly Resolution ES-11/1 (2022) ("recognizing that the military operations of the Russian Federation inside the sovereign territory of Ukraine are on a scale that the international community had not seen in Europe in decades"; deploring "in the strongest terms the aggression by the Russian Federation against Ukraine in violation of Article 2 (4) of the Charter"; demanding "that the Russian Federation immediately cease its use of force against Ukraine") (passed by 141 votes).

178 Approximately 40 states plus representatives of the European Union and Council of Europe were part of the Core Group working to establish the Special Tribunal. For discussion of the Core Group negotiations, see Chap. 7.

179 Baerbock 2023. Baerbock was elected to the prestigious position of President of the UN General Assembly for its eightieth anniversary, in 2025.

in some respects. While states are in the process of negotiating to amend the Rome Statute's jurisdiction over the crime of aggression, Russian and other nationals must not be permitted to escape accountability for the invasion of Ukraine. Yet, ensuring that the Special Tribunal has sufficient support and funding to commence operations (which must happen)[180] is simultaneously insufficient. The crime must be prosecutable more broadly. States Parties must also amend the Rome Statute to harmonize the ICC's jurisdiction over all four core crimes in order to ensure that the ICC has meaningful jurisdiction over the crime. Doing so would also enhance the legitimacy of the Special Tribunal as a step towards the universal application of the crime of aggression.

[180] On the need for support and funding for the Special Tribunal, see Chap. 7, Sect. 7.5.

Post Scriptum

This book was finalized as the United States was conducting military strikes against vessels in the Caribbean and Pacific but had not yet imposed an oil embargo on Venezuela nor abducted Venezuelan President Nicolás Maduro and his wife. Likewise, it was completed before US and Israeli strikes against Iran commenced in March 2026, or US threats to invade Greenland.

These events underscore why upholding the rule of law is not an abstract aspiration but an urgent necessity. They further emphasize the enduring importance of, and need for adherence to, the prohibition against the use of force contained in Article 2(4) of the UN Charter, which requires that states refrain from the threat or use of force against the territorial integrity or political independence of other states.

This book explicitly makes the case for prosecuting Russian (and potentially other) political and military leaders for the crime of aggression related to the invasion of Ukraine, as these were the circumstances that first inspired its drafting. Yet the argument advanced is not limited to these alleged crimes, nor does it advocate selective application of justice. The central contention is broader and more principled: whenever illegal aggression proceeds unchecked, the foundations of the international legal order are weakened. Accountability must therefore apply consistently, irrespective of geography, power, or political alignment. The unfolding situations in the Americas and the Middle East only reinforce this core argument.

If the world is to ever be more peaceful, the prohibition embodied in Article 2(4) of the UN Charter must be enforced in practice, not merely invoked in principle. The crime of aggression was created precisely for this purpose: to hold individuals accountable for the gravest violations of the international order. States should therefore expand the jurisdiction of the ICC over this crime (harmonizing the jurisdiction of all four Rome Statute crimes). Only with expanded jurisdiction can the law begin to generate genuine deterrence, and, where deterrence fails, provide a forum for investigation and prosecution.

The legacy of Nuremberg and Tokyo was the recognition that aggressive war is not simply a tragic feature of international politics but a punishable crime under international law. That legacy must be renewed rather than allowed to fade into historical memory. Until meaningful accountability for the crime of aggression becomes achievable under international law, the promise of "never again" will remain not a guarantee, but an aspiration—one still waiting to be fulfilled.

References

Abken F, Rob P (2023) Amending the Amendment: In Search of an Adequate Procedure for a Revision of the Jurisdictional Regime for the Crime of Aggression in the Rome Statute. EJIL:*Talk!* https://www.ejiltalk.org/amending-the-amendment-in-search-of-an-adequate-procedure-for-a-revision-of-the-jurisdictional-regime-for-the-crime-of-aggression-in-the-rome-statute/. Accessed 29 September 2025

Alvarez J (2025) Speech by Professor José Alvarez (2025) W. Michael Reisman Distinguished Lecture on International Law and Diplomacy, America First and the International Rule of Law. Harvard Club, New York City

Anderson J (2025) Crime of Aggression: High Pressure for ICC in New York. JusticeInfoNet. https://www.justiceinfo.net/en/147364-crime-of-aggression-high-pressure-icc-new-york.html. Accessed 19 September 2025

Andrassy J (1956) Uniting for Peace, American Journal of International Law 50: 563–82.

Bardelle A (2025) A Historic Chance Missed: Harmonization of the ICC's Jurisdiction over the Crime of Aggression Delayed Once More. Opinio Juris. https://opiniojuris.org/2025/07/25/a-historic-chance-missed-harmonization-of-the-iccs-jurisdiction-over-the-crime-of-aggression-delayed-once-more/. Accessed 19 September 2025

Baerbock A (2023) Strengthening International Law in Times of Crisis – Speech by Federal Foreign Minister Annalena Baerbock in The Hague. Federal Foreign Office. https://www.auswaertiges-amt.de/en/newsroom/news/strengthening-internationallaw-in-times-of-crisis/2573492?view. Accessed 18 July 2025

Bass G (2000) Stay The Hand of Vengeance: The Politics of International War Crimes Tribunals. Princeton University Press, Princeton

Carswell A (2013) Unblocking the UN Security Council: The Uniting for Peace Resolution. Journal of Conflict & Security Law 18: 453–80

Coalition for the ICC (2025) Coalition for the ICC Statement General Debate of the ASP Special Session on the Review of the Amendments on the Crime of Aggression. https://coalitionfortheicc.org/sites/default/files/cicc_documents/CICC%20Statement%20ASP%20Special%20session%20general%20debate.pdf. Accessed 13 September 2025

Council of Europe (nd) Frequently Asked Questions – Special Tribunal for the Crime of Aggression against Ukraine. https://www.coe.int/en/web/portal/frequently-asked-questions. Accessed 23 July 2025

Donat Cattin D (2023) The ICC at 20 From the Rome Statute's Entry into Force: Looking Backwards and Forward, or Learning From Mistakes and Building on Achievements. In: Stahn C (ed) The International Criminal Court in Its Third Decade: Reflecting on Law and Practices. Brill, Boston

European Center for Constitutional and Human Rights (2024) No War of Aggression Should Go Unpunished: ICC's Jurisdiction over Crime of Aggression in Urgent Need of Reform. https://www.ecchr.eu/en/press-release/no-war-of-aggression-should-go-unpunished/. Accessed 9 September 2025

European Council, Council of the European Union (nd) EU Sanctions Against Russia Explained, https://www.consilium.europa.eu/en/policies/sanctions-against-russia-explained/. Accessed 23 September 2025

Gevorgyan M (2025) How the ICC Assembly of States Parties Failed Small States: A Neorealist Reading of the Crime of Aggression Reform Stalemate. EJIL:*Talk!* https://www.ejiltalk.org/how-the-icc-assembly-of-states-parties-failed-small-states-a-neorealist-reading-of-the-crime-of-aggression-reform-stalemate/. Accessed 19 September 2025

Gilbert M (1981) Auschwitz and the Allies: A Devastating Account of How the Allies Responded to the News of Hitler's Mass Murder. Holt, Rinehart and Winston, London

Global Institute for the Prevention of Aggression (nd-a) https://crimeofaggression.info/the-campaign/the-global-institute-for-the-prevention-of-aggression/. Accessed 7 September 2025

Global Institute for the Prevention of Aggression (nd-b) Proposal for the Amendment of the Conditions under which the International Criminal Court Exercises Jurisdiction over the Crime of Aggression, https://crimeofaggression.info/wp-content/uploads/GIPA-model-amendment-proposal_9-September-2023.pdf. Accessed 7 September 2025

Global Institute for the Prevention of Aggression (various-dates) News. https://crimeofaggression.info/. Accessed 7 September 2025

Global Institute for the Prevention of Aggression (2022) The Need to Remove Restrictions on the ICC's Jurisdiction over the Crime of Aggression. https://crimeofaggression.info/wp-content/uploads/GIPA_Increasing-ICC-jurisdiction_29-November-2022.pdf. Accessed 26 October 2025

Global Institute for the Prevention of Aggression (2023) News. https://crimeofaggression.info/page/5/. Accessed 12 September 2025
Global Institute for the Prevention of Aggression (2024) News. https://crimeofaggression.info/page/3/. Accessed 12 September 2025
Global Institute for the Prevention of Aggression (2025a) News. https://crimeofaggression.info/page/2/. Accessed 7 September 2025
Global Institute for the Prevention of Aggression (2025b) News. https://crimeofaggression.info/. Accessed 12 September 2025
Global Institute for the Prevention of Aggression (2025c) News. https://crimeofaggression.info/. Accessed 8 September 2025
Goscha C (nd) Casualties, Indochina War, Historical Dictionary: The Indochina War (1945–1956). https://indochine.uqam.ca/en/historical-dictionary/223-casualties-indochina-war.html. Accessed 21 November 2025
Grzebyk P (2025) Myths Around the Review Process of the Kampala Amendments on the Crime of Aggression. EJIL:*Talk!* https://www.ejiltalk.org/myths-around-the-review-process-of-the-kampala-amendments-on-the-crime-of-aggression/. Accessed 19 September 2025
Human Rights Watch (2024) Human Rights Watch Briefing Note for the Twenty-Third Session of the International Criminal Court Assembly of States Parties. https://www.hrw.org/news/2024/11/18/human-rights-watch-briefing-note-twenty-third-session-international-criminal-court. Accessed 23 September 2025
Human Rights Watch (2025) Hungary: Orbán Government Withdraws from ICC. https://www.hrw.org/news/2025/06/16/hungary-orban-government-withdraws-from-icc. Accessed 16 June 2025
International Criminal Court (nd-a) Situation in Ukraine. https://www.icc-cpi.int/situations/ukraine. Accessed 12 September 2025
International Criminal Court (nd-b) Declarations Lodged Under Article 15bis(4). https://www.icc-cpi.int/resource-library. Accessed 6 May 2025
International Criminal Court (Press Release) (2025a) ICC Welcomes Ukraine as a New State Party. https://www.icc-cpi.int/news/icc-welcomes-ukraine-new-state-party. Accessed 28 May 2025
International Criminal Court (2025b) Special Session, The Review of the Amendments on the Crime of Aggression. ICC-ASP/S-1/Res.1. https://asp.icc-cpi.int/sites/default/files/asp_docs/ICC-ASP-S-1-Res.1-ENG.pdf. Accessed 18 July 2025
International Criminal Court, Assembly of States Parties (2010) Review Conference, The Crime of Aggression, ICC Doc. RC/Res.6
International Criminal Court, Assembly of States Parties (2012) History of the Special Working Group on the Crime of Aggression. https://asp.icc-cpi.int/crime-of-aggression/History-CoA. Accessed 3 September 2025
International Criminal Court, Assembly of States Parties (2017) Activation of the Jurisdiction of the Court Over the Crime of Aggression, Res. ICC-ASP/16/Res. 5
International Criminal Court, Assembly of States Parties (2025) Report of the Working Group on Amendments Regarding Its Work on the Review of the Kampala Amendments Concerning the Exercise of Jurisdiction with Regard to the Crime of Aggression. ICC-ASP/S-1/2. https://asp.icc-cpi.int/sites/default/files/asp_docs/ICC-ASP-S-1-2-ENG.pdf. Accessed 18 July 2025
Jackson RH (1945) Report
Jackson RH (1947) Second Day, Wednesday, 11/21/1945, Part 04 (1947) in Trial of the Major War Criminals before the International Military Tribunal. Volume II. Proceedings: 11/14/1945-11/30/1945. IMT, Nuremberg. https://law2.umkc.edu/faculty/projects/ftrials/nuremberg/jackson.html. Accessed 11 September 2025
Joint Civil Society (2024) Harmonization of the ICC's Jurisdiction over the Crime of Aggression: A Call to States Parties to Take the Opportunity for Reform, Position Paper. https://www.ecchr.eu/fileadmin/Offene_Briefe/Joint_Civil_Society_Statement_-_Harmonization_of_the_ICC_s_Jurisdiction_over_the_Crime_of_Aggression_ukr.pdf. Accessed 9 September 2025
Just Security (2025) Statement by the Current and Former Presidents of the Assembly of States Parties of the International Criminal Court, We Need the International Legal Order: A Call to

Protect the International Criminal Court (2025) Just Security. https://www.justsecurity.org/106856/international-criminal-court-call-for-justice/. Accessed 18 September 2025
Kopelman E (1991) Ideology and International Law: The Dissent of the Indian Justice at the Tokyo War Crimes Trial. New York University Journal of International Law and Politics. 23: 373
Kreß C (2009) Time for Decision: Some Thoughts on the Immediate Future of the Crime of Aggression: A Reply to Andreas Paulus. European Journal of International Law 20: 1129–46
Kreβ C (2018) On the Activation of ICC Jurisdiction over the Crime of Aggression. Journal of International Criminal Justice 16: 1–17
Kreβ C (2025) On Recent Events Concerning the Crime of Aggression. Journal of International Criminal Justice 23: 1–4
Labuda P (2018) The Special Criminal Court in the Central African Republic. ASIL Insights 22
McAllister J (2020) Deterring Wartime Atrocities: Hard Lessons from the Yugoslav Tribunal. International Security 44: 84–128
McDougall C (2021) The Crime of Aggression Under the Rome Statute of the International Criminal Court, 2nd edn. Cambridge University Press, Cambridge
McDougall C (2024) Expanding the ICC's Jurisdiction over the Crime of Aggression. Journal of International Criminal Justice 1: 543–64
Miller A (2023) Without an Army: How ICC Indictments Reduce Atrocities. Journal of Peace Research 60: 573–87
Neier A (2010) Letter from A. Neier, President of the Open Society Foundations, to Foreign Ministers (2010). https://www.opensocietyfoundations.org/sites/default/files/icc-aggression-letter-20100511.pdf. Accessed 15 September 2025
Niyo J (2025) Territorial Annexation and Custom: Are We at an Inflection Point in the System of International Law and Relations? EJIL:*Talk!* https://www.ejiltalk.org/territorial-annexation-and-custom-are-we-at-an-inflection-point-in-the-system-of-international-law-and-relations/?utm_source=mailpoet&utm_medium=email&utm_campaign=ejil-talk-newsletter-post-title_2. Accessed 12 September 2025
Nuridzhanian G (2025) The Newly Established Special Tribunal for the Crime of Aggression against Ukraine: Jurisdiction, Immunities and Due Process. https://ssrn.com/abstract=5359650 or https://doi.org/10.2139/ssrn.5359650. Accessed 26 October 2025
Oxford Reference, Treaty Interpretation (2014) Definition of *Effet Utile*. https://doi.org/10.1093/oi/authority.20110803095743570 Accessed 12 September 2025
Parliamentarians for Global Action (2022) Letter to Ursula Von Der Leyen and Josep Borrell. https://www.pgaction.org/pdf/2022/mep-ukraine-appeal.pdf. Accessed 11 September 2025
Permanent Missions of Costa Rica, Sierra Leone, Vanuatu, Germany and Slovenia to the United Nations (2024) Letter to the Permanent Representatives of States Parties to the Rome Statute from the Permanent Missions of Costa Rica, Sierra Leone, Vanuatu, Germany and Slovenia to the United Nations, Mandated Review of the Kampala Amendments on the Crime of Aggression (2024). https://crimeofaggression.info/wp-content/uploads/Letter-to-all-ICC-SPs_distribution-of-discussion-paper-on-review-of-Kampala-Amendments-on-the-Crime-of-Aggression_Nov-2024.pdf. Accessed 11 September 2025
Radio Free Europe/ Radio Liberty (2024) Russia Issues Warrant for International Criminal Court Judge. https://www.rferl.org/a/russia-arrest-warrant-icc-judge/33199206.html. Accessed 5 September 2025
Ratner S (2014) International Law: Rules of Treaty Interpretation. In: Dörr O, Schmalenbach K (eds) The Vienna Convention on the Law of Treaties in International Law: A Commentary. Oxford University Press, Oxford
Reuters (2025) Mali, Burkina Faso and Niger Announce Exit from International Criminal Court. https://www.reuters.com/world/africa/mali-burkina-faso-niger-announce-exit-international-criminal-court-2025-09-23/. Accessed 3 October 2025
Rubio M (2025) Marco Rubio, US Department of State, Press Statement, Sanctioning Foreign NGOs Directly Engaged in ICC's Illegitimate Targeting of Israel. https://www.state.gov/releases/office-of-the-spokesperson/2025/09/sanctioning-foreign-ngos-directly-engaged-in-iccs-illegitimate-targeting-of-israel/. Accessed 12 September 2025
Sarkees M, Wayman F (2010) Resort to War: A Data Guide to Inter-State, Extra-State, Intra-State, and Non-State Wars, 1816–2007. CQ Press, Washington, DC

Smith B (1981) American Road to Nuremberg: The Documentary Record, 1944–1945. Hoover Institution Press Publication

Trahan J (2011) The Rome Statute's Amendment on the Crime of Aggression: Negotiations at the Kampala Review Conference. International Criminal Law Review 11: 49–104

Trahan J (2012) Potential Future Rome Statute Amendments. New England Journal of International and Comparative Law. 18: 331–50

Trahan J (2018a) Views of the Future of the Field of International Justice: A Scenarios Project Based on Expert Consultations. American University International Law Review 33: 837–941

Trahan J (2018b) From Kampala to New York—The Final Negotiations to Activate the Jurisdiction of the International Criminal Court Over the Crime of Aggression. International Criminal Law Review 18: 197–243

Trahan J (2020) Existing Legal Limits to Security Council Veto Power in the Face of Atrocity Crimes. Cambridge University Press, Cambridge

Trahan J (2022a) Why the Veto Power Is Not Unlimited: A Response to Critiques of, and Questions About, Existing Legal Limits to the Veto Power in the Face of Atrocity Crimes. Case Western Reserve Journal of International Law 54: 109–140

Trahan J (2022b) Veto Use and the UN Charter Obligation to Act in Accordance with the "Purposes and Principles" of the United Nations. Journal on the Use of Force and International Law 9: 243–77

Trahan J (2023) Legal Issues Surrounding Veto Use and Aggression. Case Western Reserve Journal of International Law 55: 93–146

Trahan J (2024) Email with Carrie McDougall, 17 August 2024

Trahan J (2025a) Cyber Operations and the Crime of Aggression. Case Western Reserve Journal of International Law. 57: 77–108

Trahan J (2025b) Email with Carrie McDougall, 7 September 2025

Trahan J (2025c) Email with David Donat Cattin, 1 September 2025

Trahan J (2025d) Email with David Donat Cattin, 12 September 2025

Trahan J (2025e) Email with a legal adviser who participated in the negotiations, 9 October 2025

Trump DJ (2025) President Donald J. Trump, The White House, Imposing Sanctions on the International Criminal Court. https://www.whitehouse.gov/presidential-actions/2025/02/imposing-sanctions-on-the-international-criminal-court/. Accessed 3 September 2025

United Nations Treaty Collection (nd-a) Status, Rome Statute of the International Criminal Court. https://treaties.un.org/Pages/ViewDetails.aspx?src=TREATY&mtdsg_no=XVIII-10&chapter=18&clang=_en. Accessed 4 May 2025

United Nations Treaty Collection (nd-b) Status, Amendments to the Rome Statute of the International Criminal Court on the Crime of Aggression. https://treaties.un.org/Pages/ViewDetails.aspx?src=TREATY&mtdsg_no=XVIII-10-b&chapter=18&clang=_en. Accessed 3 September 2025

Weisbord N (2017) Civil Society. In: Kreβ C, Barriga S (eds) The Crime of Aggression: A Commentary. Cambridge University Press, Cambridge

Ziad O, Murray C, Gakidou E (2008) Fifty Years of Violent War Deaths from Vietnam to Bosnia: Analysis of Data from the World Health Survey Programme. British Medical Journal 336 (7659) 1482-86

Other Documents

Assembly of States Parties Side Event on the Review of the Kampala Amendments on the Crime of Aggression: Perspective of African States Parties, co-hosted by Ghana, Malawi, Sierra Leone, Switzerland and Africa Legal Aid ("AFLA") (2024). https://www.africalegalaid.com/blog/asp-side-event-on-thenbspreview-of-the-kampala-amendments-on-the-crime-of-aggression-perspective-of-african-states-parties. Accessed 12 September 2025

Charter of the International Military Tribunal (1945) 85 UNTS 251
Charter of the United Nations (1945) 33 UNTS 933
Chart prepared by Astrid Reisinger Coracini on file with the author
Costa Rica, Germany, Sierra Leone, Slovenia, and Vanuatu (2025) Proposal of Amendment. https://treaties.un.org/doc/Publication/CN/2025/CN.162.2025-Eng.pdf. Accessed 7 August 2025
International Court of Justice (1962) *Certain Expenses of the United Nations*, Advisory Opinion, 1962 ICJ Rep. 151
International Court of Justice (1949) *Corfu Channel (United Kingdom v. Albania)*, Judgment of 9 April 1949, 1949 ICJ Rep. 4
International Court of Justice (2004) *Legal Consequences of the Construction of a Wall in the Occupied Palestinian Territory*, Advisory Opinion, 2004 ICJ Rep. 136
International Criminal Court, ICC-ASP/23/Res.1 (2024) Strengthening the International Criminal Court and the Assembly of States Parties
International Law Commission (1966) Draft Articles on the Law of Treaties with Commentaries, 1966 Yearbook of the ILC, Vol. II
International Military Tribunal (1946) Judgment of 1 October 1946, in The Trial of German Major War Criminals. Proceedings of the International Military Tribunal Sitting at Nuremberg, Germany, Part 22 (22 August 1946 to 1 October 1946)
International Military Tribunal for the Far East (1946) Special Proclamation by the Supreme Commander to the Allied Powers at Tokyo, Amended 26 April 1946
Nuremberg Trial Proceedings Vol. 1 (nd) Indictment: Count Three, https://avalon.law.yale.edu/imt/count3.asp. Accessed 10 September 2025
Observations of the author who attended the Special Session
Oral exchange between the author and a UK representative at the AU Mission to the UN, 13 June 2025
Permanent Mission of Liechtenstein to the United Nations (2013) Handbook: Ratification and Implementation of the Kampala Amendments to the Rome Statute of the ICC
Report of the Special Working Group on the Crime of Aggression (2008) ICC-ASP/6/20/Add.1
Rome Statute of the International Criminal Court (1998) 2187 UNTS 90 (as amended)
Statute of the Special Tribunal for the Crime of Aggression against Ukraine (2025). https://search.coe.int/cm?i=0900001680b678ca. Accessed 12 September 2025
United Nations General Assembly Resolution 377A (V) (1950)
United Nations General Assembly Resolution 71/248 (2016)
United Nations General Assembly Resolution ES-11/1 (2022)
United Nations Security Council Resolution 827 (1993)
United Nations Security Council Resolution 955 (1994)
United Nations Security Council Resolution 155 (2022)
United Nations Security Council Resolution 2623 (2022)
Vienna Convention on the Law of Treaties (1969) 1155 UNTS 331, 8 ILM 679

Index

J. Trahan, *The Crime of Aggression and Russia's Invasion of Ukraine*,
https://doi.org/10.1007/978-94-6265-763-2

The manufacturer's authorised representative in the EU is Springer Nature Customer Service Centre GmbH, Europaplatz 3, 69115 Heidelberg, Germany. If you have any concerns regarding our products, please contact ProductSafety@springernature.com

Printed and bound by CPI Group (UK) Ltd, Croydon, CR0 4YY
16/09/2026
02217791-0009